Love Me Fierce in Danger

Love Me Fierce in Danger

The Life of James Ellroy

Steven Powell

BLOOMSBURY ACADEMIC
NEW YORK · LONDON · OXFORD · NEW DELHI · SYDNEY

BLOOMSBURY ACADEMIC
Bloomsbury Publishing Inc
1385 Broadway, New York, NY 10018, USA
50 Bedford Square, London, WC1B 3DP, UK
29 Earlsfort Terrace, Dublin 2, Ireland

BLOOMSBURY, BLOOMSBURY ACADEMIC and the Diana logo are
trademarks of Bloomsbury Publishing Plc

First published in the United States of America 2023

For legal purposes the Acknowledgements on p. xi constitute
an extension of this copyright page.

Cover design: ____
Cover image ©

Although this is a work of non-fiction, the author has changed the
names of certain individuals to protect their privacy.

Bloomsbury Publishing Inc does not have any control over, or responsibility for,
any third-party websites referred to or in this book. All internet addresses given in
this book were correct at the time of going to press. The author and publisher regret
any inconvenience caused if addresses have changed or sites have ceased to exist,
but can accept no responsibility for any such changes.

Library of Congress Cataloguing-in-Publication Data

ISBN: PB: 978-1-5013-6731-1
          ePDF: 978-1-5013-6733-5
          eBook: 978-1-5013-6732-8

Typeset by Integra Software Services Pvt. Ltd.
Printed and bound in the United States of America

To find out more about our authors and books visit www.bloomsbury.com
and sign up for our newsletters.

To Mike Ripley
For Getting Away with It …

Contents

List of Illustrations

Acknowledgements

I am deeply indebted to James Ellroy and Helen Knode for their unprecedented cooperation. Leslie Werner always found time for me in James's insane schedule. I am grateful to everyone I interviewed and corresponded with in preparation for this book. It took courage to discuss some sensitive issues and I hope I did you all justice. For your patience and encouragement, thank you to family and friends; Jason Carter, David Harrison, Daniel Slattery, Flávia Alves, Maylin Scott, Katherine Furman, Camille Colombel and Radu Spulber. My editor, Haaris Naqvi, believed in this book from the start. Thank you Haaris, for making the dream a reality. At Bloomsbury, I am indebted to Mollie Broad, Hali Han, Deirdre Kennedy, Christina Kowalski, and others. I would like to thank the team at Integra, particularly Elizabeth Nichols. The staff at the Thomas Cooper Library were generous with their time in granting me access to every nook and cranny in Ellroy's archive.

Finally, I am most grateful to my wife Diana.

Di, love me fierce in danger … or at least let's negotiate from there.

James Ellroy Bibliography: List of Key Works

Brown's Requiem (Oct. 1981)

Clandestine (Dec. 1982)

Blood on the Moon (Apr. 1984, book 1 in Lloyd Hopkins series)

Because the Night (Dec. 1984, book 2 in Lloyd Hopkins series)

Suicide Hill (Apr. 1986, book 3 in Lloyd Hopkins series)

Silent Terror (aka Killer on the Road, Oct. 1986)

The Black Dahlia (Sept. 1987, book 1 in LA Quartet)

The Big Nowhere (Sept. 1988, book 2 in LA Quartet)

LA Confidential (June 1990, book 3 in LA Quartet)

White Jazz (Sept. 1992, book 4 in LA Quartet)

Hollywood Nocturnes (aka *Dick Contino's Blues and Other Stories*, June 1994)

American Tabloid (Feb. 1995, book 1 in Underworld USA Trilogy)

My Dark Places (Nov. 1996)

Crime Wave (Mar. 1999)

Breakneck Pace (2001)

The Cold Six Thousand (May 2001, book 2 in Underworld USA Trilogy)

Destination: Morgue! (Sept. 2004)

Blood's a Rover (Sept. 2009, book 3 in Underworld USA Trilogy)

The Hilliker Curse: My Pursuit of Women (Sept. 2010)

Shakedown (Oct. 2012)

Perfidia (Sept. 2014, book 1 in Second LA Quartet)

LAPD 53' (May 2015, co-authored with Glyn Martin)

This Storm (May. 2019, book 2 in Second LA Quartet)

Widespread Panic (July. 2021)

Introduction

"James lives life like he was shot out of a cannon," Helen Knode, his ex-wife, tells me. Of the many women in Ellroy's life, Helen has come closest to understanding him. Understanding Ellroy, both the scope and the meaning of his extraordinary life, is a task I have spent more than a decade undertaking. I first met Ellroy in person in 2009. I was an unknown PhD candidate back then, and I was amazed at the generosity he extended towards me when there was little I could give him in return. Over the next ten years I stayed in Ellroy's orbit, authoring three books on his work and hundreds of articles before I had an epiphany: someone needed, hell, I needed, to write James Ellroy's biography.

In one sense James Ellroy needs no introduction. To be even remotely knowledgeable of twentieth-century American literature or crime fiction is to know Ellroy. With his garish Hawaiian shirts, lanky physique, mesmerizing speaking style, and penchant for barking like a dog, Ellroy makes sure he won't go unnoticed. However, his distinctive and self-styled Demon Dog persona runs deeper than its physical manifestation. It's all there in his ferocious competitiveness, tireless work ethic, and prodigious output. His writing has pushed the boundaries of genre, and he has never given up on striving for new literary achievements. This ambition, in part, stems from his struggle with addiction. His mother was a heavy drinker and, after her murder and the death of his father, Ellroy fell into a spiral of alcohol and drug abuse as a young man. He entered Alcoholics Anonymous at the age of twenty-seven and, barring a couple of relapses, has been sober ever since. But the addictive side of his character remains in everything from his unyielding ambition, voracious appetite for women, right down to the copious amounts of coffee he consumes daily.

While remarkable and often inspiring, the story of Ellroy's life is also tinged with melancholy, and not just by the various traumas he has endured. Rather, Ellroy's seven decades cover a rapidly vanishing world. He has lived through and profited from the rise and fall of Hollywood and publishing. It would be impossible for another Ellroy to ascend in the same circumstances today, but if society was to become too safe and monotonous it might create the conditions to which a self-styled polemicist like Ellroy could step into the void.

Ellroy is a brilliant reader of people's thoughts and motivations. As such, he is skilled at giving people what they want, whether it be outrage or empathy, and that sort of talent rarely goes out of style. Humor is present in everything he does. He can take sheer glee from his capacity to offend, and yet he can be equally kind and thoughtful. Ellroy has been so candid to me there were times I was unsure whether he had appointed me as his biographer or executioner, but that is entirely in keeping with his character.

Joyce Carol Oates described Ellroy as "the American Dostoyevsky." The comparison is not merely a literary one. Ellroy's extraordinary, harrowing, and inspiring life has been so mythologized, demythologized, and re-mythologized in the public eye, not least by the author himself, that it is difficult to believe that this book is his first full-length biography. All I ask is that, whether you an admirer or a detractor of Ellroy, take all your preconceptions of him and leave them at the door. Perhaps the biggest irony of all is that, in my view, Ellroy's life is the great untold story of American literature.

For the multitude of interviews I have conducted with Ellroy's friends, colleagues, and ex-partners, my subjects seemed relieved to finally give their testimony and part with the history they had witnessed in the life of an author who can be equally dazzling and infuriating. With such an abundance of voices in this story, I have avoided any ham-fisted attempts to psychoanalyze Ellroy. He is not introspective. His character can be deduced through his actions, and as such, I don't always follow a strict chronology. The structure of the book is broadly sequential, but Ellroy is often juggling a dozen projects and people at once. It is more appropriate to focus on one episode of his life at length, before moving onto another.

I feel I have talked enough about my own hand in the book and can feel Ellroy peering over my shoulder and saying, "Steve, you slimy limey, stop talking about yourself and get to the part about me."

Here goes.

Frontispiece *Ellroy's short poem "Love Me Fierce in Danger" inscribed on the back of a photograph of Helen Knode*

1

In the Shadow of Hollywood—Los Angeles (1948–1958)

On June 23, 1958, the lead story in the *Los Angeles Times* was of a tragic rail accident in Maltrata, Mexico. A passenger train had been derailed on the notoriously dangerous, winding mountain track of Cumbres de Maltrata and had plummeted full speed down the mountainside, finally crashing into Maltrata Village Station. Forty people were killed, and at least eighty were injured. One cruel twist of fate served to compound the tragedy: "the train knocked down the only telegraph and telephone lines in Maltrata village and reports of the accident were delayed."[1]

The previous year, *TIME* magazine had named the *LA Times* as the second worst newspaper in the United States.[2] Nevertheless it had the highest circulation of any newspaper based on the West Coast, and many Americans, particularly Angelenos, would have read about the Maltrata train crash in the *LA Times* on Monday morning as they began their working week. Below the Maltrata train article there lay an intriguing headline: "Blond Woman Sought in Nurse Killing."

The disturbing story that unfolded beneath the headline was more local to Los Angeles than the horrific train accident in Maltrata, and it had claimed only one life by comparison, but as with all tragedies, the ramifications would be felt by the survivors for decades. The nurse in question was Mrs. Jean Ellroy of 756 Maple Avenue, El Monte. She had been found strangled to death on Sunday morning on Kings Row, an El Monte lane leading to Arroyo High School. The blonde was an unidentified woman Mrs. Ellroy had been seen talking to on Saturday night in a local bar, the Desert Inn. The blonde was wanted for questioning by the police.

The story continued on page two and did not flinch from the disturbing details. Jean "appeared to have fought viciously to prevent her killer from winding a cotton cord and one of her stockings around her neck."[3] Jean was described as having "bright red hair, hazel eyes" and was "5 feet 6 inches tall, weight about 135 pounds." Any reader looking at the photograph the *LA Times* printed of Jean would have thought the description did not do her justice. Jean had a dazzling smile and beautiful complexion. She bore a resemblance to the Hollywood actress Jane Russell, a pinup of the era. It was difficult to believe that the vibrant young woman in the photograph with movie-star looks had been found brutally murdered only yesterday.

Next to the photograph of Jean was an equally striking portrait of her ten-year-old son, Lee Earle Ellroy. Unlike Jean, Lee did not smile. He did not seem happy. He simply stared at the camera, displaying a pensive fragility and intelligence. He had, quite literally, a long face. He was strikingly tall for his age. His hair was neatly combed over, and he was wearing a checked shirt that seemed to accentuate his prematurely adult features. Lee had the right to look uncomfortable. The photograph had been taken only moments after he had found out his mother was dead, and he had been surrounded by policemen asking questions and giving instructions. The article further stated that Jean's ex-husband Armand Ellroy was not a suspect in her murder. He was "questioned and immediately released" as he had been looking after Lee at the time of the murder.[4]

Jean and Armand's divorce had been bitter and rancorous. She had accused him of harassment, breaking into her apartment and spying on her having sex with her boyfriend. Jean and Armand were no longer on speaking terms, although they shared custody of Lee: Jean looked after him in El Monte during the week, and Lee stayed with Armand in LA at weekends. When Jean told Lee she was divorcing his father it had shocked the boy and thrown him out of his relatively comfortable existence. It had skewered his perception of his parents, leading him to despise his mother who he blamed for the divorce and idolize his carefree, languid father. As he would later admit, Lee was secretly glad that his mother was dead. It meant he could leave El Monte and live with his father in LA, which was what he had always wanted. Years later, he candidly described his emotionally cold reaction to his mother's murder: "I hated her. I hated El Monte. Some unknown killer just bought me a brand-new beautiful life."[5]

Lee was not aware that his life was about to get much worse with his mother's absence. Rather than free him from her influence, Jean Ellroy's murder would define her son, his writing, and lifelong obsessions.

Jean Ellroy was born Geneva Odelia Hilliker in Tunnel City, Wisconsin in 1915, the first child of Earle and Jessie Hilliker. Earle was a forest ranger, a big drinker, and a burly fighter. Earle and Jessie "might have been blood related. The rumor persisted."[6] They had another daughter Leoda, born in 1917. The family moved to nearby Tomah in 1930. Earle was broke and a full-blown alcoholic by the time the Depression hit America and Prohibition was in full swing. He was found drunk on the job one day by the State Conservation Boss. He was demoted and transferred to Bowler Ranger Station; one hundred miles north-east of Tomah. It appears his alcoholism also cost him his marriage and family, "Jessie refused to go with him. She stayed in Tomah. The daughters stayed with her."[7]

Jean became close to Earle's sister Norma. Aunt Norma's husband Pete owned the Tomah drugstore. Norma ran the local beauty salon. They were a well-to-do couple, and Norma was the subject of some gossip. The rumor was that Norma had a torrid affair with the local Methodist minister who had subsequently left town and committed suicide. These tales did little to sway Jean's admiration of Norma. Jean looked up to the scandalous Norma. Leoda looked up to the independent-minded Jean. Jean was an intelligent and beautiful young woman with just a shade of rebellion to her. She caught the eye of many local men, but her sights were set far from Tomah.

Jean graduated from high school in June 1934. Her ambition was to be a nurse. She applied to study nursing at West Suburban College in Chicago and moved there the same year. Norma offered to pay Jean's tuition and expenses at West Suburban. Jean must have been grateful for Norma's generosity and may have viewed her as a surrogate parent. Once Jean was settled in Chicago, "Her aunt Norma visited her. Her parents never did."[8] However, a few years later, Norma left Tomah after having an affair with another minister and Jean never saw her again.

College in Chicago proved a welcome break from small-town life. Jean dormed with a woman named Mary Evans and they became fast friends. They both had a wild side and were experts at breaking curfew, and sneaking back into the dorms at early hours, without being noticed. Mary did it to spend time with her doctor boyfriend. Jean preferred to stay out late and party. She was becoming as fond of booze as her alcoholic father. One night she came home drunk. While she sat urinating on the toilet, Jean lit a match and carelessly dropped it in the toilet bowl while she puffed away on a cigarette. The toilet paper in the bowl was set alight and singed her bottom. "Jean laughed and laughed" about the incident.[9]

Jean's first serious boyfriend was a man named Dan Coffey. Coffey was an alcoholic and diabetic. Jean must have fallen for him hard as, "She was with him every night for a solid year and a half."[10] Coffey dumped Jean abruptly. Jean was devastated but, despite this emotional setback and her increasingly heavy drinking, she was learning to balance things well. She never fell behind with her studies, and she was able to work to a high standard in class no matter how hungover she was.

In the 1930s Chicago was notorious for its gangsters, outlaws, and corruption. Jean "liked rough boys. Some of them looked like gangsters and hoodlum riffraff."[11] Jean claimed to have witnessed John Dillinger being gunned down by Federal agents outside the Biograph theater on July 22, 1934. It was "one of her favorite stories," and she enjoyed telling it to her son decades later.[12] However, Dillinger was killed only one month after Jean graduated from high school in Tomah, which suggests she either moved to Chicago promptly or may have been lying about witnessing the incident. Perhaps one of her "rough boys" gave her the inside story of Dillinger's demise and, as people tend to do, she appropriated his version as her own. Jean always told the Dillinger anecdote matter-of-factly, "She did not go into detail" her son lamented "I wish to hell she had. It would have made for a better story."[13] Despite having a rebellious streak, Jean was a surprisingly poor liar. She seldom deviated from her plain-speaking, Midwest manners.

Jean met a woman named Jean Atchison. The two Jeans became close, much to Mary's chagrin. Mary thought Jean Atchison was odd. She was ten years Jean Hilliker's senior and seemed infatuated with her; "Everybody talked about it. Everybody thought they were lesbian lovers."[14] Jean seemed to like the attention. Jean graduated from West Suburban in 1937 and immediately secured a full-time job with the college. She moved out of dorms and into an apartment in Oak Park. There may have been three or five nurses living in the apartment, accounts differ, but either way Jean was living with Mary and Jean Atchison. Whether it was for economic reasons or otherwise, "Mary had her own bedroom. Jean shared a bedroom with Jean Atchison. They slept in the same bed."[15]

In a one-off job, Jean was paid to drive an elderly married couple from Chicago to New York City. The couple were planning one last trip together, an Atlantic voyage to Europe, as the wife was dying of cancer. They were both alcoholics and Jean was tasked with keeping them sober: "The drunks wandered off at rest stops. Jean found bottles in their luggage and emptied them. The drunks scrounged up more liquor."[16] Eventually Jean encouraged them to drink so they could "pass out and let her drive in peace."[17] Once they reached New York, the couple let Jean use a hotel suite booked in their name. Jean had no trouble finding male company "She met an artist there. He drew a charcoal sketch of Jean in the nude."[18] However, she missed her girlfriends back in Chicago. Mary, Jean Atchison, and another nurse named Nancy Kirkland drove to New York to see her. They stayed in the suite where "they partied for four or five days."[19]

Mary moved out of the apartment when "her boyfriend set her up in her own place."[20] Ongoing tension between Mary and Jean was heading towards an explosion. Leoda Hilliker married Ed Wagner, a car dealer in Madison, Wisconsin in June 1939. Jean attended her sister's wedding. Jean had been through several relationships by this point. She fell pregnant around this time and may have been carrying on Leoda's wedding day. Jean asked Mary's boyfriend to perform an abortion. He refused. In desperation, Jean opted for a self-induced abortion and subsequently hemorrhaged. Mary's boyfriend treated her. He did not report the abortion. Jean "had an affair with him," possibly as a price for his services.[21] Jean and Mary fell out with each other and lost touch soon after.

Jean's move west may have been somewhat accidental. Jean Atchison entered Jean into a glamour contest sponsored by Elmo Beauty Products. The organizers wanted to find four women and crown them "Most Charming" Blonde, Brunette, Redhead, and Grayhead. Atchison sent in Jean's photo and application without telling her. Jean was angry at her friend's underhanded behavior, but this subsided as she was the redhead who won. On December 12, 1938, she flew to Los Angeles with the other winners. They stayed at the Ambassador Hotel and saw the tourist sights. Each one of them took a screen test and they were paid $1,000 for their time. Accounts of the screen test differ. Jean is variously described as having "waltzed" or "tanked" it.[22] The footage does not appear to have survived, and, in any event, Jean did not pursue an acting or modelling career afterwards, but she did make plans to move to LA.

Jean's move to LA was followed by a brief, and mysterious, marriage. None of Jean's family attended the wedding, but she told them that she was marrying the heir to the Spalding sporting goods fortune. Either Jean was lying, or she had been completely duped. Keith Spalding inherited his father's sporting goods fortune after a two-year legal battle in 1917. He was married to Eudora Hull at the time Jean married her "Spalding man." Decades after Jean's death, when her son first found about the Hilliker–Spalding marriage, he conducted his own investigation, but he was unable to determine an exact date or location of the wedding: "It wasn't Chicago. It wasn't in LA County, Orange County, San Diego County, Ventura County, Las Vegas or Reno."[23] However, a marriage license seen by this author indicates the marriage took place in Yuma County on or around November 5, 1940.

Jean married Easton Ewing Spaulding, a real estate broker who was born in Springfield, Illinois in 1902. It was his third marriage. He was married to Pearl Phelps in the 1920s. After they divorced, he wed Beatrice "Bebe" McCarthy Clark in 1931. His marriage to Bebe ended in 1940 and he married Jean the same year. They may have honeymooned together near Mount Charleston, Nevada.[24] Easton Spaulding may have been a distant cousin of Albert Goodwill Spalding, the baseball pitcher and founder of the sporting goods empire. Easton Spaulding was one of twelve children to the real estate developer Albert Starr Spaulding. Albert Starr Spaulding purchased and subdivided an area of land "between Sunset Boulevard and Fountain Avenue to the east of Fairfax Avenue."[25] Spaulding Square in Los Angeles was named after him. However, Albert Spaulding was still alive at the time Jean Hilliker married into the family, and Easton was not the eldest son. Therefore, Easton may not have been the heir to a fortune as the Hilliker family was led to believe. Perhaps he lied about that, perhaps he lied to Jean about already having a family of his own, or perhaps she played an active role in ending his second marriage. Easton was nonetheless wealthy, and his grandchildren today recall stories of how he had showered a mistress with expensive gifts. Even if he did divorce Bebe to marry Jean, Easton Spaulding's marriage to Jean fell apart quickly. Spaulding married for a fourth time, to Emile Hensel in 1945, once again in Yuma County and this marriage lasted until his death in 1986. Emile ruled Spaulding with "an iron fist," seldom letting him out of the house to visit his family from other marriages. Emile clearly felt that isolation was the cure for her husband's notoriously roving eye. Spaulding was living in Los Angeles at the time of his marriage to Jean, and he continued to live there until at least the 1970s. In that sense, he was never that far from Jean after their marriage ended.

After her marriage to Spaulding was dissolved, Jean may have stayed in LA with, or moved nearby to, a woman named Mildred Feese who she knew through a mutual friend.[26]

Mildred Feese was married to a man named Armand Ellroy.

Armand Ellroy told his life-story to his son, who documented it years later, long after Armand had died, in his own memoirs. However, Armand "was a liar. All his statements were suspect."[27] There are formal documents which shed light on Armand's life, but even here there is confusion and contradiction. Armand Lee Ellroy was born on June 30, in the final years of the nineteenth century. The exact year has been variously documented as 1896, 1898, and 1899. Peter Wolfe identifies Armand's birthplace as Lynn, Massachusetts, which is three miles north of Boston.[28] Armand's son would claim his father was born in Boston.[29] Armand would make varying statements about where he was born, but his birth certificate states that he was born in Richmond, Virginia in 1899. Perhaps if he was from an itinerant family, Armand could not be sure either of his place or year of birth. Armand's father, John Calhoun Ellroy, was a chemist from St Augustine, Florida and his mother Ida Ellroy (nee Omette) was a housewife from Shreveport, Louisiana. They were forty-nine and forty-seven years old respectively when Armand was born. His mother's relatively advanced age might suggest that Armand was the product of an unreported adoption. He bore an olive-skinned complexion and his son Lee always felt he was "Italianate" in appearance.

Armand appears to have had no formal education, but he had a gift for arithmetic and the most consistent employment he would find in later life would be inventorying drugstore stock, a role it can be assumed he developed working with his father. Armand's birth certificate lists two older sisters, Betty and Irma. In fact, Irma was his half-sister. Irma's birth certificate reveals she was born to Ida Omette and Alexander Bartolette.

According to Armand his parents died in a hotel fire when he was five or six years old, and he spent the following years in an orphanage. He claimed his heritage was Irish Presbyterian and the name Ellroy was derived from McIlroy, but "my grandfather changed it as he didn't want to be associated with the Shanty Irish."[30] As a derivation it did not catch on, there are very few Ellroys today in the US. Armand also claimed to have served in the Pershing Expedition—the ill-fated attempt to hunt down the Mexican revolutionary Pancho Villa in revenge for the Columbus Raid of 1916. Few people close to Armand believed this claim, but there is ample evidence to show that he served in a different conflict. Personnel records confirm Armand Ellroy served in the 108th Infantry, 27th Division of the American Expeditionary Forces in World War I. His record of military service shows he served abroad from May 17, 1918, to March 6, 1919. He also saw action, being present at engagements at the Hindenburg Line, Vierstraat Ridge, East Poperingue Line, and Dickebusch. Judging by the year of birth on his birth certificate, Armand was eighteen when he first served abroad, a mere month after America's entry into the war. He must have enlisted, as the first draft registration did not come into effect until June 1917 and at that point it did not apply to men under the age of twenty-one. Armand may have lied about his age to serve. He was promoted to Corporal in July 1918 and was awarded the Certificate of Merit and Conspicuous Service Cross.

After the war ended, Armand sailed from Brest to New York on the *Mauretania*. His parents long deceased, on the passenger list Armand put his next of kin as his half-sister, Irma Bartoletti. Irma married Herman August Hummel in 1920, a prolific songwriter and composer from Crawfordsville, Indiana, and they settled in Manhattan Beach. Hummel had a hit with "Yes, I got it, no hot dogs," a spinoff from the novelty song "Yes, we have no bananas." Regrettably, or perhaps not, the popularity of the song did not extend far beyond the Greater Cleveland area.

Armand had an impressive record of service for a young soldier, but as he always had something to prove, Armand liked to further embellish his tales of heroism. As he put it, he "killed lots of Krauts" and maintained a lifelong antipathy to Germans, spouting the obscenity "Fuck you Fritz" whenever someone displeased him.[31] He owned a chestful of medals and it would have been impossible to have won them all. "If he really won all those medals, he'd be as famous as Audie Murphy" his son wrote.[32] On his gravestone, Armand's army rank is listed as Sergeant, one rank above Corporal. Also engraved is the abbreviation SS-PH, indicating he was the recipient of the Silver Star and the Purple Heart. There was, presumably, not enough space to carve in the initials of all the other medals he carried around with him. He showed Lee a photo of himself in army uniform in France on Armistice Day.[33]

After being discharged from the US Army, Armand wanted to make a fortune and seduce some beautiful women along the way. He was tall, handsome, athletic and a war veteran to boot. Both of his life goals seemed attainable. In a 1924 passport application Armand put his place of residence as Short Hills, New Jersey, and his birthplace as New York. On other documents he would state his birthplace as Los Angeles. It may be that he would change the place of birth to whatever was the most bureaucratically convenient answer at any given time. On the passport application Armand puts 1896 as his year of birth. He lists his profession as a salesman, and the passport is needed for planned business trips to Brazil, British Guiana, Venezuela, Dutch Guiana, and the British West Indies. How successful these trips were is not known, but Armand sailed back on the SS *Voltaire* from Barbados to New York in early 1925.

Armand moved west, living in San Diego, and working as a deputy county auditor from 1926 to 1929. After that he worked as a salesman for a year, and then he spent a year managing a hotel. From 1931 to 1935 he worked both as a house detective and county auditor for the US Grant Hotel. After leaving these roles he became a salesman again, this time for AM Fidelity.[34] The abundance of jobs might suggest that Armand was driven and ambitious, but his biggest flaw was chronic laziness. Drifting from one role to another was often a consequence of avoiding responsibility. Armand's dream was to meet a beautiful woman and live off her money and work.

Three days before Christmas Day, 1934, Armand married Mildred Feese in San Diego. Mildred had been born in Nebraska. Like her new husband, she had probably moved west to escape boredom and find a better life. Unfortunately for Mildred, she would soon discover that Armand, who was thirteen years her senior, was restless, faithless, and temperamentally unsuited to married life. He was already leading a virtual double life in another country.

Tijuana is only twenty miles and a thirty-minute car journey south of San Diego. In the early 1930s, Armand Ellroy alternated or sometimes combined his work in San Diego with new opportunities south of the border. In Tijuana, Armand found work as a croupier and cashier at the aptly named Agua Caliente, "Hot Water," casino and hotel. The sun, lifestyle, and hedonistic reputation of TJ was much to Armand's liking. The Agua Caliente, known as the Monte Carlo of the West, was one of the most exclusive resorts in Central America in the 1930s. Colorful, vibrant, and seductive—according to local lore it served as the inspiration for Benjamin "Bugsy" Siegel to build the Flamingo Hotel in Las Vegas—the Caliente was a favorite getaway for many Hollywood stars.

One young lady who caught Armand's eye was not a star, but she was on her way to becoming one. Margarita Carmen Cansino was only twelve when her family moved her from Los Angeles to Tijuana in 1931. She starred alongside her father, famed Spanish dancer Eduardo Cansino, at the Caliente in an act dubbed "the Dancing Cansinos." Eduardo Cansino was brilliant and demanding. He was determined that his daughter would become a star now that his own fame was waning. Margarita would perform in four shows a day at the Caliente, usually not getting to bed before 2 a.m.

Armand Ellroy was by this time fluent in Spanish. He dressed and sounded like a movie idol even when he was flat broke. He was naturally persuasive and able to gain Eduardo Cansino's trust, being hired by him as a guardian to shield Margarita from "mashers," unwanted male admirers, which in a place like Tijuana, were in plentiful supply. Margarita had spent most of her childhood surrounded by older, and sometimes sinister men. She once performed with her father on the gambling ship *"The Rex,"* moored off the California coast.[35] Perhaps it was the fact that Armand was a teetotaler that impressed Cansino, and deluded him into thinking he was chaste from other vices. Armand did as Cansino instructed, but he was unable to protect Margarita from her own father. Eduardo Cansino had been sexually abusing his daughter throughout her childhood.[36] Whether Ellroy knew about this sexual abuse seems doubtful. He would later tell the writer Leonard Slater that he viewed Margarita's mother Volga as the more restrictive parent, always monitoring Margarita's behavior.

After the evening show Ellroy, along with many of the staff and performers at the Caliente, would get together for a meal or to go swimming. But Volga, an accomplished dancer herself, usually barred Margarita from attending, preferring to keep her in constant rehearsals. Armand would recall years later, "I can still see her mother sitting there, watching Rita rehearse and keeping her eye out."[37] In retrospect, Volga's protective nature was motivated in her desire to shield Margarita from her father. Barbara Leaming argues this can be seen in Margarita's unusual sleeping arrangements at the time. Margarita shared a bed with her mother Volga. Eduardo had a room to himself, and Margarita's two brothers (Eduardo Jr and Vernon) shared a room.[38] Leaming argues that Margarita's brothers may have developed a "sense that their father was among the 'men' in Agua Caliente from whom Volga felt the need to protect her daughter."[39] In which case Eduardo Cansino's hiring of Armand may have been a ploy, to cover up his own incestuous relationship with his daughter, but nevertheless, the role served Armand well. Margarita would remain an acquaintance, and occasionally his employer, for the next two decades, "My dad *did* enjoy a long run as Rita's chief stooge."[40]

One fateful evening in 1935, a Hollywood party including Winfield Sheehan, head of the Fox Film Company, and Louella Parsons, doyenne of movie columnists, was visiting the Agua Caliente. Sheehan was impressed with the young Margarita, and every performer's dream of being noticed by someone powerful enough to make you a star was about to happen. Margarita signed a movie contract with Sheehan and Hollywood beckoned. At Fox, where she was credited as Rita Cansino, Margarita's contract was for six months, and she appeared in mostly unremarkable B-pictures. She subsequently signed a contract with Columbia which was to prove more successful. At Columbia, Margarita would become a studio experiment in how to mold the perfect feminine image of a movie star. She was too plump: a crash diet would be needed. She was beautiful but she was too young, electrolysis would move her hairline back and make her appear older. Her hair was too dark: it was dyed to make her the perfect redhead. She was too Hispanic: her name was anglicized. Margarita was shortened once again to Rita and Cansino was replaced by her mother's maiden name—Hayworth.

Rita Hayworth, the movie star, was born.

It is difficult to determine the exact nature of Armand and Rita's professional relationship in the late 30s and early 40s. In 1948 his association with Hayworth became more formal, but before then he was working for her on a more casual basis. Armand was living with Mildred in LA from 1937. Being close to Hollywood was essential for his career. By this time Armand was working as a "noncertified accountant. He inventoried drugstore stock and prepared income tax returns for Hollywood people."[41] One of his clients was Rita's close friend and occasional lover Glenn Ford.[42] If Armand was securing these Hollywood clients through his association with Rita, it is safe to assume she was favoring him with her star power. However, this was ominous of darker days ahead as when Rita's fortunes changed so did Armand's. Armand put on his draft card that he was unemployed in 1942.

Armand's home life with Mildred was less happy. The marriage staggered on until June 1941, when he "willfully deserted" her for another woman.[43] Armand had grown obsessed with a beautiful redhead, but it was not Rita Hayworth.

His new lover's name was Jean Hilliker.

To Jean, Armand Ellroy looked like a "hunky drifter" and "the handsomest man."[44] She either did not know or did not care at this point about Ellroy's chronic laziness or the shallowness behind his grandiose claims as the sexual attraction was mutual and intense. "It had to be sex," their son wrote about the attraction between his ill-matched parents.[45] For Armand, Jean must have seemed like a more natural and mature beauty than Rita Hayworth.

Armand and Jean were living together on 5th and New Hampshire in LA by June 1941. Mildred Feese left her home and moved to an apartment three blocks away from where Armand was now living with Jean, either in the hope of winning him back or to see the woman who broke up her marriage get her own heart broken in return.[46] Mildred knew that behind his easy charm and imposing physique, Armand was weak-willed and ineffectual. Tellingly, Mildred did not file for divorce until September 1944, three years after she and Armand first separated. Armand ignored a court summons. In the divorce petition, the language used is strikingly blunt, even for the severe terms required to secure a divorce at the time. Armand Ellroy treated Mildred Feese in a "cruel and inhuman manner, which caused this plaintiff grievous mental suffering and distress, resulting in her becoming extremely nervous, suffering physical anguish, and becoming physically ill."[47]

The divorce was finalized in 1945. Mildred stayed in Los Angeles and married a man named William Larrabee in 1949. Armand and Jean were free to marry, but it would be another two years after his divorce before they did. They behaved like man and wife around their circle of friends and attended the occasional "movie-biz party" together.[48] They had been living together for four years now so there was no rush to the altar, or perhaps the nuptials were delayed as Jean was already having second thoughts about the handsome man she was shacking up with. Armand Ellroy and Jean Hilliker finally married on August 29, 1947. Whatever doubts Jean had about Armand were now moot. She was two months pregnant on her wedding day.[49]

That same year, a story was dominating the LA newspapers. The naked corpse of Elizabeth Short was found on 49th and Norton on January 15, 1947. Her murder, in a city with an already high murder rate, became newsworthy due to its bizarre sadism. Elizabeth Short had been brutally beaten, tortured, bisected, and exsanguinated "a horrific and painful death at the hands of a suspect or suspects who took the infliction of physical punishment to the extreme."[50] Her mouth had been sliced open from ear to ear. The corpse looked like it had been posed, as if to mimic an artistic scene, with the hands above the head, elbows bent at right-angles, and legs spread apart.

Dubbed the Black Dahlia by the LA press, Short had come to LA from the small town of Medford, Massachusetts, in search of adventure and a better life on the West Coast. In that sense she was not unlike Armand or Jean or Mildred Feese or the thousands of people who moved to LA every year. The murder occurred one year prior to Lee Earle Ellroy's birth but he claimed his parents "read about Betty Short and thought about Betty Short and talked about Betty Short in ways that I will never discern."[51] The assumption seems reasonable. Elizabeth Short's corpse was found only thirteen miles away from where Armand and Jean lived in LA at North Doheny Drive.

Just as macabre fascination with the Black Dahlia case was starting to fade, Armand Ellroy was about to enjoy his own minor Hollywood miracle. In 1948 Rita Hayworth hired him to be her business manager. Armand and Jean celebrated the birth of Lee Earle Ellroy at Good Samaritan Hospital on March 4, the same year. Their son's name was a combination of Armand's middle name Lee and Jean's father's name Earle. One can sense a certain tension in the compromise. Earle Hilliker had died in 1940 and Jean had never been close to him. She was not close to either of her parents and seldom traveled back to visit them, so it may have arisen from a sense of guilt. Whatever the intentions behind the name choice, it was something the young Ellroy would grow to hate. As his father would concede to him later, Lee Earle Ellroy, said in full, was an alliterative, tongue-twisting nightmare that sounded like a "pimp" name.[52] Still, there is no doubt that 1948 was a good year for the Ellroys. They moved out of their modest apartment in Beverly Hills, and into a larger apartment in Alden Drive, West Hollywood. It was a fashionable Spanish-style apartment with brushed-stucco walls and arched doorways.

Armand Ellroy was beginning to feel confident that he had made it in Hollywood.

Rita Hayworth's marriage to Orson Welles had ended in divorce in 1947. It would not be long before Rita fell in love again, this time with Aly Khan. Rita

Figure 1 *Armand Ellroy and his baby boy Lee. Handsome and charming, a heavy-smoking habit would gradually wear away at Armand's health.*

was wary of remarrying as by her late twenties she was already twice divorced but, as she put it, "when you're in love, you're living, you matter."[53] Aly Khan was a prince and spiritual leader of the Nizari Ismaili sect of Islam, and the heir apparent to the Aga Khan. With his dashing good looks, fondness for beautiful women, fast cars, and thoroughbred horses, Khan could rival many a movie star in terms of his lavish lifestyle. But he also had a sense of power that no Hollywood star could match. The Khans were worshipped as living deities by their Ismaili followers.

Khan had been obsessed with Rita after seeing her in the film *Blood and Sand* while stationed in Cairo during the war. He viewed the film two more times, studying her mannerisms and falling deeper in love with her.[54] While on holiday in Europe, Rita was staying at the Hotel du Cap d'Antibes in Cannes. Her friend Elsa Maxwell invited her to a local party where she first met Khan. Maxwell acted the role of matchmaker, making sure Rita and the Prince sat together at dinner. The other guests noticed how Rita and Khan seemed quite taken with each other. Khan showered Rita with expensive gifts and, for a while, affection. He had decided he was going to marry Rita from the moment he had first seen her onscreen, and once he found out Rita was also being wooed by the Shah of Iran his competitive instincts kicked in. The Shah was a much more powerful royal than Khan, and at that time, a royal had never married a movie star before. Khan felt his honor was at stake: "It was not only the prize, it was the contest itself that was taking hold of his imagination."[55]

Khan's relentless campaign to woo Rita worked. Rita and Aly Khan would soon become the most famous couple in the world.

When Khan and Hayworth were in LA together the press frenzy that followed them was relentless. To add a sense of order to the couple's frantic lifestyle, Armand worked closely with Shifra Haran. Shifra had been employed as a secretary for Orson Welles and began working for Rita after the actress's divorce from Welles. Armand and Shifra arranged for Khan to rent a pink stucco house on Rockingham Avenue, not far from Rita's red brick colonial home on Hanover Street. Armand was also tasked with wading off journalists who tried to follow the couple wherever they went, "popping up in the guise of plumbers, telephone repairmen, readers of gas meters."[56] Rita and Khan would typically travel in separate cars to split their pursuers and Armand would transmit telephone messages hoping to foil eavesdroppers. In a quieter moment, Armand introduced Rita to his baby boy at the Tail O' the Pup hot dog stand. To Armand's embarrassment, Lee managed to spill grape juice all over the movie star.[57]

When Rita and Khan first met, the prince was still married to the English socialite Joan Yarde-Buller. Once Khan's divorce came through, his wedding to Rita could go ahead. Khan planned for the union to take place at his home on the French Riviera. Armand would soon be needed in the South of France when problems began to arise with the wedding preparations. It was Armand's role to make sure the wedding went smoothly, "It was a task comparable to blueprinting a combination movie premiere—complete with reigning Number One Superstar—and a private party for a head-of-state. An impossible task, at best. At worst: a total disaster."[58] Armand flew from New York to Paris on May 12, 1949. He traveled with a suitcase full of stockings for Rita and he also brought along her pet spaniel Pookles. From Paris he made his way to Cannes for the wedding. Armand was one of only a handful of Hollywood guests in attendance. The others were Rita's agent Johnny Hyde, and her press agent Helen Morgan, Louella Parsons who had been present when Rita was first talent-spotted in Tijuana, and director Charles Vidor and his actress wife Doris Warner. Other people were conspicuous by their absence. Rita's father Eduardo Cansino dubiously claimed his invitation had not arrived on time.

After French courts denied Khan's request that the wedding be held at his home, the prince was furious to discover that it would now take place at the Town Hall and be officiated by the Mayor of Vallauris, Paul Derigon. Derigon was a communist, but he was at heart "an agreeable man in whom Marxist materialism and capitalistic enterprise coexisted as happily as two Picasso doves."[59] It was clear that Derigon saw himself as having a major role in the wedding. There was little the couple could do to stop this, but Armand's presence was making things easier for Rita and Khan. Armand set up press headquarters in Suite 131 at the Carlton Hotel. He announced that some of the press would be invited to the wedding luncheon. They would be issued special passes and be admitted to a lower terrace. Armand also designed pink passes for the regular guests. This preferential treatment seemed to win the journalists' goodwill, as there was a commotion of excitement resulting from every statement Armand read out akin to "the rush of White House correspondents to their phones after a presidential press conference."[60] Derigon was giving out his own statements to the press, opportunistically trying to talk up his own role in events and Vallauris' profile at every opportunity. But he could do little to compete with the combined glamour of a Hollywood star marrying royalty.

As a sign of his gratitude for Armand's role in salvaging the wedding plans, Khan invited Armand to a nearby casino two nights before the ceremony was due to take place. It was a 3 a.m. excursion, late enough for Khan to feel confident that reporters would not be snooping around. At one point Khan wandered away from the baccarat tables and returned with two beautiful young women on his arm. He offered Armand his pick of the two and when he declined, Khan, whose appetite was never less than voracious, disappeared with both women in tow.

Armand was growing obsessive about another woman—Rita.

Rita had matured into a beautiful, sensuous woman since Armand had first met her as a teen in Tijuana almost two decades before. Jean Ellroy may have had movie star looks, but Rita was the real thing. Rita was, as Jean had been, pregnant on her wedding day. During the wedding reception, after a long hot day, Rita sat exhausted as the Ismaili guests shuffled past her one by one to pay homage. They got on their knees, kissed her feet, and gave her gifts encrusted with pearls and gold.

Rita was not just a movie star anymore: she was a Goddess.

Armand would, several years later, tell his son Lee that he slept with Rita Hayworth, the Love Goddess: "I am fourteen years old. We're lying around the pad. 'You know,' he says, 'You know I used to fuck Rita Hayworth.'"[61] There is a lack of evidence to support Armand's boastful claim; none of Hayworth's biographers have identified Armand Ellroy as one of Rita's lovers, although circumstantially it is certainly possible that Armand and Rita had a sexual relationship. After the wedding, Rita's marriage to Khan soon came under strain. She grew tired of his constant philandering, and his lavish lifestyle had run down their finances. She may well have relied on Armand for more than just business management during this emotionally fraught time. This was the height of Armand's influence over Rita. He was twenty years her senior and a smooth-talking war hero who had first looked after her when she was a teen, far away from home, in Tijuana. Two decades later, he had done an admirable job in planning her wedding to Khan and had stopped it from becoming a fiasco. However, any sexual relationship between the two of them must have been fleeting. When she was with Khan, they traveled extensively through Europe together and embarked on a three-month tour of Ismaili communities in Africa. In addition, Rita took on almost all the parenting duties for their daughter Yasmin. Khan and Rita divorced in 1953. The coarse language Armand used to describe the actress—he "fucked" Rita and dubbed her a "nympho"—suggests this is not a woman he had a longstanding affair or relationship with.[62] He did not have the stature to consider her his mistress. As events would prove, he was the one who was disposable to her.

Rita fired Armand as her business manager in 1952, during the long separation from her philandering husband. The end of the marriage had forced Rita into a reassessment of her career and dashed her hopes of making fewer films. She needed money quickly and that meant accepting more work. She had to borrow twenty-five thousand dollars from the William Morris Agency just to stay afloat.[63] Sometime afterwards, Rita switched from the William Morris agency to the Music Corporation of America. Old family friends, especially ones as languid as Armand Ellroy, would no longer be employed by her. Rita wanted a more professional operation. She made cutbacks and Armand was one of the first to go. If there was a sexual relationship, it made sense to end that as well and cut Armand loose. He was not husband material, and besides, he was already married. Armand held a grudge for years afterwards and convinced himself that Rita had made a terrible mistake: "He had a sweet deal with Rita. She blew it—not him."[64]

The damaging effects of Armand's relationship with Hayworth lingered long into his marriage, and even after he and Jean divorced. Their son recalled overhearing parental arguments in which his father "shrieked, sobbed and bellowed" about Rita Hayworth behind closed doors.[65] This suggests Armand's feelings for Rita ran much deeper than he was prepared to openly admit to Lee. Perhaps most telling of all are the little clues. During a road trip a few years later, Jean took Lee to the theater to see a film called *Fire Down Below*. When Rita Hayworth's name appeared in the opening credits Jean glowered at the screen.[66] She knew how important the movie star had been to her husband. To Rita and her entourage, Ellroy was always known by his middle name Lee. In the Ellroy family home, he went by Armand. Perhaps alternating names allowed Ellroy, in his mind, to keep his personal and professional lives separate. The latter of which was slowly vanishing.

Armand still clung to his Hollywood connections in the vain hope that he would find another Rita and relive the good old days. Armand was friends with former child star Mickey Rooney and Rooney's business manager Sam Stiefel. Rooney was a philanderer and the source of much of Ellroy's inside knowledge on the sex lives of the stars. According to Armand, Rooney would "fuck a woodpile on the off-chance a snake might be inside."[67] Stiefel was a more ambiguous figure. He owned theaters on the East Coast that were a part of the "Chitlin Circuit"; establishments which catered to African American audiences and featured black performers who could not get work elsewhere. Stiefel's work in Hollywood would be less commendable by comparison. After persuading both Mickey Rooney and Peter Lorre to hire him as their business manager, Stiefel formed companies in both actors' names—Rooney Inc and Lorre Inc—and began to rack up massive debts that he forced the naive actors to repay.

Armand may have done odd jobs for Sam Stiefel, possibly under the pseudonym James Brady.[68] Armand took Jean and little Lee along to a party at Stiefel's showcase home in Bel Air. It is unlikely that Armand was involved in Stiefel's ongoing scheme to defraud two of Hollywood's most recognizable stars. Armand was strictly small fry, a wannabe who was not strong-willed enough to build a fortune like Stiefel had. Rooney reached out to Johnny Hyde to ask for help in cutting his links with Stiefel. Armand knew Hyde, as he was also Rita Hayworth's agent, and he was one of the guests at her wedding to Khan. Hyde encouraged Rooney to confront Stiefel, which he finally did, accusing Stiefel of extorting him to the tune of "six million, four hundred thousand, six hundred and thirteen dollars. And twelve cents"– a figure he had arrived at with Hyde's assistance.[69]

Rooney fired Stiefel, but first he was contractually obligated to appear in three films for the conman and aspiring producer. Stiefel and Rooney ended up making two films together, both of which failed at the box-office. Rooney finally escaped Stiefel's clutches when the producer passed on the third film *Francis* and moved back to Philadelphia to manage his theaters. Ironically, *Francis* was a massive hit for Universal and spawned a franchise which included six more films and the *Mister Ed* television series. It would have made both Rooney and Stiefel millions if they could have kept their poisonous business relationship going just a little longer. It should be noted that the Stiefel family to this day contest how Sam Stiefel was portrayed as a conman by Mickey Rooney. According to author Jay Stiefel, it was Rooney who ran down Stiefel's finances with his extravagant spending which Stiefel, as his business manager, was forced to repay.[70] Stiefel sold his Bel Air home and returned to live in Philadelphia to spend his last years in a relatively modest two-bedroom apartment. As it happens, Jean's connection to the Stiefel family proved more lucrative than Armand's. She worked for Stiefel as a maid and was fondly remembered by Stiefel's son, Bernard "Sonny" Stiefel.[71] With Sam Stiefel out of town and Rooney trying to rebuild his acting career, neither man had much use for Armand Ellroy. Just as he had lost his position as Rita Hayworth's business manager, Armand's last tangible links to Hollywood were slipping away.

Like many people around Armand and Jean, Lee did not spot the simmering tensions in his parents' marriage as they both, by nature, kept things bottled up. A consequence of this was that they were never particularly affectionate with each other either. Lee was left with only one unambiguously happy memory of the two of them together: "My mother passing steaks out the kitchen window to my father so he could put them on the barbecue."[72] By the early 1950s, Jean was working as a nurse at St. John's hospital in Santa Monica. Many of the patients were Hollywood stars and Jean secured a sideline as a private nurse to ZaSu Pitts, an aging actress and comedienne whose fame stretched back to the Silent Movie age. Pitts had undergone a lumpectomy in 1952 followed by a mastectomy in 1954. She had only been discharged from hospital for a week after the mastectomy before she was readmitted in acute pain. Jean was hired to care for Pitts for several weeks at her home in Brentwood.[73]

Lee overheard his parents describing Pitts as a dipsomaniac. Neither of Pitts' biographers refer to the star as having a problem with alcohol. It may be Pitts overindulged in drink temporarily to offset the pain of her illness and operation. She died of cancer in 1963. Whatever the motive behind the allegation, Pitts' reputed alcoholism was another Hollywood secret that was joked about in the Ellroy family home.[74] Lee was under the impression that Jean strictly did "wet-nursing" work for Pitts to treat her alcoholism. He was unaware that his mother was nursing a woman recovering from two major operations. Pitts' biographer Gayle Haffner speculates that Jean confided in Pitts about her troubled marriage. While this is pure conjecture as there are no witnesses or records of Jean and Pitts' conversations, there is no doubt that Jean's marriage to Armand was falling apart around this time. Jean's frustrations were mounting as she worked long hours at St. John's hospital, while Armand was unemployed and would cite his Hollywood connections every time Jean "bugged my father to get a permanent job."[75]

Gradually the rising levels of antagonism between Armand and Jean became more and more apparent to Lee as their bickering evolved into full-blown arguments. One day in 1954, Jean sat down with Lee and "told me she was divorcing my father. I took it hard. I threw a tantrum for weeks running."[76] He knew that divorced kids at school had a rough deal, being shuffled from one parent to another. Lee's fears proved well-founded. Armand moved out of the home and into an apartment on Beverly Boulevard. Lee blamed his mother for his absence. After leaving her role at St. John's hospital, Jean had secured a position at Packard Bell Electronics as an industrial nurse. She had moved out of the West Hollywood home, which was proving too expensive to maintain, and into a new apartment in Santa Monica. The money she saved on rent she spent on education. Jean pulled Lee out of West Hollywood Elementary School and moved him to the private Children's Paradise School at a cost of $50 a month.

Jean did not file for divorce until the first week of January 1955. The end of the marriage was protracted and painful for all involved. A judge ruled a temporary custody split so that Lee lived with Jean during the week, and his father at weekends. Now the real battle for Lee's heart began. In violation of a court order, Lee would meet his father after school. Time with Armand was spent watching television and eating burgers. Jean made Lee do his homework and monitored his diet. Jean was convinced Armand was spying on her: "she sensed it. She saw smudge marks on her bedroom window."[77] Armand was grilling Lee for information on his mother's movements and behavior. Not that

Lee needed any coercion in telling his father everything he saw. He was happy to spy on her. Armand told Lee he had private detectives tailing his mother everywhere she went, trying to dig up dirt that could be used against her in the divorce. When his mother took him for a drive, Lee would stare out of the rear window convinced they were being followed: "I believed it then, I know it was hoo-ha now. It didn't matter then."[78] What mattered was that Armand was succeeding in poisoning Lee's mind against Jean.

Jean began a casual relationship with a man named Hank Hart. Hart was a podgy, blue-collar worker who was missing the tip of one thumb after an industrial accident. Hart was Jean's first fling after separating from Armand, who did not approve of the relationship. Jean filed a nuisance claim against Armand as his harassment of her intensified. She alleged that Armand eavesdropped at her door. He broke into her apartment and rifled through her clothes. He followed her and confronted her while she was shopping at Ralph's Market on San Vicente Boulevard, hurling insults at her in front of the other shoppers. Armand was summoned to court. A judge appointed a court assistant to investigate the charges. Armand admitted to spying on Jean, but he tried to frame it as all being out of concern for Lee. He claimed Jean was an alcoholic, drinking heavily during the week and then without restraint at weekends. He had brought Lee home to Jean one evening and she was visibly drunk when she answered the door. He could see Hank Hart lounging around half-naked in the apartment, bottles of alcohol were scattered everywhere. He was passing her apartment later that night when he heard a commotion inside. He peered in through the kitchen window. He saw Jean and Hart "lie down on the living room sofa. They started necking. Hart stuck his hand under Jean's dress."[79] Lee wandered into the living room in his pajamas. Hart teased Lee until the boy went back to bed. Hart and Jean then had sex on the sofa.

Armand's claims were contradicted by the babysitter Jean hired, the principal of Children's Paradise School, and Jean's neighbor Eula Lee Lloyd. Ms Lloyd was particularly scathing of Armand. She had witnessed Armand peeping through Jean's window several times. When it came to Jean's turn to talk to the court assistant she did not hold back. She said Armand was lazy and spoiled their son. Armand frequently lied to Lee to impress him. Most humiliating for Armand, Jean described her soon to be ex-husband as a "latent homosexual."[80] The investigator and judge both sided with Jean. She was a good mother with a strong work ethic and displayed no overt signs of alcoholism. A formal decree was issued. Armand Ellroy was instructed not to harass Jean, break into her apartment, or loiter around the home.

Despite all the drama it had entailed, Jean's relationship with Hank Hart had never been that serious. She had several boyfriends after the divorce, and Lee had walked in on her *in flagrante* a couple of times. The first time was with Hank Hart. The second time Lee saw his mother in bed with a man he did not recognize, and an embarrassed Jean "pulled a sheet up over her breasts" at the sight of Lee entering the bedroom.[81] Lee got a longer look at his mother's body sometime later. She had just stepped out of the bath and was toweling her dripping figure when she noticed Lee was staring at her. This time she displayed no sense of embarrassment. She informed Lee that she had the tip of one nipple removed after she had developed mastitis following his birth. Although he actively disliked his mother following his parents' divorce, Lee had a childhood fascination with her figure as his interest in girls grew.

Whatever the dubious nature of Armand's slurs against Jean, there was no doubt that her fondness for men and booze was returning, fueled mostly by the unbearable pressure Armand was putting on her at every opportunity. Jean and Armand's divorce was finalized in 1956. The weekday/weekend custody split of Lee would continue. In one dramatic scene during the divorce proceedings, Lee spotted his father outside the courtroom and broke away from his mother to be with him. Armand dragged Lee into the Men's restroom to stop Jean from taking him back before he could talk to him. "My mother stormed in and whisked me out. My father let it happen."[82] While one man stood at the urinals shocked at the domestic scene that was unfolding, Armand looked on impassively. He knew that backing down and letting the incident play out would likely heighten Lee's frustration with his mother.

While Jean forced Lee to study, Armand was feeding his son's interest in popular culture. Armand's reading tastes were for historical and detective novels. He owned all of Mickey Spillane's Mike Hammer novels, and he told Lee he could read them when he was older. He subscribed to the tabloid magazine *Confidential*, as well as *Rave*, *Whisper*, and *Hush-Hush* which published exposés of the scandals and sex lives of movie stars. Lee read these magazines and found them tantalizing, "I got the scoop on Ava Gardner's nympho status and Johnny Stompanato's size."[83] For Armand, the tabloids gave him the chance to reminisce about his old Hollywood days. He also subscribed to the pornographic magazines *Swank*, *Cavalier*, and *Nugget* which reminded him of something else that he had been missing. Armand's favorite pastime was to lie on the couch, reading his novels and magazines until his eyes got tired and he drifted off to sleep, only getting up for food and bathroom breaks. He did exhibit some parental concern by skimming through the animal stories Lee was fond of reading. Armand "shitcanned the ones he knew I'd find disturbing."[84] Even though these stories were written for children, Lee was acutely sensitive to animal suffering and Armand screened each story carefully, ditching books and tearing out pages if he knew they would upset his little boy. Although his idolizing of his father would fade away over time, Lee would always remember this simple act of kindness.

Jean was jealous of Lee's close relationship with Armand and could be spiteful in retaliation. When Armand was mistakenly diagnosed with cancer in 1956, Jean relished in telling Lee that his father was suffering from the Big C. When she saw how badly Lee took the news, she informed him Armand had been misdiagnosed and "told me it was ulcers, not cancer."[85] Perhaps out of guilt, Jean told a still upset Lee that they were going on a short vacation together. Taking Lee on a trip to Mexico would give Jean time to relax and think things through. As Jean sat with Lee in an Ensenada restaurant, the boy noticed how attractive his mother looked in an off-one-shoulder dress and how other men were looking at her, "she looked startlingly fair-skinned and redheaded."[86] She seemed to like the power her looks gave her over men.

Jean could only afford a cheap hotel room for the trip and the hotel swimming pool was visibly dirty. After going for a dip, Lee emerged from the water with "blocked ears and a throbbing headache. The headache worked its way down to my left ear."[87] Jean knew immediately that her son was suffering from a severe ear infection. Thinking fast, she bundled him into the car and drove for over ninety minutes until they reached Tijuana. Tijuana was well-known for its pharmacies which sold medicines and hard drugs under the

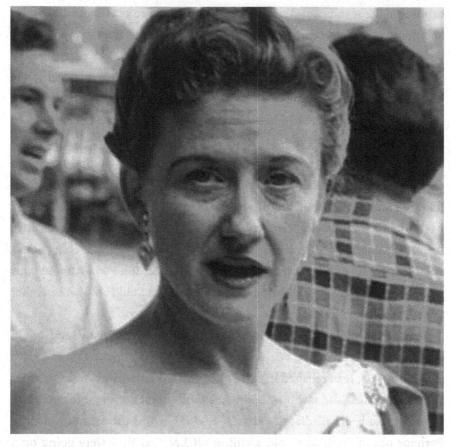

Figure 2 *Jean Ellroy pictured, after her divorce from Armand, looking striking in a one-shoulder dress during a trip to Ensenada. Photo: Courtesy of James Ellroy.*

counter. Jean got the dope, pills, and syringe she needed and treated Lee in the car. The pain instantly subsided and Lee slept soundly on the drive back to LA. This was not the first time Jean had used her medical knowledge to treat Lee personally. In 1955, Lee along with millions of other American children were among the first generation to receive the polio vaccine, then better known as the Salk vaccine. Lee was nervous about his first encounter with a needle. His overactive imagination heightened his anxiety level. He sneaked off the school bus on the appointed day and hid in the courtyard of his father's apartment. He wanted Armand to save him from having to take the vaccine. Jean left work early to find him. She drove him back to school and administered the vaccine herself while still wearing her nurse's uniform. She was not the type of mother who would give Lee much comfort talk, but her machine-like efficiency worked just as well. "She was skilled with a needle—it didn't hurt at all."[88]

Jean and Lee managed another trip away at Christmas, 1957. Shortly before the trip, Lee was spending the weekend with Armand. They went strolling through Hollywood and Armand stopped outside a building on North Cherokee Avenue. He gave Lee a comic book and told him not to roam. He would be gone for an hour. Lee later suspected that his father had gone to use a "fuckpad," but at the time he merely read until he had finished the comic book. Bored, he began to explore and stumbled across "a half-full jug of cheap wine by the mailbox bank." Lee drank the whole thing. The next thing he recalled was a "queasy cab ride." Still only nine years old, Lee had experienced his first taste of alcohol and, having already witnessed sexual activity, would soon be subjected to direct sexual contact.

Jean took Lee to visit her family in Wisconsin. Jean's mother had died suddenly of a stroke in 1950. Her younger sister Leoda was the only immediate family she had left in Wisconsin. Jean most likely used the trip to seek some advice from Leoda on how to put more distance between her and Armand. Armand did not approve of the trip. He had always disliked Jean's family and hated Leoda's husband Ed Wagner who he labelled "a draft-dodger and a kraut."[89]

On New Year's Eve, Jean, Leoda, and Ed went out to celebrate and left Lee in the care of a teenage au pair. A photo of Jean taken that night shows her in a passionate clinch with a young man. Lee, still only nine years old, had his first sexual contact the same night. He would later write about this disturbing incident with a lurid pulp sensibility. Lee was restless and frustrated that he was not spending the holidays with his father, and there was something odd about this babysitter who was watching over him. It was not just her unfamiliar German accent; it was her entire manner that gave off unsettling "Hitler-Jugend vibes."[90] She tucked him in bed that night and then started patting him lightly. Then she pulled down the covers and began fellating him. After a few seconds of being paralyzed in shock, a confused Lee pushed and kicked her off. "She talked a Kraut blue-streak and bolted the room," and she did not approach him again.[91] Jean never found out about the incident. Lee buried it deep within himself and did not talk about it for several years, when he mentioned it to Armand who "thought it was funny, because it was a girl doing it."[92]

Lee's life was about to change in a big way. The Christmas holiday had helped Jean make a key decision. Ed Wagner sold Jean a red-and-white '57 Buick at a knocked down price. She drove Lee back to LA. Lee recalled the trip for its inclement winter weather and his mother's poor driving, "We skidded in and out of mud troughs. We clipped rural fence posts and sheared off our right sideview mirror."[93] Back at home, Jean sat down with Lee for a serious talk. She often made big decisions, after much brooding, at the beginning of the year. It was time to move, she told Lee. El Monte was a small, pleasant city about fifteen miles outside of LA. They would have a bigger place there. For the first time in his life, Lee would live in a house. "My mother lied poorly," Lee would recall "She tended to formalize and overstate her lies and often embellished them with expressions of parental concern. She always laid out her major lies half-drunk."[94]

Jean was too honest and straightforward in her everyday life to lie with any conviction, and this instance was no exception. The real reason they were moving to El Monte was that Jean was running away from Armand Ellroy.

2

Murder in El Monte
(1958–1965)

When Lee first saw El Monte, he felt completely crushed. His mother had exaggerated its small-town appeal, whereas "my father got me predisposed to hate and fear the place."[1] Vehicles were parked on lawns and the residents "hosed down their cars in their underwear."[2] El Monte was only thirty miles from their old home in Santa Monica, but it was a world away in terms of culture. Its suburban mix of older residents and a burgeoning Hispanic community did not appeal to the nine-year-old Lee, "The sky was carcinogenic tan."[3] When he saw their new house at 756 Maple Avenue his mood sank further. Although it was "pretty on the outside" it was much smaller than their former home.[4] The kitchen was practically a crawl space. The toilet was so close to the bath that you could bang your leg on it when you stood up.

Their landlady was a nice, slightly anxious woman named Anna May Krycki who was prone to "agitated gestures."[5] Lee patted her Airedale dog and, to raise his spirits, Jean told Lee that he could have a puppy as a birthday present. He was going to be ten the following month. Lee asked for a Beagle, probably after spotting the breed in one of the animal stories he was so fond of. Jean happily obliged. When his birthday came around, Lee was delighted to be introduced to his new Beagle puppy. He named her Minna and smothered her with love. At some point, unbeknownst to Lee, there may have been a dog switch. In family photos which are annotated on the back by Armand, the beagle is referred to as Cleo. While she watched

Lee play happily with Minna, Jean brought up a topic which she knew would radically change his mood. She said he was a young man now and was "old enough to decide who I wanted to live with."[6] The Beagle had merely been a ploy, "a mind fuck on me in conjunction with the gift" to soften him up for this question.[7]

Lee's answer was predictable, and Jean should have seen it coming. "I want to live with my father," Lee responded. Her response was extreme, "She slapped me in the face and knocked me off the living room couch."[8] Lee banged his head on the coffee table while reeling from the force of the blow. He retreated to his room to sulk but vowed he would fight back if she ever hit him again. He was getting into fights soon enough. Jean enrolled Lee at the newly opened Anne LeGore Elementary School in El Monte, which had been named after a local teacher. He made friends with two Mexican kids named Reyes and Danny. They shared a joint with him, and Lee got high very quickly. Jean may have suspected something when Lee came home dizzy and raided the kitchen for cookies, but then marijuana was not her vice so she may not have recognized the symptoms.

Lee carried himself with increasing swagger. At least one kid at Anne LeGore school felt the full force of Lee's hair-trigger temper. One day Armand visited Lee, "a divorce decree violation," during the school's noon recess.[9] One of the schoolkids shoved Lee. Maybe he was looking for trouble or maybe it was just crowded and happened by accident; either way, Lee responded by beating up the kid in full view of Armand. He was big for his age and could handle himself well in fights. Armand likely held a tacit admiration for this sort of behavior and did nothing to stop it.

Jean, however, was less impressed with Lee's actions. Word of the fight reached the Vice-Principal, Peter Tubiolo. Jean met with Tubiolo to discuss the situation, and Lee's general lack of academic progress. From this, Lee came to believe that Tubiolo and his mother were dating: "They met and talked. They went out on a couple of dates. I reported the details to my father."[10] Sometime later, Tubiolo would strenuously deny that he ever dated Jean Ellroy. Lee assumed they were dating after he witnessed Tubiolo pick up his mother in his "blue-and-white Nash."[11] Perhaps the increasingly paranoid Armand thought the relationship must be sexual and made Lee believe it too. Armand had made these types of claims before. He said Jean had been sleeping with her divorce attorney. He was willing to think badly of any man who helped Jean. Armand told Lee that Jean only moved to El Monte as she was running away from some dangerous ex-boyfriend. He seemed oblivious to the notion that the only man Jean was trying to escape from was him. Besides, you did not leave Santa Monica for El Monte if you wanted to escape a sexualized world. El Monte, "a bustling bedroom community," had its own sordid, sex-in-the-suburbs vibe.[12]

In conjunction with the move, Jean had resigned her position at Packard Bell, where the atmosphere had been liberal and dating colleagues was common and taken up a role at Airtek Dynamics on South Figueroa, which was even more liberal in its attitudes, "Airtek was Romance City."[13] Nevertheless, Jean did not allow her newfound social life to deter her from taking an active role in Lee's education. Despite his prodigious reading habit, Lee was struggling to learn practical skills: "I couldn't tie my shoes until I was eight or nine. It took me a long time to learn how to tell time."[14] Shortly after her meeting with Tubiolo, something Lee did made her snap while they were out shopping at Jay's Market. She marched him back to the car and drove over to Medina Court, where El Monte's Latino population lived. She tried to frighten him with horrifying details, showing him how hard Mexicans worked for very little pay. Their houses were more like shacks. The implication was clear. Start to do better at school or you may end up in a crummy low-paid job. Lee ignored her, thinking to himself "I knew my father would never let me turn into a wetback."[15] He had a formula for her behavior. Every time she threatened him with work or barked instructions, he would go to his father, and he would invalidate everything she said.

Four months after her move to El Monte, things seemed to be looking up for Jean. Armand was bothering her less, as she had hoped. In fact, she never saw him anymore. For Lee's weekend visits with his dad, all Jean needed to do was drop him off at the bus depot and Armand, who had been left without a car since the separation, would pick him up and take him back to LA. No doubt Armand was still poisoning Lee's mind against her at every opportunity, but that could pass with time as Lee matured. Confident that Armand could not interfere, Jean set about enjoying her weekend.

On Saturday night, June 21, 1958, Jean left the house at around 8 p.m. She drank alone in a place called the Manger bar. Next, she was seen at Stan's Drive-In. She was in a car with a man of a swarthy, olive-skinned complexion, possibly of Mexican origin according to at least one witness. A car hop named Lavonne Chambers served them. Jean asked for the thinnest or smallest sandwich on the menu.[16] She was already a little tipsy and chatty, and Chambers remembered her as a very pleasant and attractive customer. At around 10:30 that evening, Jean arrived at a local nightclub called the Desert Inn. She was with the Swarthy Man, and a heavyset woman described as a "dishwater blonde."[17] They sat, drank, and danced together. A local drunk named Mike Whittaker crashed their party. The four of them danced together. The Swarthy Man was of a sullen disposition. He rarely spoke and looked like he could snap at the slightest provocation. Aside from that he was not physically imposing. He was short and skinny with a thin face and an extremely thin chin, which made it look like all his teeth had been removed.

Jean, the blonde, and the Swarthy Man left the Desert Inn around midnight, possibly to escape Mike Whittaker. Whittaker went to Stan's Drive-In for a snack, then stumbled around drunk until he was arrested by local Sheriffs on Valley Boulevard. They took him to Temple City Station, but the drunk tank was full, so he was transported to the Hall of Justice Jail. It was not Whittaker's lucky night. While he slept, some prisoners robbed him of his shoes and socks. He was released the next morning and walked the twelve miles home barefoot in sweltering heat: "The pavement chewed up his feet and gave him big red blisters."[18] Jean and the Swarthy Man were seen back at the Desert Inn around 2 a.m. They went to Stan's Drive-In again at 2:15, by now Jean was visibly drunk and hungry. She ordered a bowl of chili. Chambers served them again. She said Jean was just as pleasant and happy as on the previous visit a few hours earlier. The Swarthy Man was sullen and sober, he ordered coffee. They left at 2:40.

Jean Ellroy was discovered at 10:10 on Sunday morning by some kids who were out to play baseball in their local Babe Ruth League: "pearls from a broken necklace led to her body sprawled in an acacia thicket on the short lane across from the high school athletic field."[19] She had been asphyxiated with a stocking and cotton cord, both wrapped separately around her neck, and she had received multiple blows to the head. Her body had been dumped on a road beside the playing field of Arroyo High School in El Monte. Three adult coaches hurriedly pulled the kids back away from the corpse, and then found a payphone to call the police.

Lee had enjoyed a pleasant, uneventful weekend with his father in LA. They had gone to the theater to see *The Vikings* starring Kirk Douglas and Tony Curtis. Lee had been scared by a scene in which Tony Curtis had his hand hacked off, and then gets a black-leather stump guard as a replacement, "I had a nightmare about it."[20] Although his vivid dreams stemmed more from his anxiety of returning to his mother and that place, the hated El Monte. With each passing hour he dreaded going back more.

On Sunday morning Armand and Lee took the bus back to El Monte. Armand put him in a cab at the bus depot, gave the cabbie Jean's address, said goodbye, and waited for a bus to take him back to LA. As the cab approached his mother's house, Lee knew something was wrong. The place was alive with activity. There were patrol cars and ominous looking sedans, cops in uniform and others in plain-clothes. Lee would later claim that he knew what had happened before he got out of the cab, "I knew she was dead."[21]

"There's the boy," someone called out. One of the cops in plain clothes approached him, put a hand on his shoulder, leaned in and said "Son, your mother's been killed."

Again, Lee knew instinctively the meaning behind the policeman's careful phrasing, "I knew he meant 'murdered.'"[22] He was attuned to crime stories enough already to know that the police do not come out in force like this in response to fatal accidents. The cop asked him where his father was. Back at the depot, waiting for a bus, Lee replied. Another cop jumped in a car and drove over there fast. One man with a camera walked Lee over to Mrs Krycki's toolshed. He put an awl in Lee's hand and told him to pretend he was sawing wood. The whole scene, the throng of cops, the swirl of emotions was getting too much. Lee stared into the camera, frightened, and confused. The photographer wanted a second snap as a backup shot. He told Lee to improvise this time. Lee started to goof around, sawing at the wood with a "half-smile/half-grimace."[23] The cops' blank stares turned to smiles and laughter. This was a tough kid, they thought.

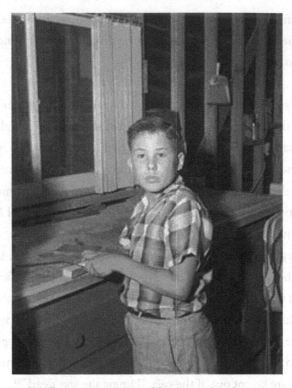

Figure 3 *Lee Earle Ellroy at ten years old, pictured only moments after he was informed his mother had been murdered. Photo: Courtesy of James Ellroy.*

Lee was then taken in a patrol car to El Monte police station. Some cops kept him company while his father, who had been stopped at the depot before he caught a bus back to LA, was interrogated by Sergeants Jack Lawton and Ward Hallinen who had been assigned to the Jean Ellroy homicide case. The cops tried to calm Lee down. The boy was nervous his dad was under suspicion and would end up going to prison. The cops asked Lee about his weekend with his father and Jean's relationship with other men. Lee described going to see *The Vikings*, and the two men he knew his mother had dated—Hank Hart and Peter Tubiolo. Armand was questioned about his relationship with the deceased. He did not hold back on his animosity towards Jean, and he lied at least once, saying he had married Jean in 1940, at which time he was still married to Mildred Feese.[24] Jean and Armand married in 1947. Armand was released, but Hallinen and Lawton said they would need to speak to him again soon. Lee ran into his dad's arms when he saw him. The cops noticed how father and son "looked both relieved and strangely happy."[25]

On the bus back to LA that night, Armand and Lee were struggling with just how strangely happy they were. Armand had grown to hate Jean and had waged a psychological campaign to turn Lee's heart against her. It was not uncommon to wish someone dead when the hatred was that intense, especially as he felt humiliated by Jean's relationships with other men. He knew that Jean had moved to El Monte because she was running away from someone. In one sense, he felt vindicated, but he also felt guilty at how well Jean's death had worked out for him. He had gotten what he wanted, sole custody of Lee, "I could tell he was really happy and in some state of serendipitous shell-shock."[26] Lee was torn as well. He willed himself to cry as he felt he owed his mother some tears, but as Armand placed a consoling arm around him Lee was secretly delighted. Earlier that day, he had a knot in his stomach as he could not bear the thought of returning to El Monte, and now he would never have to spend another night there, "some unknown killer just bought me a brand-new beautiful life."[27]

He was free to live with his father. He was free to do what he wanted.

Jean's murder seemed to jolt Armand out of his chronic laziness. He made all the arrangements for the funeral. Jean was laid to rest at Inglewood Park Cemetery. Only a few people showed up to pay their last respects. Jean's sister Leoda and her husband Ed Wagner were in attendance. Armand managed to keep his dislike for Jean's family in check, "no discernible Ellroy-Wagner hatred surfaced."[28] Lee made some excuse not to go to the service. He spent the day watching television with some of his father's friends. Armand did not object to his absence. Armand soon had his own "family" reunion. As his name had been reported in the papers in connection to Jean's murder, Irma got back in touch, and he visited her in Manhattan Beach. Armand gave instructions to Lee that he had to call her Aunt Irma. Lee remembers Irma as "raggedy-ass looking" and her husband, the songwriter Herman Hummel as "dyspeptic and misanthropic."[29]

Sergeants Hallinen and Lawton visited them again. They had few leads, and the case was not progressing well. They had interviewed Hank Hart and

Peter Tubiolo, and both were ruled out. Hart had an alibi, and Tubiolo was too plump and pale to match the description of the Swarthy Man. In addition, he vehemently denied ever dating Jean, stating that he had only ever met her once at the school when they had discussed Lee's behavior. Dating parents was against the school's code of conduct and could have cost Tubiolo his job. Unless Tubiolo was lying, Jean's relationship with the Vice-Principal had sprung from Lee's imagination, possibly planted there by Armand. Lee was not just getting into trouble at school, he was getting his Vice-Principal into trouble with him.

Lawton and Hallinen were no closer to identifying the Swarthy Man or the blonde woman Jean had been seen with that night. Before they left, Lee eavesdropped on his father talking to the two detectives in the hallway. Armand called Jean "a promiscuous drunk."[30] Hallinen and Lawton responded that "their case was dead. Jean was such a goddamn secretive woman."[31] Armand withheld information from the police which could have been useful to their investigation. He never told the police about Jean's first marriage to Easton Spaulding, which may have helped the detectives form a clearer picture of Jean's life as Spaulding was still living in LA. Armand seemed to take the view that Jean had brought her violent end on herself, a theory he later expounded to Lee by claiming his mother may have been murdered after she "balked at a three-way with the Blonde and the Dark Man."[32]

One of the most notable interviews Lawton and Hallinen conducted in the Jean Ellroy case was with the recently captured murderer Harvey Glatman. Glatman, known as "The Lonely Hearts Killer" and "The Glamour Girls Slayer," had posed as a photographer to lure his female victims with the promise of a modelling career. He tied up women in bondage poses, raped, and then murdered them. He was arrested in October 1958 and confessed to murdering three women. He was interviewed at San Quentin prison about the Jean Ellroy murder. Glatman had a photographic memory, he relished describing in vivid detail the tortures he had inflicted on his victims. He denied ever meeting Jean Ellroy and had never visited El Monte. Lawton and Hallinen left San Quentin in complete agreement that Glatman did not kill Jean Ellroy. His crimes were too sadistic, and this did not fit the profile of the Swarthy Man. Glatman was sent to the electric chair the following year. Lee read about his execution in the news.[33] Lee had taken an interest in several true-crime cases which resulted in the death penalty, including serial killer Stephen Nash and kidnapper and rapist Caryl Chessman. The execution of Chessman on May 2, 1960 was controversial as the death penalty could only be applied because the "Little Lindbergh Laws" defined kidnapping as a capital offence. Although it was widely considered a misuse of the death penalty, Lee "cheered Caryl Chessman into the gas chamber" during classroom discussions.[34] Jean's murder had imbued him with a vindictive take on justice, but he also relished how he could shock his peers.

Lee transferred from Anne Le Gore School in El Monte where Peter Tubiolo, one suspects, was happy to see the back of him, to Van Ness Avenue Elementary in LA. He was only at Van Ness briefly as, in 1959, he moved on to John Burroughs Junior High School on 6th and McCadden in the wealthy Hancock Park. Steve Horvitz was one of the pupils there and recalls how the class was informed of Lee's tragic background before his arrival, "we knew at the time, when he came into the 7th grade class, they told us his mother died. And then we heard all these crazy rumors about how she was murdered and all this stuff, but we never really knew any details or specific facts about what happened, just that she was killed."[35]

It was the fifth school Lee had attended so far, and it was the place he started to refine his crazy kid act. A few kids tried to taunt Lee about his white trash sounding name by dubbing him Leroy. He lashed back fast and hard, "A few punk confrontations killed the 'Leroy' epidemic."[36] There is no reason to doubt Ellroy's account of his temper or fighting prowess. Physical confrontations were quickly becoming a regular feature of his troubled existence and he would be equally candid about fights he lost. He was not bullied again at John Burroughs, but he was craving attention so much that he probably would have welcomed the abuse. JB, as it was known, had a predominantly Jewish student body. Lee always had trouble fitting in. Leslie Jacobson, a student at JB who Lee was crushing on, recalls "how tough it was to be a kid on the periphery" for her and Lee.[37] "On a Jewish holiday in those days the school would be empty of kids, but I would be there, he [Ellroy] would be there. So we were that other group."[38] This was the age of Camelot, and Lee and Leslie were among the sons and daughters of the cream of LA society, "These were upper-middle class kids. The girls were all beautiful. The boys were all handsome, and if you didn't feel like you were in any of those categories you sheltered yourself away from everyone and would be in small enclaves of two or three kids."[39]

Lee started toying with anti-Semitic ideas which he inherited, in part, from his father. Armand was friends with several Jewish people, but he referred to them as "pork-dodgers" in private and warned Lee they were "smarter than regular people" and "competitive."[40] At the time Lee was under the false impression that he was German-American on his mother's side. Believing himself to be Aryan and looking for trouble at JB, he became interested in the ideas of American Nazi Party founder George Lincoln Rockwell.

Lee's slide into extreme ideology coincided with his diminishing respect for his father. For years he had wanted nothing more than to leave his strict mother and live with his easygoing father. Now Armand's laziness and amorality were starting to grate. Leoda suspected Armand had murdered Jean. The belief was both sincere and absurd. Armand had been with Lee when Jean was murdered. Nevertheless, Armand reveled in the sense of power and menace he exuded over his hated sister-in-law. Leoda had become the sole executrix of Jean Ellroy's estate. Jean's murder had triggered a double indemnity clause bringing the overall sum to $20,000. Leoda told Lee she was keeping the money in trust for his college education. He could request small amounts in case of emergencies. Armand would encourage Lee to beg for money off Leoda to pay for his dental treatment, "My father paid the dentist's initial bill and pocketed the balance [from Leoda] [...] and paid a cut-rate oral surgeon twenty bucks to cut the hardware off my teeth."[41] Money was an issue from the moment Lee moved back to LA. Armand's child support payments had died with Jean, but the cost of raising Lee alone had upped his expenses considerably. The conventional solution would be to get a job, but Armand was sixty and had not been in regular employment since he had been fired by Rita Hayworth.

One of Armand's first acts after Jean died was to take possession of her red-and-white '57 Buick which had been sold to her by Ed Wagner. He managed to pocket the down payment she had made on the car and then immediately sold the vehicle. After that, he threw himself into a variety of get-rich-quick schemes. The first involved purchasing ten thousand Japanese tote seats, which he planned to sell to the LA Rams and Dodgers teams for their stadiums. Every sports fan in LA could be sitting on one, except that both clubs brushed him off. Having spent ten cents apiece for the tote seats, Armand lost a hundred bucks on the venture. A considerable sum for a man who was already broke. Rather than cut his losses and sell the totes on the street, Armand returned to accountancy and inventory work for pharmacies as the April 1959 tax deadline loomed. Ironically, by using his James Brady alias, Armand never paid taxes on his earnings from this work. The tote seats remained in the apartment, "you could have blown the cushions up and floated half the county out to sea."[42]

The apartment was becoming uninhabitable. Minna had moved with Lee from El Monte, and while Jean had done her best to housebreak the rambunctious pup neither of the Ellroy men bothered, and they let her urinate and defecate all over the carpet. The smell got worse with the summer heat as Minna's waste was absorbed into the fabric. They left the windows open as wide as possible at night to alleviate the stench and help them sleep. Despite his chronic poverty, Armand was still up to his old tricks with women, "his pal George told me he was fucking two check-stand girls at the Larchmont Safeway."[43] Lee returned home one day to the sound of sensual moans. The door to his father's bedroom was ajar. He peeked through and saw his father in bed with a "zaftig blonde." Minna was walking up and down on the mattress, trying to find a peaceful spot amidst the entangled bodies and bouncing bedspring.

Lee was increasingly disappointed with Armand. He no longer believed his dad's stories about how he won his medals during the war. In fact, Armand's military record suggests at least some of his war stories were accurate. But then Lee was something of an oddity in being a child in the 1950s whose father was a World War I veteran. Many of Lee's peers at school would have had fathers who served in World War II. The effects of the conflict were deeply embedded in American culture, so much so that Lee recalled how he thought the war was still happening as a child and his mother had to disabuse him of the notion.[44] By contrast, in the late 1950s, World War I was an obscure part of history which many Americans had only a dwindling memory of and even less interest in. It is regrettable that Lee could not learn more from his father's experiences of wartime, but then Armand's chronic lying had begun to undermine everything he said.

Lee began to question all of Armand's statements. Armand first mentioned Rita Hayworth to Lee when he was eleven years old, "he launched into a song and dance about being her business manager."[45] Lee did not believe him, nor his claims that he slept with the movie star.[46] Despite Lee's dwindling respect for Armand, they had developed a bond of sorts. If Lee told Armand he studied penguins at school on a particular day, Armand responded "Yeah? Well, I'm a penguin fucker from way back."[47] He would repeat the gag when Lee told him he had studied giraffes, tigers, lions, and the two of them would laugh uproariously. When Armand lazed around on the couch, occasionally spouting "fuck you" and "suck my dick" when some TV pundit upset him, Lee still felt a great deal of affection for the old man. Armand was a casual bigot; it would never occur to him to actively seek to harm anyone in a minority group. Lee, on the other hand, was in danger of becoming a full-blown reactionary. He was determined to push his classroom Nazi act to the limit.

As Lee was underperforming at school, he relied on his dad more and more for his social and cultural education. The first mystery stories Lee ever read were the Hardy Boys books. Armand would limit him to two books a week. Lee would devour the two books so quickly he would go out and steal some more. Once he had finished the Hardy Books, he moved onto his father's Mickey Spillane collection. He dug private eye Mike Hammer's brutal methods as a vindication of his own worldview. Hammer was scarred and ugly, both physically and emotionally, but he was irresistible to women. Armand and Lee did not discuss the plots of the books together, so Lee absorbed and internalized the narrative structure on his own.

Armand was more influential as an educator in terms of the throwaway remarks he would make to Lee about the Hollywood lifestyle. Armand claimed that the actress Christine Nelson, "flashed her snatch" to him at a Hollywood party.[48] While Lee knew his father's claims were often dubious, he still "sensed there was a secret world coexisting with the outwardly more placid world."[49] Hollywood existed by this duality, its secret and sexual world was becoming much more fascinating to Lee than its idealized, and to an extent sanitized, appearance.

For his eleventh birthday, Lee received two books as gifts from his father. One was an anthology of Sherlock Holmes stories and the other was Jack

Webb's *The Badge*. *The Badge* was a companion piece to the TV show *Dragnet* which starred Webb as LAPD Sergeant Joe Friday. *Dragnet* was known for its semi-documentary style, Webb's monotone performance, and its favorable portrayal of the LAPD. *The Badge* featured cases considered too disturbing for television. Completely disregarding the Sherlock Holmes book, Lee plunged into *The Badge*. He read about the Club Mecca firebombing which killed six people. He read about the "Two Tonys" murder and the LA underworld, "This book taught me. This book gave me heroes and fiends."[50] But there was one case that stood out from all the rest. There was a ten-page summary of the murder of Elizabeth Short, aka the Black Dahlia, that haunted Lee and spawned an obsession that would last for the rest of his life, "It's an unsolved crime—just like my mother's case. Betty Short claims me."[51]

Webb's account follows Detective Finis Brown's increasingly frustrated attempts to solve an impossible case. Webb concludes on the Black Dahlia case with a warning. When it comes to finding the killer, "You are free to speculate. But do him a favor—don't press your deductions on Finis Brown."[52] But speculate Lee did. He devised scenarios. Solve the case in his mind and catch her killer in one dream, and then rescue her and become her lover in another dream. Sometimes the grisly details of her death would get too much for Lee and he would awaken from a nightmare in a cold sweat, "My nightmares had a pure raw force. Vivid details burst out of my unconscious."[53] The Dahlia case reminded him of his mother's murder and brought memories of her flooding back.

Armand had warned Lee not to dwell on his mother's death. He kept some newspaper clippings on Jean's murder hidden in the apartment. Lee found them and read-through them all looking for answers. Lee's obsession with murder, which he developed in tandem with the onset of adolescence, was beginning to affect his schooling. Graphic images of severed organs would come to him in class when he was supposed to be working. He would skip school and go to the LA public library. He read the newspaper coverage of the Dahlia case on microfilm readers. He found a kindred spirit in Elizabeth Short: "She told whopping lies with no small flair. She concocted grand love affairs with doomed army pilots and stillborn babies."[54] Perhaps she had lied to the wrong man one day, a man brimming with hatred and violent fantasies towards women. Lee may have envisaged Elizabeth Short's murderer as similar in misogynistic motive as his mother's killer. He later wrote of the night his mother was murdered: "She was drunk. She said 'yes' or 'no' or 'maybe' or some encoded combination, she said, 'no', finally."[55]

In his three years at John Burroughs Junior High School, Lee only earned the respect of one teacher. Walter McIntosh taught Social Studies in a small, bunker-like room below the main auditorium. Lee enjoyed McIntosh's lessons. Perhaps as it was a small class and he had no audience to play his Nazi schtick too, or maybe it was because McIntosh was brilliant at conveying the "Big" ideas of history that Lee became more attentive and involved with his work. As he put it in a letter to McIntosh years later: "I learned a lot, laughed a lot and generally had a blast."[56] McIntosh too, saw some creative spark in Lee. "McIntosh was the only teacher who took me aside and said, 'you've got talent.'"[57] The art teacher Alan Hines introduced Lee to Beethoven's Fifth Symphony, sparking a lifelong obsession with classical music.

It was either McIntosh or another teacher who warned Lee that his Nazi act was just making students laugh at him and not with him. It was not enough to deter Lee. The attention he received, good or bad, was payment enough. When a teacher called Armand to notify him of Lee's worrying behavior in class, Armand replied that Lee only did it to get attention and it was best to ignore him. This was almost impossible advice for any teacher to follow. Lee could always turn up his act a little when he felt he was being ignored. He was taking it out of school as well. He spouted Nazi slogans at a ban-the-bomb rally and threw eggs at the peace protestors, no doubt testing their pacifism to the limit. His act began to fuel his inner imagination and from it he could conceive a narrative, "A liquor store heist might play into Nazis picketing the film *Exodus*."[58] This was one of the first non-Dahlia crime plots that Lee formed in his teenage mind. Although many of his behavioral problems began to develop while studying at JB, Lee still found it to be the only school he ever enjoyed attending. He was already displaying potential as a richly creative youth, even if it was partly in the chaos he created, "I gave oral book reports on books that did not exist."[59] A few of Lee's friends in class were in on the ruse and struggled to contain their laughter.

After graduating from JB in 1962, Lee was set to go to Los Angeles High School. Armand knew what would happen there. Lee would spout his Nazi schtick and "they'd kill me the first time I opened my mouth."[60] Armand had not shown much interest in Lee's schooling before now. Lee would give his math homework to Armand who, with his accountant's brain, would get through it in minutes. Armand was happy to do Lee's homework, and yet he was too lazy to teach his son arithmetic: "I can't do arithmetic to this day very well." Lee would concede twenty-five years later.[61] Armand did, however, come up with a clever scheme to get Lee into Fairfax High School located in the plush Melrose Avenue, a ZIP code well above their budget.

In one of his numerous get-rich-quick schemes, Armand had managed a show at the Cabaret Concert Theater. The show was called *Tantrums at 9*, sometimes retitled *Tantrums at 9:45* if they were forced into a different slot. It featured a mixture of comedians and singers, but it folded in a matter of weeks. The performers were rarely paid and worked with the hope that a talent scout might spot them. Lee visited and was haunted by the combination of talent and melancholy in the performers, "This wasn't Broadway, and they weren't doing a Stephen Sondheim show."[62] Armand's role in the theater did have an upside: "My father got tight with a comic named Alan Sues." Armand and Sues opened a hat shop together: "Sues designed the hats. My father kept the books and flogged the hats by mail order."[63] It soon went out of business. Armand put down Sues' address in West Hollywood as his own to gain Lee a place at Fairfax High. Sues would go on to great success. Some of the characters he created for his nightclub act he developed as a regular on the TV show *Laugh-In*. Sues once visited Armand and Lee at their apartment, but the stench of dog shit was so foul he couldn't get past the corridor.

Fairfax High's student body was ninety percent Jewish and boasted several distinguished alumni, including Armand's old friend Mickey Rooney. Armand had placed "his Nazi son down in the heart of the West LA shtetl."[64] The American Nazi Party had an enclave in Glendale. Lee visited and, despite living off pocket money from his broke father, bought himself an assortment of fascist memorabilia including bumper stickers, swastika armbands, racist tracts, and the record "Ship Those Niggers Back" by Odis Cochran and the Three Bigots.

At John Burroughs school, Lee had been tolerated as a clown but now he was dealing with students who were older and tougher. He went around school handing out hate tracts and spouting racist spiel and the other kids responded by pushing and shoving him around, and once or twice giving him a good thrashing. He was there only a matter of months before "A big Jewish kid cornered me in the rotunda and kicked my ass soundly."[65] It was not enough to change Lee's behavior. He knew in his heart that racism was repugnant and absurd, but he was just desperate for an audience. When he attended a Nazi rally and sang the Horst-Wessel song he did not know whether to laugh or cry at the wretched, ugly sight of his fellow believers, "You could not imagine a more pathetic bunch of fools."[66] He never showed off or tried to shock them. They were not an audience worth having, but he did learn a little about controlling an audience. Lee witnessed a mesmeric speech by Gerald L.K. Smith, founder of the America First Party, at the Embassy Auditorium on 9th and Grand Avenue, "He could still crank it up."[67]

Armand was finally losing patience with his Nazi son. He started calling Lee "Der Fuhrer" and wore a yarmulke around the apartment to torment him.[68] As was so often the case in the Ellroy family, sex would be the issue that changed everything. Lee developed a crush on a Jewish girl at school. He wrote a song criticizing Nazi party leader George Lincoln Rockwell to impress her.[69] It did him no good. She knew about his rep as the school racist and wanted nothing to do with him.

Lee's first consensual sexual contact had been with another boy. He had discovered masturbation while still a student at John Burroughs and was doing it as often as he could. Between lessons Lee and his friends had "jerked off in adjoining toilet stalls."[70] Lee was friends with another kid who lived close by. Lee and his friend, who he does not name in his memoirs, engaged in mutual masturbation while looking at Playboy centerfolds. It was more exciting doing it with another boy, and yet he felt it was wrong as "I knew I wasn't a homo."[71] But he was worried that it might make him gay. He shared a room with his father. Lee was worried he would blurt out gay fantasies in his sleep. Armand was a homophobe who referred to gays as "fruits" or "faggots," but like much of his casual bigotry he never let his prejudice consume him. After all, his friend Alan Sues was gay. Armand liked to take Lee to the theater to see westerns starring Randolph Scott. After one showing, while strolling through Hollywood Ranch Market, Armand told Lee the truth about the heroic cowboy they had just seen on the big screen: "My father laid out the straight dope on Randolph Scott. He was one notorious homo."[72] He knew it from his days in the movie biz. He told Lee gay men did serve one purpose, "their presence expanded the pool of available women."[73]

Lee started ignoring the friend who had become his masturbation partner. He sought refuge in the Kinsey Reports to explain the episode. While skimming through the reports at his local library, he was relieved with Kinsey's findings that adolescent mutual masturbation was not necessarily indicative of sexuality "It is not improbable that nearly all boys have some pre-adolescent genital play with other boys or with girls."[74] The friend would not leave him alone though. He asked Lee to take over his paper route while he went on a family vacation. Lee agreed and then ditched all the newspapers in the trash. Once he got back from vacation and realized the betrayal, the friend challenged Lee to a fight. Lee agreed, and a time and place was set. Lee had a week to prepare. He worked himself up into a fit of outwardly straight, macho anger. Describing the fight years later, Ellroy did not shy away from its homoerotic undertones. The two kids "heaved, lurched, thrashed, flailed and powder-punched the shit out of each other."[75] By the time it was over they were "dehydrated and falling-down dizzy."[76] Lee lost the fight, but he felt like he had redeemed himself through violence. He never saw his former friend again.

Lee was too proud to renounce his Nazism at Fairfax High, and his reputation was too far gone for it to make much difference. He was suspended after one particularly obnoxious racist rant in early 1965, and when the suspension was over, he went straight back and disrupted the school's Folk Song Club with "an obscene song of his own creation."[77] This time he got expelled. He turned his back on racism and Fairfax High. The school has never acknowledged Ellroy as one of its many famous students, even though they do acknowledge other future celebrities who attended but never graduated such as Demi Moore. Lee could not blame them for hating him, and he held no animosity against the school or anyone who attended. As he walked away from Fairfax, he realized how desperate his situation was. A wave of fear and desire overcame him.

He did not want to yield to his self-destructive urges. He wanted to bring something tangible out of the fantasy world he had concocted for himself.

Armand Ellroy's health had been in steep decline for the past few years. He had suffered from stomach ulcers since before Jean Ellroy had died. As time went by and the pain got worse, he became increasingly reliant on Alka Seltzer drinks to numb his discomfort. But it was also his, and to a lesser extent Lee's, lifestyle that was contributing to his ill health. They were frequently broke and shared a sugar and starch diet of milk and cookies for breakfast and hamburgers and hot dogs for dinner. Armand smoked three packs of Lucky Strikes a day. Lee noticed how red-faced and out of breath his father was becoming. He would have coughing fits and dizzy spells with increasing regularity. They fell behind on the rent and had to move to a smaller apartment. The landlord was furious with the stench Minna had created and said the apartment would need to be fumigated, "A five-year accumulation of dog effluvia had left the place uninhabitable."[78] Minna was quick to mark her territory in their new apartment. She was now too old for housebreaking, and there was something more than laziness behind Armand's inability to train her. He was depressed with how his life had turned out and he knew the end was near.

Lee came home from school on November 1, 1963, to find his father sitting in a pool of his own urine and feces. His physique, once lean and taut, was now weak as his skin had gone slack, "he was twitching and weeping and babbling and drooling."[79] Lee fought back his own tears and called Armand's doctor. An ambulance arrived and Armand was transported to a Veterans Administration Hospital. A doctor telephoned Lee and gave him the news. His father had suffered a stroke. Lee visited him every day in the hospital. At first the prognosis was good. The doctors were confident they could restore Armand's speech and physical mobility with the right treatment. Armand learned to speak again using children's primer texts. Lee cheered his father with stories as often as he could. They were full of bravado and questionable authenticity. His favorite tale was how he would make a fortune as a bestselling novelist and pay for his healthcare. As his father's health declined, he was noticing how much he was his mirror image.

Armand was discharged from hospital on November 22, 1963. It was the day President Kennedy was assassinated in Dallas. Armand, a Republican to the core, had always referred to Kennedy as "that Catholic cocksucker."[80] He could still spout obscenities and tell old Hollywood tales, but his heart was no longer in it and Lee could tell. Lee did his best to look after his father and hated to see him suffer, but his constant whining and neediness was a lot to take for an adolescent. He began to look for reasons to stay away from the apartment. He had taken to stealing their food and other essentials. Armand never wanted him to be gone for long. It was not just that he needed him at home in case he had another stroke, Armand was convinced that Lee's mere presence was a good luck charm that could ward off strokes and heart attacks. Nevertheless, Armand resumed a lifestyle that sent his health back into steep decline. He lived on his diet of fatty food, Lucky Strikes, and Alka-Seltzer, "he was hellbent to die."[81]

Lee had been shoplifting books ever since he had developed his prodigious reading habit. Lee would steal a book then ride away on his Schwinn Corvette, which he kitted out with "gooseneck handlebars, plastic saddlebars, rhinestone-studded mud-flaps and a speedometer."[82] The last addition was rather ironic, as the already cumbersome bike was "heavy and hard to propel."[83] Shoplifting enough food to last for two people every week was a lot riskier than stealing the occasional book. In May 1964, a shopworker caught Lee stealing six pairs of swimming trunks. Terrified that the man was going to call the police on him, Lee listened to his angry lectures for several hours until "he jabbed me in the chest and made me sign a guilt waiver."[84] Finally released, Lee rode home as fast as he could. He got back at 10:00 p.m. His father had been alone for far longer than planned. When he arrived, an ambulance was parked outside. Two medics were carting his father on a stretcher into the back of the ambulance. One of them told Lee what had happened, his father had suffered a mild heart attack. Armand recovered well enough to be released from hospital again. Lee was his carer and all that stood in the way of Armand spending his last days in a nursing home.

The stress was pushing Lee over the edge. Now expelled from school his behavior became ever more extreme; he'd peep through bedroom windows searching for sexual gratification, make obscene phone calls, and he claimed to have "called in bomb threats to high schools throughout the LA basin."[85] As he had no money, he was increasingly reliant on shoplifting. His clothes were tatty and stained. His hair was greasy. He looked and felt awful. Something drastic was called for.

Lee came up with the idea of joining the Marine Corp. As his father was a veteran, Lee may have seen it as a form of escape that would still honor the old man. Perhaps he felt that serving his country would atone for his dalliance with Nazism. He would continue to make gestures to address this dark period of his life in the coming years. Armand would not give his consent for Lee to join the Marines, as the Vietnam War was already escalating, he dreaded the thought of his son being sucked into it, but he was not, in principle, opposed to Lee enlisting in the US Army. This was his initial reaction. Lee passed the induction test without incident. He telephoned his father to tell him he had been accepted into the Army, "he broke down and sobbed" on the other end of the line.[86] Armand knew this meant he would die alone, and Lee was already feeling guilty about what he had done. Within days, Lee's guilt would turn to fear as he discovered the harsh reality of army life.

Lee caught a plane to the Advanced Infantry Training Center at Fort Polk, Louisiana via a connecting flight in Houston. Fort Polk was hot, humid, prone to heavy rain, and swarming with mosquitos. It was considered a perfect climate for training soldiers to be sent to Vietnam. Lee was drenched in sweat, from nerves as much as the heat, as he stood in line waiting to be processed while mean looking sergeants barked orders at the new recruits. He wanted out fast. He telephoned his father, "The old man was incoherent."[87] Was he having another stroke, Lee wondered. He knew he needed to get back to LA for his father's sake, as much as his own.

While he was reading out the oath of enlistment, something inside him snapped. He started faking a nervous breakdown. It came partly from the extreme agitation that he was feeling, but he was still calculating enough to embellish his performance. An officer marched him to the infirmary. The army doctor had seen this kind of behavior before from dozens of work-shy and troubled young men. He gave Lee a shot of a high-powered tranquilizer, "I woke up after evening chow."[88] He was hungry, depressed, and lonely. He continued the act the next day, and this time made out that he could not speak. The platoon sergeant thought he could be genuine, and when a stuttering Lee managed to write down his concern for his sick father the sergeant telephoned Armand in LA and agreed that he sounded very ill. Nevertheless, Lee was assigned to Company A, 2nd Battalion, 5th Training Brigade where he went through two days of basic training, all the time maintaining his manic, nervous breakdown act. "I hated the army," Ellroy recalled in one of his first literary interviews. "They took me away from my Nero Wolfe books and made me get up at 5:00 a.m. and do push ups."[89]

Lee was so terrified that he would not be able to escape the military that he could have easily had a genuine breakdown at any moment. The sense of control that performing gave him was probably the only thing that stopped it. The other recruits egged him on, enjoying having something to laugh at to alleviate their burdens. Finally, the company commander summoned Lee to his office. He had bad news, "he said the Red Cross was flying me home for two weeks. My father just had another stroke."[90]

Armand could barely talk, but "the old man looked surprisingly good."[91] Lee visited him every day for two weeks and promised to be out of the Army soon so he could take care of him. Now that he was far away from Fort Polk, he prided himself on looking dashing in his army uniform. He kitted it out with as much war surplus insignia as he could find and spent his time outside the hospital travelling around LA, enjoying the privileges of being a war hero. When the two weeks were up Lee had no choice but to fly back to Fort Polk. He resumed his crazy man act, and he was convincing enough to fool an army psychiatrist who examined him. He approved Lee's discharge, but the paperwork would take a month to process. However, a few days later the Red Cross called again, "My father just had another stroke."[92]

Lee got back to LA just in time. Armand was emaciated, with tubes coming out of his nose and running up his arms. He was mumbling to himself. Lee leaned in close to try and make out what he was saying, "His last discernible words were 'Try to pick up every waitress who serves you.'"[93]

Lee was not in the room when his father died. He recalled a nurse hurrying him into a waiting room, possibly as Armand's ECG was flatlining. A few minutes later a doctor walked in and told him his father was dead. The date was June 4, 1965. Armand was a few weeks shy of his sixty-sixth birthday.

Lee caught a bus back to his motel. He willed himself to cry, "just like I did with the redhead."[94] He had felt relieved at Jean Ellroy's death as his ten-year-old self carried a simple childlike hatred of his mother's strict ways. As time had passed, he began to realize that his mother was right and much of his desperate lifestyle was inherited from Armand's shallow personality. He took after his father in other ways too. He had joined the army in a time of war, and as he was still only seventeen, he was now legally an orphan. It was horrible to see his father suffer. It was a relief to know that his pain was over.

He wiped away the tears. He was free of his parents. Free of a domineering mother. Free of a terminally ill father. Soon he would be free of the US Army too. He was free to pursue his ambition to become a great writer, and he was free to live a life of vice.

He was free.

3

Down and Out in the City of Angels (1965–1975)

Armand Ellroy was laid to rest at Los Angeles National Cemetery. Few people attended the funeral. Shifra Haran, Rita Hayworth's former secretary, looked on disapprovingly as Lee swigged from a bottle of whisky and engaged in some drunken playacting: "I stood over my father's grave and flaunted my army greens replete with unearned regalia."[1] A wreath was sent by the movie producer Bryan Foy, another Hollywood friend Armand had done some odd jobs for.

After his father's death, Ellroy was obligated to return to Fort Polk while his discharge was being processed. His remaining time there was a lot easier than it was for the other recruits "headed for advanced infantry training and probable Vietnam duty."[2] He passed the time reading crime fiction. His most onerous task was keeping up his crazy man act around the other soldiers. Ellroy "stuttered and lurked around the Company A mess hall" just in case anyone doubted his mental problems and put his discharge in jeopardy. Ellroy was formally discharged "Under Honorable Conditions" in July 1965, one month after his father's death. He was right to feel relieved at avoiding service in Vietnam. More military personnel were shipped from Fort Polk to Vietnam than from any other Training Base in the US. Soldiers who voluntarily enlisted, as Ellroy had, outnumbered draftees in Vietnam by more than four to one.[3]

One of the consequences of Ellroy's discharge was that he was now ineligible to be drafted. After his brief taste of army life, he was elated at the news, "I scammed the entire US army."[4] By successfully manipulating his army superiors, Ellroy had found renewed confidence as a performer. Ellroy had developed acting skills long before he had shown any interest in writing. As his schooling had been so erratic, the seventeen-year-old Ellroy had little experience of writing essays. Ellroy's acting skills were quite sophisticated by comparison and rooted in his childhood. Every child learns how to test their parents for weakness through a mixture of play-acting and manipulation. Ellroy had grown particularly skilled at this due to his parents' divorce and their contrasting personalities. Armand and Jean could not agree on anything regarding Ellroy's upbringing. Ellroy had exploited their differing parenting styles to the limit. As he flew back to LA, with five hundred dollars in his wallet as a parting gift from the US Army, Ellroy had only one thing on his mind.

He was on the cusp of adulthood, sexually obsessed, and a virgin.

Ellroy's behavior increasingly resembled that of his father, despite his long-standing disillusionment with him. One of his first acts upon returning to LA was to forge "my father's name to his last three social security checks."[5] Armand would not have hesitated to pull off a con in different circumstances. Ellroy needed money and a place to stay quickly. The apartment he had shared with his father was "locked and boarded," and Armand's belongings had been seized "in lieu of back rent."[6] Any potential family mementos had been lost. Ellroy's only remaining family was two thousand miles away in Wisconsin. Ellroy occasionally spoke on the phone with Leoda. They had a tense relationship. Leoda had always felt, in some abstract way, that Armand had been responsible for her sister's death: "She was glad my father was dead."[7] She may have seen things in Ellroy's behavior that were an unhappy reminder of Armand. Nonetheless, Leoda was generous to Ellroy. She sent him one hundred dollars a month from his mother's estate and signed him up for survivor benefits as the child of deceased parents. Acutely aware of how Ellroy lacked any qualifications, she urged him to go back to school. The benefits terminated when Ellroy reached eighteen, but he could continue to receive them until the age of twenty-one if he was in full-time education. Ellroy calculated that the child stipends were not worth the work that re-entering education for another three years would entail. The combination of army money, his father's social security, and Leoda's monthly payments had swelled

Ellroy's bank account to around a thousand dollars—a considerable sum for a seventeen-year-old in 1965.

Ellroy found himself a "one-room pad at Beverly and Wilton," but he did not have a plan for how he would maintain the rent over the long term.[8] To his credit, Ellroy was good at finding employment. His problem was that he could never hold down a job. Through a "Great Society" domestic program Ellroy obtained a job shelving books at the Wilshire Branch Library. He only worked there for a few weeks, but "it's where I learned that all the great crime writers were published by Knopf."[9] He ran his finger over the Borzoi logo on the spine of a dozen Ross Macdonald novels and dreamed of becoming a crime writer.

Ellroy got a job handing out flyers but quit out of boredom after a week. He was hired as a busboy at the very first Sizzler steakhouse in Culver City but was fired for dropping dishes. Ellroy landed a kitchen role in a Kentucky Fried Chicken restaurant only to be dismissed for poor hygiene. He had lost three jobs in two weeks. Ellroy "opted for a work-free summer" and reverted to his old shoplifting habits, stealing clothes from stores such as Silverwoods and Desmonds.[10] This fashionable attire, "madras shirts, crew-neck sweaters, thin-wale cord pants" made him feel confident that he could fit in with his better-off friends.[11]

In his memoir *My Dark Places*, Ellroy uses pseudonyms for three principal friends that he spent time with during this period, "Lloyd, Fritz and Daryl." As with many youthful friendships, they were something of a clique with Ellroy having to prove himself among people he may have, rather insecurely, viewed as being smarter than himself. Fritz was planning to attend USC, another friend named George had been accepted at Caltech. As the only one among them who did not live with his parents, Ellroy was aware that having an apartment made him a "viable flunky" in the group. The three of them used to enjoy meeting Ellroy at his apartment which he decorated with "right-wing bumper stickers and playmate of the month foldouts."[12] They were more than happy to sponge off Ellroy who spent his money "taking them out to steak dinners and movies."[13] Although his companions may have somewhat looked down on Ellroy, one friendship stood out and would endure over the next decade, eventually leading Ellroy on a path to reform and sobriety that probably saved his life.

Lloyd's real name was Robert Randolph Rice, known to all as Randy.

Randy Rice may not have been as outwardly impressive as Fritz or George, he was only finishing high school by comparison, but Ellroy still looked up to him and considered Randy a kindred spirit. Randy had wild, wavy hair and "light-blue eyes so light it looks like he sends them out to be bleached."[14] Like Ellroy, Randy was an only child. His parents divorced when he was nine. His father was killed after being struck by a car when Randy was only eleven. The similarities between Randy and Ellroy were striking. They both had a wild streak and loved to tell stories. Randy's mother Elizabeth was a strict Christian Scientist who worked at the William Andrews Clark Memorial Library at UCLA. After her husband's death, she remarried a Sicilian grocer who was hot-tempered and volatile. He had little time for Ellroy and Randy's behavior and once chased them out of the house while brandishing a knife: "We got away easily but still." Ellroy introduced Randy to the Black Dahlia case, and he became obsessed with every detail, "We used to spend hours hashing over the Black Dahlia case and talking about crime fiction."[15]

The other members of Ellroy's friendship group had equally colorful families. George's father Rudy was a highway patrolman with far-right political views. His constant drunken ranting annoyed most members of the group, but Ellroy liked Rudy and considered him a romantic dreamer. Ellroy's friendship with Rudy is telling for several reasons. Although Ellroy felt shame for his anti-Semitic past, he was not averse to making friends with extremists like Rudy, even going so far as to showing him racist paraphernalia he once purchased. Rudy would be the first of many police officers Ellroy would befriend, although most of them came in later life when he was a celebrity writer. If his behavior around Rudy was obsequious at first, then it contrasted sharply with friends with liberal views who Ellroy could not resist goading with outrageous right-wing opinions. Rudy would soon prove a useful friend to have.

Ellroy was caught shoplifting at a Liquor and Food Mart in August 1965. Two clerks detained him while they waited for the police to arrive. At the booking station, Ellroy told a juvenile officer that both of his parents were dead. Ellroy was informed that he was not legally allowed to live alone until he was eighteen. He was transported to the Georgia Street Juvenile Facility. Ellroy's first arrest was a traumatic experience. He was not as tough as the other juveniles, and they took delight in taunting him. He managed not to look too scared in front of them but as soon as the lights went out, Ellroy admits that he "cried myself to sleep."[16] Now he was faced with the prospect of being housed in an institution full of aggressive juveniles all visibly tougher than he was.

Rudy came to his rescue. He used his policeman clout to obtain Ellroy the status of "emancipated juvenile" and six months on probation which would end shortly before Ellroy reached eighteen. Rudy became his "informal guardian."[17] Race riots erupted in the Watts neighborhood of LA in August '65 and Rudy was called to duty. Ellroy was both thrilled and horrified by the riots. Randy and Ellroy got as close to the riots as they could, rather foolishly carrying BB guns with them. Ellroy saw himself as a Mike Hammer figure who needed to suppress the anti-American communist uprising. They soaked up the atmosphere and shouted racial slurs, but they must have come across as harmless as "some cops made us go home" after threatening to "call your parents."[18] On the third day of the riots, the National Guard were deployed to restore order in the city. Ellroy was smart enough not to venture near the riots once the violence intensified. The riots allegedly began after police used excessive force in arresting a 21-year-old black man, Marquette Frye, for a driving offense. It was an everyday incident that led to an eruption of chaos after decades of distrust between LA's African American community and the LAPD. Thirty-four people were killed in the riots.

By the time of his eighteenth birthday in March 1966, Ellroy had completed his probation. Another consequence of attaining adulthood was that his survivor benefits abruptly stopped. Reviewing his desperate finances, Ellroy decided that he might have to return to education. Randy was attending Culter Christian Academy at the behest of his mother. It was a school he openly detested. He had briefly attended Principia School in St. Louis and was enjoying it and making friends but his mother moved him to Culter so that he could have a Christian education closer to home.

Randy warned Ellroy that Culter Academy was a miserable, oppressive institution but Ellroy felt he had no other option. Randy told him that in order to gain admittance he needed to convince the Principal that he was a born-again believer. Ellroy enjoyed acting and possessed a religious streak.

He performed well-enough in front of the Principal to win a place: "I believed what I was saying for the length of time I was saying it. I possessed a chameleon soul."[19] It would not last, however. Ellroy found the student body at Culter was made up of "born again psychos and doper malcontents."[20] The ethos was to completely renounce your past life and devote yourself to Christ. Ellroy could not stand the misanthropic strand to Evangelical beliefs. As someone who was just discovering, and had yet to experience, all manner of sins, he was not inclined to renounce them yet. To make matters worse, there was a $60 a month tuition fee which Ellroy had to pay out of his survivor benefits. It didn't seem worth it. Ellroy attended a few classes sporadically before dropping out completely after two months.

There were several attractive girls who Ellroy got to know through his friendship group, and, with youthful impulsiveness, he tried to date all of them. His first date was with a young woman named Kay Olmsted, a friend of Fritz's sister who attended the exclusive all-girls Marlborough school in Hancock Park. They went to see *The Sound of Music*. Kay enjoyed the movie and Ellroy didn't, but he was savvy enough to lie so as not to displease her. The ploy worked as after the movie they were "hugging and kissing sans tongues."[21] They went on several more dates, but Kay would not allow their physical intimacy to develop any further. She invited Ellroy to her house, and several of her Marlborough School girlfriends' houses in Hancock Park. It was the start of another obsession for Ellroy. He had often lived close to Hancock Park but had never experienced the lifestyle of its upper-middle class families. He was fascinated by the houses, "I liked the plush furnishings. I liked the big rooms. I liked the wood panels and oil paintings."[22]

Kay ended things with Ellroy with a kiss-off letter stating she was a Christian and only dated "saved" men. Ellroy was insulted by the letter. Kay had never mentioned religion before. In response, Ellroy asked out Kay's friend Ann DeArmand. They went to see the movie *Harper*, starring Paul Newman as Lew Archer. After the movie he and Ann kissed sensually. Ellroy enjoyed this new physical experience, but he was impatient for more intimacy. He asked out a string of girls in the Marlborough School/Hancock Park set.

By this time, Ellroy's reputation among this friendship group was well-known and they all coldly rebuffed his overtures.

Ellroy's revenge on the young society women who had rejected him was in one sense extreme, and yet it was subtle enough that they never discovered what he had done. Fritz's family lived in Hancock Park. Fritz maintained a little room adjoining the family garage. It was the young adult version of a treehouse where Fritz and his friends could smoke dope without fear of discovery. His family were strictly forbidden from entering. Fritz made the mistake of giving Ellroy a spare key to the room. The room had excellent views of the main house. In December 1966, Fritz and his family went on vacation for Christmas. Ellroy took advantage of this and let himself into Fritz's room. He observed the main house for potential weak spots that could act as entrance points. He settled on the pet-access hole in the kitchen door. Ellroy crouched down on the ground beside the kitchen door. He was tall but stick-thin. It was easy to go unnoticed when the Hancock Park mansions were designed to give residents as much privacy as possible. He tripped a latch on the kitchen door and entered the house. He did not turn the lights on. It was too risky as Fritz's neighbors might have known the family was away. He explored the house in relative darkness. He found the room of Fritz's sister Heidi. She was about the same age as Ellroy and had curtly rejected his advances. He performed fetishistic acts with Heidi's lingerie and "stole a pair of white panties."[23]

Ellroy was sober when entering the house. He couldn't afford booze and dope when his friends were away, and it made sense to have his wits about him when engaging in such dangerous activity. However, he did find some painkillers which he took with a double scotch. He washed the whiskey glass and put it back in its place. He made sure everything was exactly as he had found it before he left. What he had taken was not enough to arouse suspicion. Neither were the panties he stole enough to maintain his sexual interest. He knew he had "touched another secret world," and his voyeuristic cravings would spur him into more burglaries.[24] Fritz had already given Ellroy partial access into his property. The next burglary would be more difficult. There were many attractive young women who lived in Hancock Park. Ellroy knew them socially. To fulfill his sexual fantasies with these women, Ellroy would need to devise more creative burglaries.

Kay Olmsted's house would be his next target. Ellroy was still smarting over the letter Kay had written ending their brief dating experience for religious reasons. Given Ellroy's shambolic appearance there may have been more than doctrinal issues at stake in Kay's decision to spurn his advances. He telephoned Kay's house from Fritz's room, and no one picked up. Answering machines had been introduced to the US market in 1960 and were still rare. An unanswered call was a good indication that a house was empty. Ellroy entered Kay's house through an open window which had been shabbily covered by a screen held down by bent and rusty nails. He had found the house's weak spot and pried away at the nails. He did not find any drugs or alcohol in the house. Kay had not been lying about her strict Christian upbringing. He gorged on some food in the fridge before settling on his real prize of the night—Kay's bedroom.

He writhed around on Kay's bed and stole some of her lingerie.

His next target was Kathy Montgomery whom Ellroy had first met at John Burroughs Junior High School. Ellroy carried a torch for Kathy that shone a bit more brightly than it did for the other Hancock Park girls, "She was my longtime secret love."[25] His clandestine exploration of her house was farcical as he belatedly discovered that nothing matched the expectations he had built up of Kathy in his mind. He drank some "weird-ass liqueur" he found in the drinks cabinet, and subsequently failed to identify Kathy's bedroom.[26] Ellroy had to content himself that apples do not fall far from the tree as he stole two sets of differently sized lingerie, unsure as to which one belonged to Kathy and which pair belonged to her mother.

Ellroy would return to burglarize the houses of Kay, Kathy, and Heidi periodically and invade the homes of young women whom he names as Missy, Julie, Peggy, and Joanne. He always knew his victims. He never strayed from the relatively small area of Hancock Park that he considered his burglary-voyeur stomping ground. He was in command of his impulses enough to abort the burglary if an entrance point had been secured or a pedestrian looked at him suspiciously, or even if an unexpected noise in the night spooked him. He was walking a fine line between being thrilled by his actions and living in abject fear. It was fear and sexual insecurity that had pushed him down such an extreme path. As he said of Kathy, "I was afraid of her for no justifiable reason."[27]

On August 9, 1969, four members of the "Manson Family" invaded the home of the actress Sharon Tate Polanski at 10050 Cielo Drive in Benedict

Canyon. They murdered Tate, who was more than eight months pregnant. They also murdered Tate's three guests: celebrity hairstylist Jay Sebring, producer Wojciech Frykowski, and his partner, the heiress Abigail Folger. They also murdered the eighteen-year-old Steven Parent (a former El Monte resident who had lived half a mile away from Jean and Lee Ellroy), who had been visiting the property's caretaker. Charles Manson was not present at these murders but the following night, Manson led the four murderers and two more of his followers and invaded the home of Leno and Rosemary LaBianca at 3301 Waverly Drive in Los Feliz. Leno, a supermarket executive, and his wife Rosemary were both murdered. The subsequent police investigation and media coverage of the trial, which pored over every lurid detail of the murders and the absurd apocalyptic beliefs of the Manson cult, caused widespread revulsion, morbid fascination and—particularly among LA's upper middle-classes who had never been targeted so brutally before now—panic.

In her essay, "The White Album," Joan Didion wrote of how she received the news shortly after the murders occurred:

> I was sitting in the shallow end of my sister-in-law's swimming pool in Beverly Hills when she received a telephone call from a friend who had just heard about the murders at Sharon Tate Polanski's house on Cielo Drive. The phone rang many times during the next hour. These early reports were garbled and contradictory. One caller would say hoods, the next would say chains. There were twenty dead, no, twelve, ten, eighteen. Black masses were imagined, and bad trips blamed. I remember all of the day's misinformation very clearly, and I also remember this, and I wish I did not: *I remember that no one was surprised.*[28]

For Ellroy, the murders committed by the Manson Family heralded much more than the symbolic end of the sixties. It placed him in a different type of danger than what Joan Didion felt. "I started to see more and more alarm tape on windows, people were getting dogs, there were stickers for the Bel Air Patrol and Hollywood Patrol, private companies that patrolled the swankier areas."[29] Ellroy, who by this time was on probation for an unrelated trespassing offense, stopped breaking and entering into houses as he knew it was inevitable that he would be caught or killed eventually. The voyeuristic thrill was receding and his sense of shame, which could be periodically quite acute, was increasing. In one of his final burglaries, he violated one of his own rules, stealing all the money in a purse he found. He could never go back to that house once he had clandestinely announced his presence, and he was losing all desire to.

Although the burglaries made for good authorial anecdotes and contributed to his mythos, Ellroy regretted his actions and sometimes despaired of media interest in this period of his life: "I broke into houses fifteen, eighteen, twenty, twenty-two times between Christmas time '66 and the summer of '69, circumspectly, very, very cautiously, great concern to cover my tracks. Shamefully, I knew it was wrong. And in-between each one of those little episodes I'd read twenty or thirty books. So, the amount of time spent housebreaking was proportionately tiny."[30] By ceasing the burglaries Ellroy could assuage one part of his conscience, but he was still aggressively pursuing what Didion described as the "mystical flirtation with the idea of 'sin'" in other forms.

Ellroy was succumbing more and more to his self-destructive behavior. He never once drank alcohol with moderation and spurned beer as the alcohol volume was too low. He preferred to drink large quantities of liquor very quickly to get high. Even Rudy grew tired of Ellroy: "he figured out I was worthless and not a sincere right-winger."[31] The feeling was mutual. Although Ellroy had friends who shared his conservative views, if their views veered towards the far-right then he soon tired of them. Ellroy befriended a black homeless man who he knew only as Flame-O. Flame-O had gained his nickname for repeatedly setting himself on fire during his binges on Thunderbird wine. He lived under a freeway embankment. Ellroy occasionally, when he had money, paid Flame-O to buy his liquor for him. Flame-O recognized the symptoms of alcoholism in Ellroy and called him "wino-bait."[32]

Ellroy could still count on one loyal friend. Minna had been in kennels since Armand's death, but now he had his own apartment Ellroy brought her home with him. Minna was older now and needed less exercise. Many nights she would curl up on the bed next to Ellroy while he masturbated compulsively. He turned to drugs to enhance his sexual pleasure. Ellroy had first tried smoking marijuana at school in El Monte but had been careful to hide this incident from his parents and it had not become a habit. By the 1960s, the moral panic around marijuana had abated. Drug use was becoming somewhat normalized in the liberal middle classes. Fritz took speed to help him study through the night and cope with the constant supply of work at USC. Ellroy took speed and went on masturbation sessions for "12 to 18 hours straight."[33] As he later conceded, "I masturbated myself bloody."[34] Ellroy and his friends were taking a wide array of pills: Seconal, Nembutal, and Dexedrine. On one occasion Ellroy took LSD, but the "transcendental message left me cold."[35]

Ellroy returned to his apartment one day and Minna had disappeared. He roamed the streets looking for her and put a lost dog ad in the *LA Times* but to no avail. He suspected his landlord, an unpleasant man who hated dogs and found Ellroy to be a difficult tenant generally. The disappearance of a beloved pet is a traumatic event for the owner in any circumstances. For Ellroy, it was particularly upsetting as Minna was one of the last tangible links he had to his mother. She gave him the pet only months before she was murdered. As with many things experienced in childhood, looking after Minna had a profound effect on Ellroy's character. He became a lifelong dog lover, later owning three more dogs, and even styling his authorial persona as "the Demon Dog." It is probably not a coincidence that Ellroy's drug use rapidly increased after Minna was gone. Upset, but also free of the last remaining responsibility that dog ownership required of him, Ellroy embarked on a destructive binge until, like Minna, he became a stray animal.

Ellroy's actions, when cornered and in danger, could be animalistic and desperate:

> At 19, one night in his fear's worst epiphany, he met his own demon dog. 'After stealing a bottle of wine in Hollywood,' he explains, 'I hopped a fence into a lumber yard, and a Dobermann attacked. I thought it was over. I thought at the very least he was going to get my nuts. I killed him with a two-by-four. I kept hitting him long after he was dead because I thought he was going to jump up at me, like in a horror movie. I couldn't hold food down for a week after it, and I had flashes for months, because I love animals and this animal was just doing his job.'[36]

Around this time, Ellroy squandered his remaining money on booze and drugs and got locked out of his apartment for unpaid rent. Leoda, who was tired of Ellroy's wanton self-destructiveness, refused to advance his allowance.

He stayed with Fritz first and then Randy until both of their families evicted him. With nowhere else to go, Ellroy "stole some blankets from a Goodwill box" and settled for the night in Robert Burns Park.[37]

It was his first taste of homelessness.

Ellroy spent three consecutive weeks living in Robert Burns Park. He could handle the cold and sleep through the noises of the night, but the most humiliating moments came when he would wake up drenched by the sprinkler system. The system operated at "irregular intervals."[38] Even when he retreated to a dry spot, Ellroy found it might be next in line for a watering. Ellroy kept "a bust of Beethoven stashed in a bush in Robert Burns Park."[39] The bust was a gift from Randy. Classical music was something that Ellroy could memorize and return to, providing him with solace and company no matter where he was or how squalid his conditions were.

Ellroy turned to the California State Employment Office to find a way out of his predicament. He was given some job referrals and landed a post handing out flyers for a psychic named Sister Ramona. Ellroy found Sister Ramona to be a despicable racist who practiced her phony healing act on lower-income Black and Mexican communities. The job did give Ellroy insight into the workings of a successful con-artist, but he quit as he couldn't handle the verbal abuse he was getting while handing out flyers. Temporary employment had served its purpose. He paid his back-rent and reclaimed his apartment at Beverley and Wilton.

In March 1968, after an agonizingly long wait, Ellroy would finally lose his virginity. He was "Bombing around looking to steal a bottle of wine on Oakwood and Westwood Avenue. Ran into a guy I knew in High School called John Theiss. And he started talking shit about all the women he'd had, and I knew he was jiving me, and he said he had a roommate named Ralph Rickman and they got this woman" cohabitating with them. Ellroy accompanied Theiss back to his apartment in Clinton, lower Hollywood. Rickman was there and so was a woman named Susan Helenius. Ellroy was immediately taken with Susan. She was an attractive "best looking legs I ever saw," 29-year-old, fast-talking Finnish American leftist from San Francisco.[40] Ellroy tried to counter her left-wing views with his conservative outlook but found "I just couldn't keep up with her." She suggested they get high, and Ellroy obliged by stealing a bottle of Romilar cough syrup from a nearby pharmacy, "You had to drink a milkshake with it or a pint of heavy cream just to keep it down. It was a hallucinogenic and it was horrible, but she seemed to enjoy it, and from that point on I was her toady."[41] Romilar cough syrup was withdrawn from the over-the-counter market in 1973 due to its frequent misuse as a recreational drug.

Susan wanted a new place to live and bluntly informed Ellroy she would sleep with him if she could stay at his apartment. Ellroy readily agreed and lost his virginity to Susan on Friday, April 12, 1968. The sex was fumbled and disappointing, and Susan only reluctantly agreed to sleep with him on four occasions, but he allowed her to remain at his place as he was growing obsessed with her. They visited San Francisco and stayed at her parents' home in November of that year. Ellroy spent some time exploring the city with Susan's brother Chris, looking for a record store which had a copy in stock of The Beatles newly released *White Album*. They found a copy in North Beach and got stoned listening to it.

Back in LA, Susan began a relationship with a woman named Colleen McKay and announced to Ellroy that she was a lesbian. Her coming out entailed she was moving out. Ellroy was devastated. He wasn't offended at her being gay although he was surprised as he didn't "detect a lezbo vibe in her."[42] He was going to miss their arguments about politics. They stayed in touch for a little while, but that ended abruptly when Ellroy made derogatory remarks about her brother over the phone and Susan hung up on him. Susan and Colleen became notable figures in the Gay Liberation movement in LA. Colleen ran LA's first feminist restaurant, the Women's Saloon and Parlor, at 4908 West Fountain Avenue in East Hollywood. Susan wrote for the gay journal *Everywoman*. Her style wasn't subtle and hopefully she didn't have Ellroy in mind when she wrote, "Men have exhausted the pornographic possibilities of nearly everything for the sake of the god dollar and ego-throbbing fascism."[43]

Susan would be the first of many women Ellroy would date who held staunchly left-wing views.

Ellroy came out of his obsession with Susan by going on a drink and drugs bender. He was soon evicted and in the Fall of 68, the nights were too cold and rainy for Ellroy to sleep in Robert Burns Park. He went in search of shelter. Ellroy found a "deserted house at 8th and Ardmore."[44] There were "no interior lights and no running water."[45] The only furnishings were a closet and a "moldy faux-leather cloth," but it was more than enough for Ellroy's needs. He stayed at the house for some time. He did not know that he was being watched. A neighbor reported Ellroy to the police. According to Ellroy, his arrest was dramatic and violent, "Four cops kicked my door in and charged me with shotguns. They threw me to the floor and handcuffed me. They stuck those big 12-gauge pumps in my face."[46] The irony was not lost on Ellroy. He had burglarized some of the most exclusive houses in Hancock Park and never faced any consequences and now, through a karmic twist of fate, he was being carted off to Wilshire Police Station and charged with burglary when he was just a homeless person looking for a place to stay.

Figure 4 *Booking photo of Lee Earle Ellroy for a drunk driving charge one week after his twenty-third birthday. Photo: Courtesy of LAPD.*

Once Ellroy was at Wilshire Station his situation improved a little. He told a detective during his interview that he was not burglarizing the house but merely crashing there. He made the following statement, which was typed in block capitals on his arrest report:

I HAVE BEEN STAYING AT DIFFERENT FRIENDS HOUSES WHEN I DON'T STAY HERE. I DON'T REMEMBER THE FRIENDS NAMES. I CAME FROM SAN FRANCISCO APPROX ONE MONTH AGO. I STAYED WITH DIFFERENT PEOPLE BUT I DON'T KNOW THEIR NAMES: OR WHAT ADDRESSES I STAYED AT IN SAN FRANCISCO[47]

The friends in San Francisco were Susan Helenius and her family, who Ellroy felt honor-bound not to name. The detective reasoned that Ellroy was telling the truth and that he wasn't cut out to be a burglar. The charge was knocked down from burglary to trespassing. Ellroy's account of this arrest, his first as a legal adult, is verified by the available documentation. His rap sheet reveals he was charged twice on November 30, 1968. Firstly, for 459 PC Burglary and latterly for 602.5 PC Trespassing. On the arrest record Ellroy lists both his parents as deceased. Curiously, he told booking officers his father's name was James Ellroy.

Ellroy was moved in with the inmates charged with misdemeanors. It was the weekend and Ellroy had to spend two nights at Wilshire before he could be arraigned. Then on Monday morning he was escorted by a Sheriff's bus to the Lincoln Heights Division and placed in the drunk tank. It was crammed and uncomfortable. Sheriff's Deputies tossed the prisoners food bags. If you failed to grab a bag you missed lunch. Ellroy ate his lunch while the daily horrors of life in the drunk tank unfolded before him, "A dozen winos suffered alcoholic seizures."[48]

Prisoners were escorted to the courtroom and appeared before a judge in groups of ten. Ellroy was warned that the resident Judge Mary Waters had a fearsome reputation, "The guys in the tank said she was a nasty old cunt."[49] Ellroy pled guilty, but that did not stop him from getting a blast of contempt from the bench. Judge Waters scorned Ellroy for looking like a draft dodger. She was a veteran of the WAVES, United States Naval Reserve, and had no time for people who refused to serve their country. Ellroy was hooked up to a "12-man shackle train" and herded onto a bus that took him to the Main County Jail.[50] Judge Waters ordered Ellroy to be held without bail pending sentencing. It was a harsh decision given that he was unlikely to receive a custodial sentence for trespassing. Ellroy would have to spend three weeks in LA County Jail before he would be formally sentenced on December 23rd.

Ellroy was to grow accustomed to the bus journey from court to jail over the next few years. Sometimes violent or bizarre incidents would break the deadening monotony of jailhouse life. The bus was gender segregated and on one journey a female prisoner took off "her jail smock and banged her pubus up against the grate."[51] A male prisoner on the other side of the partition put his head to the glass, so that he was as close to her crotch as possible and started miming cunnilingus.

Being processed at the Main County Jail was a long and exhausting process. Ellroy and the other prisoners would receive a blood test, inoculation, and chest X-ray. If Ellroy's drug use was detected it was not acted upon by the staff. He received no drug treatment in jail. There would be periods of isolation. The inmates would be moved from one holding cell to another. Ellroy had to strip naked and undergo a skin search, all bodily orifices were checked for contraband or weapons. He was covered in a delousing spray and given jailhouse denims to wear. Ellroy was questioned about his medical history, "At one point they said who's a homosexual and they'd get isolated."[52] The entire induction process took up to fourteen or fifteen hours, and it was past midnight before Ellroy was shown to his cell. He was sharing a cell with five other inmates and had to slide his mattress under the bottom bunk and sleep there. After breakfast the following morning, Ellroy was transferred to the Hall of Justice Jail. This facility was even more crowded and Ellroy had to sleep on the catwalk on the thirteenth floor. He was getting used to carrying his mattress round with him and being moved from one cell to another. Ellroy's time in jail largely passed by without incident. He was smart enough not to talk back to either the inmates or the Sheriff's deputies, all of whom were tougher than he was.

Ellroy only ever instigated one jailhouse fight and it ended disastrously for him. During one induction, a Mexican drag queen started patting Ellroy's knee and saying playfully in an effeminate voice "Hi, I'm Peaches." This was causing the other inmates to laugh and an annoyed Ellroy felt that he had to prove himself. He got to his feet, punched Peaches, and watched him fall to the floor. The other inmates were cheering in approval, but then "Peaches gets up, and Peaches has hands like Muhammed Ali, and Peaches kicked my fucking ass!"[53]

Ellroy was fortunate not to receive any sustained physical abuse from the other inmates, but he was in no doubt that they looked upon him with contempt. Randy came to visit one day. Like Ellroy, he would do time in jail for minor offences and "probably served more time aggregate than me as he had tougher probation officers."[54] Randy didn't want Ellroy to return to homelessness once he was released from jail, so he arranged for him to move into a small apartment for $80 a month on 6th and St. Andrews. It would necessitate a return to paid employment. Ellroy now had something to work towards which helped him to count his days down.

Judge Mary Waters sentenced Ellroy to three years of probation on December 23rd. It effectively ended his first stint of jail time, and he was back to being a free man. It was the last time Ellroy would see Judge Waters, but she remained the scourge of lowlife in Los Angeles Municipal Court for the next three decades.

When he was out of jail, Ellroy's preoccupation with sex soon returned. Despite both of his parents being good-looking and sexually confident, Ellroy was awkward and gangly by comparison. His lifestyle didn't help. He lived off the one hundred dollars a month Leoda sent him. As his rent was $60, Ellroy tried to stretch the remaining $40 by stealing all his food and drink, and only taking drugs if it could be scrounged off his friends. A poor, inconsistent diet made him dangerously skinny, which in turn made shoplifting relatively easy as he could hide food in his pants or under his shirt without arousing suspicion. His lack of nutrition gave him a bad acne problem, particularly on his back which was covered from top to bottom with acne scars. He could not afford acne cream. He always popped his zits, but it only compounded the problem and left him in excruciating pain.

Despite these hardships, Ellroy soon found himself dating another woman, and the relationship seemed far more promising than his tawdry arrangement with Susan. Ellroy met a young woman named Brenda on the Wilshire

Boulevard bus. She was closer to his age than Susan and much more interested in him as a person. Ellroy told her he was a "great-writer-in-waiting."[55] She told Ellroy that he had a strong voice and might make a good actor. However, Brenda ended things when she felt the relationship was compromising her values. Ellroy quickly found another girlfriend when he met Chrystine Mollett. Chrystine was "the archetypal early seventies hippy from the San Gabriel Valley" and was somewhat curious about Ellroy's acne-riddled anatomy.[56] At one point "she bit my right-middle knuckle down to the bone to scope out the cartilage."[57] Chrystine had left home and was sleeping in her car, putting up a quarantine sign on her windshield so she wouldn't be disturbed. She would periodically sleep in Hancock Park with Ellroy, where their sleep would be interrupted by the sprinkler system. Chrystine recalls Ellroy was "fast and agile" and could awake and find a dry spot quickly.[58] However, she worried that drug use was taking its toll on his health as "his skin was the bitterest thing I ever tasted."[59]

Ellroy discovered Chrystine had also been seeing Randy Rice. Ellroy got into a physical altercation with Randy over the betrayal, "We fought until we were so exhausted that we collapsed in each other's arms on the hood of a car."[60] Chrystine recalls Ellroy as somewhat sweeter in temperament than Randy, and in better shape. Randy was red-faced and bloated. Ellroy confided to her that he didn't like the name Lee. "He liked being called Ellroy."[61] One evening, Chrystine returned to her car to discover that it had caught fire. Chrystine telephoned her father who arranged for the car to be towed, and she subsequently moved back home. Consequently, she lost touch with Ellroy. Had it not been for this incident, she believes the relationship would have "undoubtedly" continued.[62]

Ellroy had taken to selling his blood plasma as a way of making money. After one trip to the blood bank in the Summer of 1971 he met Randy at the Pacific Palisades and they drank alcohol. The combination of blood loss, lack of food, and alcohol made Ellroy woozy fast. Ellroy could recall haranguing some hippies on the beach with his right-wing views. That was the last thing he remembered before blacking out, "the curtain drops."[63] When Ellroy awoke he found himself naked in bed with a morbidly obese woman who "weighed three bills easy."[64] He put on his clothes. His wallet was on a bedside table. There was more money in it than there had been before he blacked out. But the biggest shock came next. Not willing to give the woman another moment of his time, a mortified Ellroy threw on his clothes quickly while she was asleep. He sneaked outside her door and found himself in an apartment corridor and "weaved my way past hippies."[65] Out on the street he failed to recognize his surroundings. It didn't look like any part of LA he was familiar with, and then it dawned on him.

"I was on Fell Street, San Francisco."[66]

The incident would prove to be one of the most bizarre blackouts Ellroy had ever experienced. He had no idea of how he had travelled the 380 miles from the Palisades to San Francisco, except he had a vague notion he may have gone hitchhiking and been picked up by another group of hippies. The obese woman likely paid for the sex, making this the first and only time that Ellroy played the gigolo. As embarrassing as the whole affair was, it did not deter Ellroy from his drug and alcohol addiction.

Throughout these years Ellroy was hired and fired from more than a dozen jobs. In 1969 he got a job in the mailroom at KCOP-TV. Listeners would send money in the post in response to radio ads. Ellroy would recognize a potentially lucrative envelope by its weight and the jangling of coins. He found that stealing the contents of the envelope supplemented his income nicely. He was never caught stealing, but he was fired after crashing the company van and being forced to admit that he did not possess a driver's license. Ellroy later found work at the Porno Villa bookstore. His feelings about pornography were ambiguous. Ellroy loved *Playboy* magazine and regarded Kaya Christian, Playmate of the Month November 1967, as his favorite model. And yet even *Playboy* had a certain literary merit that raised it above the hardcore material at the Porno Villa, and the Playmates were essentially modelled on the Girl-Next-Door type which matched Ellroy's fascination with the hidden sexuality of suburban life.

It was the height of the "Golden Age of Pornography." *Deep Throat* had been a mainstream box-office success in 1972. The porn industry had decamped from New York City to LA to take advantage of low rents and easy access to movie technicians. Pornography laws had been liberalized and material was becoming increasingly hardcore. Many of the images Ellroy saw left him cold. The women were engaged in an "ugly pandering business."[67] Ellroy did get a laugh out of some of the sex toys, such as the strap-on Donkey Dan Dick Extender. The bookstore was full of two-way mirrors to deter same-sex assignations. Men would come in cruising and brush up against each other while pretending to examine stock. Ellroy was under instructions to break-up such encounters, shouting "Hey, cut it out. Stop it," and the skittish men would scatter at the sound of his voice.

Ellroy was fired after he was caught stealing from the till. He had been stealing the store's pornographic material for some time. Pornography may have meant little more to Ellroy than a means to self-abuse, but it did allow him to indulge in a fantasy that, no matter how ludicrous, transcended mere sexual desire. He examined the images of the naked women during his nightshift, and at home after he had stolen a fresh batch of material. He indulged in some male-savior fantasies, "I gave my girls names and prayed for them every night."[68] In this, he was not unlike Randy who, "had a bent for tortured women hooked up to abusive men. He tried to rescue them and got into fights with dope-dealer sleazebags."[69] Ellroy toured the streets with Randy who acted as his guide and taught him the strata of LA lowlife, "I met bikers, fruit hustlers and Gene the Short Queen—a 4' 10 transvestite."[70] It was an education to Ellroy, but he often found there was nothing poetic in the squalor. In his banter with Randy, Ellroy developed a schtick he would later term "Dog Humor." Ellroy defined Dog Humor as "Profane. It's nihilistic. It's sexual. Why mince words. It's racist and homophobic and full of inventive use of foul language. It celebrates the crassest and most debased in human behavior. It's a way of taking the most obvious and broadest strokes of satire and making it funny in context."[71] It would serve him well as an author known for his outrageous Demon Dog persona. But its initial use was as a survival instinct. A way of coping with the more squalid aspects of his life and turning them into minor narratives at a time when opportunities to be creative through writing were not available to him.

Without a job, and continuously behind on his rent, the landlord evicted him from his apartment permanently. Ellroy was by now more accustomed and prepared for outdoor living. He found a dry spot by a toolshed in Robert Burns Park. Randy let him shower at his house and he kept a spare set of clothes there. He still received $100 dollars a month from Leoda, now mailed to Randy's house, and he didn't have to worry about spending it on rent. He was not outside all day. He spent as much time as he could in public libraries and continued to read as many crime novels as he could. He enjoyed the hardboiled classics by Raymond Chandler, James M. Cain, and Dashiell Hammett, but he spent a lot of time perusing the new releases section. George V. Higgins debut novel *The Friends of Eddie Coyle* was published in 1970 and LAPD Police Officer Joseph Wambaugh's first novel *The New Centurions* was released in 1971. Ellroy ranked both authors among his favorites and, in time, they would prove influential on his writing.

Ellroy was not the only homeless or vagrant person who frequented the public libraries. One day Ellroy met "a freak at the Hollywood public library" named Marvin.[72] Marvin introduced him to a new and dangerous drug habit. Up until then Ellroy's drug use had been serious but had not strayed too far from the middle-class tastes in narcotics at the time. He had been taking the same drugs as his friends who were planning to attend university. Now that they were gone, Ellroy's drug supply had dried up. Marvin recommended Benzedrex inhalers. The inhalers were a small white tube designed to be inhaled through the nose to alleviate congestion. They could be utilized as a recreational drug if the user removed the cotton wad, which was soaked in propylhexedrine, from inside the tube and swallowed it. Furthermore, the inhalers were cheap and could be bought over the counter at any pharmacy.

Ellroy stole three Benzedrex inhalers from a local pharmacy and resolved to take them all at once. He nearly choked washing down the cotton wads with root beer, but within half-an-hour he was feeling the desired effect. Ellroy went on an eight-hour high that allowed him to masturbate through the night. On the comedown he was feeling "dingy and schizzy."[73] He drank alcohol to come out of it. Ellroy had discovered his most destructive habit yet—a cheap and plentiful supply of drugs that would eat away at his mental and physical health over the coming years.

From 1970 to 1973, Ellroy's Probation Officer was a woman named Elizabeth Heath. Liz was "gracious, intelligent, stern-willed and funny."[74] Ellroy may have mistaken her firm and courteous personality, as required by her role, as a sign of affection. He had a painful crush on her, doing his best to look smart and clean-cut before each of their meetings. Liz eventually left LA. She made a farewell telephone call to Ellroy, and her manner was warm and encouraging. Ellroy was "glib" in response.[75] He knew he was never going to see her again, and it was the best way to deal with the emotional pain.

Ellroy was fortunate that for three years he had such a sympathetic Probation Officer in Liz, as he was in almost constant trouble. Ellroy later claimed that he was arrested "sixty-five, seventy" times.[76] His rap sheet lists fourteen arrests or field incidents, and a total of fifteen booking photos of Ellroy were taken from 1968 to 1975. He was arrested on March 17, 1971, one week after his twenty-third birthday, for shoplifting. A department store worker named Carol McClure observed Ellroy place a bottle of peach-flavored brandy into his trousers. He was detained and the police were called. Ellroy was arrested again for shoplifting at Savon Drugs pharmacy on December 23, 1971. Ellroy shoved a handful of Benzedrex inhalers into his trousers and attempted to run past the registers but was apprehended by the security guard Kenneth Boros. Upon this arrest Ellroy, rather optimistically, listed his occupation as a writer. He was arrested twice more in 1972. In 1973, Ellroy had the most arrests in a single year. Two arrests were particularly humiliating. He was booked for 314.1 PC Indecent Exposure and 647a PC Lewd Conduct in Public.

His initial arrests were all in LA, but when he was in possession of a car he ventured further afield, frequently intoxicated while he did so. He was arrested in Santa Monica and Santa Barbara for driving offences. Ellroy learned that Sheriff's Deputies were more corrupt and prone to violence than the LAPD, "I saw them do some pretty brutal numbers."[77] Ellroy insists there are gaps on his rap sheet, although certainly not enough to justify his claim he was arrested up to seventy times. On May 9, 1973, Ellroy was arrested for DUI. Two officers in a patrol car observed Ellroy driving a 1962 Blue Ford Falcon. He was weaving erratically and straddling lanes on Rosewood & Poinsettia. After pulling him over the officers noticed Ellroy's "alcoholic" breath, "flushed" face, and "rapid" speech. His walk was "unsteady," clothing "disarranged." He admitted to drinking three glasses of white port and beer and "pkd at scene."[78]

On October 24, 1974, Ellroy was arrested for 647f PC Public Intoxication. A police officer arrived at Olympic and La Cienega Blvd and found three witnesses and a wounded Ellroy. Ellroy had been crossing the road drunk and was hit by a truck driven by witness one—William Reynolds. The officer "obs that the deft's eyes were bloodshot and watery and his speech was slurred and thick. Ofc could smell an odor of alcoholic beverage emitting from the deft's breath."[79] Given the serious nature of the traffic accident Ellroy appears to have escaped relatively unscathed. He was taken to Culver hospital where he was treated for "abrasion to his upper lip."[80]

By the mid-70s Ellroy had passed through the LA County Jail system several times and was used to it and bored of it. Passing through jails did have its advantages as it made him appreciative of life's little luxuries. He enjoyed reading in the toilets after lights-out at Biscailuz Center Jail. Sobriety made him feel healthier and working out in the gym gave him muscle tone and a more imposing physique. Although there were narcotics passing through the jail system, Ellroy did not indulge in drug use while in custody. That would have brought him into closer proximity with the jailhouse gangs and a danger level he could not control. Ellroy's withdrawal from criminal life was predicated on the knowledge that he was not tough enough to survive the state prison system, which would have been his fate if he was convicted on felony charges. This self-awareness, his continuing ambition to become a writer and the subsequent steep decline in his physical and mental health all contributed to the slow end of Ellroy's criminal behavior from 1974 onwards.

At one of sentencing hearings in 1973, the judge remarked to Ellroy that "he was sick of seeing him in my court." He gave Ellroy a choice: he could serve six months in LA County Jail, or he could reside at the Salvation Army Harbor Light Mission on Skid Row for ninety days. It would entail taking Antabuse, attending church, and performing whatever menial task was asked of him. But as an alternative to jail, it was an offer too good to refuse. At the Mission, Ellroy was struck by the kindness of the volunteers. He was sober, working, and in good spirits. He struck up a friendship with a former Catholic priest named Bill Conroy. Conroy was a charismatic figure. He had a PhD in Physics from Fordham University, and Ellroy was impressed by how he could hold court on a variety of subjects, from theology to trigonometry. At night, they would walk through Skid Row taking in the dubious sights of the LA slums, "He's Conroy. I'm Ellroy. We had a blast."[81] Conroy had left the priesthood after finding celibacy a difficult proposition. Likewise, Ellroy was not ready for a clean and sober life. Despite being touched by the kindness of the people he met there, Ellroy bailed on the Mission before his ninety days were up. Aware that he still had Antabuse in his system, Ellroy abstained from alcohol for as long as he could. Although he inadvertently made himself sick one day when he doused himself with a stolen bottle of cologne and the alcohol content seeped into the pores of his skin.

Ellroy's health had been gradually worsening for some time. He had built up an immunity to Benzedrex inhalers and had to swallow a dozen cotton wads at a time to get high. He became increasingly paranoid, hearing voices and believing that his landlord and fellow tenants were spying on him. During one particularly unpleasant drug trip Ellroy's fear and delusions overcame him as he couldn't stop the voices in his head. He left the apartment, abandoning all his belongings. Ellroy stormed through the streets with no idea where he was heading. He found a convenience room where he could stay for $39 a month in Sunset and Micheltorena. The moment he moved into the small fleapit room the voices started in his head again, "the tenant next door started hissing through the air vents."[82] Ellroy took more inhalers to silence the voices. They made them worse. He ripped apart his blanket and pillows in a frenzy and filled his ears with foam rubber. The voices penetrated through his makeshift earplugs. He spent one night in the room before fleeing the voices the next morning. He moved back to the familiar setting of Robert Burns Park.

Ellroy was homeless again. He knew what he needed to do to survive on the streets. He stole new clothes when the ones he was wearing became too grimy. He discovered the dine-and-dash con. He would go to a restaurant, order a big meal, and sneak out before the time came to pay the bill. He did this until he ran out of restaurants that didn't recognize him. He continued to spend hours at a time in libraries and read dozens of crime novels. He was becoming quite knowledgeable about the structure and plotting of crime fiction. He could spot the clues in the text for moments that would be paid off later in the story. He could recognize the differing style and authorial voices of Chandler and Hammett and Ed McBain. He was growing confident that he could imitate them in a crime story of his own. But as he had still not tried writing anything himself it was a knowledge that would not have any practical application for a few more years.

As much as he tried to pragmatically and intellectually stave off the health challenges that homelessness entails, Ellroy continued to abuse drink and drugs and the voices in his head would not go away. He was having chest pains which he ignored until the pain became too acute. He took a bus to the County Hospital and was diagnosed with pneumonia. He stayed in hospital for a week while a course of antibiotics slowly worked its way through his system. He went straight back to his regular habits once he was discharged.

Although Ellroy was locked in a spiral of self-destruction, there was a part of him that was looking for an escape. His religious faith, always fragile, would intensify with time and give him some much needed emotional strength. In 1975, Ellroy had a vivid religious experience. It was late, he didn't have a place to stay, and he was walking down Pico Boulevard in heavy rain, "I passed a run of storefronts. One doorknob seemed to glow. I put my hand on it. The door opened effortlessly."[83] Ellroy had found shelter for the night, and the next morning his damp clothes had dried, and he felt completely revived, but his health problems would recur soon afterwards. The incident might seem mundane compared to some of his other experiences while homeless, but Ellroy felt that he had been both saved and chosen. "God left that door open for me. I have no doubt of that."[84] The vision of the glowing doorknob and Ellroy's easy entry into the building can be rationally explained. Malnutrition and drug use can cause hallucinations. Ellroy had a history of breaking and entering. He was increasingly blacking out and waking up in unfamiliar locations. Seeking shelter in an office building was not unusual to him. In any event, Ellroy would soon endure hallucinations more visceral than any of his religious experiences.

As Ellroy describes it, he was relieving himself in Randy Rice's bathroom when the first hallucinations occurred, "A monster jumped out of the toilet. I shut the lid and saw more monsters seep through it. Spiders crawled up my legs. Little blobs hurled themselves at my eyes."[85] Ellroy stole Randy's liquor to try and drink-away the images. He got so drunk that he passed out and woke up terrified on the roof of Randy's apartment building. The voices and hallucinations were ironically pushing Ellroy closer to reality. He could no longer control his vices and the simple truth was that if he didn't get sober soon then he would die. He hitchhiked his way to the hospital, drinking liquor along the way. He took one last swig of the bottle on the hospital steps "and turned myself in."[86] Jail had always given him brief stints of sobriety. Now Ellroy was hoping the hospital staff could help him achieve it permanently. Ellroy spent two days at the County Hospital before being transferred to Long Beach State Hospital Addiction Recovery Program. The journey to Long Beach did not imbue Ellroy with confidence. He went in a hospital van with three alcoholic men much older than himself. They swapped stories that terrified Ellroy. They were locked in a cycle of alcoholism and occasional bouts of hospital treatment and enforced sobriety. They talked as though only death could stop their addiction. Ellroy was younger, fitter, and determined to do better. At Long Beach, Ellroy was once again prescribed Antabuse every day.

Ellroy was starting to feel physically better, and the voices and hallucinations had ceased. However, he couldn't stand the group therapy sessions. The endless series of self-hating monologues reminded him of the salvation testimonies at Culter Christian Academy. When it came to his turn to speak Ellroy couldn't resist launching into preposterous stories of his sexual exploits to impress several attractive women on the program. Ellroy once claimed in an interview that he was "kicked out for disrupting group therapy," but in his memoirs he claimed to have completed the program.[87] Not all the therapy sessions were mandatory, so it is likely the staff asked him not to attend if he refused to contribute in a positive manner.

Before he completed the program, Ellroy was examined for a hacking cough he had developed. Ellroy was given a muscle relaxant and a doctor placed a penlight attached to a tube down his throat. Nothing unusual was detected. The failure of the examination to diagnose Ellroy's lung condition would cost him dearly in the long-term. Once he had completed the program, Ellroy returned to living on Randy's roof. He was still on Antabuse and had been sober for over a month, but his living conditions were miserable. In hospital he had been fed three warm meals a day and had a roof over his head. Now he was back to being virtually homeless with a roof beneath his feet. In June 1975, at the age of twenty-seven Ellroy endured a nervous breakdown. He awoke abruptly from a nap with a craving for cigarettes. He resolved to obtain some but felt paralyzed by some unknown force. Then Ellroy realized he could not think or say his own name, "he kept missing the synapses."[88] After spending about an hour lying against the fire door, quivering with fear, Ellroy started to scream. The screaming was so intense and prolonged that it was noticed by people in the streets and in Randy's building. Luckily, Randy was home and called an ambulance and then carried him downstairs in his arms. The paramedics arrived and Ellroy was strapped to a gurney. In the hospital, Ellroy was still screaming and hearing voices. His paranoia was raging, and he believed the hospital staff were his enemies. He thrashed and writhed away at his restraints until he was injected with a sedative.

When Ellroy awoke his throat was raw from screaming himself mute. Although he was groggy, Ellroy was able to recall a thought that had eluded him when he was breaking down. He remembered his name—Lee Earle Ellroy. Then slowly his memory began to recall every detail of his breakdown. Ellroy was in an emotionally fraught state. He had once fled from the voices in his head. Now he wanted to purge his memory. The trauma of the past few hours made him weep uncontrollably in his hospital bed. Ellroy claims a doctor diagnosed him with the condition "post-alcohol brain syndrome." It was, he said, the cause of his breakdown. It's possible Ellroy misremembered the diagnosis. Ellroy was most likely suffering from alcohol withdrawal syndrome and delirium tremens (DTs). Although DTs commonly occur when an alcoholic has been sober for three days. Ellroy had not touched a drink for more than thirty days when his hallucinations started "Sober drunks went through it sometimes."[89] The medical staff also found the cause of Ellroy's heavy cough and shortness of breath. He had an abscess the size of a fist on his left lung, a common condition for alcoholics. Ellroy spent a month in isolation in the hospital. He was heavily medicated on tranquilizers and tried to sleep as much as he could. There were too many painful and fearful memories tormenting Ellroy when he was awake. His natural inclination had always been to keep on the move when he was mentally tortured. Ellroy checked himself out of the hospital against the doctor's advice. It would be less than twenty-four hours before he was back again.

Ellroy may have suffered a partial seizure as he was walking away from the hospital.[90] Nevertheless he kept moving, stealing gin from a liquor store, and finding his way back to Randy's apartment. Once he was there Ellroy kept drinking, determined to get as drunk as possible to ease his torment. He had another seizure and blacked out. Randy called an ambulance again. The paramedics managed to revive Ellroy, and he walked, with their assistance, down to the ambulance. Ellroy was placed on the lung ward. He was given antibiotics again but some of the most effective treatment for abscesses is postural drainage. A nurse would massage and clap on his back. The mixture of gravity and percussion dislodged the mucus in his lungs and Ellroy would spit globs of it into a bottle. Gradually his lungs healed and Ellroy began to recover.

Lying in his hospital bed Ellroy spent a lot of time in prayer and thought. At the age of twenty-seven he had come close to a terrifying death. Ellroy was depressed by the thought that so much of his life had been spent in squalor and he had no real achievements to his name. He resolved not only to embrace sobriety, but to work with a new sense of urgency and competitiveness. Once he had his life on track, he could pursue his dreams of becoming a writer. But for the time being Ellroy focused on getting better and thanked God that the voices in his head had stopped and he had retained his sanity. It's important not to overstate Ellroy's religiosity. Prayer provided solace but Ellroy "understood the preposterous aspect of all divine contracts." He knew that even the most determined recovering addicts were still in danger of a relapse and the mental breakdown that could accompany it. "My brain could blow tomorrow or in the year 2000."[91]

It was a prediction that would prove chillingly prescient.

4

Debris by the Sea
(1975–1981)

Once he was discharged from hospital, Ellroy returned to his spot on the roof of Randy's apartment building. It was not somewhere he wished to stay for long. He was sick of sleeping rough and the place held some traumatic memories for him. In hospital, Ellroy had taken to memorizing "magazine ads and slogans on milk cartons."[1] It gave him confidence and helped to ward off his fear of losing his ability to speak and remember his own name. Out of hospital, Ellroy returned to the library. His love of novels was now of great benefit to his recovery. He memorized passages from books, and it helped him to grow mentally stronger. His recovery was aided by a run of good luck.

Kurt Trostorff was one of the tenants in the same skid-row hotel where Randy was staying. Trostorff had once been the equipment manager for the Detroit Tigers and Los Angeles Angels, hence his nickname "Tracker" Trostorff. He was also an accomplished ice skater who had performed with the Ice Follies. He had at one point entertained the notion of becoming an actor but had fallen on hard times due to his weakness for alcohol. He was now working as a golf caddy at the Hillcrest Country Club. He informed Ellroy that it was "good tax-free work."[2] Ellroy put on his best outfit and visited the Hillcrest. He was promptly hired by the caddy master.

Ellroy was nervous and fumbling during his first week on the job. But he wasn't going to repeat the mistake of his past and walk away from a regular salary. He started caddying with one golf bag at a time, then moved on to two and quickly memorized the different types of irons. In the beginning, Ellroy caddied for the "ducks" who were the older members who attended regularly and were well-known for being miserly with the caddies. Anthony Kafesjian was one of the younger caddies who recalls that experienced caddies "jealously guarded the regular high-tipping players," but Ellroy was a "strong personality" who made his presence known.[3] As his looping skills improved, Ellroy started making a minimum $200 a week. He used the money to get himself a permanent room at the Westwood Hotel for $25 a week. It was a modest "piss and sink room" but it was a roof over his head.[4] The Westwood was close to the major country clubs of LA and caddies, or "loopers" as they were also known, rented out most of the rooms.

The Hillcrest had an almost exclusively upper-middle class Jewish membership while some gentile celebrities, including Frank Sinatra, were granted honorary membership. It had been founded as an alternative to the

Figure 5 *"Pari-Mutuels" by Tim Morneau. A caddy attends to his ducks "members known to be bad tippers" at the Hillcrest Country Club. Morneau was Ellroy's closest friend at the Hillcrest. Credit: Tim Morneau.*

major country clubs of LA which barred Jews as members. With any feelings of anti-Semitism long behind him, Ellroy enjoyed taking in the culture at the Hillcrest. He listened in on the conversations of the doctors and lawyers he caddied for, absorbing their dialects, and observing the joys and stresses of their lives. In the caddy house it was a different world. Ellroy's fellow caddies were blue-collar guys who passed the time between "loops" playing card games, drinking, and smoking pot.

Tim Morneau was "a smart young caddy going to college part-time."[5] Morneau stood out from the rest of the loopers. He was studying at UCLA and was fascinated by American history and loved literature. He and Ellroy became close friends. Morneau recalls the day he met Ellroy, "I was called up from the caddy house to get a golf cart from the cart barn. Like the caddy house, the cart barn was a large shed concealed down below the first tee. It was the station where all the carts were hooked up to chargers. I saw Lee [Ellroy] there alone, a new guy, and went up to say hello. I introduced myself, and immediately I realized there was something special about this fellow."[6] Ellroy and Morneau spent a lot of time together going on nocturnal walks and "sharing stories, talking history and literature, music, my stories of Hillcrest caddies, favorite movies, culture, women, etc.; his stories, of his mother's murder in 1958, the corruption of the LAPD in the 1950's."[7]

At Morneau's apartment they watched on television the presidential inauguration of Jimmy Carter on January 20, 1977. They shared a deep interest in history and politics. Morneau schooled Ellroy on the culture at the Hillcrest. With its easy money and untaxing work the lifestyle of a caddy was seductive and, for younger loopers like Ellroy and Morneau, it would have been all too easy to be sucked into this world permanently. The older loopers would say to them, "Kid, you'll never get out of here. You've got the grass in your shoes."

California weather usually made caddying a year-round job in LA, but the winter of 1977 was notable for the torrential rain in the area. Once the rains cleared, rodents would swarm over the damp course. Ellroy, whose working day often finished by 2 p.m., was given $5 a day "rain money" and stayed holed up at his room in the Westwood. The lack of work gave him plenty of time to think. He had wanted to be an author for years, had devised and played with stories in his mind, but he had never worked up the courage to take the first step and start writing. He felt that the time to start was approaching and he didn't want to let it pass by. He loved crime fiction and "didn't buy the old canard that you had to start by writing short stories."[8] Only a novel could encompass Ellroy's obsessions, and his most all-consuming obsession was crime and the Black Dahlia case. John Gregory Dunne's *True Confessions*, loosely inspired by the Dahlia case, was released in 1977 and was an instant bestseller. Ellroy loved the novel but felt a twinge of jealousy that Dunne had adapted the Dahlia case into fiction before him. Dunne was already an established author prior to *True Confessions*, whereas Ellroy was an unknown golf caddy. It made sense to avoid the Black Dahlia case until he had more experience of writing. Ellroy admitted that "the success of the book [*True Confessions*] deterred me from writing" about the Black Dahlia case.[9] He needed to write about other crimes. A story was forming in Ellroy's mind. It would be set in LA and draw upon Ellroy's immediate experience of caddying, his interests in classical music, obsession with sex, and intricate knowledge of LA's criminal history. Frightened of losing the story, but also nervous of the prospect of writing a novel, Ellroy began jotting down his ideas.

Around this time, Ellroy and Randy were spending a lot of time with a young couple they had befriended. Sol Abrveaya and Joan Levitt shared a garage apartment in West Hollywood. Abrveaya was a short "yogi" type of character who was popular with women. Randy liked him as he was more prone to "hero-worship," but Ellroy could see through him "to a core I didn't like."[10] He suspected that Abrveaya thought he and Randy were both losers. Ellroy was more taken with his girlfriend Joan. She had dark brunette hair and striking blue eyes. One day, the four of them were in Abrveaya's living room when Joan reached over the coffee table, "She's reaching for a ciggie. She always wore jeans and a blouse or a man's shirt, and I can see her breast, and I think, oh shit, I have to change my life."[11] Determined to create something positive out of his two fair-weather friends, Ellroy made them characters in the story he was plotting.

As so many of the caddies smoked pot it was a potentially dangerous environment for a recovering addict to be in. After four months of sobriety,

Ellroy gave into temptation and started smoking Thai Stick regularly. Ellroy smoked a lot of pot with Morneau. He was confident that his newfound vice would not lead to a relapse into his former addictions. "I'd rather ingest rat poison" he told Morneau about the thought of consuming alcohol again. He still occasionally gave people alcohol as a gift. He once gave Morneau a six-pack of beers. Although Morneau suspected that this was something of a test as a couple of weeks later Ellroy checked Morneau's fridge and, seeing that the six-pack had gone untouched, said to him, "Good for you, Tim—you're not an alcoholic." Morneau got his pot supply from a fellow caddy "who planted pot gardens right there on Hillcrest property, very scientifically, designed to grow the best, with watering systems, rabbit-proof wire fencing, etc."[12] Ellroy was at first careful not to smoke pot at the Hillcrest, but after a while he got lazy and started lighting up whenever he could.

Ellroy's behavior started to slip at the Hillcrest. He could still be unpredictable when pushed. A Latino caddy named Rudy was known as the club bully. Short in stature and temper, Rudy suffered a Napoleon complex about his height. He called himself "Killer" and liked to intimidate some of the meeker caddies. Morneau witnessed Rudy try his tough-guy act on Ellroy, "When he started to pull this stuff on Lee, instantly Lee spun around on him and said, 'Fuck you, greaseball! Come on! Let's go! Right now!' Rudy beat a fast retreat. He got off easy, I'm sure Lee was ready to pulverize him."[13]

One day Ellroy was caught smoking weed by a club member's son. The guy also worked as a caddy and Ellroy disliked him intensely. When he started berating Ellroy for smoking on club premises Ellroy lost his temper and decked him, possibly to impress a "good-looking woman" who was standing nearby.[14] Ellroy was fired immediately and escorted off the premises by a security guard. But Ellroy wasn't ready to give up caddying just yet. It had immeasurably improved his quality of life and was an integral setting to the novel he was planning. Ellroy visited the Bel-Air Country Club looking for work. He was still on good terms with Mark Rhodes, the caddy master at the Hillcrest, and had with him a letter of introduction. He talked up his experience as a caddy at the Hillcrest and neglected to mention his dismissal. The caddies at the Bel-Air were no different from those who worked at Hillcrest, "drug addicts, winos, compulsive gamblers, ex-cons and generally shitbirds."[15] Ellroy looked clean-cut by comparison and was hired. If working at the Hillcrest had been a good job, then caddying at the Bel-Air was a dream come true. The course was even more beautiful, and the members included many Hollywood stars.

Ellroy found himself caddying for celebrities such as George C. Scott "he had an anger in him," Dinah Shore "a good tipper," Farrah Fawcett "very lovely and gracious" and Howard Keel "we used to call him Howard Cruel, he was a mean sonofabitch."[16] He smoked weed with Glen Campbell and had a memorable encounter with Robert Goulet. Goulet told him to get some extra balls out of his golf bag, "I reached in for the balls and there was a loaded, cocked 45 automatic."[17] Ellroy loved to observe the rich and famous at play. Ellroy caddied for Telly Savalas. Savalas chain-smoked and was dressed entirely in black on a hot summer's day. He never spoke to Ellroy, merely pointed at the irons he wanted. Ellroy was growing tired of Savalas' rude behavior when at the ninth hole, they came across a dead gopher with all fours in the air near the putting green. Savalas took a golf iron, prodded the gopher curiously, grinned and said his Kojak catchphrase "Who loves ya baby." He then tipped Ellroy generously and walked away.

Ellroy had another notable celebrity encounter with Charles Bronson. Bronson's Bel-Air mansion adjoined the country club. Ellroy occasionally caught glimpses of Bronson in his garden. He was especially pleased when he caught sight of Bronson's wife, the actress Jill Ireland, sunbathing. Occasionally Bronson's dog, a white German Shepherd, would jump the gate and come onto the course. Ellroy would pet it before shooing it back to the house. Bronson would stand by the gate, talk to the caddies, and occasionally give them cans of beer. Bronson held a grudge against the Bel-Air. He felt that his movie star status warranted a free membership with the club. No such offer was forthcoming. Bronson loved to badmouth the club to the caddies who were more than happy to reciprocate in return for free beer. Perhaps Bronson hoped he could sow dissent or distract the caddies so much that it would drive down business at the club. It seemed an odd method of revenge for the star of *Death Wish* to take. Business at the club carried on much as before, and Bronson and his wife soon grew tired of the motley bunch of caddies loitering around their home. Bronson conceded defeat and thereafter the caddies no longer felt welcome near his home.

Finally, on January 26, 1979, Ellroy made a fateful decision. It was a Monday, when members didn't play, and he was caddying for a divorced man named Bob Briscoe who was taking his young son round the course. They were on the eighth hole when "I actually sent up a prayer to my seldom sought, blandly protestant God."[18] Ellroy prayed that he would be able to start writing. He had notes but no outline, but Ellroy knew that if he left it any longer, he would never build up the confidence to start and "wanted to take this impetus from a divine source."[19]

That evening, at his room in the Westwood Hotel, Ellroy started writing. He didn't have a desk, so he wrote standing up resting the paper on his dresser. He wrote in block capitals with a black pen on white paper, with a red correcting pen to hand. The first line he wrote was "Business was good. It was the same every Summer." He had a feeling that "I would succeed from that first sentence."[20]

During the Summer of 1977, while Ellroy and Randy were both staying at the Westwood hotel, Randy urged his friend to embrace full sobriety. Ellroy was skeptical at first. He loved smoking Thai Stick. But there was always the danger that it could lead to a relapse. Finally, Ellroy followed Randy's advice and attended his first Westside AA meeting on August 1, 1977. Ellroy was always grateful to Randy for giving him the courage to make the decision, "He'd gotten sober first; I just sorta followed his lead."[21]

There was another compelling reason for him to attend AA. It was difficult for Ellroy to meet single women. He tried approaching women in bookstores. They found him weird and imposing and backed away. He needed to find an environment in which women felt comfortable around him. AA would prove the perfect setting.

In AA, Ellroy soon made new friends and met a diverse cast of characters. His first sponsor was a man named Mark McGuire. McGuire had been crippled in a surfing accident. He was in constant physical pain and used his time and energy to help addicts. Ellroy credited McGuire with helping him to turn his life around, "He did not have a long life-expectancy. There was a gravity to him."[22] In addition, many of the attendees were actors, writers, and dancers. But no matter how talented the people at AA were, they all attended because alcohol and drug addiction had brought them to the brink. "I heard stories that topped mine for sheer horror," Ellroy recalled.[23] There were funny stories too. One young lawyer told the group that he had once blacked out during a bender and woke up on a cruise liner, days later, dressed as a Rabbi on a "Jewish Singles" tour of the Caribbean. Henceforth he was always known as "Rabbi" at AA.

"Rabbi" later became a District Attorney.

Ellroy met and befriended Gerald "Jerry" Chamales at AA. Chamales was the son of the author and OSS veteran Tom T. Chamales. Jerry Chamales encouraged Ellroy to pursue his writing ambitions and "I introduced him to a writer I was in a relationship with named Roberta Ostroff as I thought it would be encouraging to him."[24] Ostroff had written a biography of the war correspondent Dickey Chapelle. Ellroy was unmoved by her advice. He was certain he knew how to write.

Ellroy briefly worked for Chamales, as Chamales was pursuing his own dream of setting up a computer products company. Ellroy was one of the first employees of Omni Computer products and went to work in Chamales's Venice Beach apartment selling printer cartridges over the phone. Years later, a *Fortune* Magazine article described the average working day of the two ambitious men:

> A BACH CONCERTO FILLS a Venice Beach, California, apartment – just loud enough to drown out the periodic gun shots that emerge from a nearby drug deal gone awry. It's 1978. Two friends, one a struggling scribe, the other a scrappy entrepreneur, are soothed by the music as the sun begins to rise. Outside, the denizens of this bohemian enclave push shopping carts in search of a prime spot to display their paintings or play their music. Inside, the two men set up their own marketplace, preparing for a day of phone sales. Bach is soon replaced by *The Psychology of Winning* audio tape; Dennis Waitley's preachings form an armor that will protect the two salespeople from the rejection telemarketing invariably brings.[25]

Although both men were wrestling with a fear or rejection, Ellroy proved himself to be a smooth salesman, landing the fledgling company the Neiman Marcus account. He only worked for Chamales for a few weeks however, before his restlessness drove him back to the golf course and to writing his manuscript. Chamales renamed his company Rhinotek Computer Products and developed it into a multi-million-dollar business.

Westside AA meetings often took place in a church and ended with the Lord's Prayer. Ellroy took the meetings more seriously than he had when he was hospitalized. He still liked to impress women when it was his turn to speak, but he soon discovered that there was no need to show off to hook up with a woman. AA had a Christian heritage, but its meetings were followed by a party atmosphere in which promiscuity was on the menu. Sex was a thrilling alternative to booze and drugs. Hot Tub parties were the latest craze sweeping LA. After meetings, Ellroy and his friends would party at "Hot Tub Fever" at 3131 Olympic Boulevard, Santa Monica, which became a byword for casual sex and orgies. People could rent out a hot tub with their partner or with someone they just met in the club. Each cubicle had a vending machine which sold condoms, KY jelly, and sex toys.

On December 8, 1980, Chamales and Ellroy were driving through LA. They stopped at a light and spotted two attractive women who were both in tears on the sidewalk.

"Hey ladies, what's wrong?" Ellroy called out.

"John Lennon's been shot," one of the sobbing women blurted out.

Neither Chamales nor Ellroy were going to let this opportunity pass up. Feigning an interest in Lennon's music and The Beatles, the two men persuaded the ladies in mourning to go for a coffee with them. They took them to a diner where they chatted and told jokes, and everyone seemed to be enjoying themselves. However, Chamales recalls that any hopes of a seduction were suddenly dashed as "we lost our momentum with the two lovely ladies when James suggested we should all go to Hot Tub Fever!"[26] Realizing that Chamales and Ellroy's intentions may have been less than honorable, the two women made their excuses and left.

Hot Tub Fever was rebranded as an "environmental health experience" in the mid-1980s when the Aids crisis began to change attitudes towards sex. In addition to his nights in Hot Tubs, Ellroy attended local wife-swapping parties and met attractive women for one-night stands. Ellroy was not averse to engaging the services of a prostitute. They were a common sight on "Sunset & Highland all the way out to Sunset & Crescent Heights" during the weekend.[27]

He would take them to a cheap motel on Holloway & La Cienega Boulevard. They tended to be women who had full-time jobs but made extra money in prostitution on the weekends. Perhaps out of guilt, Ellroy tried to persuade one of them to attend AA meetings with him.

Ellroy had finally developed an active sex life, but there was a sadness underlying this sexualized atmosphere. Ellroy wanted more than casual sex. He wanted a relationship that would last more than a night or two. Fellowship after AA meetings was not always seedy. Ellroy took part in arranging the AA Christmas parties. His contribution was to write and perform profane poems. After meetings, Ellroy, Randy, and another friend Rick Swirkal would sit in all night cafes and discuss their mutual love of crime fiction. They discussed all the greats—Chandler, Hammett, Ross Macdonald. Years later, Swirkal attended one of Ellroy's book readings and recognized his shtick on crime writers being the same, word for word, as their former late-night chats.[28] Ellroy paid Swirkal to conduct research on the 1957 Club Mecca firebombing for him, which he planned to incorporate into his novel.

Swirkal recalls telling Ellroy that he had started writing his own novel. A look of apprehension came over Ellroy's face. Writers are prone to petty jealousy and fear of rejection, but Swirkal's news would prove to be a good motivator for Ellroy who was already telling his friends that he was going to be the greatest crime writer who ever lived.

Ellroy was writing his first novel at a furious pace. When he was not writing at home, he would write on a bench at the Bel-Air Country Club, and in the caddy house "with card games going on around me."[29] The style was inspired by Raymond Chandler, who Ellroy found to be "a very easy writer to imitate." Morneau recalls Ellroy reading a copy of Frank MacShane's newly published biography of Raymond Chandler, around the time he was writing the manuscript.

Despite the Chandler influence, Ellroy thought the concept of the hardboiled private detective solving murders to be too implausible, so he made his PI, Fritz Brown, specialize in car repossession. Ellroy modelled Brown on himself. Brown came "from my old neighborhood, gets involved with a bunch of caddies. All that's me."[30] Ellroy had briefly worked as a process server for Mark

Zorne, a fellow caddy who aspired to be a private detective. A detective license could be granted if the applicant had a certain amount of hours experience in process serving, which Zorne was working towards. Zorne's father was an attorney. Ellroy and Zorne would pick up writs and subpoenas from Zorne Snr's hole-in-the-wall office in South Beverly Drive.

Ellroy put on his best jacket and tie, carried a notebook and pen around with him and talked to people at the County Clerk's Office hoping to pick up the trade. Ellroy and Zorne were tasked with finding a Latino man named Omar Gonzalez who worked as a bartender at gay clubs. One evening they were dining at Barone's Pizzeria in Valley Glen after a frustrating day chasing down leads that went nowhere. Ellroy had not yet earned a cent as he was paid on a contingency basis, and he was beginning to have doubts about the job. They received a tip that Gonzalez was working at the lesbian nightclub Peanuts at 7969 Santa Monica Boulevard. They drove to Peanuts but Zorne, who Ellroy found to be nebbish and not cut out for detective work, was too embarrassed to go inside. Ellroy entered the club alone and caught the attention of every woman inside who made him for a cop. He talked to the bar staff and a few patrons. No one had heard of Gonzalez. He checked the Men's Room as a formality. All the stalls around the toilets had been taken down and Ellroy discovered a woman was perched on one toilet while another woman went down on her.

"Excuse me ladies," Ellroy apologized cheerfully, before exiting.

He returned to the parking lot where he informed his sheepish detective partner, "Zorney, he ain't in there and I've gotta go back to the golf course as this ain't working out."

His brief stint as a process server gave Ellroy some much needed insight into detective work. In the novel, Brown's client, Freddy "Fat Dog" Baker, with whom he shares a quixotic friendship, also represents another side to Ellroy's personality. Fat Dog is an unapologetic racist, who sleeps on golf courses and has bad hygiene and no social skills. Ellroy was fond of the character. Therefore, he doesn't give the reader a showdown between Brown and Fat Dog. Halfway through the novel Brown finds Fat Dog murdered in Mexico. The story pivots towards a confrontation between Brown and a corrupt LAPD captain Haywood Cathcart.

Ellroy was deep into the writing of his first novel when the Westwood Hotel was sold-off to developers to be converted into office suites. It was in a prime real estate area and its status as a fleapit hotel was a glaring incongruity. Ellroy, Randy Rice, and the ragtag bunch of loopers and pensioners who comprised the residents of the Westwood Hotel were all forced to find alternative accommodation. When Ellroy moved out he drifted from one apartment to another, staying with friends and sleeping on their couch or on the floor. He stayed with a friend from AA, Sam Barker, for a short period.

Ellroy stayed with Mark McGuire until they had a falling out. McGuire disapproved of how Ellroy was becoming increasingly obsessed with writing and felt that it was drawing his attention away from AA's 12-step program. McGuire was one of the "Step-Nazis," longstanding AA members who had an almost religious belief in the program. He gave Ellroy an ultimatum to quit writing or leave. Ellroy found McGuire's manner increasingly abrasive, and he had no intention of abandoning his novel. Ellroy was forced to leave McGuire's apartment and get a new sponsor at AA. Ellroy rewarded his friends for their generosity in letting him stay. He paid them at least $100 a week from his earnings as a caddy. Ellroy briefly lived with an eccentric artist Danae Fulmer at her apartment in Marco Court, Venice. It was a purely platonic arrangement and she put him up as a favor while he looked for somewhere else to stay.

Danae was in a relationship with a friend of Ellroy's in AA, Alex Nicol. Nicol visited Danae in her apartment one evening while Ellroy was there. Ellroy asked Nicol to take a photograph of him. The photograph would be a little unusual, Ellroy told him, as he needed to pose naked in it. Ellroy planned to use the photo as an advert in a Swingers magazine. Nicol took a polaroid shot of Ellroy nude, lounging in a high back wicker chair, trying his best to look seductive.

Alas, no one responded to the ad.

After a few weeks, Danae asked Ellroy to leave so her friend Deirdre Kennedy could move in. Deirdre recalls "it was upon her [Danae's] kitchen table that Ellroy scribbled his first book. I recall that table as being the typical 50s style bright yellow with chrome around the edges. I thought Ellroy was so eccentric to be writing out a whole novel by hand."[31] Ellroy and Deirdre became friends, and he freely admitted later that he "chased" her. Neither of them knew at the time that they were distantly related by marriage. Deirdre was the stepsister of Catherine Judd, who was the granddaughter of Easton Ewing Spaulding, the first husband of Jean Hilliker.

Norman Winski replaced Mark McGuire as Ellroy's AA sponsor. Winski was a "swishy, pompadour" character who could not have been more different from the stern McGuire.[32] Winski wrote semi-pornographic books dressed up as sociological studies. His titles included *Sex Behavior of the American Bachelor* (1965) and *The Homosexual Explosion* (1966). Winski was a writer for the soft-porn *Velvet* magazine, and in late 1979 he became the editor of its sister publication *Velvet Talks*. Winski offered Ellroy a one-off job. He would pay Ellroy to lend his "strong deep voice" to a vinyl record which would come attached to Winski's debut issue of *Velvet Talks* as editor. Ellroy traveled to the offices of *Velvet* at 6th and Western. Also on the audio recording were three women, one of whom was the noted adult actress Pat Manning. Ellroy had a great time performing the scripted scene, which did not require physical contact, with the three women. Although they could barely get through the raunchy dialogue without cracking up.

Winski lived in a bungalow at 517 Ocean Front Walk, Venice Beach. He moved out and arranged for Ellroy to move in. Winski was dapper and foppish, so when Ellroy arrived at the bungalow he was surprised to find it was a "pigsty."[33] He paid Danae $200 to give the apartment a deep clean before he moved in. The Ocean Front Walk bungalows had supposedly been bought by Charles Chaplin as a place for his celebrity friends to stay when they were visiting, although this has since been debunked by LA historians. The Chaplin connection was widely believed at the time and was talked up by Ellroy's landlord Mr Frank, an elderly man who often visited the property with his octogenarian girlfriend. Frank could be cheap on the upkeep of the bungalows. There was sand coming through the floorboards and broken glass scattered around the premises, but it was still a pleasant place to live with a spectacular view of the sun going down over the Pacific every evening.

Many of the Westside AA residents lived in Venice Beach and they called themselves "Debris by the Sea." Before the 80s property boom gave the area a Disneyfied atmosphere, Venice Beach still had an independent, bohemian vibe. Artists and performers were a common sight on the Boardwalk. The shops and restaurants were family-run, idiosyncratic, and affordable. Ellroy enjoyed the sea breeze, long walks on the beach, and drinking espressos at the nearby Victory Coffee Shop.

One of the residents at Ocean Front Walk was a woman named Sybil Blazej who worked for the Los Angeles Library System. She recalls first meeting Ellroy, "He was asking every young woman I knew the same thing: 'Can I take you to dinner and will you read my manuscript?'"[34] She turned him down but as he was so persistent, she eventually agreed to go on a date with him. "He had an old Volkswagen at the time. I was sure the car was going to blow up as he drove me to dinner."[35] Sybil refused to read the manuscript he hauled around with him in a large envelope. Nevertheless, they became friends and bonded over their mutual love of libraries. Sybil began a relationship with Randy Rice and for a while, Ellroy, Rice, and Sybil were all neighbors at Ocean Front Walk. Sybil and her friends were fascinated by Ellroy's use of language, "He was like a pre-rapper. He would talk in rhyme and poetry constantly."[36]

Ellroy called his bungalow "his pad" or "the hovel." If someone knocked on his door during a writing session, he growled at them in displeasure. His writing routine never varied. According to Sybil:

> He would take one bottle of instant coffee and he would pour it into a cup and then he would take it to the sink, and I never would have believed this unless I had seen it myself, he would pour hot water straight from the faucet into the cup, stir it up, drink it down and then he would sit and write for hours.[37]

Ellroy had finished the manuscript in a matter of months. He titled it "Concerto for Orchestra." Brown, like Ellroy, is obsessed with classical music and becomes romantically involved with the cellist Jane Baker, who is Fat Dog's sister. Writing the novel was a thrilling experience, more exhilarating than any other addiction Ellroy had fed. But the comedown was difficult. Ellroy had no idea how to get the novel published, but he suspected it was going to be a long, arduous process. To make use of the excess energy writing had given him, Ellroy threw himself into writing another novel.

Ellroy's second manuscript, *Clandestine*, is set in the 1950s and concerns Freddy Underhill, a LAPD cop who has a one-night stand with a woman named Maggie Cadwallader, who is subsequently found murdered. Feeling both guilt and fear at his proximity to the murder, Underhill begins to investigate. As with "Concerto for Orchestra," the narrative changes dynamic halfway through the novel when the investigation is derailed (in a brilliantly sustained interrogation scene) by LAPD Lieutenant Dudley Smith, a demonic Irish American cop who forces Underhill out of the LAPD. Underhill loses his career and his marriage, but several years later begins a private investigation which leads him into a relentless pursuit of Maggie's killer. Ellroy based Maggie on his mother. Her murderer "Doc" Harris was based on his father and their ten-year-old son, Michael, was based on Ellroy himself as a child. Ellroy modelled Doc Harris on his father to address emotions shared by Armand Ellroy and him after Jean's death. Prior to her murder they had both hated Jean enough to wish her dead in their uglier thoughts. They had both, to a degree, benefited from Jean's death in that Armand had gained sole custody. Leoda always held Armand responsible for her sister's death and never forgave him. However, writing the novel did not significantly alter Ellroy's opinion of his mother at the time. Maggie has a weakness for men and alcohol, a trait for which Ellroy always judged his mother harshly. Ultimately, Ellroy wrote *Clandestine* as an objective exercise in emotional distance, "I wanted to get rid of the story. I wanted to prove myself impervious to my mother's presence and to get on with it."[38]

During an AA meeting, an actress had mentioned to the group that she had written a novel which had been accepted for publication by Harper & Row. Excited by her news, Ellroy asked the actress for advice on getting his own novel published. He remembered her attitude as dismissive. She advised him to find an agent through the anthology *Writer's Market*, but Ellroy could tell she didn't want to help him any further. Ellroy checked out a copy of *Writer's Market* from the library. In the entire volume there were only four agents listed who accepted unsolicited manuscripts. Ellroy decided to send his novel to all four of them, but there was a problem. The manuscript was entirely handwritten. Ellroy didn't know how to type, and he was too restless to learn now.

Ellroy paid one of his friends in AA, Bill LeVallee, to type up the handwritten manuscript. Then he went to Kinko's to xerox three more copies and posted a manuscript to each agent individually. Almost all his earnings went on the costs of hiring LeVallee, the xeroxing, and postage. Ellroy prayed that his investment was going to pay off.

Richard Huttner had worked as an editor at Fawcett's Gold Medal Paperbacks before starting his own literary agency in 1977. He operated the agency from his house in Turtle Bay, Manhattan and had signed some notable clients, such as David Madden. "One day in the mail arrived a manuscript" Huttner recalled.

The manuscript was titled "Concerto for Orchestra" and the author's name was James Ellroy.

> My policy was I would read the first ten pages of a manuscript anybody sent me. Because it was rare that something would come in, somebody sent me unsolicited, that would be marketable. But his (Ellroy's) book got my attention from the first page so I read the whole book, and I had the feeling that this was a very talented individual and this was going to be a saleable book.[39]

Ellroy received a telephone call early one morning. His instinct told him it was going to be one of the agents he had contacted. Sure enough, it was Richard Huttner who called to tell Ellroy that he had written a fine novel and offered to represent him. Ellroy later claimed that of the four agents he sent the manuscript to, all of them wanted to represent him, "and I went with the guy who sounded the most intelligent and aggressive."[40] In fact, Huttner was more diplomatic than aggressive in style. He wrote Ellroy a memorandum on the novel, tactfully suggesting changes which would improve the chances of selling the book to a publisher. Huttner felt that Ellroy's weakness was his portrayal of women, and the romance between Fritz Brown and Fat Dog's sister Jane was corny and implausible. "What didn't ring true and what I gave editorial suggestions [about], in his first book, was his depiction of female characters. He did not have any kind of a realistic relationship, in my opinion, with women. He couldn't create flesh and blood characters who were women because it seemed like he just didn't know women or have much relationship experience."[41] Ellroy dutifully accepted Huttner's advice. He was working with a professional and he wanted to make the most of Huttner's guidance. A few cheesy lines remained in the finished text. Brown meets Jane in Robert Burns Park, and they bond over classical music. He suggests they listen to chamber music in his apartment and then the first-person narration informs the reader, "we didn't listen to chamber music, we made our own."[42]

Securing an agent was a significant achievement but getting a publisher to buy the book would be the next challenge. By this time though Ellroy was in a race to succeed. He sent Huttner a typewritten copy of his next manuscript *Clandestine*, asking Huttner to call him the moment he finished reading it. Huttner didn't call, but he wrote to Ellroy on December 15, 1980, as "I felt I could better express myself in a letter." The letter contained more promising news:

> CLANDESTINE is a powerful, moving novel even more complex and finely crafted than CONCERTO FOR ORCHESTRA. It has strong possibilities for commercial and literary success.[43]

However, with his characteristic diplomacy Huttner suggested some changes that could be made to the manuscript. Many of these he wanted to be cuts as "in its present form, the manuscript is too long to be economically published. That is, a publisher would have to print and sell an enormous number of copies to break even on the high production cost."[44] In its first draft *Clandestine* was 642 pages long, and as Ellroy was a new and unknown author "the chances of garnering such a publisher commitment must be judged as slim."[45] Thus, the novel needed to be shortened. Ellroy duly followed his agent's advice and began cutting the text. He trusted Huttner, and his faith in him would prove to be well-judged.

Ellroy met Patricia "Penny" Nagler in a supermarket checkout line in June 1979. They started chatting and Ellroy took her phone number. Penny was twenty-six and Ellroy was thirty-one. She was from New York City and her ambition was to be a lawyer. He was also ambitious, he told her. Ellroy had refined his social act in AA and exhibited enough confidence around Penny without tipping into arrogance. They went on dates. Ellroy kept his impatient nature in check and played the boyfriend role well to begin with. Being with Penny was teaching him more social skills. She had family, friends, and a

good education. It was the sort of upbringing Ellroy felt that he had missed
out on. Penny was Jewish, "That appealed to me. It would force me to atone
for prior anti-Semitism."[46] Penny inspired Ellroy to create the character of the
Jewish attorney Lorna Weinberg, the romantic interest of Freddy Underhill in
Clandestine.

Ellroy could still be erratic and unpredictable. During bouts of insomnia,
he would reenact Hemingway's suicide with a shotgun, following ritualistically
its description in Carlos Baker's *Ernest Hemingway: A Life Story* (1969). Penny
insisted that he seek help, or the relationship was over. Ellroy reluctantly agreed
and spent ten months in therapy with the psychiatrist Dr. Carol Shahin. The
sessions gave Ellroy the opportunity to talk through his issues. He was not
prescribed any medication, and he may not have accepted any if offered, as
many AA members were leery about pharmaceuticals. However, Ellroy was
dismissive of his experience of therapy afterwards, "I think she [Dr. Shahin]
was turned on by me."[47]

One afternoon Ellroy came home tired after his shift at the Bel-Air. He had
been caddying for the actor Robert Stack and Stack's constant talk about guns
was wearisome. Stack had set two world records in skeet shooting and he was
known for being loquacious on the subject. Ellroy wanted to unwind or work
on the *Clandestine* manuscript. The phone rang and it was Richard Huttner.
He had good news. "I submitted it [Concerto for Orchestra] to Avon books.
Avon at that time was part of the Hearst Corporation and the editor there
made me an offer of a $3,500 advance, half on signing and half on approval of
the author's final manuscript."[48]

Ellroy was going to be a published author and he anticipated becoming
rich fast. His first check was $1,404. He paid his back rent, bought a cashmere
sweater and a $500 1964 Chevrolet Nova.[49] He took Penny to Santa Barbara for
the weekend. They visited The Copper Coffee Pot on State Street three times.
Ellroy had heard that Ross Macdonald was a frequent patron and, knowing
what he looked like from his author photograph, he hoped to bump into him
and give him a copy of the *Clandestine* manuscript unsolicited. They never
saw Macdonald. By the time they got back to Venice Beach, Penny had to loan
Ellroy $5 so he could buy himself a burger for lunch. Ellroy frittered away his
advance over the weekend on the boyishly naive assumption that all published

authors were wealthy. He was about to discover that this was not the case, and that while writing a manuscript was hard work, editing was far more arduous.

Ellroy's first editor at Avon was Richard Sewell. His second editor was Nellie Sabin. "The credit for 'discovering' Ellroy goes to a young male editor [Sewell]," Nellie recalls, "Ironically he was fired shortly thereafter."[50] In his correspondence with Nellie, Ellroy became flirtatious, although there is nothing to suggest that she invited this. He did reveal to Nellie the motive behind a very personal decision. His author's name was to be James Ellroy, not his legal name Lee Earle Ellroy. All his friends called him Lee, and were surprised when he changed it, "Oh, so you're James now are you!" Deirdre Kennedy remembers saying with skepticism.[51] Ellroy had been using the name James in all his correspondence with Huttner. When Nellie quizzed him on his choice of author's name, he replied that James Ellroy sounded "simple, concise and dignified—things I am not."[52] He had taken it from a pseudonym his father had used occasionally—James Brady. However, as with his father, he never really settled on a single name. In the coming years, many of his friends and girlfriends called him James, Jimmy, or simply Dog. Dog was another name he was determined to develop as an author, and he referred to himself as the "Demon Dog of American Crime Fiction" in at least one of his letters to Nellie. As Ellroy's writing career developed one rule became more important than anything else.

No one was allowed to call him Lee.

When it came to typesetting the manuscript, Ellroy did not at first understand the symbols of editing. Even with the symbol key Avon sent him he still found it difficult, tedious work. Ellroy decided to ask Bill LeVallee, who had typed up his handwritten manuscript, to make the requested editions.

Nellie offered to send Ellroy a cheque for $100 dollars for him to buy a typewriter, "because longhand will simply not do for a big-time author."[53] Ellroy declined but said he would accept a few thousand dollars so he could buy himself a "state of the art IBM Selectric."[54] This was probably a ruse by Ellroy to get more money. He had no interest in learning to type. Ellroy's biggest point of contention with Avon was over the title. Ellroy's editors felt that "Concerto for Orchestra" would be confusing, misleading, and a difficult title to market as a crime novel. Ellroy reluctantly conceded but felt that Nellie's suggestion of "Concerto for Murder" and "Music for Murder" were too cheesy. Ellroy concocted the title *Brown's Requiem*, as "even the dumbest private-eye reader knows that Requiem connotes death. That it also connotes music is the final indicator."[55] The final section of the novel was retitled "Concerto for Orchestra," a title Ellroy had originally chosen as a direct reference to the orchestral work by Béla Bartók. *Brown's Requiem* was scheduled for publication in October 1981.

In his correspondence with Nellie, Ellroy began to make increasingly forward comments. In a letter dated December 15, 1980, he wrote, "I was hotfooting it down the Venice Boardwalk an hour ago when unexpectedly ardent thoughts of you ambushed me."[56] He informs Nellie that, "I have a feeling that I will be writing to you beyond the bounds of the writer-editor relationship. If my letters become too romantic let me know. I will then tether my leash to a distant phone poll and bark in other directions."[57] Despite telling Nellie that he has "recently rekindled an old flame," by which he meant Penny, he goes on to say he is contemplating visiting New York for a Christmas vacation and warns, "Beware—I will be coming armed for romance. Be sure to carry a can of mace to keep me at bay across the luncheon table, or I will be barking outside your window like a hungry dog."[58]

In a letter to Nellie dated April 14, 1981, Ellroy opens with his typically bizarre humor. He tells the story of Louie and Loretta, two cockroaches in his apartment who crawl out of their "re-converted rent controlled roach hotel" and dance the "cockroach cadenza" every time he plays classical music.[59] As an author he is already entertaining plans of moving on from crime fiction which he describes as full of "macho bullshit" and "cheap pathos."[60] For Ellroy, there are only "two crime writers at the level of genius"—George V. Higgins and Ross Macdonald. But Ellroy talks as though he alone is touched with genius when describing his latest manuscript "LA Death Trip," a narrative suffused with:

> Murderous passion, runaway inflation, a physical landscape becoming more and more blighted, sex becoming more and more available and less and less satisfying, soaring crime rates and the resultant paranoia, alcoholism

and drug addiction becoming epidemic, nostalgia deified, punk rock, blasted innocence, inoperative machinery, religious fanaticism, ambiguous change—your life claptraps abounding—an in, under, all about and around these things, the search for a perfect spiritual and physical love; profound in its ardor, heartbreaking in its selfishness, astounding in its misplaced tenderness. Such are the chaotic elements that will make crime fiction the relevant, passion inducing voice that it must be.[61]

Amidst the boasting and joking, Ellroy finds time to talk about his religious views and probe Nellie (as a potential partner) about hers:

Do you believe in God? I do, although faith is difficult for me, even in the light of the miracle of my sobriety and all the other miracles that have resulted because of it. What a strange, powerful paradox—that the world should be so insane, yet life so beautiful! I firmly believe that God is alive and that he (she?) loves the most monstrous person on earth as she (he?) loves the most loving. It's funny, but until I got sober, I never gave God much thought. I have never been a Christian, Jew, Buddhist, Hindu, Moslem or philosophy lover. I have never actively sought enlightenment. Yet through this mad citybound life of mine, directionals of pure love have pointed me to a God who can do for me what I cannot do for myself.[62]

Ellroy ends the letter as he began it, with a strange and humorous tale, although this one seems designed to encourage Nellie's belief in the professional partnership they have embarked upon:

A cordon of friendly short-haired dogs are dancing around a bonfire in a rainforest. These magical hounds know most of the secrets of life and impart them to certain humans who they feel can understand their knowledge and manifest it in loving ways. The dogs are holding paws and swaying to the music. They bark out your name, and mine, and Rich Huttner's and Dick Sewell's, and the names of many of our friends. The wisdom that follows is barked in code, a code that we assimilate verbally. The fire grows dim, and the dogs recede into our imaginations, becoming so diffuse that we all wonder if we are hallucinating. Just as we are about to shake our heads en masse and relegate the experience to some kind of mass hysteria the dogs reappear bright as day and as they wave goodbye, bark out their credo, which is from a poem from WH Auden:

He then quotes "Death's Echo," which ends "Dance till the stars come down from the rafters; Dance, Dance, Dance till you drop."[63]

Nellie wrote back a few days later, thanking Ellroy for his long letter and, rather delicately, tried to pour cold water on his crush. "I'm glad you've toned down your notions of immediate fame and fortune," Nellie wrote. "Those, too, can be unhealthy."[64] Nellie had misjudged Ellroy in this regard. Ellroy was burning with ambition and convinced of his impending fame. In AA, he had befriended the newly published fantasy author Niel Hancock. Hancock was a Vietnam veteran who published his first novel in 1977, quickly followed by a series of successful novels known as the Circle of Light Quartet. Hancock's personality was just as strong and imposing as Ellroy's. According to his sister-in-law Marya Ursin, "Everything became a moment of light quirky observation which then became a story. Back in the day, he was a riotous drinker, lived on the islands, ran guns for a bit, told tales of a drunken bassett hound."[65] Hancock was one of the first writers who spotted Ellroy's potential after reading the "Concerto for Orchestra" manuscript. He agreed to take some author photos of Ellroy which were then mailed to Avon. By this time Ellroy's racy letters to Nellie had become the subject of some gossip at her office.

An Avon staffer sent the photos on to Nellie with a note, "N, Well, now we know. Here's James Ellroy."[66]

To his friends, Ellroy talked incessantly about his new writing career and all the great novels he was going to write. Inevitably, it drove a few of them crazy. Sybil was displeased with how Ellroy tried to pressure Randy, who liked to write in his free time, into pursuing a writing career. "Eventually he began to resent me," Sybil recalls "as he felt I was taking Randy's interests away from him, being able to focus on becoming the great writer that he was intended to be. He projected his energies and enthusiasms onto his best friend as well. If he was going to become a great writer then his best friend was also going to do that and he must have the same ambitions."[67] For years, Ellroy had looked up to

Figure 6 *Ellroy and Randy Rice: sober, healthy, and happy in Venice Beach. No other friend had such a formative influence on Ellroy as Randy. Photo: Courtesy of Rae Jones.*

Randy as the stronger of the two of them. He had done better at school, turned his back on petty crime and quit booze and drugs all before Ellroy did. Ellroy had achieved sobriety at his urging, but now the aspiring writer was surging ahead, and their friendship began to wane.

While old friendships may have been under strain, Ellroy was beginning new relationships. Cindy DePoy attended UCLA where she became friends with Tim Morneau. Ellroy met Cindy on the Venice Beach Boardwalk in the Fall of 1980. Morneau may have played matchmaker a little. "He described him to me," Cindy recalls "as a former alcoholic, drug addict, had been in jail. Told me the whole story, and that he was recovered and was just about to have his first book published."[68] Ellroy and Cindy immediately hit it off and began dating. Ellroy appreciated how Cindy didn't judge him harshly over his past, "I didn't consider it such a horrible thing that he had addiction problems because I knew that addicts were people too."[69] However, Ellroy's sobriety did affect their social life together. At one party they attended, Ellroy couldn't cope with a large group of people drinking and chatting so he retreated to a bedroom to write poetry, "I didn't have the sensitivity to realize that would be a really hard situation for him," Cindy recalled.[70]

In other situations, Ellroy could be blind to other people's feelings or social niceties. Cindy's brother-in-law was a cop with the LAPD and Ellroy tried to grill him for information about his work, "My brother-in-law wasn't very open about it. He didn't understand where he was coming from."[71] Ellroy's relationship with Cindy continued into the Winter of 1981 but cracks were beginning to show. Ellroy was seven years older than Cindy, and while he was starting to think about marriage, she was not ready to make that commitment. Ultimately, they broke up and Cindy moved to Spain to pursue a career as a teacher and later a translator of academic texts. Ellroy recalled Cindy as "the one that got away" and said, "her song was 'Image of a Girl' by The Safaris."[72] Cindy continued to hold Ellroy in high regard but admitted that his politics was a problem "Even though he denied it, I think he was pretty right-wing. I was not right-wing at all, and still am not, so I just couldn't accept that."[73]

Ellroy had become as obsessive about politics as he was about writing. Now that Reagan was in the White House, Margaret Thatcher was two years into her premiership in the UK, and Pope John Paul II was leading an anti-communist crusade from the Vatican, Ellroy liked to talk about how this triumvirate of conservative leaders would begin a new golden age.

It was not the sort of talk that made him popular in Venice Beach, but it did little to quell women's initial attraction to him.

Anne "Vandy" Van der Vort met Ellroy at a party hosted by the actress Helen Shaver in her Hollywood Hills home. Vandy was unaware that Ellroy had already made a pass at Shaver, and had managed to obtain her phone number, but she never returned his call. Amidst all the artists and celebrity party guests, "For some reason I made a beeline towards him," Vandy recalls.[74] She found Ellroy to be charming and they started dating. All went well at first, but tension flared up when they attended a rock concert featuring a band "of my choosing."[75] Ellroy detested rock music and wouldn't speak to Vandy all evening. Finally, she managed to prise out of Ellroy what was bothering him so much.

"You didn't dress preppy enough," he told her.

Ellroy was developing a fixation on well-educated, intelligent, middle-class, and all-together "preppy" women. Rock music broke the mystique of his ideal woman.

At the time Vandy was sharing an apartment with the teen actress Sandra Bogan. Her relationship with Ellroy ended abruptly when he visited her apartment, and he was furious for some reason which he would not divulge. He picked up a glass-topped coffee table and threw it against the wall, smashing the glass everywhere. No one was hurt in the incident, but Ellroy departed immediately afterwards, leaving Vandy to clear up the mess. The next time Vandy heard from Ellroy it was equally abrupt. He wrote her a letter stating that he had moved to Eastchester NY and, tongue firmly in cheek, he was joining a rock band.

5

The Road to the Dahlia
(1981–1985)

On June 13, 1981, Ellroy was standing on the golf course at Bel-Air when he made the sudden decision to move to New York. It was a typically beautiful, sunny day at the Bel-Air and the decision may have struck the religious-minded Ellroy as an epiphany, but there were longstanding reasons behind the move. His relationships with Penny, Cindy, and Anne were over. The social scene at AA was beginning to bore him. Ellroy now felt confident in his sobriety. His new drug was writing, and he was completely hooked. New York City was the world capital of book publishing and it made sense to move there. Ellroy felt that he was making up for lost time: "I had never been anywhere but LA. It was time to move."[1] An excited Ellroy wrote Nellie while on a break at the Bel-Air caddy shack patio, "I am moving to New York," he declared, "I have been thinking about it for some time and decided on Saturday to do it."[2]

However, moving from the West Coast to the East Coast was going to be logistically difficult. Although he now enjoyed regular employment, Ellroy spent money recklessly and was frequently broke. He couldn't afford a flight to New York or to hire a removals company to take his belongings there. The solution came through a friend in AA. Ellroy had stayed at Sam Barker's apartment when he was forced to leave the Westwood. Vandy recalls that Ellroy and Barker were close friends, although when she was dating Barker a few years after her relationship with Ellroy had ended, the friendship didn't stop Ellroy from coming on to her. He wanted to have sex with Vandy in Barker's garage. Vandy declined.

Barker found a company that paid drivers to transport cars across the country and was given an assignment to drive a car for a customer to Long Island. Drivers only had to pay for their own gas. Ellroy arranged to rent a room in a house in Eastchester, NY. He took with him the bare minimum of possessions and a letter of introduction from the caddy master at Bel Air to be presented to the Wykagyl Country Club in New Rochelle, where Ellroy hoped to work as a caddy. Ellroy and Barker alternated driving duties. They had enough money between them for one night in a motel, but for the rest of the journey they slept at roadsides. They made it to New York in about a week.

Ellroy's landlady in Eastchester was a woman named Edith Eisler. She was the widow of Paul Eisler, who had served as professor of music at the Manhattan School of Music and New York University. She shared Ellroy's love of classical music and proved a kind and generous landlady. When Ellroy fell behind with the rent she would wait patiently while Ellroy found a job until he could afford to pay her. She was more annoyed at Ellroy for monopolizing the use of her telephone. Ellroy would spend hours talking to women on Edith's phone. He subsequently had a separate line installed in his room. Edith's house was near Wykagl Country Club. Ellroy's modest room was in the basement, and he described it as his "my all-time darkest brood den."[3]

The day after he arrived in Eastchester, Ellroy visited the Wykagl and handed his letter of introduction to Pasquale "Big Pat" Argentina. To his surprise, Argentina put him to work right away and Ellroy, still exhausted from the cross-country journey, rather grumpily began looping the course, which he found to be hilly and challenging. Ellroy became close with the caddy master, Pasquale "Little Pat" Mandarano who he found had "a calming influence on the caddies."[4]

Life in his new home seemed good to Ellroy at first. His small basement apartment was perfect for his needs, "music kept lilting through the vents."[5] Eastchester was ideally located to commute into New York City. His caddying job was going to bring in regular income, and most importantly he had his writing career and a new manuscript "LA Death Trip" to occupy his time.

Ellroy had his first face-to-face meeting with Richard Huttner in Mumbles pub on Third Avenue one week after moving to the East Coast. Huttner found Ellroy to be personable but was surprised at the ease in which he could describe horrific events from his past, from his mother's murder to his periods of homelessness and jail time. "He seemed like an affable, normal guy and then he would tell this incredible story of compulsive masturbation, and all these things that he would come out with which were beyond my ken. But he did everything in publishing just the way it should be. He did the revisions. He was cooperative."[6]

Ellroy may have been cooperative and hardworking in his newly established role as an author, but he was not above showing off. Nellie Sabin recalls his first appearance at the Avon offices, "He commanded a lot of attention—a guy over six feet tall, walking down the hall in his Brooks Brothers suit holding a little bunch of flowers in front of him. Who was he? He found me in my little office, and the first thing he said was, 'You don't sound the way I thought you would.' So already there was a disparity between his dream editor and me."[7]

They went out to lunch and Ellroy clearly wanted to make some progress on the flirtatious remarks he had made to Nellie in their correspondence.

"So, Nell, is there a special man in your life?"

"I'm married, James. You know that."

Nellie was shocked at his response. "'YOU'RE MARRIED?!' James bellowed in the tiny restaurant, sweeping things onto the floor with a crash. The other patrons looked at me disapprovingly. How could I have been so cruel to the gentleman in the Brooks Brothers suit? I was certain I had made it clear to James already that I was married, but obviously there had been a miscommunication."[8]

By the time they got back to the office any disappointment Ellroy felt about Nellie's marital status had evaporated. He displayed his usual swagger. Ellroy was exiting the bathroom as a senior editor, Robert Wyatt, was going in. Nellie observed their conversation:

> James admired the other man's tie, and said, "Are those Golden
> Retrievers on your tie?"
> The Hearst executive was very pleased. "Why yes, they are."

"Do you have a Golden Retriever?" asked James, showing interest.

"Why yes, I do," the Hearst executive said proudly, by this time feeling at ease. "Her name is Daisy."

The two men were face to face in the hall while I leaned against the wall and waited.

James said, "When Daisy dies, are you going to have her roasted or stuffed?"

As the face of the other man turned to disbelief and horror. I took James by the elbow and got him out of there.[9]

Ellroy did not feel any regret at embarrassing a senior editor. He felt comfortable and unthreatened in his position as an Avon author, later joking about the incident in another letter to Nellie:

Tell Dave that the stuffed dog idea is passe. I have a better idea—a barbecue! Dave supplies the dog, Avon supplies the guest list and I supply the soy sauce! We can roast the noble hound in Central Park, and in lieu of an apple in its mouth we can use Avon books that have flopped such as *Sea Trial* by Frank De Fellitta. If Mr. De Felitta objects to this, we can roast him as well.[10]

Ellroy had heard a rumor that, after writing several bestsellers, De Felitta had secured a one-million-dollar deal to publish *Sea Trial* with Avon and it had flopped. Ellroy believed that he could do better, but he was about to receive one almighty humbling.

Richard Huttner had some serious news that was liable to change Ellroy's cocky demeanor. Huttner had accepted a position at Rodale Press and had decided to wrap up his literary agency. The publishing industry was contracting at the time, "From 1980 to 82 it was very difficult to sell books."[11] On a personal level, Huttner was going to miss Ellroy's easy charm and raw talent. But he had serious doubts about "LA Death Trip." "That book is written in a very different style than the first two. The first two were straightforward crime books that everybody would love. Then, when he wrote the LA one, he embarked upon this hard-bitten terse style, and I didn't particularly think it was very commercial."[12]

Brown's Requiem was published September 1981. It gained some respectable reviews and was nominated for the very first Private Eye Writers of America Shamus Award. Ellroy discovered the book had been nominated while working a 5 a.m. to 1 p.m. shift as a dishwasher at a Max Factor plant in Tuckahoe. After finally seeing his novel in print, Ellroy found the whole experience anti-climactic. He disliked the cover art, "Fuck—a man with a gun on a golf course."[13] They had ignored his suggestion of an image of a woman playing a cello. They also declined to print his author photograph and presented Ellroy with few opportunities to publicize the book.

Clandestine was scheduled for publication the following year, but Ellroy's professional relationship with Avon was waning, partly as there were reservations about "LA Death Trip." Nellie described it as "page after page of slicing and dicing women. I thought his writing was getting worse instead of better. I asked other people to read it too, and no one was enthusiastic. So, I had to send it back, and I hoped his next effort would be better."[14]

Ellroy was beginning to think he had been cut loose. He had arrived in New York thinking "I was extremely hot shit" and had swaggered around the Avon offices accordingly.[15] Ellroy didn't realize that Avon had been monitoring his sales and progress as a writer very carefully, and what they found was not encouraging. According to Nellie Sabin:

> Paperback houses would lead with one blockbuster per month, then fill out the list with 'midlist' titles, both reprints and paperback originals, and finally throw in some trade paperbacks. If a midlist book sold 30,000 copies, I believe that was good enough. But within a year or two the publisher eliminated any midlist or quirky titles that might not have robust sales. That's when the doors really closed to new writers. Avon would pay millions for the latest manuscript by a romance author with a known track record, or for the rights to a bestselling hardcover, but nothing to promising new writers.[16]

Ellroy's "midlist" sales had been in the low thousands.

Richard Huttner had given Ellroy three referrals to other agents—Knox Burger, Howard Morhaim, and Martha Millard. Burger was the most high-profile of the three, but Ellroy had heard he was obnoxious and never contacted him. Ellroy sent Morhaim and Millard a copy of "LA Death Trip," then wrote to Nellie "Morhaim has read part of it and has arranged a meeting with me. I assume this means acceptance on his part."[17] Ellroy was being presumptuous. Morhaim thought that Ellroy's writing displayed a lot of potential but urged him to make extensive revisions to the manuscript as a prerequisite of any offer of representation.

After his meeting with Morhaim, Ellroy walked to meet Martha Millard "at my office/apt in Chelsea."[18] Martha's first impression of Ellroy was "Just from his galvanizing presence, before I even read the work, I knew he was a unique and special writer."[19] Ellroy and Martha began dating and she agreed to represent him. According to Ellroy, Martha, "loooved the book and thought I was cute."[20] Contrary to Ellroy's recollection of how she responded to "LA Death Trip," Martha claims "I tried to get him to soften it, to be more like his first novel, but needless to say, he wouldn't. He was unswerving in his opinions, and it was clear he was NOT open to my attempts to make the book 'saleable.'"[21]

One of the first contacts Ellroy made when he moved to New York would prove to be among the most important in influencing his career. Otto Penzler was possibly the most renowned publisher and editor working in the crime fiction genre at the time. He had opened The Mysterious Bookshop on West 56th Street in 1979. Crime writers would come to the store with the hope of speaking to Penzler and receiving advice on how to secure an agent and get their book in print. Ellroy walked to the Mysterious Bookshop directly after his first meeting with Nellie Sabin at the Hearst offices on 57th Street. He climbed the spiral staircase which led to a mezzanine where Penzler sat at his office desk.

Penzler recalls a tall, well-built, and imposing man walking towards him with a large envelope package in his left hand.

"Are you Penzler?"

"Yes."

Ellroy stuck out his right hand and introduced himself with characteristic brio.

"My name's James Ellroy, and I'm the next great one."

"Mr. Ellroy," Penzler replied, shaking his hand "would you excuse me if I reserve judgment on that."

The two men shared a similar sense of humor and Penzler decided he would read the "LA Death Trip" manuscript Ellroy gave him, but by the time the meeting was over Ellroy had not secured any guarantee that Penzler would work with him. Since that first meeting with Penzler, Ellroy had made no progress in finding a publisher for "LA Death Trip." Martha kept submitting it and it was continuously rejected. After the relatively straightforward publication of his first two novels by Avon, Ellroy was feeling frustrated by the constant rejection and delay. He decided to take Morhaim and Martha's advice to make substantial rewrites and began to carefully revise the manuscript. It was a slow, arduous process and Ellroy was getting bored with the story. As he was still writing by hand, Ellroy needed to employ a new typist. Ellroy's neighbor in Eastchester was a man named Mike Garcia who worked as a clerk at the FBI office in White Plains. Garcia recommended Beth Lalli, a typist he knew, to Ellroy. Ellroy and Beth got along well, and she would remain his typist for more than twenty years. In the early 80s, Ellroy was often so broke that he would walk to Beth's house in New Rochelle and drop the manuscript off by hand.

Frustrated by the lack of progress on "LA Death Trip," Ellroy decided to start working on another novel. It would be an epic work of historical fiction inspired by Saul Bellow's picaresque *The Adventures of Augie March*, which Ellroy had read years earlier in LA while heavily abusing drugs. Ellroy completed 398 pages of a manuscript he titled "The Confessions of Bugsy Siegel." This was only half the length of how he envisioned the novel. He portrays Siegel as a sexual voyeur much like himself as a younger man. But even Ellroy had doubts about the project.

Martha had submitted "LA Death Trip" to seventeen publishers and received an equal number of rejections. According to Ellroy, she informed him that it was unlikely that the book would be accepted for publication and dropped him as a client. She also ended their romantic relationship. Ellroy was displeased that he still had to pay her $150 in xeroxing fees. He was broke and had to work a few extra shifts at Wykagl to settle the debt. Martha's account of their parting is different, "He dropped me […] I was sorry because I knew he'd be a success, but as my goal at the time was to grow my agency, I could do without such a high maintenance, opinionated writer. What a character!"[22]

Despite the continual setbacks with "LA Death Trip" and the end of his relationship with Martha, Ellroy was increasingly confident with women. He was tall, muscular, with a striking moustache and still possessed a good head of hair that gave him a raffish look. For the first time in his life, he was starting to feel like a handsome guy.

One morning Ellroy was sitting drinking coffee in the kitchen of a house owned by his "ten-second girlfriend" Joyce. She was reading the latest edition of *New York* magazine. She passed him the magazine and said, "Didn't you tell me you knew these guys?"[23] The magazine was running an ad for the newly formed Mysterious Literary Agency. It was a joint venture between Otto Penzler and his close friend, the literary agent, Nat Sobel. According to Sobel, "We did a whole thing where our letterhead had no address and no phone number. If you wanted to find us, you had to solve the mystery."[24] Ellroy knew Penzler was based at the Mysterious Bookshop, so it was easy to reconnect with him. Penzler had read *Brown's Requiem* and thought Ellroy was a "very powerful stylist, but they weren't particularly well constructed plots."[25] Of "LA Death Trip" he was blunter, "It was just awful, but there was no denying the raw talent."[26] Ellroy originally wanted Penzler to represent him, but Penzler insisted that it was a job for an agent.

Ellroy met with both Penzler and Sobel at the Mysterious Bookshop. The two men informed Ellroy that "Siegel was out to lunch but 'LA Death Trip' could be reworked."[27] It was a lifeline for Ellroy. Nat Sobel agreed to be his agent and Ellroy was the first client of the Mysterious Literary Agency. Penzler later claimed he never read "The Confessions of Bugsy Siegel," but Sobel did and "hated it."[28] The manuscript to "LA Death Trip" would still need to be extensively revised. Ellroy enjoyed working with Sobel. He found him to be "a stickler for the logic of the dramatic scenes" and "character motivations."[29] Thus, Sobel questioned why the novel ends with the lead protagonist, Detective Lloyd Hopkins, committing suicide with a rocket launcher at the Silverlake power plant in his confrontation with the serial killer, Theodore Verplanck. A real detective would never do this knowing that the explosion would also kill hundreds of innocent people. Ellroy wanted to write a novel in which "LA burns to the ground."[30] Sobel and Penzler insisted the novel would have to be more conventional, if it was to be marketable.

Sobel was abrasive compared to the diplomatic Richard Huttner and the encouraging Martha Millard. After writing Ellroy a "rather lengthy editorial report" about the novel, Ellroy wrote back what looked like "a kidnap letter. It was written in red pencil on yellow legal paper, and some of the words on it were like an inch high: I AM NOT GOING TO DO THIS."[31] Sobel thought Ellroy was "loony," but he had to concede "it was a very smart letter. He was very smart about what he would do, why he wouldn't do certain things."[32]

Clandestine was published by Avon in 1982 and received strong reviews and an Edgar nomination for Best Paperback Original. It lost out to *Triangle* by Teri White. John Douglas was an editor who hosted the Avon nominees table that evening. It "was the first piece of bad news that Avon and Ellroy got to share," Douglas recalls of Ellroy losing out on the award.[33] Douglas had started reading Ellroy's work that same day and, encouraged at what he found, was hopeful of working with him. When he met Ellroy that night he was impressed by the author, although he was surprised that, among a crowd of male authors decked out in tuxedos, Ellroy's "choice of evening wear was an outfit highlighted by a golfer's set of Plus-Fours."[34] Douglas soon discovered that the prospect of working with Ellroy was slim as "the editor [Nellie] who had chosen Ellroy initially had turned down the manuscript on the third book and then left the company."[35]

Nat Sobel was still submitting "LA Death Trip" to publishers without any success. Ellroy never revealed to Penzler and Sobel, until long after the novel was published, that Martha Millard had already received seventeen rejections for the book when she had represented Ellroy. Ultimately, Penzler and Sobel agreed it was unlikely that a publisher was going to buy "LA Death Trip." They also agreed that Ellroy was an extraordinary talent, and they didn't want to lose him. Penzler had founded the Mysterious Press in 1975. He thought it would be a good home for Ellroy's novel, but to avoid a potential conflict of interest, he insisted Sobel pitch it and work directly with his colleague at Mysterious Press, Michael Seidman.

Ellroy was paid a $5,000 dollar advance by Mysterious Press for "LA Death Trip," which was subsequently retitled and published as *Blood on the Moon* in 1984. Unlike his first two books, the published novel was very different from the original manuscript. Lloyd Hopkins no longer committed a spectacular suicide in the finale. There were pragmatic reasons to keep Hopkins alive. Both Sobel and Penzler thought Hopkins had potential as a series character, which would help build Ellroy's commercial profile. Ellroy was coming round to this point of view as well and started drafting a second Hopkins novel. The Lloyd Hopkins character also brought Ellroy back to Avon. The Mysterious Press would publish the Hopkins novels in hardback and, "after some negotiation," John Douglas recalls "Avon concluded a mass-market reprint arrangement" in paperback.[36]

After such an arduous journey to publication, Ellroy was disappointed with the low sales for *Blood on the Moon* despite some favorable reviews. He had few publicity opportunities. Ellroy attended Mystery Writers of America meetings but failed to make any valuable contacts as he was hoping to meet attractive women, and the MWA was largely a Gentlemen's Club at the time. Ellroy would grow agitated at the meetings and start showing off. His behavior reached a nadir on December 20, 1983, when he appeared on a panel for a discussion titled "The Police in Fiction" at New York Public Library.[37] His fellow panelists were Dorothy Uhnak, Robert Volpe, and Hillary Waugh, all of whom were well-established in their writing careers and received glowing introductions from the panel moderator Carol Brener. This triggered Ellroy, "I didn't know how to do anything but talk about myself and shoot my mouth off. I'd get randomly aggressive with people in the audience. I'd talk over people. I was pissed off and insecure."[38] After the disastrous panel discussion, Ellroy knew his behavior would have to change. From now on when he met fellow authors Ellroy went on a charm offensive, forging genuine friendships and useful contacts in the process.

Ellroy developed an idea which he hoped would generate publicity for *Blood on the Moon*. *Armchair Detective* was a quarterly journal founded by the crime fiction historian Allen J. Hubin in 1967. It was well-regarded by fans and critics of the genre as one of the best sources for interviews, reviews, and essays. Ellroy had only ever done one interview, by phone for an Illinois-based radio host, and it hadn't led to more requests. He was itching to get his voice out into the public arena. Ellroy had befriended the actor Duane Tucker back in LA. He asked Tucker whether he could use his name as an "interviewer" and essentially write the interview himself. Tucker agreed. Penzler, who was publishing *Armchair Detective* through the Mysterious Press at the time, also agreed. The published interview makes for compelling reading and shows that Ellroy was brimming with ambition at a time when few readers and reviewers knew who he was.

Ellroy is grandiose in describing his future projects to "Tucker":

I'm going to write three more present-day LA police novels, none of which will feature psychopathic killers. After that, I plan on greatly broadening my scope. How's this for diversity: a long police procedural set in Sioux City, South Dakota, in 1946; a long novel of political intrigue and mass murder in Berlin around the time of Hitler's Beer Hall Putsch; the first complete novelization of LA's 1947 "Black Dahlia" murder case.[39]

Ellroy hadn't given up on his "The Confessions of Bugsy Siegel" manuscript, claiming he was "reworking, rethinking and rewriting" it.[40] Ellroy mentions his mother's murder, but he keeps his comments about Jean Ellroy brief and refers to *Clandestine* as "a heavily fictionalized account of her murder—a fact-fiction pastiche."[41] Ellroy ends the interview with a pledge: "To crime fiction readers everywhere. I pledge to never relent in my determination not to flinch and my determination never to grow stale; never to give you anything less than my best."[42] Ellroy's self-penned interview with Duane Tucker for *Armchair Detective*, although contrived, was an important first step in what would develop into an ingenuity for publicity and self-promotion.

Nellie Sabin believed that Ellroy "may have had a compelling romantic vision of moving to New York, marrying his editor, and becoming famous immediately."[43] While it is not unusual to have relationships with people who work in the same business, Ellroy had developed a strong liking for the many attractive women in publishing which suggests Nellie had read him correctly. There wasn't much of a social scene in Eastchester. Ellroy described it as "sexile."[44] The place to meet women was at the publishing parties in Manhattan. Ellroy began a relationship with Meg Ruley, an agent at the Janet Rotrosen literary agency. But monogamy did not come easily to Ellroy. One day he was visiting Nat Sobel's home, where the junior agents worked in a basement office, and he met Betsy Lerner, "James blew into the office with all his mad energy and when we were introduced, he kissed my hand," Betsy recalls, "The next time I had to send him a royalty statement, I included a brief note with my phone number."[45]

They began seeing each other. Betsy found Ellroy to be charming and he seemed to be on the cusp of a great writing career, "The Demon Dog persona was just beginning to emerge. He was barking but not quite howling. But all the talent and ambition were evident."[46] At the same time he was very supportive of her ambitions, "We are twelve years apart. James often noted that we were both born in the Year of the Rat. I was in graduate school for writing when we met and no one encouraged me more than James or was more generous."[47] Nevertheless, the relationship came to an end. Ellroy and Betsy parted amicably, both returning to their former partners. Ellroy resumed his relationship with Meg, until that too came to an end.

Thomas Harris's *Red Dragon* had been published in 1981, introducing the character of Dr. Hannibal Lecter to the world. Ellroy did not read *Red Dragon* until after *Blood on the Moon* was published. Ellroy found the novel to be riveting and its impact could be felt in genre publishing. Suddenly publishers were determined to find the next big psychological thriller novel. Why then had *Blood on the Moon*, which featured "mano-a-mano duels of cops and serial killers," not even come close to the success of *Red Dragon*?[48] Ellroy had to concede that *Red Dragon* was "a far superior book," and for the second Hopkins novel he set about the dangerous task of imitating Harris's formula.[49]

Ellroy was living frugally in Eastchester. Although he occasionally attended book parties in Manhattan, his life was far from glamorous. The night train back from New York to Eastchester reinforced this, "a lot of very nicely dressed, turned-out stockbrokers would piss and shit in the stairwells."[50] New York State's seasonal weather entailed that Ellroy could not work as a caddy all-year round. The royalties he received from his books were minimal. He had to find alternative sources of income. He obtained a job working for a company run by two Italian brothers on Huguenot Street, New Rochelle. The company sold a cheap knock-off of HomeGuard Security. Ellroy's job was in tele sales, cold-calling people and pitching an "engraving tool, a registry number and nationwide registry of your possessions, a sign for your window."[51] Ellroy worked from home and was fired after failing to make any sales as he was too preoccupied flirting with women on the phone. His late-night conversations with a woman named Joan became increasingly racy and Ellroy agreed to visit her in Detroit.

Ellroy spent just over a week with Joan in Detroit. Joan had a job at the Fisher Body Plant, so while she was at work Ellroy would spend the day at Wayne State University Library working on the second Lloyd Hopkins novel. Once the brief fling with Joan was over, Ellroy returned to Eastchester. He accepted a position as a caretaker at a large house in Rhinebeck. It was winter and the region received heavy snow. Ellroy did basic maintenance jobs in the house and found it a perfect place for writing as he was getting deeper into the novel. One of his responsibilities was looking after the owner's two large Akita dogs. As a dog lover, Ellroy relished his time with the Akitas. He would take them for long walks in the country and they would sleep in his bed during the cold nights. They became attached and territorial towards Ellroy, growling at him when he tried to leave the bed to use the facilities during the night, and fighting over their spot next to him.[52]

Ellroy titled the second Hopkins novel *Because the Night* after the song by the Patti Smith Group. The characters use variations of the phrase to justify their dark philosophy: "Because the night was there to provide comfort and the nourishing of brave dreams, and only someone willing to fight for its sanctity deserved to claim it as his citadel."[53] The novel is more polished than *Blood on the Moon* but suffers from a less compulsive narrative drive. Part of the problem stems from the distracting influence of *Red Dragon*. Ellroy claims he wanted to make "Hopkins as great a character as Thomas Harris' Will Graham."[54] But Hopkins has not changed substantially since the first novel, and Ellroy is more interested in his nemesis, the sinister psychiatrist Dr. John Havilland. Havilland's malevolence, narcissism, and gift for manipulation bear more than a passing resemblance to Hannibal Lecter, minus the cannibalism.

Ellroy creates a more plausible psychopath in Havilland. He is not enamored with the character, and as the narrative progresses Havilland's sexual repression and obsession with voyeurism renders him increasingly pathetic. His eventual fate is wretched and ironic. He is viciously beaten by one of his own patients and left in a vegetative state, thus, depriving him of his intellect, which was both the cause of and solace from his misanthropy. The novel was published in 1984, the same year as *Blood on the Moon* and to the same respectful reviews and disappointing sales. Ellroy had not managed to imitate the successful serial killer formula Harris's *Red Dragon* had formed, but he could just not help himself in making Havilland a more believable villain than Hannibal Lecter.

There was some debate between Ellroy, Penzler, and Sobel as to how many books there should be in the Lloyd Hopkins series. Penzler and Sobel wanted Ellroy to keep writing Hopkins novels for as long as possible. They were convinced that this was the route for Ellroy to reach a commercial success that matched his burning talent. Ellroy was tired of the character, but he appreciated the plotting skills that he was acquiring by writing the novels. His long-term ambition was to write an epic novel on the Black Dahlia case and then to move onto writing historical fiction permanently. He needed to finish the Hopkins series before he could realize that goal. *Because the Night* was billed as the second novel in the "Hopkins in Jeopardy" Quintet, the title was a homage to the Ross Macdonald omnibus *Archer in Jeopardy*. Ellroy privately doubted that he could write another three novels in the series. In the event, the third Hopkins would be the final and best novel in the series.

Ellroy considered using "LA Death Trip" as the title for the third Hopkins novel but, remembering that manuscript's difficult gestation, he decided against it. He also considered the elegiac title "For the LA Dead," before settling on *Suicide Hill*. As with *Because the Night*, the title was a musical reference, being both a fictional place in LA and a play on the Fats Domino song "Blueberry Hill." The novel begins with an LAPD psychiatric evaluation of Hopkins, criticizing him for his past conduct and assessing his continued suitability for police service. This false document verisimilitude would become a staple of Ellroy's novels, and he would expand upon it to include newspaper reports, journal entries, transcripts of covertly recorded conversations, and other mediums in his later fiction.

Most of *Suicide Hill* centers on the misadventures of the luckless ex-convict Duane Rice. Rice is deeply in love with his faithless girlfriend Vandy, and he makes increasingly foolish attempts to win her heart. The more things go wrong for Rice the more the reader roots for him. Escaping from an armed robbery, he kills a uniformed cop who is the son of a powerful police captain Fred Gaffaney. The devoutly religious Gaffaney (loosely based on LAPD Assistant Chief Robert "Bible Bob" Vernon) has come into conflict with Hopkins as his traditionalist views contrast sharply with Hopkins' womanizing and unconventional detective methods. Hopkins views Gaffaney's attempts to mentor a cadre of Christian officers within the LAPD as a threat to the department. The novel ends on a tender note. Gaffaney has murdered Rice as revenge for his son's death. He then clumsily attempts to shoot himself with his service revolver. Hopkins consoles Gaffaney and the two adversaries share a moment of solace together. Most of the narrative's breathtaking set-pieces feature Duane Rice and not Hopkins. Ellroy was growing bored of Hopkins.

Ellroy was increasingly confident that he now had the skills to write his Black Dahlia novel, but before he began his formal research a lucrative writing opportunity came his way. Ellroy's friendship with John Douglas had grown with time. The two men formed what they jokingly referred to as the "Meat and Violence Club," of which they were the only members. Meat and Violence nights consisted of a steak dinner followed by a slasher or crime film at one of the sleazy cinemas that were dotted around Times Square, "one of the first meetings was *Cobra*, a star-vehicle for Sylvester Stallone," Douglas recalls. "The dinner was fine, but Leonard Maltin was not kind in his review."[55] Douglas wanted Ellroy to write a first-person novel from the perspective of a serial killer. Ellroy had never been invited by a publisher to write a novel before now, and he was already bored with the serial killer craze, "serial killer novels are just as dead as private eye novels," he claimed.[56] However, Douglas was offering Ellroy a $10,000 advance. Ellroy was behind on his rent at the time, caught between caddying seasons and working at a Jewish Deli to scrape a living. It was an offer too good to refuse.

Ellroy wrote *Killer on the Road* in three weeks. He borrowed heavily from his own life-story in creating the serial killer Martin Plunkett. Plunkett is born and raised in LA, the son of an alcoholic mother and languid, promiscuous father. After his father walks out on the family and his mother commits suicide, aided somewhat by Plunkett spiking her medication, Plunkett is free to indulge in his psychopathic urges. After meeting members of the Manson Family, he becomes briefly obsessed with cult leader Charles Manson. But when Plunkett is serving time in the LA County Jail, for a minor offense, he meets Manson and is disappointed with his shambolic appearance and incoherent ramblings. He verbally humiliates Manson and, once he is released, Plunkett embarks on a killing spree while driving across the US. Ellroy delivers a stunning but implausible twist halfway through the novel. Plunkett is arrested by State Trooper Ross Anderson in Wisconsin. Anderson knows Plunkett is a murderer, as he is a serial killer himself. Anderson seduces Plunkett, thus leading him to confront his sexuality, the repression of which has led to his sexually violent urges. Plunkett is ultimately captured when Anderson, facing the death penalty, betrays him to FBI Agent Thomas Dusenberry. Plunkett is imprisoned but he claims one last victim in Dusenberry. Plunkett refuses to cooperate with Dusenberry in any way. Shocked by the evil he encounters in Plunkett, Dusenberry slips into a depression which costs him his career, his marriage, and ultimately his life.

Killer on the Road is one of Ellroy's weakest novels. It is compulsively readable from beginning to end but it just contains too many implausible moments which Ellroy, who was writing at great speed and with little conviction, never attempted to revise. John Douglas insisted on changing the title to *Silent Terror*, based on the ending where Plunkett drives Dusenberry to death just by maintaining his silence. Ellroy did not like the title but felt that he could not object as it was "the only book I ever wrote for the money as I needed some dough".[57] For Ellroy, the novel was a brief but lucrative distraction from his long-standing ambition and artistic goal. The Lloyd Hopkins novels had not been a commercial success: "The combined sales in hardcover," Penzler recalls "were less than 5,000 copies, just disastrous."[58] They had at least helped Ellroy to hone his skills as a writer and led to the one-time lucrative offer from John Douglas. Ellroy knew that writing a Black Dahlia novel was his best chance of receiving the critical and commercial success that he craved. Otherwise, he could have been facing the possibility of being dropped again.

All his instincts were proved right. Ellroy's Black Dahlia novel would completely change his life and career.

6

Sweet Smell of Success (1986–1990)

Ellroy began his research on the Dahlia case in the New York Public Library. He converted $300 into its equivalent in quarters and carried the coins in "three triple-reinforced pillowcases" which he would use to order, via interlibrary loan, the original newspaper coverage by the *LA Times*, *Herald*, and *Examiner* of the Dahlia investigation.[1] Ellroy examined the newspapers on a microfilm reader and made photocopies he could refer to when working on the outline to the novel.

There were still other writing jobs that occupied Ellroy's time. Sobel and Penzler both felt that he should finish the Hopkins in Jeopardy Quintet, or at the very least write a fourth novel in the series. Ellroy reluctantly began outlining another Hopkins novel he provisionally titled "The Cold Six Thousand." In it, Hopkins has been demoted to uniform duty. The title refers to the aspirations of Lynn Dietrich, a hooker who has a dream of saving up $6,000. This is the money she needs to retire to the small town of Xuatapul, Mexico, where you can live like royalty for a year for precisely $6,000. Every time her savings get close to the required sum however, she deliberately squanders the money and sabotages her dreams. Ellroy wrote an 84-page outline for "The Cold Six Thousand" before abandoning the project. He just had no interest in the series anymore. However, he did make a mental note of the title, which he liked, and the idea behind it.

After studying hundreds of newspaper articles on the Dahlia investigation, Ellroy got the urge to revisit Los Angeles. He wanted to visit the spot where Elizabeth Short's corpse was discovered and other locations in the outline, which grew to be 144 pages long. Serendipitously, Ellroy's return to LA coincided with growing Hollywood interest in his work. In 1984, Ellroy had been contacted by the screenwriter Joseph Stinson. Stinson had scripted the Dirty Harry film *Sudden Impact*, in which he coined the phrase "Go ahead. Make my day," a saying which entered the lexicon after being co-opted by President Reagan. Stinson wanted to write and direct a film adaptation of *Clandestine* and had contacted Ellroy about securing the rights. He was struck by the candor of Ellroy's response: "I've got $200 in the bank and caddy season is three months off—I think we can make a deal."[2] Ellroy complimented Stinson on the success of *Sudden Impact*, claiming he saw it in the theater and "people were coming all over the screen!"[3] For Ellroy, to have a screenwriter like Stinson use his own money to buy the rights to one of his novels was a major boost. Ellroy and Stinson would talk for hours on the phone and became close friends.

Ellroy had made arrangements to sleep on the couch of his friend Alan Marks for his visit to LA. Ellroy employed Marks periodically as a researcher. Sleeping on his couch was the sort of modest arrangement Ellroy was used to. He was more vexed by Marks' chain-smoking habit. However, Ellroy was about to get his first taste of Hollywood glamour. Ellroy attended a party in Malibu hosted by an acting coach who was a friend of Duane Tucker. He noticed a "tall willowy, unadorned woman."[4] He asked around for some details about the woman and was informed her name was Amanda and was she a call girl who charged $1,000 a night. Ellroy had barely scraped together the money to fly to LA. However, earlier that day Sobel had contacted Ellroy. They spoke on a payphone outside Marks's home. Sobel informed Ellroy that the director James B. Harris had optioned *Blood on the Moon* for $5,000, minus $500 for Sobel's commission. Ellroy approached Amanda and the next morning he awoke with $3,500 to his name.

Jimmy Harris had produced some of the early, critically lauded Stanley Kubrick films before turning to directing himself. Harris offered to pay Ellroy $2,000 a week for his time while he was in LA and took him to some of the best restaurants in town. Ellroy was under the impression Harris wanted him to adapt *Blood on the Moon* into a screenplay. Harris was adamant that he was going to write the script himself, he just wanted to throw around ideas with Ellroy. Ellroy, by nature energetic and impatient, found Harris's working style to be plodding and circumspect. But after a while, he began to relax and enjoy Harris's company. Harris was a natural raconteur and regaled Ellroy with stories about Hollywood and working with Kubrick.

Harris took Ellroy out for breakfast, lunch, and dinner and always picked up the check. For Ellroy, who seldom ate three meals a day, it was a real treat. They would have lunch at Nate and Al's deli in Beverly Hills. For dinner they would move onto Matteo's, an Italian restaurant on Westwood Boulevard. Ellroy would never forget Harris's generosity, and the two men became lifelong friends. In Matteo's Harris introduced Ellroy to Fred "Private Eye to the Stars" Otash. Otash's name had come up repeatedly in Ellroy's research on 1950s LA. However, the lighting was low in Matteo's to flatter aging movie stars. Ellroy barely recognized Otash and he made little impression upon introduction.

Once he returned from LA, Ellroy retreated to his basement apartment to write the novel. His intense writing schedule did not deter him in his pursuit of women. He joined a poetry reading group connected to the renowned *Little Magazine*. Meetings took place at the Upper West Side apartment of the science fiction writer Samuel "Chip" Delany. Delany recalls meeting Ellroy "for a handful of monthly meetings," and even though Ellroy's ulterior motive for attending was to find a girlfriend, Delany thought Ellroy "was smart, worked hard. I liked him, certainly, and thought he was a *very* talented writer. It was unpaid work and done out of love for the English language."[5]

At the editorial meetings, Ellroy met and began dating the poet and short story writer Susan Palwick. Ellroy had previously dated Susan's friend, the writer Ellen Kushner. At first, Susan was bowled over by Ellroy's charm and generosity. Walking through Manhattan together one day, a homeless person approached them asking for money. The man seemed to be heavily under the influence of drugs. To Susan's surprise, Ellroy emptied his pockets and gave the man all the money he had on him. When Susan asked him why he had been so generous when the man would likely spend it on drugs, Ellroy replied:

"When I was living on the streets of LA, I survived by people giving me money."

Although he was very generous, Susan witnessed Ellroy's competitive streak. He took her to a dinner party at Otto Penzler's house. The other guests were Harlan Ellison and his wife Susan Toth. Ellison read his short story "Soft Monkey" in its entirety. Although the story would go on to win an Edgar Award, no one present, apart from Ellison, enjoyed the reading and Ellroy said he was "flabbergasted by the move."[6] Susan thought the evening descended into a "battle of the egos" between Ellroy, Ellison, and Penzler. Ellison, in a vile mood, approached her and asked, "What are you doing with this loser?" Susan recalls, "I was tempted to ask his wife the same thing."[7]

Within a few weeks of dating, Ellroy was already talking about marriage with Susan. She was still in thrall to him at this stage, but she began to find the level of control he wished to exert over her worrying. He would dictate to her what she was going to wear. At one point he stated their first daughter would be named Eleanor. Susan replied that she had never liked the name. Ellroy was not impressed by her response "as I had broken the image of what his perfect woman should be."[8]

Susan invited Ellroy to spend Thanksgiving dinner with her parents. At first, Ellroy was all charm, giving Susan's mother an inscribed copy of one of his novels. Then Susan said something which elicited an icy response. Ellroy was eating crackers and Susan noticed that the crumbs were dropping onto his shirt. Susan suggested that he use a plate. Ellroy glared at her and then very slowly crushed the cracker in his hand and released the crumbs onto the carpet. Susan was also disappointed that Ellroy was not more encouraging in helping her pursue her writing career, "He paid lip service to the idea."

> I had a story published in *Asimov's* while I was with him ["Elephant," in the November 1986 issue]; he read it and dutifully told me it was a good story. But once when I was trying to write during a weekend visit with him, he kept interrupting me in ways that made it clear he wanted to be the only writer in the room. He came across as weirdly insecure, given that I'd sold two or three short stories at that point, and he'd published several novels and was pulling in movie deals.[9]

Ellroy informed Susan that the relationship was over during a brief phone call on December 8, 1986. Susan was shocked. Although there had been some tense moments, only a few weeks earlier Ellroy had been talking about marriage. The relationship had lasted ten weeks in total. Susan had confronted Ellroy when he joked about using the names of his ex-girlfriends as dead hookers in his novels. She found the idea repulsive. These were often the same women he had dedicated novels to when the relationship was going well.

A few years after the relationship ended Susan was dining with the author Robert LeGault. He mentioned that Ellroy had used her name in his latest novel *LA Confidential*. She rushed out to a bookstore and started frantically skimming through a copy. Sure enough, she found her name:

Sharon Susan Palwick, 20, hooker, DOD 8/29/53, Bakersfield, California. The same specs: no suspects, no leads, case closed.[10]

Susan's debut novel *Flying in Place* was published in 1992. Around that time, she saw Ellroy at a book festival. He was contrite and visibly embarrassed at how shabbily he had treated her. He inscribed her copy of *The Black Dahlia*, "To: Susan—with love, amends, regrets, much respect and admiration for your new haircut. Dog."[11] At one point, Ellroy had reached out to her saying that he wanted to get back together. Susan was reluctant to even entertain the notion. A friend advised her that Ellroy was a control freak, and that she should give him a specific date and time to call. If he stuck to it, that would be a sign that he had changed. Susan followed this advice and Ellroy did not call.

After ending his romance with Susan, Ellroy's next relationship was with Glenda Revelle who he met at a publishing party in the Spring of '87. Glenda was an academic specializing in Developmental Psychology. According to Glenda:

The host of the party was a book collector and had the books in his collection (each ensconced in its own individual plastic bag to protect it) on his bookshelves. James and I struck up a conversation, and we both seemed to be enjoying it. At some point James walked over to the host's bookshelf and pulled the paperback of his first novel, *Brown's Requiem*, off the shelf, took it out of its plastic bag and signed it with a note, hopeful about romance, and gave it to me.[12]

On their first date Ellroy "was doing a bit of the Demon Dog shtick, and I started asking questions to try to get him out of the shtick and into being real with each other."[13] Glenda found that while Ellroy's Demon Dog persona could be "bombastic, arrogant and overbearing," in his relaxed, more personal manner he was "gentle, kind, generous, and always respectful of me and my thoughts and feelings."[14] She got to know him partly by reading his novels "I think it was while reading his second book, *Clandestine*, that I started falling in love with him. We had not spent much, if any, time together since that first party at this point. He seduced me with his words."[15]

The relationship became more serious with Ellroy travelling to Fort Smith, Arkansas to meet Glenda's parents, "My dad had always been pretty hard on my boyfriends, but he seemed to warm to something in James."[16] Glenda's father had also been reading Ellroy's work. "Since I Don't Have You" was published in the journal *A Matter of Crime*. The main protagonist, Turner "Buzz" Meeks describes himself as an "Armadillo Poacher" from Oklahoma. This caused amusement among Glenda's family, who were all sure that there weren't any armadillo poachers in Oklahoma. Ellroy and Glenda and her parents, in separate cars, took a road trip from Fort Smith to Fayetteville to visit Glenda's brother.

"On the drive, my dad spotted a roadkill armadillo on the side of the road. My dad actually picked the thing up and put it in the trunk of his car to present to James when we arrived in Fayetteville."[17] Ellroy was amused by the gesture and Glenda took it as a good sign as "My dad was always reticent about any encounters with bugs or critters of any kind, so the fact that he would do this to share a laugh with James was huge."[18]

In addition to his voracious appetite for women, Ellroy was equally adept at making friends. At an AA meeting in New York in 1983, Ellroy met and befriended the poet Thomas Lux. After meetings they would go out for burgers together at a restaurant called Tumbledown Dick's in Bronxville. Lux taught at Sarah Lawrence College. Like Ellroy, he was a ladies' man, and Ellroy recalled that Lux "liked the girls at Sarah Lawrence."[19] Ellroy taught Lux's class on a number of occasions where his intense persona left quite the impression on a number of students.

Lux's literary career was firmly established by the time Ellroy met him. Ellroy also formed friendships with several authors who were at the beginning of a promising career. Ellroy met Steve Erickson "at a bookstore on Westwood Boulevard not long after the publication of my second novel (*Rubicon Beach*), and he congratulated me on the attention the book had gotten."[20] Ellroy and Erickson became friends, and Erickson would go on to write a long profile on Ellroy for the *LA Weekly* "He's not a hard interview except maybe just trying to contain him – parts of the profile I wrote were just monologues of his related verbatim."[21] Ellroy admired the profile so much he had it framed in his Eastchester apartment. Erickson wrote that the major theme of Ellroy's novels was "a glory that costs everything and means nothing" which Ellroy later used as a metafictional epigraph to *LA Confidential.*[22]

Another friend of this era was the psychologist, Jonathan Kellerman. Kellerman's debut novel *When the Bough Breaks* was a smash-hit and Kellerman met Ellroy at the 1986 Edgar Awards in New York City, a black tie event where he recalls Ellroy was wearing "a blue blazer and parrot green pants."[23] Kellerman had read Ellroy's novels, recognized him from his author photograph and approached him even though "people warned me away from him, booksellers would say 'Don't talk to that guy, he's crazy.'"[24] However, Kellerman found Ellroy to be "lovely, very shy, and he insisted on calling me Dr. Kellerman."[25]

Ellroy would visit Kellerman when he was in LA. They would dine at the Pacific Dining Car where Kellerman noticed how the staff would treat Ellroy like a celebrity. One night they were driving home from dinner when they stopped at a light and Ellroy turned to Kellerman and said,

"Jon, you know Dutch [Elmore Leonard] is getting kinda old, and Bob Parker's getting kinda old. So, who do you think will be the next king of American crime fiction, you or me?"

"You James," Kellerman replied gamely.

Kellerman also witnessed Ellroy's more vulnerable side. Ellroy talked about his mother in negative terms, describing her as a "whore" and an "alcoholic" and using language Kellerman thought was inappropriate but which he recognized was coming from emotional wounds. On one occasion the two men were sifting through Kellerman's collection of True Crime magazines when Ellroy suddenly came across an article about his mother's murder, which

Figure 7 *Rising Stars of the Genre: Ellroy and Jonathan Kellerman at Vagabond Books, LA, in 1986. Credit: Susan Palwick.*

featured a portrait of her on the front cover. Within seconds of seeing the article Ellroy burst into tears, "All that bravado and all that inappropriate talk just melted away and it was really a touching scene," Kellerman recalls.[26]

Ellroy met and befriended the author James Grady at an event at The Mysterious Bookshop. Grady had enjoyed huge success with his debut novel *Six Days of the Condor*. Grady lived in Washington DC, where his wife Bonnie Goldstein worked as a Senate aide. On the night they met, Grady bought a copy of *Blood on the Moon* and Ellroy inscribed it:

> Hail, Fellow Writer—Continue guarding the nation's capital, but leave the White House open to Guerrilla attack! I will attack certain women, you will attack political malfeasance, and together we will storm the literary establishment.[27]

But Ellroy's best friend, without question, was Otto Penzler. Penzler had the ability to give tough editing advice without provoking Ellroy's ire. They spent a lot of time together, often taking in fights at Madison Square Garden or watching them on television at Penzler's home. Penzler witnessed how Ellroy struggled to contain his pent-up energy. While watching one slow-moving boxing match, Ellroy dropped to the floor and did a hundred push-ups in frustration.

The writing process for *The Black Dahlia* took nearly a year. Ellroy made some changes in structure between the outline and the finished novel. The outline ends with the murderer Ramona Sprague slashing her own mouth open to mimic her method of killing Elizabeth Short. Deciding this was too gothic, Ellroy rewrote the scene so that Bucky Bleichert leaves the terminally ill Ramona to die of cancer, judging it to be punishment enough.

Ellroy "wrote the last page and wept."[28] His progression as a writer had undergone a massive leap forward between *The Black Dahlia* and his six previous novels. He had created remarkable characters with whom he had spent much of the past year: Bucky Bleichert, the Warrants squad cop with a dubious family history who gets sucked into the Dahlia investigation. His cop partner and boxing rival, the aggressive, intelligent, and self-destructive Lee Blanchard. The woman that comes between them is Kay Lake, a South Dakota country girl who has been Blanchard's companion since he rescued her from a brutal pimp, but who finds herself increasingly attracted to Bleichert. Out of this triumvirate, Ellroy honors the memory of Elizabeth Short, the ill-fated woman he had been obsessed with since childhood. Hovering allusively over the text is the presence of his mother Jean Ellroy. Ellroy dedicated the novel to her. The connection between two murdered women, Elizabeth Short and Jean Ellroy, was something that the author was readying himself to exploit.

One morning Penzler received a call from Nat Sobel who told him, "You have got to read this."[29]

The Black Dahlia

"I never knew her in life" is Bucky Bleichert's opening line in the prologue to *The Black Dahlia*.[30] "Her" is Elizabeth Short, the eponymous victim, who Bleichert learns to know in death. Short's brief life did not amount to her becoming much more than "a sad little girl and a whore—at best a could-have-been," but as harsh as that sounds, Bleichert, and by extension, Ellroy, does not judge her for her flaws, as this is "a tag that might equally apply to me."[31] Bleichert's identification with Short is more than a representation of who he is. Their paths did not cross in life and knowing Short in death has sinister undertones. Bleichert becomes intimate with Short through the investigation and later in the novel, his spiritual union with the object of his obsession is made flesh through a sexual relationship with a Short proxy.

Short's murder was one of the most brutal in Los Angeles's history: the torture inflicted on her is enough to turn the stomach of even the most experienced homicide detective, let alone an unseasoned cop like Bleichert, whose response to the murder exceeds his professional obligations and simultaneously compromises his police career. Despite his inexperience, Bleichert first gets dragged into the investigation as he is near the scene when Short's corpse is discovered, and the LAPD devotes all its available manpower to a murder which quickly becomes a media sensation.

The lurid newspaper coverage of Elizabeth Short's murder ensured that, although the victim finally gains the recognition she sought, she is as exploited in death as she had been in life. Nevertheless, Bleichert surmises that "as brutal as the facts were, she would have wanted all of them known."[32] However, the tabloid narrative is not enough. Bleichert feels a debt of gratitude to Short which he can only repay through the written word, "since I owe her a great deal and am the only one who does know the entire story, I have undertaken the writing of this memoir."[33] Bleichert's memoir will not become part of the public record on the case. Rather, his manuscript is an act of private remembrance, akin to the Anne Sexton poem which is quoted in epigraph, wherein a woman periodically takes out photographs of her father to study before quietly putting them away, "Now I fold you down, my drunkard, my navigator/My first lost keeper, to love and look at later."[34]

Bleichert first encounters violence several years before he ever hears Elizabeth Short's name, "Before the Dahlia case was the partnership, and before that there was the war."[35] The reference to wartime is bittersweet. Bleichert is insecure at how he never saw combat duty and his only taste of blood occurs during the Zoot Suit riots of June 1943. Bleichert comes to the aid of Officer

Lee Blanchard who, in the chaos of the riot, has found himself cornered by "three marines in dress blues and a pachuco in full-drape zoot suit." Once they have fought their way out of trouble, violence, like sex, is followed by domesticity. Bleichert and Blanchard quietly sit out the rest of the riot and soon return to "the polite conversation at roll call."[36] The riots may have just been a historical footnote to a global conflict, but to Bleichert and Blanchard they are crucial in forging the friendship and rivalry that will define their lives over the next few years. Blanchard and Bleichert are given the nicknames Mr. Fire and Mr. Ice respectively. They are partners and boxing rivals in Central Division, and they work the Good Cop/Bad Cop routine to great effect, "Our boxing reputations gave us an added edge of respect on the street, and when Lee rabbit-punched for information and I interceded on the punchee's behalf, it got us what we wanted."[37]

"Cherchez la femme," the intercession of a woman is what pulls this macho friendship apart. Blanchard's partner is a former gun moll from Sioux City named Kay Lake. Bleichert is instantly attracted to Kay but resists the urge to act on it out of loyalty to Blanchard. Her presence solidifies the friendship at first, and the trinity of Bleichert, Blanchard, and Kay form what Jim Mancall describes as a "pseudo-family," providing Bleichert with the sort of comfortable, even loving, environment he lacked in his upbringing.[38] The first six chapters show their friendship at its height, with Kay acting as the lover/friend/mother figure to her two boys. Cracks in the trinity begin to appear after a police shooting in which Bleichert and Blanchard kill four men. They return to Blanchard's home before he abruptly departs leaving Bleichert alone with Kay:

> Kay was standing nude under the shower. Her expression stayed fixed in no expression at all, even when our eyes met. I took in her body, from freckled breasts with dark nipples to wide hips and flat stomach, then she pirouetted for me. I saw old knife scars criss-crossing her backside from thighs to spine, choked back tremors and walked away wishing she hadn't showed me on the day I killed two men.[39]

Kay's direct sexuality is exuded through her nude posing. Her fixed expression admits a sense of being watched, which is heightened by her performance, her ballet-like pirouette. This strange movement ironically adds to her vitality as the revealing of her full figure expresses the vividness of her sexuality—from which Blanchard is precluded as the two are celibate. Blanchard and Kay's living arrangements might appear progressive, to the point where it could damage his police career as "shacking's against the (LAPD) regs," but it is built on a lie as he leaves Kay emotionally and sexually unfulfilled, and by leaving her alone with his male friend Blanchard is either taunting Kay or willfully oblivious of either Bucky or Kay's feelings.[40] Kay's revealing of her scars, a souvenir from her upbringing in Sioux City, provokes an ambiguous sexual response in Bucky as he "choked back tremors" possibly through anger at what she has been through but also in guilt, the scars could become emotionally deeper if he betrayed Blanchard. Bleichert's reaction to violence earlier in the day is not that of a professional detective. It is emotional and personal, and at the mercy of Kay. She runs a bath leaving Bucky "feeling the steam, knowing it was all for me."[41] It is in this moment, preceded by violence and arrested by violence that the trinity begins to reformulate, and Bleichert will eventually step into the domestic role which has been vacated, quite literally as he disappears, by Blanchard.

Bleichert's viewing of Kay's scars are also a portentous omen of the imminent discovery of Elizabeth Short's corpse as the man who slashed his mark onto Kay's flesh, her former pimp Bobby DeWitt, has the same initials (BD) as the Black Dahlia. The branding of Kay, turning her into a form of male possession is paralleled by Bucky's first glimpse of Betty's corpse when it is discovered at 39th and Norton, and which plunges Bucky into a sexual obsession that goes far beyond his desire for a woman who is in a relationship with his best friend:

> The mouth cut ear to ear into a smile that leered up at you, somehow mocking the brutality inflicted. I knew I would carry that smile with me to the grave.[42]

At first sight, Bleichert and Betty Short are in a relationship of sorts, as she has claimed him with her death smile. However, as with many relationships in Ellroy's work, the role of the dominant partner is fluid. Bucky foresees that he will "carry" her smile with him for life, essentially molding her into a fantasy figure he can love which may have little to do with the woman she was in life.

Bleichert and Blanchard's official role in the homicide case is relatively modest, but when Bleichert begins his own private investigation, it brings him closer to the truth than any homicide detective on the case. Like Betty Short, Bucky becomes a fantasist, dreaming of the glory that will come his way when he unmasks the killer. Bucky chases a lead about a Dahlia-lookalike, Madeleine Sprague. He approaches Madeleine outside a lesbian bar and, genuinely attracted to her "superficially similar" resemblance to Betty Short which she enhances through "hairdo and makeup" and professionally intrigued, he begins a relationship which gives him access to the enigmatic Sprague family.[43] Bleichert's relationship with Madeleine is mutually exploitative from the start. Although she comes across a heartless femme fatale, Madeleine is coerced into sex by Bleichert in exchange for keeping her out of trouble with the law. Slowly, Bleichert deludes himself into thinking their relationship is genuine and each favor he performs for Madeleine potentially jeopardizes his policeman role.

Bucky's introduction to the Sprague family has faint echoes of Ellroy's brief acquaintance with several families who lived in Hancock Park in the mid-1960s, in that a young man from a modest background is being introduced by his girlfriend to her upper-crust family. On the surface, the Spragues are very successful, with wealth and all the furnishings you'd expect to find in an expensive home. The only visible oddity is a stuffed dog with a newspaper in his mouth. During a rather surreal dinner party, Bucky is informed that the dog Balto was shot by her father Emmett Sprague "the day Daddy learned he'd made his first million," a blackly comic example of the male urge to freeze living beings into inanimate ideals.[44] Balto had been performing its role in a way that sealed its unlucky fate, as it had been bringing the daily newspaper which carried a report that Emmett had become very wealthy. Every member of the nuclear family is ostensibly present at the dinner— mother, father, siblings, even the stuffed dog. However, each member, is to some degree a fraud and behind their secrets lies the solution to Elizabeth Short's murder. Balto was stuffed by Georgie Tilden, a disfigured World War I veteran and associate of Emmett's since they grew up in Scotland together. Bucky discovers that Georgie has been having an affair with the matriarch Ramona Sprague, and that Madeleine is his illegitimate daughter. Madeleine's overtly sexual behavior towards Emmett is a tacit acknowledgement that only Martha is Emmett's biological daughter. The merging of bloodlines seals the fate of the unwitting Elizabeth, as when Madeleine brings her back to the Sprague home Ramona is incensed by Betty's resemblance to the daughter (Madeleine) whose very existence is proof of her adultery and loveless marriage to Emmett.

Surface is essential in this world, speaking as it does to success but also when penetrated, exposing twisted sexual desires and psychotic motivations. During the homicide investigation, Bucky and Blanchard are both emotionally shaken after viewing a stag film "Slave Girls in Hell" featuring Elizabeth Short. Although Short appears to have nominally consented to appear in the film, she is taking instructions from off-camera and can be seen pleading to stop as her humiliation grows worse with every act. The same evening, Bucky is intimate with Madeleine, but his performance is stymied by the graphic images from the film which he can't dispel. He wants to go slowly but as Madeleine approaches climax she urges him "Don't hold back. I'm ready."[45] As she lies in his arms, naked and sweating from the sex, Madeleine looks the very essence of female sexuality. But Bucky tries to alter the image, "Smile at me. Look soft and sweet." This attempt to reverse Madeleine back to innocence backfires as her "Pollyanna grin" reminds Bucky of "the Dahlia's death smile." During their pillow talk, Madeleine reveals she had sex with Betty, Bleichert felt "like I was sinking; like the bed was dropping out from under me."[46] He is attracted to her because of her resemblance to Short, but he does not want Madeleine to be sexually attracted to the same qualities in Short or to have had a relationship with Short that is impossible for him. Madeleine confesses she was attracted to exactly those qualities, "I just did it to see what it would be like to be with a girl who looked so much like me."[47] Although his concept of the feminine ideal has once again been breached, it reveals a vital clue in the puzzle as Elizabeth Short was killed for upsetting the delicate status quo in the Sprague family. Madeleine has intuited Bleichert's feelings for Betty and is prepared to fully exploit to create another false family. "I'll be Betty or anyone else you want me to be," she tells him.[48] Ellroy concocted Betty and Madeleine's relationship from his research on the case. He was struck by the sensationalist tabloid coverage of the investigation which, ironically, was prohibited from referencing Betty's sexuality, "they couldn't use the word 'lesbian.' They said, quote: 'The affection of women came as easily to Elizabeth Short as the affection of men.'"[49]

The Black Dahlia ends with the mystery storyline resolved, but with the characters reliving the story, both through their memories and their relationships. Bleichert receives a letter from Kay informing him that she is carrying his child. The letter is postmarked Cambridge, Massachusetts as a tentative invitation for Bleichert to follow, and reminding him of a previous trip to Elizabeth Short's hometown of nearby Medford. The novel ends with Bleichert lost in thought aboard a plane flying to Boston: "I reached for Betty then; a wish, almost a prayer."[50] He may have avenged Betty by solving her murder, but this has not diminished Bucky's necromantic engagement with the female victim, although he has become less possessive in the way he conducts it, "I asked Betty to grant me safe passage in return for my love."[51] By seeking permission from Betty he is acknowledging the control she exhibits over him, and how he needs to step back from his obsessions to fulfill his new role as father and husband. *The Black Dahlia* ends with Bucky surrendering himself to women he previously tried to control.

Penzler and Sobel were both floored by the manuscript to *The Black Dahlia*, and Penzler initially bought it for Mysterious Press. However, the novel was generating a buzz in publishing circles and Warner Books, which would buy Mysterious Press in 1989, optioned it for $50,000. This sum was more money than Ellroy had earned through all his previous advances and royalties combined. But rather than go on a spending spree (as he had done in the past) Ellroy was minded to reinvest the money back into the book. Penzler informed Ellroy that the publicity budget was likely to be a modest $15,000, "as none of the books had succeeded up until then."

Ellroy made an offer to Penzler. If Warner doubled the publicity budget to $30,000 then he would personally invest $45,000, his entire fee from Warner's minus Sobel's commission, giving the novel an overall publicity budget of $75,000. The new budget was agreed and soon Ellroy found that the money could buy him publicity beyond anything he had experienced before. *The Black Dahlia* had a front cover feature on *Publisher's Weekly* and a full-page ad in the *Times Book Review*. One of the conditions of his investment was that Ellroy would be able to promote the book in a three-month nationwide tour.

The tour was organized by Edna Farley, a renowned freelance publicist who planned book tours from her Fort Lauderdale home, pioneering a work from home method which was rare at the time. Ellroy spoke with Farley on the phone before he set off. She planned a nationwide tour and used her established media connections to make sure Ellroy got the exposure he needed. It was either Farley or another publicist at Warner who advised Ellroy to talk about the novel's emotional connection to his mother's murder. Even the active schedule Farley planned for Ellroy was not enough to fill three months. The California leg had gaps between engagements, and Ellroy used this time to drive from city to city, phoning bookstores and offering to make appearances for book signings.

Ellroy was a natural performer and soon discovered how to work a bookstore audience. According to Sobel, "James has a nearly photographic memory, he remembered every single person he met, and he single-handedly made his book successful."[52] The responses were not always enthusiastic. At one bookstore Ellroy found that he didn't sell a single book and was reduced to begging a customer to buy a copy.

Life on the road was invigorating but demanding. At night, in his hotel room Ellroy liked to unwind by talking on the phone to women. He had met several women through Singles Ads and, juggling them on the phone, he rather rashly assumed that his phone calls were covered by the fee for the room. When he returned to New York, Ellroy discovered that he had racked up a phone bill of thousands of dollars. However, Larry Kirshbaum at Warner was so impressed by the energy and dedication Ellroy had put into promoting the novel that he agreed the company would split the phone bills with him. Kirshbaum began at Warner as a Marketing Executive and eventually became CEO of the company. Ellroy liked him and did much to cultivate a friendship, "He [Ellroy] called me 'The Godfather' which I loved. (I considered myself a rather dull, blue-and-gray suit.)" Kirshbaum recalls.[53] "He would love to get down on his knees and grab my ring finger and pretend some kind of overblown subservient gratitude which was a big, bullshit, dramatic act."[54]

One of the women Ellroy was talking to on the phone was Glenda. Their romance had been fizzling out, so Ellroy asked her to fly out and join him on the San Francisco leg of the tour in the hope that it might revive things. Glenda agreed and they stayed at the Fairmont Hotel together. Ellroy wanted to see the sights from the movie *Vertigo*. They dined at Ernie's restaurant and went hiking in Muir Woods. The weekend was pleasant enough but both parties knew the relationship was over. According to Glenda, "It just lived out its natural course."[55]

In San Francisco, Ellroy was interviewed by Edvins "Ed" Beitiks, a reporter for the *San Francisco Examiner*. Ellroy had grown accustomed to interviewers who had failed to read his book, or they had done little research prior to meeting him, but he was soon to discover that Beitiks knew his subject well. Born in Germany, in the dying days of World War II, Beitiks' father had been killed on the Eastern front and he emigrated with his mother to the US after the war. He served in the US Army's First Cavalry Division in Vietnam, where he was seriously wounded and exposed to Agent Orange. It left him with a pockmarked, florid complexion. A porkpie hat was permanently lodged on his head, embellishing his already striking features. He had spent much of 1987 travelling the South, covering the tenth anniversary of Elvis Presley's death, and making a pilgrimage to William Faulkner's house, Rowan Oak in Oxford, Mississippi.

Ellroy was grateful that Beitiks had read *The Black Dahlia* and was struck by his incisive intelligence. Ellroy talked about his fictional solution to the case. In the novel, a gruesome painting hangs in the Sprague family home. It is a portrait of Gwynplain, a character in Victor Hugo's novel *The Man Who Laughs* whose mouth is slashed open from ear to ear. This serves as the inspiration for Ramona Sprague and Georgie Tilden's murder of Elizabeth Short as they cut her mouth open in a similar way. Ellroy had invented the painting after someone told him about the Hugo novel.

"What did you think of my explanation?" Ellroy asked Beitiks, somewhat nervously hoping for his approval.

"It was a very fine but still inadequate explanation of the horror visited upon Elizabeth Short," Beitiks replied. "We are trying to frame that horror within some kind of reference," he said, shaking his head. "There is no cultural reference. There is no artistic reference of the horror inflicted upon her. No level of detail can do that horror justice."

Ellroy was stunned by Beitiks' response. He felt a degree of guilt at how he had profited from turning Elizabeth Short's murder into fiction, even visiting her grave for one publicity event, and exploited the connection with his mother's unsolved murder during the book tour. It had been a whirlwind three-month trip but listening to Beitiks that day reminded him of the ugly suffering Elizabeth Short had endured, and the futile nature of trying to rationalize it. "It was a sobering conversation," Ellroy recalled.[56]

The Black Dahlia received glowing reviews and became Ellroy's first bestseller. The paperback edition peaked at number fifteen on the *New York Times* bestseller list. The incredible effort Ellroy had expended on researching the case and writing the manuscript, followed by an exhaustive nationwide tour had paid off. Flush with success, with money in the bank and the realization that he now had some clout as an author, Ellroy plunged himself into writing his new novel, which he had already started prior to *The Black Dahlia* tour. The research and writing process for *The Big Nowhere* was a faster and smoother process for Ellroy than it had been for his previous novel.

Ellroy had been toying with the main plot idea of *The Big Nowhere* for years. In 1980, Ellroy had gone to the cinema with Randy Rice to see the William Friedkin film *Cruising*. Al Pacino plays a NYPD cop who, after a series of murders of gay men in Greenwich Village, goes undercover in the hardcore S&M subculture. In doing so, he becomes attracted to gay culture, questioning his sexuality, and bringing his relationship with his girlfriend under strain. Ellroy thought the film's premise was fascinating, but the result was disappointing. The film was "bad, it's elliptical, it's just full of shit."[57]

He took the premise and tried to improve upon it in the character of Danny Upshaw, a Los Angeles Sheriff's Deputy Detective investigating a series of brutal murders in early 1950s LA. Upshaw also must go undercover, in a separate investigation into communist activity in Hollywood. The twin roles of investigating murders with a homosexual angle and submerging himself in a promiscuous and libertine environment force Upshaw to confront his heretofore repressed homosexuality, with tragic consequences. Built around

Upshaw's story is a detailed period novel encompassing the Red Scare, gangland wars, and police corruption. Ellroy developed a subjective third-person narration alternating between three main characters—Upshaw, LAPD lieutenant Mal Considine, and bagman, fixer, and retired armadillo poacher Turner "Buzz" Meeks.

The Big Nowhere was released in September 1988 and was met with critical acclaim. *Publisher's Weekly* described it as "taut and densely detailed, this is a mystery with the grim, inexorable pull of film noir."[58] Writing in the *New York Times*, John Gross described the novel as "a big, sprawling book which lays on the atmosphere rich and thick," and that Ellroy's "characters are drawn with a firm brush, he has an excellent line in flinty, sardonic dialogue."[59] Not all reviewers were impressed. Also in the *Times*, Sarah Schulman complained that the "text is bursting with racial epithets against blacks, Mexicans and Jews."[60] Schulman also found "Ellroy saves his most unrelenting negative stereotypes for the many gay men who appear in his novel."[61] The novel sold only half as many copies as *The Black Dahlia* in hardcover. Otto Penzler described the sales as "disappointing, with an author you want growth."[62]

The Big Nowhere was a more accomplished and moving novel than *The Black Dahlia*, but its sprawling narrative lacked the *Dahlia*'s irresistible premise of a real-life unsolved murder. Nevertheless, it marked a major step forward for Ellroy as a writer and, contrary to Schulman's criticism, he handled the tortured sexuality of Danny Upshaw sensitively, partly as the subject fascinated him so much. He had portrayed gay cops in three previous novels, but never with as much insight and empathy as he had with Danny Upshaw. From *The Big Nowhere* onwards he would continually return to the macho law-enforcement or underworld figure hiding his sexuality to protect himself from his hypocritical culture. Another key decision Ellroy made with *The Big Nowhere* was to bring back the character of Lieutenant Dudley Smith. Smith had appeared briefly in *Clandestine*, and his charismatic, scheming, and malevolent personality had left a big impression. He would evolve into the main antagonist of a series of novels Ellroy was now referring to as the LA Quartet. Evil and attractive in equal measure, with a backstory that includes revolutionary Ireland and post-World War II Paraguay, Dudley Smith is undoubtedly Ellroy's most famous creation, as firmly associated with the author as Tom Ripley is to Patricia Highsmith.

Ellroy embarked on another ambitious book tour to support the novel, but the response from readers was more muted than it had been for *The Black Dahlia*. Nevertheless, Ellroy would meet a screenwriter on the tour who was to have a major effect on his career. Brian Helgeland was in his mid-twenties and had recently gained his first writing credits on low-budget horror movies. He was a fan of Ellroy's and went to see him at a bookstore signing on Hollywood Boulevard "to see what a real writer looked like."[63] Only three other people attended the signing, so Helgeland was able to monopolize the author's time. The two writers—one at the beginning of his career, the other enjoying a run of great success—got along well. Ellroy and Helgeland's paths would later intersect on a project that would bring them both unprecedented success.

The film adaptation of *Blood on the Moon* was retitled *Cop*. Released in March 1988, it gained some positive reviews, but it was not a box-office success. The fiercest critic of the film was Ellroy himself. Lacking anyone to see it with, he asked his ex-girlfriend Glenda to accompany him, and they watched the film in an almost empty cinema in Greenwich Village. He was deeply disappointed and did not hold back his opinion to Jimmy Harris. "Never having a film made of one of his works," Harris recalls,[64] "I don't think he realized that some dialogue was going to be changed and putting those words into the actors' mouths, the actors have their own ideas at times and you have a certain departure from the original."[65] Nevertheless, the two men remained close and, with Ellroy's blessing, Harris purchased a two-year option on *The Black Dahlia*. At the time Ellroy was represented by Stuart Miller at the Agency for the Performing Arts. Miller was shopping around the film rights of Ellroy's novels with the inflated asking price of one million dollars. Ellroy thought it was impossible that Miller could secure such a sum, nor did he think it was a good negotiating tactic to demand it.

According to Jimmy Harris, "The deal on *The Black Dahlia* was made at a place called The Hamburger Hamlet. At that time, he needed the money to buy a car."[66] Although he had been driving for years, Ellroy had finally passed his driving test at the age of forty. "If you give me the money for a car you can have the rights to *The Black Dahlia* and that was the deal. It was $25,000 for an option on the book. He said I should call his agent in the morning and make an offer. The agent of course will think it's too small."[67] Miller did think it was too small and informed Ellroy. To Miller's astonishment, Ellroy readily accepted.

Miller called Harris back and said, "I don't believe this, but my client has actually accepted the offer."

"We had a scam going on the rights," Harris fondly recalled.[68] Harris began adapting the novel into a screenplay with the intention of casting James Woods in the role of Bleichert and keeping it as faithful to Ellroy's narrative as possible. It would be a long time, however, before *The Black Dahlia* was filmed and by then it was in very different circumstances to what Harris and Ellroy had envisaged.

On February 17, 1988, Ellroy and Duane Tucker visited the Museum of Modern Art in New York. Ellroy was restless. He was never a big fan of museums, and he was only there as it was Tucker's birthday. So, when he spotted two attractive women wandering through the galleries together his interest was piqued.

Mary Doherty recalls Ellroy approaching her, "His exact words as he walked up to me while I was gazing at a painting were, 'Would you hang that piece of shit on your wall?'"[69] Mary and Ellroy started talking. In terms of background, they could not have been more different. Mary was from a moneyed, conservative family in Akron, Ohio. She was working as a business executive for the NYNEX corporation when she met Ellroy. The attraction between them was mutual. "I thought he was a little nerdy but sweet and quirky," Mary recalls.[70] Ellroy described Mary as "a righteous human being and devoid of pretense [...] I liked her very much."[71] When it came time to leave the museum, Ellroy was completely unfazed when Mary told him she lived in Boston.

"That's why God invented airplanes," he replied.

He mailed her a copy of *The Black Dahlia* and a *People* magazine feature on him. It was the first of many gifts, "He often sent sweet love letters and flowers."[72] True to his word, Ellroy would visit Mary in Boston. Ellroy enjoyed the trips to see his new sweetheart, although he didn't much care for Boston,

"His right-wing pronouncements kind of rolled off me at first. When the flush of infatuation wore off, I became more rattled by them," Mary recalled.[73]

NYNEX relocated Mary to a large house in Greenwich, Washington County. Ellroy was delighted that she would be closer to him. The company paid for the rent on the house and Ellroy spent so much time there that "he pretty much moved in when I got the place," although he retained his Eastchester apartment as an office.[74] Ellroy and Mary christened their new residence "the Zebra pad." Mary described it as "oddly garishly decorated with lime green walls and zebra patterned lampshades."[75] Living together was a precursor to their engagement. Ellroy had proposed to several girlfriends over the years, never with much sincerity. Mary was from a Catholic family and their relationship had proceeded so far that marriage was the next logical step.

Ellroy and Mary planned their wedding together. It took place in December of 1988, less than a year since the couple first met. The ceremony was held at St. Andrew's Catholic Church in Bluffton, South Carolina, near to where Mary's family was living at the time. Ellroy agreed to go to Pre-Cana seminars as a condition for having a Catholic wedding. He regarded the course as "hilarious" as it was clearly designed for couples who had been raised in the Catholic faith. Seminars would be titled "Preparing to leave the family home." Ellroy quipped to one priest, "I haven't been in the family home for twenty-three years, Father."[76]

Otto Penzler served as Ellroy's best man. On the day of the ceremony, Ellroy and Penzler were stood "in a little room behind the pulpit, waiting for the bride to walk down the aisle and all that and Ellroy looked over at me and said,

> Do you think I should do this?
> "James … yeah!" he replied, exasperated. "She's terrific."
> I don't know. I don't know. I'm nervous about this. I'm nervous.
> "Of course you're nervous, every groom is nervous."[77]

When nervous, Ellroy tended to exaggerate his Demon Dog schtick. At the reception afterwards Ellroy used the groom's speech to shock several people in attendance, including Mary's family. "He talked about pissing on car seats in parking lots," Penzler recalled. "The kind of thing that astonished, in a very bad way, his wife's family."[78] As Ellroy and Mary jetted off to St. Thomas and St.

Barts in the Caribbean for their honeymoon, Penzler and Sobel caught a flight back to New York.

"So, what do you think?" Sobel asked Penzler.

"Eighteen months," he replied.

It had not been a typical wedding.

Now married, Ellroy and Mary bought a house together at St. John's Place in New Canaan. It was the first property that Ellroy owned and, as Mary put it, "a huge turning point in his life."[79] Built in 1912, the house had six bedrooms and covered 4,000 square feet. It reminded Ellroy of the houses he used to break into in Hancock Park. If anything, the "turning point" Mary recognized in Ellroy may have come too soon, "Our home was too spacious and airy [...] My office was too bright. My yard was too big."[80] Ellroy did not want to return to the squalor of his old LA life, but he was missing the excitement that came with performing his "shtick of seduce and explain" to every attractive woman he met.[81]

"Mary wanted kids and I didn't," Ellroy recalls.[82] He suggested a compromise. Ellroy would try mentoring to see if being a father-figure suited him. Ellroy approached the organization Big Brothers Big Sisters of America to volunteer for mentoring. His criminal record meant that he failed their background check. At the time, Ellroy was friends with the author and attorney Andrew Vachss. With his eyepatch, love of big dogs, and severe expression Vachss had an intense demeanor to rival Ellroy's, but Ellroy "admired him greatly."[83] His legal practice represented children and youths exclusively and Vachss suggested that Ellroy try mentoring one of the youths in his charge. Vachss warned him in advance that, "this kid was absolutely without a conscience. His life had been such that he was an ambulatory sociopath."[84] Ellroy travelled "up the Saw Mill River Parkway" to visit the boy who was a product of a broken home.[85] They had a couple of meetings but Ellroy found "I just had no rapport with him."[86] The mentoring experiment had not been a success but Vachss remained grateful for Ellroy's efforts, "I give him full and proper respect: he did try. But nobody could have succeeded. I don't care: Dr Phil would have blown his brains out."[87]

To bring some company to their large, mostly empty house, Mary adopted a dog "He talked often about his love of Bull Terriers. I knew it would make him happy if we got one. I found Barko from a breeder through the AKC and had him shipped to LaGuardia. It was exciting picking him up at the airport. We were dog parents I guess you would say."[88] Mary presented Barko to Ellroy as a birthday gift on March 4, 1989. Barko was Ellroy's first dog since Minna. Ellroy and Mary liked to create dialogue for Barko:

"Barko, are you getting enough love?"

"No!"

As much as Ellroy and Mary doted on Barko, his presence was not enough to fill the void in their relationship. But for a while, the breakneck pace of Ellroy's work schedule took his mind off domestic issues.

Ellroy first visited France in 1988. He came at the invitation of Rivages editor François Guérif. Ellroy was, by this time, already acclaimed in France but the conditions that had made this possible had often come about through the work of other people. Guérif had read *Blood on the Moon* and:

> I was absolutely under shock, and I wanted to publish it. But I discovered that all the publishers in France had rejected his previous books and so his agent said, 'no, you can't buy *Blood on the Moon*. You have to buy the three—*Blood on the Moon, Because the Night, Suicide Hill*. Of course, I am an editor, but I did not own the publishing company and the owner of the publishing company did not want to publish Ellroy. He said, 'it's too much of a risk, he's unknown' and I said, 'Yes you must and if not, I'm going away.'[89]

After threatening to leave the company, Guérif secured a deal to publish the three Lloyd Hopkins novels. The next challenge would be to find a translator who could do justice to Ellroy's telegraphic prose. Guérif approached two translators who turned him down flat, remarking that the language was "too difficult" and one of them labeled Ellroy a fascist.[90] It was Freddy Michalski, the son of a Polish miner, who finally agreed to translate the novel, with astonishing results. Describing Ellroy's prose as "Dry tongue, extraordinarily rhythmic, dissociated, burst, in the syntax which resembles the staccato of a machine gun," Michalski would go on to win a Trophée 813 for his translation of *White Jazz*.[91]

At first, the critical reaction to Ellroy was ambivalent. Guérif recalls that the critics "did not know what to think. They did not know if Ellroy was an extreme-right guy. They were troubled." Guérif turned to his friend Jean-Paul Manchette. Manchette was "the greatest writer of Roman Noir and he was a critic, and he was a very leftist guy. And I told him on the phone that nobody wanted to talk about the book and someone even told me it's a fascist book."[92] Manchette read Ellroy's work and wrote an article in *Libération*, praising his skills as a writer and even declaring his politics "un peu marxiste."[93] Guérif recalls this as the turning point of Ellroy's reputation in France, "That piece was published at the beginning of July 1987, and Ellroy got big on that day. It was if Manchette was telling his followers to like James's work. He became very famous suddenly and he never stopped."[94]

Ellroy's brash, intense personality was a hit with the French public. He appeared at a Noir festival in Grenoble in October 1989. To ramp up publicity, all the authors invited to the festival travelled on Le Train Noir from Paris and arrived, amid much fanfare, in Grenoble after a five-hour trip. John Williams was on the train and recalls the only drinks being served were champagne, cognac, and coffee. Most of the authors were drunk by the time of arrival and chain-smoking Gauloises, but Ellroy quietly sipped coffee and ignored the drunken revelry. Whenever he toured Europe, the ubiquitous presence of alcohol could be a problem for Ellroy. Some authors did not take kindly to his abstemiousness. At a party held in Guérif's Paris apartment, the British author Derek Raymond tried to force a bottle of whiskey into Ellroy's hand. Ellroy politely declined at first, but Raymond was so persistent that a furious Ellroy forcibly pushed the bottle and Raymond away from him.

Ellroy appeared on the French culture show *Cinéma Cinémas* and declared, "I am obsessed with violence. I am obsessed with twisted sexuality. I am obsessed with jealousy, greed, overweening ambition. I am obsessed with obsession."[95] As it happens a new obsession was consuming Ellroy back in the US, its scope was bigger than anything he had handled before, and it would lead to another seismic reinvention of his writing style.

In May 1988, Ellroy attended the American Booksellers Convention in Anaheim. Some of the big books being promoted that year were the celebrity memoirs of entrepreneur Lee Iacocca, former child star Shirley Temple Black, and magician Orson Bean. But the only book to catch Ellroy's eye was a galley copy of a novel titled *Libra* by Don DeLillo. The novel was a speculative biography of Lee Harvey Oswald. Ellroy was gripped by the novel and immediately began testing DeLillo's narrative by comparing it to the non-fiction books that had been written on the Kennedy assassination. Ellroy held no firm opinions on the assassination up until that point. As it had happened on the same day his father was discharged from hospital, Ellroy had always conflated Kennedy's death with personal, rather than political events.

He surmised that DeLillo had deftly avoided the more fanciful conspiracy theories and cherry-picked the more intriguing unanswered questions of the assassination. Ellroy resolved that he could develop this structure into "a physically larger, physically broader book that would track all the harbingers of the assassination from five years earlier. I mean DeLillo just lobbed me that one."[96] It was the beginning of a confluence of events which not only inspired Ellroy to write the novel *American Tabloid*, but also instigated a complete departure in his literary career.

One Sunday evening, Ellroy visited a video rental store to find a film to watch with Mary. Ellroy selected the BBC documentary *Say Goodbye to the President: Marilyn and the Kennedys*. Once he got the tape home and put it in the VCR player, Ellroy knew he had found a revisionist style that he wanted to emulate. The documentary mixes fact and speculation freely and traces the final days of Marilyn Monroe and her links to the Kennedy brothers—John and Robert. Several claims made in the film are controversial—it is implied that Marilyn's mental and physical decline was exacerbated by her toxic relationship with the Kennedys, especially her brief affair with John. Then it is suggested that Robert Kennedy was given time to leave LA before news of Monroe's death was announced to the media. Ellroy did not so much care about the veracity of the claims, he was more impressed by the narrative verisimilitude created by the interviews conducted by the urbane Irish author Anthony Summers. Summers interviewed, among others, private detectives John Danoff and Fred Otash who had wiretapped Marilyn's meetings with John Kennedy at Peter Lawford's house in Santa Monica.

Ellroy recognized Fred Otash as the man Jimmy Harris had introduced him to in LA. He had learned more about Otash's sordid reputation since then and was using him as the model of "Trashcan" Jack Vincennes in *LA Confidential*, the manuscript he was currently working on. Otash had served in the LAPD from 1945 to 1955. He left the force as he was distrusted by Chief Parker, who shuffled him from division to division to make him as uncomfortable in the department as possible. Otash served as Head of Security at the Hollywood Ranch Market. He worked as lead investigator for *Confidential* magazine, the tabloid magazine which specialized in celebrity scandals. After losing his PI license over his involvement in a horse doping scam, he worked as a freelance troubleshooter for organized crime figures. Ellroy decided he needed to meet Otash and discuss, at length, his relationship with the LAPD, *Confidential* magazine, and his role in wiretapping the Kennedys. He also took a closer look at the work of Anthony Summers. He admired Summers' biography *Goddess: The Secret Lives of Marilyn Monroe* for its portrayal of post-war Hollywood, but he found many of Summers' claims to be fanciful and distrusted his tendency, as a non-fiction writer, to gravitate towards conspiracy theories.

While he was conducting research on the political history of the US, Ellroy was deep into the drafting of *LA Confidential*. Working from an outline of around 250 pages, with a cast of over eighty characters moving between "eight inextricably linked plotlines," Ellroy submitted a manuscript that was over 800 pages long. Ellroy considered the novel dramatically inviolate, but once again his authorial vision was about to collide with the economic realities of publishing. Sobel telephoned Nancy Nieman, a senior editor at Warner Books, and informed her that the manuscript was ready for submission. But when Sobel told her the length of the manuscript, she was unswerving in her view that it would have to be drastically shortened, by up to a quarter, for mass market publication.

This presented a dilemma for Ellroy. It was not just ego that prevented him from wanting to make cuts. At the heart of the narrative are three cops—Ed Exley, Bud White, and Jack Vincennes. Sobel recognized that you couldn't just "take out one of the cops."[97] Ellroy was even more uncompromising. He was convinced that the novel only worked by adhering to the outline, scene by scene, that he had written, and any deviation would render the narrative incoherent.

According to Sobel, the solution occurred serendipitously:

> I had the manuscript on the desk in front of me, and as a joke I said to
> James, 'Well, maybe we could cut out a few small words.' I meant it entirely
> as a joke. But I started going through a manuscript page and cut out about
> a dozen words on the page. James said, 'Give me that.' I gave him the page.
> And he just kept cutting. He was cutting and cutting and cutting. When he
> was done with the page, it looked like a redacted piece from the CIA. I said,
> 'James, how would they be able to read this?' He said, 'Let me read you the
> page.' It was terrific. He said, 'I know what I have to do.' He took the whole
> manuscript back and cut hundreds of pages from the book and developed
> the style. That editor never knew what we had to do, but she forced him
> into creating this special Ellroy style, which his reputation as a stylist is
> really based on. It came from her, sight unseen, saying 'Cut 25 percent of
> the book.' He wound up cutting enough without cutting a single scene from
> that book.[98]

The discovery and development of a style stripping the text of adverbs,
adjectives, and conjunctions would prove fortuitous for Ellroy. Not only was
LA Confidential another tremendous critical success, but he could also now
write directly in this style, experimenting with its sparseness and elasticity
from book to book.

LA Confidential was published in June 1990. In October of that year, a book
was published which featured the most scathing criticism of Ellroy that had
ever been put in print. Mike Davis's *City of Quartz: Excavating the Future in
Los Angeles* is both a history of LA and a commentary on its contemporary
identity. Davis once worked as a trucker and his knowledge of the topography
of the city was impressive, although his opinion of it is far from flattering.
He saves his true ire for the work of Ellroy. Davis describes Ellroy's work as
"an almost unendurable wordstorm of perversity and gore" and argues it is
defending or reflecting "the actual moral texture of the Reagan–Bush era."[99]
Even one of Davis's footnotes is disparaging of the author, noting that Ellroy's
"potboilers" are written "3,000 miles away" from LA in a "basement office in
Eastchester."[100] He fails to mention that Ellroy was born and raised in LA.

Davis's criticism came at a time when Ellroy's critical reputation was ascending, and it did nothing to halt that trend. Although his tone was sneering, there was nothing written about Ellroy in *City in Quartz* that was beyond the pale. That would come three years later when Davis was being interviewed by Marcos Frommer for the *Chicago Review of Books*:

> Now let me tell you who I can't stand, and to top the list I would put that neo-Nazi in American writing who is James Ellroy … And to begin with he's not a good writer. He's a kind of methamphetamine caricature of Raymond Chandler … Each of his books is practically a Mein Kampf, it's anti-communistic, it's anti-Mexican, and it's racist.[101]

Although it is doubtful Ellroy considered being called "anti-communistic" as much of an insult, he did admit that some of Davis's other charges "bugged me in the moment."[102] He was not about to engage in a literary feud with Davis. However, when asked about his character's frequent use of racial epithets he would respond that the racism of his protagonists "was a casual attribute, not a defining characteristic."[103] The issue of race was always secondary to the historical narratives, although contrary to how Davis characterized him Ellroy described his work as "the story of bad white men."[104] He just wasn't about to judge characters from another era based on contemporary values and reduce his text to a moralistic rant. Ironically, Ellroy's political views were never that far from Davis's, especially about LA which Ellroy had never tried to romanticize. Davis described himself as being on the revolutionary left. Ellroy was undoubtedly conservative, but much of his readership held left-wing views and he admitted "I may have a little bit of a Marxist social sense and distrust of authority, but in the end, I'd rather err on its side than on the side of chaos."[105]

Ellroy had provided a robust defense of his work. Davis's attempts to label him as a racist did not stick.

With the help of Alan Marks, Ellroy was able to obtain Fred Otash's phone number. Otash was more than happy to talk to Ellroy. He flew to Miami to visit Otash at his apartment at 1111 Biscayne Blvd, the Jockey Club. Even before his first face to face meeting with Otash, Ellroy already had an idea about how he would use the celebrity PI. Otash would be the lead character in his book on the Kennedy assassination. In Ellroy's alternative history, Otash would be the man who pulled the trigger on John F. Kennedy.

As a living symbol of a time long past, Otash did not disappoint. Olive-skinned, with a penchant for velour suits, Otash suffered from emphysema and high blood pressure, but his eyes still lit up as he happily reminisced to Ellroy about the sexual peccadilloes of Hollywood stars. They chatted away on Otash's large balcony overlooking Biscayne Bay. Otash told Ellroy that Robert Kennedy did not have an affair with Marilyn Monroe, but John Kennedy did. Otash recorded a series of Kennedy and Marilyn's trysts which led him to discover that Kennedy was strictly a "two-minute man" in the bedroom. Ellroy regarded all Otash's stories with a degree of healthy skepticism. He inadvertently offended Otash when he asked, as his parents were from Lebanon, whether he was a Muslim. Otash snapped back, "You motherfucker, my people were Christian."[106]

Ellroy offered to pay Otash $30,000 for him to be the lead character in his Kennedy assassination novel. One of the stipulations was, to maintain narrative credibility, Otash did not publicly contradict anything that happened in the novel. Otash agreed and Ellroy was already feeding him cash just to maintain their conversations. He had learned from Jimmy Harris that you pay people for their time. But as soon as he was on the plane back to Connecticut, Ellroy began to have doubts. It was partly his personal reaction to Otash. Ellroy loved discussing LA lore and often used racial and sexual humor for shock effect, but there was something about Otash's callous attitude to all the lives he had destroyed that irked the sterner side to Ellroy's character. While the deal with Otash was still on the table, Ellroy began formulating a new lead character as backup—Pete Bondurant. Bondurant is a former US marine, LA Sheriff's deputy turned enforcer for Howard Hughes. Ellroy was drafting an extensive outline to the novel in which Bondurant featured prominently, and the more he wrote about him the more he preferred the character to Otash.

In the Fall of 1990, Ellroy informed Mary that the marriage was over, and he walked out of the family home. As he put it, "I wanted out, so I got out."[107] The end of the marriage had been foreseen by many, not least the couple themselves. They had enjoyed a whirlwind romance and a couple of happy, active years together, as Mary recalls:

> We traveled on book tours to London, Paris, Frankfurt, and Geneva. We had a great time on the tours, and I loved the people involved in his business. It became apparent though, that as fun and exciting as those travels were, he and I as a couple were missing something. The fun and excitement of the tours put the reality of our incompatibility on the back burner. We began to realize we were two nice people trying to find things in common and over time it became apparent that we didn't have much.[108]

They agreed to a speedy and amicable divorce, which Ellroy did not contest. Ellroy returned to his Eastchester basement apartment, "I had to be back in that dark hole."[109] Although he tried to make the divorce as painless as possible for Mary, Ellroy had not been faithful during their marriage. A brief fling with a screenwriter named Shelley, who he had met at Vagabond bookstore during the *LA Confidential* tour had ended messily. Shelley later sued Ellroy in a dispute over a two-picture option the two of them had struck with the director Walter Hill. The matter was settled out of court.

As his marriage would soon be legally over, Ellroy was free to pursue other women and one disastrous affair would not deter him. In fact, before separating from Mary, Ellroy had already met the woman who would become his new obsession, soulmate, and bride.

Her name was Helen Knode.

7

Enter the Borzoi
(1990–1993)

In October 1990, Ellroy was invited to LA to do an interview for *Rolling Stone*. His interviewer was the author Mikal Gilmore. Mikal was the brother of the convicted murderer Gary Gilmore, the subject of Norman Mailer's *The Executioner's Song*. Mikal met Ellroy in the Pacific Dining Car. He brought along an ex-girlfriend of his, Helen Knode, who was at that time a journalist for the *LA Weekly*. Ellroy was jetlagged, Helen was recovering from dental surgery, but even if they both felt fuzzy headed there was no doubt that a genuine attraction developed. Helen had not read his novels and did not know, at first, who Ellroy was. He tried to impress her with a string of one-liners which "all fell flat."[1] Helen described herself as a "Girl-Bolshevik" at the time, and Ellroy may have verbally softened some of his right-wing views so she wouldn't be put off by him.[2] In the interview, Ellroy accuses Ronald Reagan of "sleepwalking through his presidency," which is in stark contrast to his usual glowing assessment of Reagan.[3]

Ellroy had not yet separated from Mary at this point, but his strong attraction to Helen would give him the impetus to walk out on what he and his wife knew was a failing marriage. In subsequent interviews, Ellroy would place his first meeting with Helen as occurring after he and Mary separated, to spare Mary's feelings.

Ellroy called Gilmore and asked him for more details about Helen. She had a fascinating background which tantalized Ellroy. Born in Calgary, her family had worked in the oil business for four generations. Her father's alcoholism and mismanagement of the family wealth had broken up his marriage to Helen's mother. Helen developed a peripatetic existence as a young woman. She studied at the University of Kansas and then did an MA at Cornell. She then moved to Europe where, by her own admission, she was something of "a wild one" traveling and partying in London, Paris, and Berlin. Her journalistic career started as a film reviewer for the *Cornell Daily Sun*, then the New York based *East Village Eye*, before she moved to LA. Having grown tired of reviewing films, Knode was now writing her "Weird Sister" column for the *LA Weekly*, which gave her the scope to cover a wide range of subjects. Ellroy and Helen began corresponding, but there was a tacit understanding between the two of them that the relationship would not become intimate until his marriage to Mary was over.

In March 1991, Gilmore called Ellroy to request another interview. Ellroy accepted on the condition, as he had been obsessing about Helen, that it took place in LA. Gilmore told him that the magazine wouldn't cover the costs of another flight. Ellroy paid for the flight himself. The interview eventually ran in *Rolling Stone*'s sister publication *Men's Journal*. Since their last meeting Helen had read three of Ellroy's novels that he had mailed to her. She had been entranced by *The Black Dahlia*, "I was stunned and hit by how sympathetic he was to her—Elizabeth Short. He didn't blame her for being a tart, for being a nomad, all that kind of stuff, rolling around LA. And you'd have plenty who'd think, well of course she's gonna end up like that [murdered], maybe not quite so grotesquely."[4] She wanted to write a piece on the Dahlia for the *LA Weekly* and asked Ellroy to give her a tour of the crime sites. "There was an intellectual spark," she said.[5] For Ellroy there was so much more. He had fallen in love with Helen and, now separated from Mary, he was free to take the relationship forward at his usual warp speed.

Ellroy proposed to Helen at the Mondrian Hotel on Sunset Boulevard. Ellroy liked to stay there when he visited his home city and luxuriated in its Hollywood opulence "it's a weakness of mine." He had booked them a suite and, even though he was facing hefty alimony payments, Ellroy was spending cash at an uncontrollable rate. He over-tipped all the hotel staff, who knew Ellroy as a regular and had taken to calling him "El Jefe." Knode laughed at Ellroy's "gauche white-trash glee" attitude to the hotel's first-class service.[6] Here was the buffoon she had first met in the Pacific Dining Car who was now pulling out all the stops to impress her with boyish enthusiasm. She accepted his proposal. They rented a house in Laurel Canyon where they lived while planning their wedding. Ellroy's divorce from Mary was finalized in September. He married Helen the following month on October 4, 1991.

Ellroy's wedding to Helen was so diametrically opposite to the Catholic ceremony of his previous marriage, that anyone who attended both weddings might be forgiven for wondering if this was the same groom. The wedding took place at the venue Ellroy and Helen had first met—the Pacific Dining Car. Ellroy wore a kilt and black tie. Helen wore a "pink-peach '40s vintage dress," possibly as a reference to her favorite Ellroy heroine Kay Lake, who at her wedding to Bucky Bleichert wore "a pink dress to satirize her lack of virginity."[7] Ellroy had insisted on a Christian pastor to conduct the ceremony. Helen agreed on the condition that it was a woman. The pastor did not like Ellroy and warned Helen the marriage would not last. Their jointly written vows were a hybrid of Christian and New Age values.

Figure 8 *Ellroy and Helen on their wedding day, October 4, 1991, at the Pacific Dining Car. Photo: Courtesy of Helen Knode.*

Ellroy wanted Helen to move with him back to Connecticut. Helen was reluctant. Her career was in LA. Ellroy insisted and they rented a house at Ponus Ridge in New Canaan. It was only a ten-minute drive, and very similar in size and design, from the house he had bought with Mary. Ellroy liked the arrangement as he could still see Barko on the weekends. Ellroy candidly admitted that, as a husband, he was not easy to live with. He "refused to cook," nor could he "read credit-card bills or balance checkbooks," and never cleaned up after himself, treating the house as his "personal trough."[8] Seeing Barko was one of the more pleasurable aspects of living in the house for Helen. Relations between Ellroy, Helen, and Mary were all very amicable, "I was very fond of Helen Knode to whom, with James, I entrusted Barko-care while traveling after our divorce," Mary recalled.[9]

Ellroy received a call one day from Nat Sobel. Sobel had intriguing news— Sonny Mehta wanted to meet him. Ellroy was excited. It wasn't specified what the meeting would be about, but Ellroy could guess—Mehta was the editor-in-chief at Knopf, a publisher Ellroy had always longed to write for.

Born Ajai Singh Mehta in New Delhi in 1942, the son of a diplomat, Mehta had read History and English Literature at St. Catherine's College, Cambridge where he had worked as an editor at *Granta* magazine. It was the start of a spectacular career in publishing. Mehta established his reputation as an editor of high-quality literary and genre works at Granada publishing, Pan Books, and at Paladin, the latter of which he co-founded. He moved to New York, and to Knopf, in 1987, becoming its third editor-in-chief. By the early 90s, Mehta was one of the biggest names in New York publishing, an industry which, in the pre-internet age, was thriving. The restaurants of Fifth Avenue were clogged with agents, editors, and authors looking to make deals.

Ellroy met Mehta for lunch at the Four Seasons in Manhattan. It was the venue where many of the biggest literary deals were informally brokered. Excited, but also nervous that he might somehow blow his chance with Mehta, Ellroy put on his smartest suit and tie and did his best to charm the legendary editor. Mehta was very different to Ellroy in terms of personality. Urbane and enigmatic, he chain-smoked, barely touched his food, and drank several glasses of wine, topped off with a scotch with no discernible effect on his sobriety.

Ellroy could be judgmental when people drank alcohol in his company. He didn't like it if a person had two or three drinks, but around Mehta he kept this opinion to himself.

Mehta said very little and Ellroy felt entranced by his "fixed stare" which, like a skittish date, made Ellroy talk too much. A pivotal moment came halfway through the meeting. Ellroy had wolfed down his meal whereas Mehta's hamburger patty lay untouched on his plate. By now, Ellroy had developed his own fixed stare on the hamburger which was distracting him from the conversation.

"James," Mehta said. "Do you want to eat that hamburger patty?"

"Yes," Ellroy replied, taking the hamburger off Mehta's plate to their mutual amusement.

Now that they had developed a rapport, Ellroy asked Mehta why he had requested the meeting. Mehta informed Ellroy he had read *The Black Dahlia* and *The Big Nowhere* and thought that he was an extraordinarily talented author. Would Ellroy be interested in writing for Knopf?

Ellroy was overjoyed, but his reputation was ascending so quickly at the time that Knopf was not the only publisher interested in acquiring him. A literary auction took place at Nat Sobel's brownstone home on East 19th Street. The final bids were made by Avon and Knopf. Both publishing houses were offering six-figure sums, but Avon's offer was slightly higher. However, the money was less important to Ellroy than the status of becoming a Knopf author. He instructed Sobel to accept Knopf's offer. "By the time the discussion about making an offer to keep James with Avon came to be, it was a long-shot at best," John Douglas recalled.[10] "James was much attracted to the Knopf operation and was very impressed with the heavy-weight genre writers who were in multi-volume commitments."[11]

It had been just over ten years since Ellroy moved to the East Coast upon the publication of his first novel, and after several humbling setbacks he was now in the middle of an incredibly hot streak. Ellroy's concluding novel of the LA Quartet, *White Jazz*, was scheduled for publication with Warner Books, but now that he had signed Ellroy, Sonny Mehta made enquiries about acquiring the novel for Knopf. Ellroy was very grateful to Larry Kirshbaum for allowing Knopf to buy the novel and bringing Ellroy's journey with the revered publisher forward. "Ellroy left in part because Otto was not involved," Kirshbaum recalls, adding that losing Penzler was the greatest mistake of his career, "and we let him out of his *White Jazz* obligation because he made it very clear in a personal appeal to me that he wanted to pursue a more literary path with Sonny Mehta."[12] Ellroy did his homework prior to the move. Andrew Vachss had been a Knopf author since 1987, and Ellroy approached him with "a long list of questions about the operation."[13]

However, no sooner had Knopf acquired the novel than Mehta expressed doubts over the lean prose style. Ellroy started writing *White Jazz* in a "normally discursive style" but soon decided it "felt flabby" and began cutting words from the text with more ruthlessness than he had with *LA Confidential*, creating a first-person narrative of his lead protagonist Dave "the Enforcer" Klein which reads like a fever dream, as Klein's multiple roles of policeman, mob hitman, slum landlord, and overprotective sibling to his attractive sister begin to fall apart. The result was a harsh, stripped-down tone that worried Ellroy's new editor-in-chief. Mehta called Ellroy over to his apartment one Saturday morning and said, "It's just too inaccessible. Will you put some words back?" Ellroy agreed once "Mehta showed him passages where additional 'ands' and 'buts' would fatten up the prose."[14] He spent twenty days reworking the manuscript at a rate of forty pages a day. Once he was finished, he immediately returned to the *American Tabloid* outline.

The extensive reworking of *White Jazz* did not stop Ellroy's debut novel at Knopf from being a minor commercial disappointment. The reviews were strong. Todd Grimson wrote, "Ellroy has truly crossed over beyond the 'crime novel.' *White Jazz* is avant-garde."[15] But even admiring critics were apprehensive about the prose style, "I think I'd have sold 75,000 copies in hard cover with all that publicity if every reviewer hadn't said, 'Wow, this book is tough.'"[16] The novel was published in September 1992, and Ellroy found himself being bumped from television shows due to the wall-to-wall coverage of the presidential election.

White Jazz is the shortest novel of the LA Quartet, which adds to its lightning strike power as the reader is inexorably drawn to its hyper-violent conclusion and the unforgettable final line, "Love me fierce in danger." As Helen Knode recalls, "*White Jazz* was in manuscript some months into my acquaintance with James. I was very struck and moved by that sentence, as I'm struck by many, many of James's final sentences—and more, struck by how he dramatizes tenderness and longing for women in all his books."[17] A photo exists of Helen, presumably taken by Ellroy, looking striking in a dark coat and staring hypnotically at the camera. The back of the photo is inscribed with a short poem by Ellroy:

> Love me fierce and ferociously
> in danger, in despair, densely, with dedication
> —in death
> Love me

At Knopf, Ellroy would meet the graphic designer who would establish the distinctive pulp-art designs that had been lacking in his earlier novels. Ellroy first met Chip Kidd in Sonny Mehta's office. Still in his twenties, Kidd had established himself as the pre-eminent book cover designer of his generation with his artwork for Michael Crichton's novel *Jurassic Park*. Ellroy and Kidd

Figure 9 *A striking photo of Helen Knode from the 1980s. Although the photo was taken before she met Ellroy, he would later inscribe it with the poem "Love me fierce in danger." Photo: Courtesy of Helen Knode. Credit: Nicola Atkinson-Griffith*

became good friends. Kidd was impressed with Ellroy's knowledge of DC Comics. Ellroy professed to be a fan of the relatively obscure character Snapper Carr, which surprised Kidd who had not expected Ellroy to be a comics fan. In terms of designing the cover of *White Jazz* the process was simple, "Here's the manuscript, you read it and get your own ideas. I read it, got an idea of the milieu."[18] For the cover he found a photograph of a bullet-riddled door of an LAPD squad car, "The image is sort of misleading. That door was used for target practice by the LAPD. You're meant to think it's a shootout."[19]

It wasn't just Mehta and Kidd who would become good friends with Ellroy. In the coming years at Knopf, Ellroy would form friendships with editors such as Jason Arthur, Edward Kastenmeier, Andrew Weber, and the publicity director Paul Bogaards. He would prize these relationships above all other friendships and was generous in sending expensive thank you gifts (usually bottles of Dom Perignon or Johnnie Walker) to every one of them whenever one of his books reached publication. Ellroy also liked to reach out to authors who joined the Knopf family.

Bret Easton Ellis's novel *American Psycho* had been scheduled for publication in March 1991 by Simon & Schuster. The publisher withdrew, citing "aesthetic differences" most likely stemming from the novel's extreme violence. *American Psycho* was published by the Knopf imprint Vintage later that year. Ellroy wrote to Ellis, expressing his support for the novel. Ellis wrote back to Ellroy in October, 1992, apologizing for the delay which he put down to complications surrounding his father's sudden death, which entailed "dealing with sleazeball attorneys and demented trustee's [sic] and my father's gold-digging 24 year-old girlfriend and whether my father was a suicide or not, an overdose of insulin, questions, major trouble with the IRS."[20] If Ellroy had been fishing for compliments from Ellis, then he would not be disappointed. Ellis described *Killer on the Road* as "the best novel about a serial killer that I have ever read. Bloodcurdling. And the sequence when the two killers first meet and find their common ground in that motel room ranks among the best you have ever written."[21] Ellis ended the letter on a generous note, "Though I hate admitting this to other writers: I'm a big fan."[22]

Donna Tartt's debut novel *The Secret History* had sparked a bidding war between publishers before being acquired by Knopf and becoming a bestseller, an unprecedented feat for an author still only in her twenties. When Ellroy met Tartt he found her to be "full of herself."[23] He and Helen were invited to a birthday party thrown for her in New York but left early as it was "cacophonously noisy."[24] Prior to these meetings, Ellroy and Tartt had corresponded briefly. Tartt wrote Ellroy a postcard in which she was generous about his writing, "I am a tremendous fan of yours, read (and recommend) your novels with relish."[25] Her note also had a flavor of Southern coquettishness, "Well, I think you're just swell. Ain't nobody around who writes like you do."[26]

As his reputation as an author continued to grow, Ellroy was meeting more prestigious figures in the literary community. Ellroy was introduced to William Styron by Styron's son-in-law, the actor Darrell Larson. Ellroy had been friends with Larson for several years. Larson vividly recalls the first time Ellroy approached him, at a book event, and declared dramatically, "They put a bag on your head. They dumped your body at a garbage dump."[27] Ellroy was referring to Larson's character in the film *Mike's Murder*. Despite being critically acclaimed and starring Debra Winger in the leading role, *Mike's Murder* had only secured a very limited theatrical release, but Ellroy had managed to see the film in the theater and admired it. At Larson's request, Ellroy would give readings of his work at the MET Theatre in East Hollywood. Ellroy met Styron at his estate in Roxbury, Connecticut. Ellroy described the meeting as "flat as a pancake" as Styron was silent and withdrawn, suffering from the depression that plagued him in later life.[28] Ellroy was ready to give up on the conversation when he mentioned offhand that he was a dog-lover and suddenly Styron "perked up."[29] Styron owned several therapy dogs to treat his depression, and Ellroy was pleased that Styron felt that dogs should sleep up on the bed with their owner, rather than be kept in another room at night. A view Ellroy shared.

Fred Otash died on October 5, 1992, "He was having a heart attack and called a cab rather than an ambulance," Ellroy recalled mordantly.[30] The cab got stuck in traffic and by the time it reached Cedars Sinai, Otash was dead. Earlier that year, Otash had flown from Paris to LA (he lived part of the year in Cannes). His health was worsening and Otash requested that Ellroy upgrade his ticket to

Business Class so he could sit apart from the smokers. When he arrived in LA, Ellroy told him the deal was off. He had grown wary of Otash's appearances on tabloid-style TV shows which were gaining popularity at the time. Ellroy thought Otash was too indiscreet to maintain the suggestion that his character in the novel could have committed all the acts attributed to him, "I didn't trust him not to betray me on this."[31] Ellroy paid Otash some more money just to cut him loose.

Ellroy spoke to Otash on the phone a few days before he died. They had haggled over Ellroy gaining access to Otash's FBI file. Sometime later, Ellroy did obtain a copy of Otash's FBI file. It contained nothing more than a brief summation of his career and a copy of *Confidential* magazine, "He was yesterday's man."[32] Ironically, Otash's death was the only factor that might have revived Ellroy's interest in him, as he could now use him without fear of contradiction or legal action. In time, he would return to Otash as a character repeatedly. But for his immediate plans, Ellroy had Pete Bondurant and a whole host of fictional and real-life characters to work with in the novel he was writing.

Ellroy submitted an extensive outline for *American Tabloid* to Mehta. In it, he had four main viewpoint characters—Robert F. Kennedy, FBI agent Ward Littell, Lenny Sands (a gay entertainer with Mob ties), and a final viewpoint character to be revealed in the epilogue, the FBI agent and Mafia fixer Kemper Boyd. Ellroy devoted an entire section to the death of Marilyn Monroe titled "Goddess," in reference to the Anthony Summers biography, in which Lenny Sands murders Monroe before she can compromise the Kennedy brothers. After reading the outline, Mehta called Ellroy into his office. He showed him a recently published novel, *The Immortals* by Michael Korda, which fictionalized Monroe's overdose as being staged to protect the Kennedys. Mehta told him, "You can't write something as similar to this cheesy book here. Go back and rethink it."

Ellroy skimmed through *The Immortals* and dubbed it "one of the worst novels I've ever read."[33] He knew that Mehta's advice was sound and began to rewrite the outline from scratch. He took out the Monroe murder plot and reduced Lenny Sands and Robert Kennedy to supporting characters. He made Pete Bondurant a viewpoint character which proved to be a sage choice, as it gave the novel authenticity as a secret history of the period seen from the perspective of Underworld characters.

Critical interest in Ellroy's work, particularly in Europe, was on the rise. Reinhard Jud and Wolfgang Lehner were two young aspiring filmmakers from Vienna. Jud had begun reading Ellroy's novels a few years earlier and thought he would be a good subject for a documentary. They managed to secure a meeting with Ellroy in Rome in 1991. "The meeting was five minutes at most, but a connection was made," recalls Lehner.[34] Back in the US, Ellroy telephoned Jud and Lehner and informed them that a French production company was also interested in making a film about him and he would cooperate with whoever secured the funding first.

Shortly thereafter, Jud and Lehner secured funding and filming could begin. They shot some footage of Ellroy writing and talking to Barko in his Eastchester office. Most of the filming was in LA. Ellroy was touring *White Jazz* and he was filmed giving typically exuberant readings. Lehner noticed during one bookstore reading that "the women couldn't take their eyes off him."[35] Ellroy was filmed at various iconic locations in LA. Jud and Lehner shared credit on the script. Jud was the director and Lehner was his cinematographer. "We read his books and got the fever," Jud recalls.[36] It was that fever, the energy in Ellroy's prose, that took the two men through the production, as they were shooting fast and on a low budget. They were able to use some gruesome crime scene photographs in their footage, including one of the murder scene of "the Two Tonys," an event Ellroy had fictionalized in *White Jazz*.

James Ellroy: Demon Dog of American Crime Fiction was screened at the AFI in Washington DC in June of 1993. Ellroy's friend James Grady had some experience with the AFI and knew that their screenings usually attracted only small audiences. For Ellroy to get a good turnout for his film, Grady asked his wife Bonnie, who at the time was working for Senator Howard Metzenbaum, to bring along some of her colleagues from Capitol Hill. A dozen or so respectable looking DC civil servants filed into the screening, "Five minutes into the film we hear this uproarious laughter," Grady recalls.[37] "Everyone turns their heads thinking there is a lunatic in the audience, and it's Ellroy laughing at his own schtick onscreen."[38] When the film was finished, Grady witnessed most of the Senate staff hurriedly making their way towards the exit, hoping to avoid Ellroy. Ellroy himself was in a buoyant mood, leaving the screening to meet Helen who had flown into DC to see him.

In 1992, Ellroy was interviewed by Paul Scanlon for *GQ* magazine. At the time, Ellroy was fond of Reyn Spooner Hawaiian shirts. Scanlon suggested to Ellroy that he should write a fashion piece for the magazine on his love for this colorful attire. Ellroy's article "Prints Valiant" appeared in the June 1993 edition of *GQ*. It was the start of a long and productive relationship with the magazine. Ellroy subsequently met Art Cooper, *GQ's* editor-in-chief, at the Four Seasons. "The first word James uttered was 'Woof!'—and thus did the Demon Dog of American Literature enter my life and *GQ's*."[39] Ellroy discussed with Cooper his potential role at the magazine. Ellroy's pitch was to write investigative journalism on major crimes and celebrity scandals in a prose style that sometimes aped the salacious tone of *Hush Hush* magazine. Ellroy may have had reservations for taking on such a demanding role, requiring extensive travel, when he was already drafting an epic historical novel. Helen told him repeatedly that he was working too hard, but Cooper was offering him free rein to choose his subjects and the promise of handsome commissions. A recurring trait of Ellroy's personal and professional life was that he just couldn't say no.

Ellroy wrote an article for *GQ* titled "Out of the Past" which was structured as a short biography of "the World's Greatest Accordionist" Dick Contino, Ellroy's childhood memories of Contino, and later attempts to track him down. Contino was a singer and a major star of the late 1940s. His onstage charisma with an accordion had the same sexual intensity to teenage girls as Elvis Presley's gyrating hips. Contino's career fell apart when he was drafted for the Korean War and, in a panic, he fled from pre-induction barracks at Fort Ord. He was subsequently sentenced to six months imprisonment, which he served at McNeil Island Correctional Center in Puget Sound.

Ellroy wanted to meet Contino but wasn't even sure if he was still alive. He hired Alan Marks to compile a factsheet on Contino, but all information on the entertainer petered out in 1989. As Marks was unable to find an obituary for Contino, he assured Ellroy that he probably was still alive. Eventually, Marks discovered that Contino was living and still occasionally performing in Las Vegas. Ellroy and Contino spoke on the phone. As Contino reminisced about his showbiz career it initiated a flood of memories in Ellroy of his childhood growing up in LA. Now that the LA Quartet was complete, Ellroy was "suffering some separation pangs from Los Angeles" and decided that Contino should be the hero of a narrative which would be a mystery structured around the LA production of Contino's 1958 comeback vehicle, the grade-Z film *Daddy-O*.[40] Ellroy flew to Vegas to meet Contino and make the deal. He would pay Contino money for permission to use him as a character on the condition that he didn't publicly contradict any of the events in the story. It would barely have mattered if he did as "Dick Contino's Blues," which was first published in the 1993 Winter issue of *Granta* was fairly preposterous and written in an outrageously comic style "entirely in keeping with Contino's personality."[41]

"Dick Contino's Blues" was deemed too comic for Knopf. Therefore, it was reprinted in the anthology *Hollywood Nocturnes*, which was published by Otto Penzler Books, one of many publishing businesses launched by Penzler. *Hollywood Nocturnes* featured short stories such as "Dial Axminster 6-400" which Ellroy had written for his friend Richard Layman, who had briefly revived *Black Mask* magazine in 1985. He could now cannibalize the material he wrote for *GQ* and other publications to appear in anthologies to be published between novels, thus greatly enhancing his income. Ellroy toured the book, often appearing onstage with Contino. Ellroy read excerpts from the text while Contino would perform his signature hit "Lady of Spain."

The book attracted the attention of Hollywood. The actor Tony Denison and director Jeff Stein optioned "Dick Contino's Blues" and began adapting it into a screenplay, with the help of screenwriter Darrell Fetty. Ellroy became good friends with Denison, Stein, and Fetty and was amazed by the quality of their screenplay, which remains his favorite adaptation to date. Ellroy allowed them to keep renewing the option for free in the hope that they could get "Dick Contino's Blues" made for either cinema or television. He wrote a supportive letter to Stein:

Your screenplay adaptation of *Dick Contino's Blues* is without question one of the best screenplays I have ever read and easily the finest adaptation of one of my own works. You caught it all; the horror, the pathos, the buffoonery and basic lost quality of showbiz bottomfeeders lives. LA in the late 50s, the meeting ground of kitsch culture and high truth and most of all the truth of Dick Contino's noble, pathetic, stupid, brave life. I will probably never see my LA Quartet novels successfully captured in this form, but you have nailed *DCB*, an alternative picaresque remodelling of the era with astonishing clarity.[42]

Ellroy worked non-stop on a variety of projects and big deals. He was deep into the drafting of *American Tabloid* and another, more personal, obsession was about to be reawakened in the author which would evolve into an all-consuming book project between novels. Aside from the massive work it would entail, it also required Ellroy to confront, without the use of a fictional screen, the most traumatizing event in his life—the murder of Jean Ellroy.

8

On the Trail of Swarthy Man (1993–1995)

On Christmas Day, 1993, Helen and Ellroy exchanged gifts. Ellroy was intrigued when Helen handed him his wrapped, rectangular gift with "trepidation" and said, "I hope you won't be upset."[1] The gift was a framed photograph of Ellroy at ten years old. It was taken from the *LA Times* article on his mother's murder. Helen had put a great deal of time and effort into acquiring the photo. Ellroy wasn't upset. The image instantly unleashed a cascade of memories, and he was letting himself "spin/fall with it."[2] And with memory would come opportunity, but at a cost.

The following month Ellroy was contacted by the reporter Frank Girardot. Girardot was writing a piece for the *San Gabriel Valley Tribune* about the LA County Sheriff's Unsolved Unit. The article would focus on five unsolved murders, one of which was the murder of Jean Ellroy. Girardot and Ellroy became friendly and Ellroy visited him at his LA home to watch a boxing match with some of Girardot's colleagues. Girardot recalls they ordered pizza and, while most of the men present simply ordered pepperoni and cheese and tomato, Ellroy specifically requested a variety of toppings which led to some of the other guests trying to contain their amusement.[3]

Girardot informed Ellroy that he planned to view his mother's homicide file. Ellroy's immediate reaction was a desire to see the file himself. He called Paul Scanlon and asked whether *GQ* would run a piece about him viewing his mother's murder file. Scanlon was very enthusiastic about the idea. After

Girardot read the file, he delicately told Ellroy that his mother had been raped prior to her murder, a detail he found that Ellroy was reluctant to accept. Girardot put Ellroy in contact with two LASD detectives he had been dealing with—Sergeant Bill McComas and Sergeant Bill Stoner. Stoner, at first, spoke with Helen on the phone as Ellroy was in the UK on a book tour,"I said [to Helen] I need to review the file to make sure there's nothing in it we don't want released to public knowledge, which I did and called her back and said—Yeah, if he wants to come in and view the file I'll wait for him. I said, I retire in two weeks so he needs to hurry up and get here!"[4] Ellroy called Stoner from his hotel room and promised he would visit him as soon as possible. He arranged for a copy of *White Jazz* to be sent to Stoner in advance.

Ellroy booked a flight to LA, but his plans were delayed by the Northridge earthquake that occurred on January 17, 1994. Dozens of people were killed, and many buildings were destroyed or condemned, including the Hall of Justice. Sheriff's Homicide was forced to move into a leased facility. Their files were stuck in transit. Ellroy eventually flew to LA in March. He booked a suite at the Mondrian and spent the night before he was due to see his mother's file alone and in deep thought, "I turned out the lights and let the redhead take me places."[5] The next morning Ellroy met Stoner at the Homicide Bureau. "The first thing I said to him (after reading *White Jazz*) was 'Don't you know any legit policemen? They're all crooks!'"[6]

Ellroy was impressed by Stoner. He found his perceptions "were sharply lucid and devoid of commonly held police ideology" and was surprised when Stoner described the LAPD as a "racist institution."[7] Stoner warned Ellroy that some of the photos in his mother's murder file were graphic and offered to remove the more disturbing ones, but Ellroy insisted he wanted to see the file in full. Stoner left Ellroy alone so he could study the file. Ellroy visibly suppressed any emotional response to what he discovered. He was too busy focusing on gathering material for his article. The file was revealing and helped to disabuse him of preconceptions he had of his mother. A witness described Jean's male companion, "the Swarthy Man," as Mexican which surprised Ellroy as he considered his mother to have been "right-wing and obsessed with appearances."[8] He had thought that openly dating a Mexican man would have been taboo for her. Ellroy discovered that Jean was working at Airtek from

September 1956, whereas he thought she was at Packard Bell at that time. The autopsy report revealed that Jean's lungs were severely congested after years of heavy smoking. Lung cancer could have been a real possibility for her in later life. The ethnicity of the "Swarthy Man" was a point of contention based on the fallibility of witness statements. Lavonne Chambers, the carhop who had served Jean and the Swarthy Man, said he was likely "Greek or Italian."[9]

When Ellroy was finished with the file, Stoner was struck by how dispassionate he seemed. "I later realized he was in shock."[10] Back in New Canaan, Ellroy wrote about the experience in a *GQ* article, "My Mother's Killer." Even before the article went to print Ellroy knew that this was not the end of the matter. Viewing the homicide file had given him the desire to know more. It gnawed away at him. He now wanted to investigate his mother's murder as formally and as thoroughly as possible, and he knew he was going to write a book about it. The next step was to get people on board.

Ellroy met with Sonny Mehta and found him to be typically supportive, "He said that he heard about the *GQ* piece and was hoping I would want to expand it."[11] Mehta subsequently read the article and was so impressed that a deal with Knopf began to take shape. Ellroy needed someone with professional experience to help him with the investigation and, ever since his first meeting with Stoner, he had only one candidate in mind. Stoner, however, had reservations, "I still wasn't sure I wanted to work with him. He spoke very negatively, very ugly, about his mother at times. Calling her an alcoholic and basically describing her as a whore. I wasn't sure I wanted to work with somebody who was going to be reacting like that." [12] Stoner made an agreement with his wife Ann. They wouldn't spend any of the fee Ellroy was offering and then, a few weeks into the investigation, if he felt that Ellroy was harassing witnesses or behaving unprofessionally he would withdraw his assistance and return the fee.

Ellroy had all the pieces in place he needed to conduct the investigation and write the book, but he had to be careful in how he conducted himself. He was used to hiring researchers who would comb through newspaper archives and compile factsheets. Now he was going to be interviewing mostly elderly witnesses about a crime that was uniquely personal to him. Stoner's fear was "Do I wanna walk up on an eighty-year-old woman, knock on her door and ask for her cooperation and have James start yelling, 'C'mon bitch, give it up.' I wasn't quite sure how he was going to respond once we started this investigation."[13]

Ellroy and Stoner's investigation began in September 1994. Ellroy flew to LA on Labor Day. Stoner met him at the airport, and they drove straight to Arroyo High School in El Monte. They spent time at the scene where Jean's corpse was found thirty-six years earlier. There had been some development in the intervening years. The location was not quite the secluded lovers' lane it had been the night Jean was murdered, but Ellroy could still picture the scene and feel her presence. This was Stoner's intention. He often drove by murder scenes, returning to the same spot repeatedly to develop a sense of what the victim must have felt and what the murderer was thinking. Ellroy and Stoner sat in the car and talked before driving away. It was during this conversation that Ellroy realized Stoner's thinking on the case was very different to his. Ellroy's theory was that Jean and the Swarthy Man had consensual sex after leaving the Desert Inn. The Swarthy Man then drove Jean by this quiet spot because "he wanted to ditch this desperate woman and get on with his life."[14] Ellroy believed Jean wanted "more sex or more male attention" causing the Swarthy Man to snap. He killed her but he did not rape her as, in Ellroy's view, the Swarthy Man was not a serial killer with psycho-sexual urges.

Stoner told Ellroy that the theory lacked credibility. In Stoner's view, the Swarthy Man wanted sex. Jean was on her period and said no, "Jean wanted to cool him down. She said, Let's go back to Stan's Drive In."[15] Witness statements confirm the Swarthy Man's foul mood at Stan's Drive In. He's getting tired of waiting for sex and won't take no for an answer. They drive by Arroyo High School. The Swarthy Man demands sex for a final time. When Jean says no, he "hits her on the head five or six times."[16] He rapes her while she is unconscious and then decides to kill her. The hypothesis was so graphic and disturbing to Ellroy that he could no longer control his emotional reaction. He started shaking in the car. It was a hot summer day. Stoner turned on the air conditioning and gave Ellroy a moment to compose himself.

Within a few days, Ellroy underwent another emotionally wrenching experience. Stoner wanted Ellroy to come to the Sheriff's Academy to examine the physical evidence from his mother's case. It was another hot day, and the evidence warehouse was stiflingly warm. A clerk brought them several transparent bags, "I opened the third bag and saw the dress and brassiere my mother wore to her death."[17] Stoner recalls Ellroy holding the dress close to his face. When he removed it there were tears in his eyes and he said, "I can smell her."[18] Ellroy then examined the contents of the fourth bag. It contained the cord and nylon stocking that had been used to strangle his mother.

Ellroy stayed at a rented apartment in Newport Beach, close to where Stoner lived. Ellroy hung a corkboard on the wall to pin files and photos connected to the case. The moment Ellroy and Stoner began working together they developed an instant rapport, which helped to assuage Stoner's initial doubts about Ellroy. Stoner did much of the initial legwork, and he estimated that the investigation could take at least ten months. This gave Ellroy time alone at his apartment where he could think about the structure of the book. Stoner and Ellroy agreed that the chances of them finding the culprit were extremely low. They were going to be interviewing elderly people whose memories of Jean and the events surrounding her murder had faded with time. Ellroy planned the book on the presumption that they wouldn't find his mother's killer. He wanted to show "the metaphysic of the unsuccessful homicide investigation."[19] When it came to publicizing the book Ellroy would be coy on this point. He knew readers were unlikely to buy the book unless it promised answers.

There were other narrative strands Ellroy could layer into the book. He and Stoner spent a lot of time together, traveling across the country to interview witnesses. Stoner talked about his work on the Roy Radin homicide case. Radin was a show business promoter trying to break into the movie business. He was attempting to raise finance for the gangster musical *The Cotton Club* when he was murdered by contract killer William Mentzer. Mentzer had been hired by Karen Greenberger (a notorious cocaine dealer), who was angered when Radin forced her out of a producer's role for the film. The more Stoner began to trust Ellroy the more he would reveal, including details of how a police career had placed strain on his marriage to Ann and the raising of their twin sons. This was material which Ellroy felt, with Stoner's blessing, warranted inclusion in the book. Stoner later said, "it really made me feel complete as a policeman."[20] Ellroy revealed to one interviewer "I see the book thusly. It would be my autobiography, my mother's biography, Bill Stoner's biography."[21]

This structure was subject to change depending on the findings of the investigation. There would be surprises along the way. Early in the investigation, Stoner called Ellroy with startling news. He had found an unsolved homicide file which bore striking similarities to his mother's case. Ellroy and Stoner studied the case of Elspeth "Bobbie" Long. Bobbie was a waitress who was found beaten and strangled to death with a nylon stocking on January 23, 1959, seven months after Jean's murder. Her corpse had been abandoned on a road in La Puente, four miles out of El Monte. It was not only the details of the two murders which were "point-by-point twins."[22] Bobbie's lifestyle was, in some respects, like how Jean had been living at the end of her life. She was secretive and lied about her age. Two identification cards were found in her belongings, for Elspeth Long and Bobbie Long, which listed addresses in New Orleans, Miami, and Phoenix. She was fond of men and money, and her neighbor said she had been seeing a "rich guy" who the police were never able to identify. Stoner's discovery of the Bobbie Long case was a major development in their investigation. If a definite link could be found between the murders of Jean Ellroy and Bobbie Long, then that would validate Stoner's theory that the Swarthy Man was a potential serial killer. There was the possibility that a clue in the Bobbie Long murder might lead to a breakthrough in Jean's case.

The first interview Ellroy and Stoner conducted together was with Ward Hallinen. Hallinen had been one of the original investigators in Jean Ellroy's murder and had also investigated the murder of Bobbie Long. He had enjoyed a long career in law enforcement, in which he had witnessed the dark side of Hollywood glamor as he once booked the troubled starlet Frances Farmer into LA County Jail on a drunk driving charge. Hallinen was eighty-three years old and living in San Diego County when Ellroy and Stoner went to visit him. On the phone he had warned Stoner that he couldn't remember the case. Ellroy could remember him well though. The moment he saw the frail octogenarian he had a vivid flashback to Hallinen giving him a candy bar to keep him amused at the police station. Stoner had brought along the murder file in the hope that it might spark something in Hallinen's memory.

Ellroy asked Hallinen about Jim Boss Bennett. Bennett had been arrested for attempted rape in La Puente in 1962. He had been picked out of lineup by two witnesses from the night of Jean's murder as the Swarthy Man. Bennett was released as there was insufficient evidence to charge him with the attempted rape or Jean's murder. Hallinen could not remember Bennett or the lineup. Ellroy wrote that Hallinen was "fighting his incapacity full-bore."[23] Despite straining to remember some pertinent detail, Hallinen could barely recall the case and was unable to give them any useful information. He apologized to Ellroy that he "didn't nail the bastard" and Ellroy responded cryptically that he was "up against a very cunning victim."[24] Jean, like Bobbie Long, had led a secretive life which her own family had struggled to understand, and its shielded nature had impeded the police investigation.

More interviews followed. Ellroy and Stoner flew to Sacramento to interview retired LASD detective Charlie Guenther. Guenther had worked with Stoner on the Cotton Club case and had a reputation as "the man who *really* broke the Charles Manson case."[25] Guenther had investigated a tip from Shirley Miller who reported her ex-husband Will Lenard Miller as confessing to Jean's murder. Guenther remembered the case well. Shirley Miller said her ex had dated Jean and was angry with her for refusing to process his medical claim when they both worked at Airtek. Miller had a criminal record for passing bad checks. In 1970, Miller was arrested on a probation warrant and Guenther interviewed him about the Jean Ellroy murder. Miller denied killing her and passed a polygraph test. Guenther recalled Miller as being a "goddamn crybaby."[26] He did not fit the description of the Swarthy Man. Ellroy and Stoner surmised that he was not a plausible suspect. This became a recurring problem of the investigation. Men who might have had a motive to kill Jean would never quite fit the profile of the Swarthy Man. Jim Boss Bennett, like Will Lenard Miller, was described as "skinny white trash" who "did not look Greek or Italian or in any way Latin."[27] Jean was happy and relaxed around the Swarthy Man the night she was killed.

He was moody and seductive.

Perhaps the most heartbreaking interview Ellroy and Stoner conducted was with Lavonne Parga (nee Chambers). She had been working as a carhop at Stan's Drive-In the night Jean was murdered. Lavonne was one of the witnesses who picked Jim Boss Bennett out of a lineup. Stoner traced her to Reno. Ellroy and Stoner visited Lavonne's home only for her son to answer and inform them that she had been admitted to hospital after an asthma attack. Her son remembered Jean's murder. He was only a toddler when it occurred, but it was something his mother had talked about for years. Ellroy and Stoner visited Lavonne at Washoe County Medical Center. Lavonne appeared to be strong and resilient despite her health problems, and she proved to be a good witness, "Her answers jibed with the background details in the file."[28] She told Ellroy his mother was a beautiful woman and was deeply moved at the sight of Jean's son as a fully grown man. The police had told her the Swarthy Man might be local, and she had kept her eyes peeled every night she worked at the Drive-In just in case she ever saw him again. One detail from that night left her wracked with guilt. Carhops were supposed to take the license plate numbers of every customer in case they drove off without paying, but Jean and her male companion looked perfectly respectable, so Lavonne had not regarded it as necessary. "The case could have been solved that night," Stoner observed ruefully.[29]

Ellroy's detective skills were now developing quickly. He knew when to put aside his brash personality, which had always been partly an act, and let people talk without fear of being intimidated by his competitive streak. "Stoner was my teacher," Ellroy wrote.[30] The two of them became "very close friends" or as Stoner put it, "almost like brothers."[31] They interviewed Michael Whittaker in San Francisco. Whittaker had danced with Jean, the Swarthy Man, and the Blonde in the Desert Inn the night Jean was murdered. He had been arrested for drunken behavior the same night. Whittaker hadn't changed much in the intervening thirty-seven years, although his lifestyle had taken its toll. He was living in a rundown apartment in the Mission District. The neighborhood was plagued with crime. Across the street from Whittaker's building Stoner and Ellroy witnessed a shooting when a black youth, "sprayed the playground with some kind of assault weapon."[32] Fortunately, no one was hurt in the incident.

Whittaker proved useless as a witness. He was on methadone for his addictions, and it affected his memory. He claimed to have visited the Desert Inn with "some fat Hawaiian guy who knew karate."[33] He only visited the bar once, "the place put a hex on him."[34] Whittaker continued to make fanciful claims until they cut the interview short. Ellroy, always generous even though Whittaker had annoyed him, left him a hundred-dollar bill.

One aspect of the investigation in which Ellroy had more expertise than Stoner was in drumming up publicity. A producer from the ABC *Day One* show called Ellroy. He wanted to film a segment about the investigation. Stoner agreed that nationwide publicity might unearth some new leads. Ellroy and Stoner spent four days filming with the *Day One* show crew, and Ellroy had a toll-free line installed on his apartment phone so he could receive any tips that might come in once the segment aired.

Ellroy was contacted by Nicola Black, a Scottish director who had previously interviewed Ellroy in Partick Police Station for a documentary on Allan Pinkerton. Black wanted to make a documentary about Ellroy and his work, in which the investigation would feature prominently. The subsequent production, titled *White Jazz*, was filmed in LA over the course of ten days. Ellroy was a natural performer. "He would do these amazing pieces to camera, almost as a one-off," Black recalls.[35] Black was deeply impressed by Stoner, "The relationship between Bill and James was really tangible. There was a great empathy between them. Bill is a very empathetic and sensitive man."[36] *White Jazz* features a reenactment of Jean's murder by the Swarthy Man. Black asked for Ellroy's permission before filming the scene. It's a chilling visualization of the murder with Jean and the Swarthy Man arguing in his car about him supposedly flirting with the Blonde woman in the bar. The argument gets more intense and when Jean tries to exit the vehicle the Swarthy Man violently attacks her. Black was apprehensive about how Ellroy would react to the scene, but he was impressed with the production. More than two decades later, the author still regards *White Jazz* as his favorite of the many documentaries produced about his life and work.

Many of the interviews Stoner and Ellroy conducted were with people he knew as a child. In many cases his recollection of events clashed with theirs. They interviewed Peter Tubiolo, the former vice-principal of Anne Le Gore Elementary School. Tubiolo repeated to them what he had told the police at the time, that he had never dated Jean Ellroy and only met her once for a meeting about her son's behavior. Ellroy admitted to Tubiolo that he had given the police the information about the two of them dating. The misunderstanding sprang from when he had seen Tubiolo pick up his mother from their house in his "blue and white Nash."[37]

"I loved that car," Tubiolo replied cryptically.

Ellroy and Stoner travelled to Kanab, Utah to interview Anna May Krycki, Jean's former landlady in El Monte. Mrs Krycki was elderly and shrill. Stoner telephoned her in advance. She said she remembered "Leroy Ellroy" as a "spasticated boy" who didn't know how to use a broom.[38] She repeated the claim when they saw her in person. Mrs Krycki said her husband had tried to teach "Leroy" how to push a broom to no avail.

Her memory of the case was more revealing. She remembered Jean telling her "I think this place will be safe." She thought that Jean was hiding in El Monte. She stood out from the locals as she was "cultured and refined."[39] Mrs Krycki had told the police that Jean didn't drink, but Ellroy had a vivid memory of seeing the two of them drunk together. Many of her statements to them contradicted what she had told the police. She told Ellroy and Stoner that she suspected Jean had a drinking problem and often smelt liquor on her breath.

Just as the interview was winding down Mrs Krycki gave them some potentially explosive information. In 1952, while living in El Monte and separated from her husband, Anna May Krycki had gone on a date with a man named John LoPresti. They went to the Coconino Club. She described LoPresti as "smooth and calculating." Afterwards, he drove her out to Puente Hills, and he made some forceful sexual advances on her. When she resisted, he turned violent and shoved her in the backseat. He ejaculated prematurely and "wiped his pants off with a handkerchief."[40] He made some crass sexual comments and then drove her home. She saw him around a few times, but he didn't bother her. She hadn't reported him to the police as she was locked in a custody battle with her husband at the time. She told Ellroy and Stoner that she had warned Jean about John LoPresti.

It was an ugly and plausible story, although Ellroy didn't believe Mrs Krycki's final point about the warning to his mother. If LoPresti could be the Swarthy Man, then why would Jean have been so relaxed in his company if she already knew of his violent reputation?

It was a long drive back to Newport Beach with Stoner constantly teasing Ellroy about his lack of broom-sweeping skills. Nevertheless, they had a firm suspect in John LoPresti that they could now pursue. They discussed

LoPresti and agreed that it was theoretically plausible that his capacity for sexual violence could have grown from the assault on Anna May Krycki in 1952 to the murder of Jean in 1958. Other aspects of the case were cohering in Ellroy's mind and challenging his memory of events. People had lied or withheld information about Jean which had clouded the police's understanding of the victim. Armand had told the police he married Jean in 1941 when they married in 1948, and he most likely never told them about Jean's first marriage which may have been, at least tangentially, useful information as Easton Spaulding was still living in LA at the time of the murder. Peter Tubiolo picking Jean up in his car appeared odd for a teacher/parent conference. Mrs Krycki lied to the police about Jean's heavy drinking. An El Monte cop named Keith Tedrow had seen Jean's naked cadaver and, mistaking her mastitis for something more sinister, spread a rumor that the killer had bitten off her nipple. Tedrow appeared to struggle with misogyny. He was shot to death in 1971 by a woman he was trying to coerce into performing oral sex on him. Witnesses lied and the mystery around Jean grew. But no one lied for sinister reasons, they lied for petty, stupid reasons to protect their reputations.

Ellroy and Stoner traced LoPresti through records held in the El Monte Museum. They visited him and the moment he opened the door for them they knew he wasn't the Swarthy Man. He did not resemble him in any way, nor did he look particularly Latino. He chain-smoked and told them he was having heart surgery the next day. He admitted going to the Coconino Club and the Desert Inn back in the fifties and gave them some names of people in the same social scene. As they got ready to leave Stoner made a parting shot at LoPresti, "We heard you mauled a woman named Anna May Krycki and shot your load prematurely."[41] A humiliated LoPresti gave a barrage of panicked denials, but it was a moot point as Ellroy and Stoner knew he wasn't the Swarthy Man.

Ellroy and Stoner interviewed former deputy Bill Vickers. They interviewed a former bartender at the Desert Inn named Al Manganiello. They interviewed former LASD captain Vic Cavellero. They talked to Keith Tedrow's ex-wife Sherry. They talked to El Monte police chief Wayne Clayton. They interviewed as many people as they could find. Their leads started to dry up or go nowhere.

Stoner and Ellroy still disagreed on whether the Swarthy Man was a serial killer. Stoner believed he was, but he warned Ellroy "not to lock into any given theory or hypothetical reconstruction."[42]

Criminal profiling was in vogue at the time. Stoner commissioned retired LASD homicide detective Carlos Avila to compose a psychological portrait of the Swarthy Man. After studying the case files, Avila wrote a lengthy report in which he concurred with Stoner's view that Jean's murderer was a serial killer, "Unless the offender was arrested and incarcerated for some extended period of time, we would expect the offender to have continued killing, if not in this state, in others."[43]

Profiling has been discredited in recent years, notably after the DC sniper attacks when profilers got almost every detail of the perpetrators wrong. However, at the time, Avila's profile made Ellroy more receptive to the idea that the Swarthy Man was a serial killer or, at the very least, murdered both Jean Ellroy and Bobbie Long. Ellroy and Stoner were running out of options, but nationwide publicity could potentially offer new leads. The *LA Weekly* ran a piece on the investigation which, at Ellroy's insistence, included the toll-free tip-line number he had installed in his apartment. They were inundated with calls as soon as the article was published. Most of the callers were cranks. People would call and hang up. Psychics called to solicit business. Callers would name OJ Simpson as the killer. A woman named Janice Knowlton called repeatedly. Janice was the victim of sexual abuse by her father, George Frederick Knowlton, and accused him of murdering Elizabeth Short in the book *Daddy was the Black Dahlia Killer* (1995). She also wrote to Ellroy and said her father was the Swarthy Man. Ellroy did not take her claims seriously. Janice Knowlton committed suicide in 2004.

The *Day One* segment aired in April 1995 but, much to Ellroy and Stoner's chagrin, it did not run Ellroy's 1-800 number as it violated the program's Standards and Practices code. Ellroy decided he would formally end the investigation on December 15, 1995. He now had a mass of information and needed time alone to write the book. Stoner told him they should look up Jean's family in Wisconsin. The prospect made Ellroy nervous. He had never enjoyed a close relationship with his mother's family and, as an author who had done so much to reinvent himself, he didn't like the thought that "they might welcome me back and try to turn me into a docile stiff with an extended family."[44]

The Lee Earle Ellroy they had known was long gone. James Ellroy had abolished him.

Ellroy and Stoner increasingly had to juggle the investigation with their other commitments. Stoner was involved in pre-trial work in the 1981 rape and homicide case of Tracy Lea Stewart. Robert Beckett Sr went on trial for Stewart's murder at LA County Superior Court in 1995. Ellroy attended most of the two-week trial of Beckett. The trial of OJ Simpson was happening in the same building and Ellroy appreciated the sideways view it gave him of the proceedings. Ellroy had already written a piece on Simpson and the Nicole Brown/Ron Goldman murder, which was published in GQ in December 1994, one month before Simpson's trial began. Ellroy essentially portrays the former footballer turned actor as an empty celebrity, suggesting he should either take a guilty plea or commit suicide, adding "he didn't have the soul or the balls" to commit to either option.[45] His brief glimpses of the trial confirmed his view that celebrity had become the biggest factor in the case. He noted that Johnny Cochran wore more expensive suits than any of the lawyers in the Beckett trial.

The trial of Robert Beckett was a "box-office dud" by comparison.[46] Beckett was found guilty of the murder of Tracy Lea Stewart. Ellroy did not attend the sentencing hearing. He expressed skepticism about the relatively new procedure of the victim's family being able to confront the defendant once they were convicted. But as their own investigation was coming to an end, Ellroy knew it was a form of resolution that he was never going to experience. Beckett's conviction had brought justice to Tracy Stewart's family. It brought relief to Bill Stoner who spent years working on the case. But Ellroy and Stoner were no closer to solving the murder of Jean Ellroy.

Ellroy spent two weeks with the Los Angeles Sheriff's Homicide Bureau and went out on some active calls, witnessing the aftermath of "two gangland killings. I saw bloodstains and bullet holes and grieving families."[47] He wrote about the experience in GQ in an article titled "The Tooth of Crime." Ellroy wanted to call the article "the Bulldogs" after the LASD's mascot and informal name for themselves. It would have been the stronger title given Ellroy's focus on how the Bulldogs identity had evolved over the past fifty years. Ever increasing urbanization had led to an expanding jurisdiction and a crushing level of responsibility, "There were 14 Bulldogs in 1958. There were 140 today."[48] In the aftermath of the Rodney King police brutality scandal, the role and reputation of law enforcement was still being debated in LA and throughout the US.

Ellroy was extremely grateful for all the assistance he had received from various levels of law enforcement. He counted many cops, including Stoner, as his best friends. He was determined to portray them honestly. He presented himself as a lone voice defending the role of the police against a prevailing media narrative that had become increasingly skeptical of law enforcement. Sometimes Ellroy would make arguments that many of his friends would balk at. He defended the actions of the police officers who arrested Rodney King, "The fifty-six hammer blows that put Rodney on the ground, and the contact slash don't look good, but moment to moment the entire three minute tape leads me to say, and I realize this is revolutionary, I don't think they did anything wrong."[49] Ellroy did suggest, tongue-in-cheek, that Sheriff's Homicide could benefit from a rebranding, "In truth, bulldogs are lazy creatures prone to breathing disorders and hip dysplasia. The vulture should replace the bulldog as Homicide's mascot."[50] Ellroy enjoyed his experience with the Bulldogs so much that he began developing a TV pilot based on the work of Sheriff's Homicide.

Whether it was beneficial or not for his reputation as a crime writer, there is little doubt that Ellroy was quickly becoming the most prominent celebrity apologist of the LAPD and LASD.

9

Demon Dog of American Crime Fiction (1995–2000)

One of the producers of *Unsolved Mysteries* contacted Ellroy. She wanted to make an episode based on the Jean Ellroy case. The show was popular with an elderly demographic. It might spark a memory in an older witness. If the Swarthy Man had been a serial killer, then the episode might remind a retired cop of a similar case. The episode was shot in four days. Ellroy agreed to do a reenactment scene of him first opening the evidence bag which contained the stocking used to strangle Jean. Even though the stocking was a replica of the actual murder weapon, Ellroy's composure in playing the scene still earned praise from the director. Most of the shoot was good fun, with Ellroy developing a rapport with the actors who played his mother, the Swarthy Man, the Blonde, and the young actor cast as the ten-year old Lee Ellroy.

The episode aired in March 1996. On camera, Ellroy struck an optimistic note about their chances of solving his mother's murder: "There are people out there who know elements of this case, who know names, who've heard the story. And it's just a question of tapping into those people."[1] It was an optimism he was not feeling in private. He had concluded the investigation was over and the case would go unsolved. This was borne out by the phone tips that came in after the show. Most of them did not amount to credible leads and many could be dismissed outright. Janice Knowlton phoned in repeatedly, getting upset at times. The phone operators decided to let her talk, without interruption, although her claims were not plausible. Ellroy hoped that Jean's family in Wisconsin would see the show and get in touch. In the event, they did not see the episode, but Stoner was able to locate them in Cross Plains, Wisconsin.

Leoda had died in 1989. Her husband, Ed Wagner, was gravely ill in hospital with congestive heart disease. Their daughter, Janet Klock, informed Stoner of Jean's brief marriage to "the Spalding Man," which occurred prior to her marrying Armand. Ellroy was floored by the news but no one in the family knew the man's full name, and he and Stoner were unable to discover his identity.

Ed and Janet were equally stunned that Ellroy was still alive and had become so successful. They had no idea "Lee" had become a bestselling author and had assumed he was long dead. Ellroy and Stoner made plans to visit the family in Cross Plains, but Ed Wagner died in hospital before they arrived. Janet gave Ellroy several family photographs of Jean which he had never seen before. Janet's sister, Jeannie, showed Ellroy his family tree and he was shocked to discover his heritage was British. He had assumed his grandparents were German immigrants, "I don't know where I got that idea."[2] Ellroy may have just assumed it, given the sizable German American community in Wisconsin, or he may have got it from Armand, whose dislike of Jean's family may have been tied to his anti-German sentiment. Regardless, this discovery of his British heritage would filter into Ellroy's thinking. He would increasingly describe himself as an anglophile and talk about his books, and the works of artists he admired as being concerned with "the defense of the West."

Janet and Jeannie were welcoming to Ellroy. According to Janet, "I had so hoped it would become a relationship of some sort, seeing as Jeannie and I were the only family he had but ..." and Jeannie "James visited us when he wrote his book about his mother, and it was clearly foreign territory. I would have liked to keep in touch with James, but he clearly did not want that."[3] At the time, Ellroy carried very negative associations with the concept of family, and it was reflected in his civil but guarded behavior around his cousins.

Ellroy and Helen moved to Kansas City in 1995. Helen had never fully settled in at New Canaan, where she had moved at Ellroy's insistence after their wedding.

Living in Kansas City would allow her to be close to her mother and her aunt. Ellroy may have been reluctant to leave New Canaan at first, but he soon began to love his new life in the Heartland of America. Ellroy and Helen bought a large Tudor-style house in Mission Hills, an affluent and relatively undiscovered neighborhood, and Ellroy settled into an environment where he felt the safest. His new house covered 4,000 square feet, had six bedrooms, with striking white walls offset by a dark oak-paneled floor. Mission Hills resembled New Canaan with its rows of mansions, immaculate lawns, and exclusive country clubs. It was both self-contained and far removed from the gritty urbanization of Kansas City, which Ellroy bluntly described as a "dump."[4] Ellroy left the planning and logistics of moving thousands of miles across the country entirely to Helen, which caused some tension between them, but then Ellroy's working schedule was so demanding that he probably couldn't have helped even if he wanted to.

Ellroy described the various projects he had been juggling in a letter to Sonny Mehta. Of the investigation into his mother's murder, Ellroy wrote "I've been at it for ten months—interrupted by four book tours, the filming of the British documentary (*White Jazz*) about me, and a third European tour later this month."[5] Ellroy apologized to Mehta for the delays in completing *My Dark Places* but insisted that "to curtail the investigation would severely impact the quality of the book."[6] He also claimed, with some justification, that his time was being "eaten-up" by "publicity commitments and a one-month screenwriting assignment I took out of sheer greed."[7]

The hard work was paying off. *American Tabloid* was published in February 1995 and was a bestseller which garnered terrific reviews and won *Time* magazine's Best (Fiction) Book of 1995, beating Philip Roth's *Sabbath's Theater* into second place, a feat which delighted Ellroy.

American Tabloid

Ellroy wanted his readers to ponder the historical authenticity of *American Tabloid*. By the mid-90s conspiracy theories were rife across a wide range of subjects. Ellroy needed to make his novel historically credible and for it to stand out in a crowded field of work, particularly conspiratorially minded work, on the Kennedy Presidency. To this end, he began the text with a short, single-page prologue addressing the reader, a practice that he had never used before for a first-edition novel. Ellroy is abrasive in his condemnation of the popular trend to idolize Kennedy and America: "*America was never innocent. We popped our cherry on the boat over and looked back with no regrets.*"[8] The style of Ellroy's direct address reflects his abrasive personality, in the same way that Bucky Bleichert's opening monologue establishes an unusually personal relationship between a detective and a murder victim he never knew in life. Ellroy's voice is starkly contrasted by the prose style of the novel, which is consistently dry even its description of extreme violence. Ellroy's places events within a wider timeframe: the corruption of the US is an inevitable component of its national character and not a recent moral decline: "*You can't ascribe our fall from grace to any single event or set of circumstances. You can't lose what you lacked at conception.*"[9] Ellroy's Christian upbringing imbued him with the belief that mankind is fallen, and it cannot redeem itself by acts or a humanistic reverence for Kennedy. The moral shortcomings of one man are paralleled by the failings of a society which worshipped him, despite his evident flaws which Ellroy will push further to the surface. From the outset, Ellroy makes it clear that the novel will deglamorize the aura surrounding JFK: "*Jack Kennedy was the mythological front man for a particularly juicy slice of our history.*"[10] The importance of timing, in this case a premature death, supersedes the substance of events and creates heroes, as with Kennedy. Timing seems more important than the man, ensuring, through the eulogy of character, that his legacy has been woefully distorted: "*Jack got whacked at the optimum moment to assure his sainthood. Lies continue to swirl around his eternal flame.*"[11] In *American Tabloid*, Kennedy is not only stripped of his reputation as a heroic martyr, he is also relegated to a supporting character in the events that unfold, unaware of the debt he owes to the Underworld and his monstrous father, and therefore unable to repay it. Martyrs die for a cause, yet Ellroy denies Kennedy this moral significance as the continuation of the Underworld as an economic and political force is the primary motivation of the conspirators whereas Kennedy himself is portrayed as self-interested.

The novel is concerned less with revelations about the assassination, thus maintaining its minor role as but "one murder in a whole series of murders," than with uncovering other hidden stories of the time. Ellroy deliberately does not employ Lee Harvey Oswald as a character, partly out of deference to Don DeLillo's *Libra* but also to pour scorn on the official record of events. This is just one area in which journalism, or more specifically, the tabloid journalism of the title, is vitally important to the novel. *American Tabloid* reads as a curious blend of history and investigative journalism in which the author gives the reader the inside scoop on the story behind the story. However, one narrative rewrites the other, as the hidden story reveals the true movers and shakers: "*They were rogue cops and shakedown artists. They were wiretappers and soldiers of fortune and faggot lounge entertainers. Had one second of their lives deviated off course, American history would not exist as we know it.*"[12] Political office is shown to be another façade. History is retold from an Underworld perspective. Ellroy's vision of the assassination conspiracy is that disparate criminal elements came together in a loose association with the tacit backing of Hoover and rogue Intelligence operatives. Ellroy is reordering the historical story. But Ellroy does more than simply uncover a new ruling set who operate alongside historical figures, he also employs optimistic, patriotic language to cynically congratulate them:

> It's time to demythologize an era and build a new myth from the gutter to the stars. It's time to embrace bad men and the price they paid to secretly define their time.
> Here's to them.[13]

The style of revisionism Ellroy had embraced, after discarding his initial outline and its warmed-over Marilyn Monroe murder plot, led him to realize "that this isn't just one novel. This is a trilogy about America between the years 1958 and 1973."[14] Ellroy had created such a compelling historical vision of Underworld dominance that he was now planning to extend it to distort mainstream perceptions of the recent American past over a much longer period than he first thought possible.

On the eve of publication of *American Tabloid*, Ellroy wrote a letter to Don DeLillo, whom he had never met in person, thanking him for writing *Libra* and promising to credit the novel as the inspiration for *American Tabloid* at every opportunity. DeLillo responded in a letter dated March 4 (Ellroy's forty-seventh birthday), but he mistakenly put the year as 1955, a typo which Ellroy felt "seemed appropriate."[15] DeLillo informed Ellroy that "writers who look into the assassination tend to become haunted by it, of course, and maybe it will happen to you."[16] He then gives an example of how that obsession led him to visit the Texas Theatre where Oswald was arrested, and where he reenacted one of Oswald's more minor crimes:

> When I was in Dallas chasing Oswald's ghost, I walked through the lobby and into the theater without a ticket—the ticket taker was distracted by something, and I realized this is exactly how Oswald got in, with sirens wailing in the streets—he snuck in.[17]

Ellroy appeared, at least in part, to believe in the conspiracy theory regarding JFK's assassination he had worked into the novel. The plot is convoluted but he elaborated on the basic theory when publicizing the novel. In an interview with Ron Hogan, Ellroy stated "I think organized crime, exile factions, and renegade CIA killed Jack the Haircut. I think your most objective researchers do as well."[18] However, his views were malleable, both on and off the page, "The one question I never answer specifically about *American Tabloid* is what's real and what's not."[19]

It was the beginning of an ambitious project of historical revisionism in his writing. Ellroy had decided *American Tabloid* needed to be followed by two direct sequels, each covering five years of American history successively. The first sequel would end with the assassinations of Martin Luther King and Robert Kennedy and the concluding novel would end with the death of J. Edgar Hoover. Both novels would offer an alternative, conspiratorial version of these events. Ellroy would call the series the Underworld USA trilogy, in tribute to Samuel Fuller's film *Underworld USA* (1961). Ellroy professed to be a huge fan of Fuller, although his one meeting with him, at MystFest in Cattolica in 1990, was not memorable, "I found him to be a crusty old cocksucker—and a motormouth. He wouldn't let me get a word in—and all I wanted to do was tell him how much I loved his films."[20]

Chip Kidd produced one of his most memorable cover designs for *American Tabloid*, in which a large single eye peers over the title, evoking Ellroy's themes of voyeurism and the dawn of the surveillance era. Kidd used a photograph of Frank Sinatra's eye taken from a *Confidential* magazine cover. It was around this time that Kidd discovered just how unique a friend Ellroy could be.

Kidd had been having trouble with an ex-partner, a man he had been in a relationship with for six years, before he left him for someone else. "He went ballistic, harassing me day and night via the phone. He'd get drunk, call me up late at night with threats."[21]

Ellroy knew Kidd's ex-partner, who Kidd describes as an "older upstanding citizen, a businessman," but he was not aware that things had deteriorated to such a level. One day, Ellroy and Kidd were talking on the phone.[22]

"What's wrong?" Ellroy asked. "You sound really rattled."

Kidd explained the situation with his ex-partner. Ellroy's response startled him.

"It sounds to me like he's just blowing off steam. Give it another month and if it doesn't stop, I know some guys in New York that will scare him. They're not gonna hurt him, but they'll scare the shit out of him, and he'll go away."

Ellroy's analysis proved correct. The ex-partner did stop harassing Kidd within a month and no further action proved necessary. "I was so grateful. It sounds sinister, but it was really sweet. I'm sure he was quite sincere," Kidd said. "No other author has offered to threaten my ex-boyfriend!"[23]

Ellroy could be generous in more conventional ways. The author Michael Connelly contacted Ellroy for permission to use elements of Jean Ellroy's murder in the backstory of his detective character, Harry Bosch, whose mother is also the victim of an unsolved murder. Ellroy encouraged Connelly to pursue the theme, "I do not hold the patent on murdered mothers" he told him.[24]

Even when Ellroy inspired other writers he often did so under a cloud of controversy. The renowned Bouchercon convention was held in Nottingham from September 28 to October 1, 1995. Ellroy was the international guest of honor. Despite being the city of Robin Hood, Nottingham was considered an odd choice to hold the crime fiction convention which had only taken place outside of North America once before. Events got off to a rocky start when P.D. James decided to cancel her appearance after making classist statements which were reported in the press. Ellroy arrived in the city jetlagged and exhausted. Unable to sleep in his hotel room he spent the evening roaming the streets half-dazed. He was much amused by the sight of some drunken football hooligans scrapping outside of a pub. They were hardly dangerous compared to the street gangs of LA. Ellroy casually sidestepped the brawlers as they ineffectually threw punches at each other.

According to the writer Mike Ripley, on the day he was due to speak Ellroy received a briefing from "the CWA (Crime Writers Association) asking him not to swear and offend the blue-rinse brigade. He took absolutely no notice."[25]

Ellroy may have been profane, but he still inspired many of the writers in the audience, one of whom was Ian Rankin. Despite writing a string of crime novels, Rankin had not yet produced a major bestseller and was in fear of being dropped by his publisher. He looked to Ellroy for inspiration:

> He was a huge influence, because I read all the LA novels, the big LA Quartet and I was just coming up to the writing of my novel *Black and Blue* and I was in a fairly grim place career-wise in that my writing, my books, my sales were seen as being midlist (i.e. I'm not a beginner any more but I'm not making waves, I'm not getting to the bestseller lists). And I was always in danger of being dumped by my publisher and I thought, ok the next book you write has got to be the big one, and that was *Black and Blue*. And I took on some of the stuff I'd learned from Ellroy.[26]

Rankin was struck by Ellroy's claim at Bouchercon that "If you've got the stones you can make history do whatever you want it to do."[27] He bought a tape of Ellroy's talk and studied it while writing *Black and Blue*, "For the first time in one of my books I used a real unsolved murder, a series of murders, a killer called Bible John who was operating in the late 60s in Glasgow and he became a character in the book, and that was a lesson I learned from Ellroy."[28]

Black & Blue was the bestseller Rankin needed and became regarded as hallmark text in the Tartan Noir genre. For years, a rumor persisted that Ellroy had dubbed Rankin the originator of "Tartan Noir." But as Rankin has now conceded, he asked Ellroy to write those words when he was inscribing one of his books and was happy to let the legend develop,

> I pretended that he invented the term Tartan Noir. I said, he wrote it in a book to me and he came up with that title Tartan Noir. I told him to write

that. I basically said to him, what I write you could describe as Tartan Noir. And then he wrote 'you rule Tartan Noir' and I said he invented it. The truth is I invented it.[29]

Although Ellroy could be a mesmerizing public speaker, he was just as likely to offend his audience as inspire it, even when he was dealing with celebrities who naturally admired him. Ellroy had given a reading at Waterstones in London in February 1995. In attendance was the musician Nick Cave. Cave was such a fan of Ellroy that he hung a signed photo of him in his study, next to portraits of his other key inspirations—Jesus Christ, and the Blues musician John Lee Hooker. Ellroy in turn had been enthusiastic about Cave's songwriting ability. At a reading in New York a friend of Cave's asked Ellroy to sign a copy of *White Jazz* which he then sent on to the singer-songwriter. Ellroy wrote "Nick, feel those evil rock 'n' roll chords of doom. That song in *Until the End of the World* really kicked my ass."[30] *Until the End of the World* was a film directed by Wim Wenders for which Cave had contributed to the soundtrack. With such mutual admiration between them, one might assume that Ellroy and Cave would hit it off in person. However, the opposite proved to be the case.

Ellroy invited Cave and "a herd of publishing types to dine with him" after the reading, "he ranted on about rock 'n' roll being nothing more than 'institutionalized rebellion,'" Cave wrote.[31] Ellroy was also dismissive of Cave when asked about the encounter two years later, "He [Cave] was a big bore. He was number 7 on my list of the 8 most boring people I have ever met. He was also number 8 on my list of the 8 most pretentious and self-absorbed people I have ever met."[32] Cave wasn't the first rock star who became a huge fan of Ellroy. In the late 1980s, Thurston Moore and Kim Gordon of the band Sonic Youth would visit Ellroy when he was making an appearance at Vagabonds Bookstore. Their song "The Wonder" was inspired by Ellroy's writing, and the band would dedicate performances to the author during their concerts.

The success of *American Tabloid* led to an increase of interest in Hollywood for Ellroy's work. Joel Gotler reached out to Ellroy through Nat Sobel. "I've been a literary film agent for fifty years and I've never met anyone like James Ellroy," Gotler recalls.[33] The two men met over lunch and developed an instant friendship. Gotler and Ellroy both felt that the author had not received adequate representation in Hollywood. Gotler had the connections to provide Ellroy with a steady supply of television and screenwriting assignments. Ellroy knew that most screenplays he worked on would not be made into a film, but it didn't faze him. If anything, it made him even more appreciative of the money that could be made through screenwriting, "Compared to writing novels, writing screenplays is very easy and for a very quick turnaround on your buck."[34] Some of the most prominent actors and directors at the time would request meetings with Ellroy.

Nick Nolte had been working on the neo-noir film *Mulholland Falls* about the LAPD "Hat Squad." Aware that this was a subject Ellroy had covered in his novels, Nolte requested a meeting with the author. Nolte wanted to be certain that his film did not plagiarize Ellroy's work. Ellroy liked Nolte. They were both dog lovers, although Ellroy was taken aback by the fact that Nolte had once eaten dog food as it was required for his role as a homeless man in *Down and Out in Beverly Hills*. The discussion soon moved on to how they could work together on their own project. Ellroy suggested an adaptation of *White Jazz* in a contemporary LA setting with Nolte in the leading role of Dave Klein. Work began on the project. Ellroy became good friends with the producer Clark Peterson, and the two men would become frequent collaborators on film projects. He appears to have been less than enamored with the co-producer Greg Shapiro, as he defaced letters Shapiro sent him requesting scene changes.

The *White Jazz* adaptation would languish in development hell for years, until finally falling apart. Although this may have been disappointing to him, Ellroy was about to achieve a new level of celebrity status due to events that were taking place largely outside his purview. He would describe the film adaptation of *LA Confidential* as "the greatest thing that happened to me which I had nothing to do with."[35]

Brian Helgeland, the screenwriter who had first met Ellroy in a bookstore in 1988, had been lobbying for the assignment of adapting *LA Confidential* into a screenplay. He discovered the task had been assigned to the director Curtis Hanson. He approached Hanson, who was busy filming *The River Wild* at the time. Hanson told him he wouldn't have time to work on the screenplay for at least six months and encouraged him to plough on with a first draft. Helgeland had completed a first draft by the time Hanson was able to start work on the screenplay.

Hanson and Helgeland met with Ellroy at the Pacific Dining Car. After his experience with *Cop*, Ellroy was skeptical that any more of his novels would be filmed. Joe Stinson had been trying to get *Clandestine* filmed for years without success. Jimmy Harris had endured similar experiences with *The Black Dahlia*, as had Maurizio Grimaldi with *The Big Nowhere*, as well as Tony Denison, Jeff Stein, and Darrell Fetty with *Dick Contino's Blues*. Ellroy's only period fiction to have been adapted was the short story "Since I Don't Have You" for the TV series *Fallen Angels* in 1993. Ellroy had been reasonably pleased with the results, but it was going to be a lot more difficult adapting a novel into a film than it was to create thirty minutes of television from a short story.

Of all his novels, Ellroy considered *LA Confidential* to be the most unfilmable, describing it as "unsavory, unapologetically dark, untameable, and altogether untranslatable to the screen."[36] But Hanson assured him that the film would be made. Hanson had secured funding through Arnon Milchan of Regency Enterprises, by pitching the story to him using a series of vintage

Figure 10 *Wrestling it out. Ellroy and LA Confidential screenwriter Brian Helgeland. Photo: Courtesy of Brian Helgeland.*

LA postcards. Milchan thought that some of Hanson's casting decisions were risky. Two relatively unknown Australian actors, Russell Crowe and Guy Pearce, were cast in the leading roles of Bud White and Ed Exley respectively. Although he was concerned this would harm the commercial prospects of the film, Milchan would prove to be a laissez-faire producer and Crowe and Pearce would give star-making performances.

Ellroy embarked on a whistle-stop nationwide tour of Australia in March 1996. He was invited by Random House Australia and the tour was organized by publicists Stuart Coupe and Alan Davidson. Ellroy met Russell Crowe in Sydney. They took a boat tour around Sydney Harbour and discussed the forthcoming production of *LA Confidential*. In Sydney, Ellroy was greeted by the Premier of New South Wales, Bob Carr. Carr was an Americanist and a fan of Ellroy's work. Ellroy was impressed by how approachable Carr was compared to US politicians, although he still regarded him as "a gasbag."[37] He was given a tour around King's Cross, one of the more crime-stricken areas of the city, but Ellroy thought the place looked harmless compared to LA. Ellroy dined with Carr at his home and spent the evening watching the Australian mini-series *Blue Murder*, a non-fiction crime drama.

In Melbourne, Ellroy met with Guy Pearce. Pearce attended one of Ellroy's readings. Already a recognizable actor in Australia, he took his place in the audience incognito. Ellroy was asked whether any of his novels would be adapted into film. He responded that *LA Confidential* was in pre-production and two Australian actors had been cast in leading roles, which caused the audience to erupt with laughter as they clearly thought Ellroy was joking. Pearce slowly sank into his chair.

Ellroy found the Australian public was very receptive to his outrageous Demon Dog persona. At several gigs, Ellroy was supported by the band The Jackson Code. He loved the band members' Australian sense of humor and became friends with the lead singer Mark Snarski. As part of his act, Ellroy sang "This Could Be the Start of Something" by Steve Allen. Ellroy considered it a "great swingers' song" and rewrote it with profane lyrics. The original song begins "You're walking along the street, or you're at a party." Ellroy changed this to "You're beating up Rodney King and starting a riot" and the lyrics got progressively more offensive as the song went on

Ellroy performed his version of "This Could Be the Start of Something" at the MET Theater at a gig organized by Darrell Larson and at the Beverly Hills Public Library with the backup band Pink Floyd the Barber. Ellroy had great stage presence, but he couldn't hold a note. Although that hardly mattered as the lyrics were so profane that Rick Moors, the bass player at several events where Ellroy sang, recalls "a steady stream of blue haired old ladies making a beeline for the exits."[38] Australian audiences tended to be much harder to shock, although Ellroy confided to Snarski that he would never record the song for fear of being sued.

LA Confidential began principal photography in May 1996. Ellroy visited the set and witnessed the filming of a scene in which Bud White rescues a

Figure 11 *Ellroy with Mark Snarski in March 1996. Ellroy toured Australia with Snarski and his band The Jackson Code. Photo: Courtesy of Mark Snarski.*

bound and gagged Inez Soto from her kidnappers. Ellroy developed a rapport with the main cast, with the exception of Kevin Spacey, describing him as "a venomous individual" and James Cromwell who he regarded as "aloof and imperious."[39] Ellroy shared many of Milchan's concerns about the casting. He looked at the cast and saw people who did not look or sound like the characters he had created on the page. Helgeland recalls that during one rehearsal an actor disagreed with Hanson about how to play a scene and had even brought an "expert" on set to prove his point. "Curtis disappeared for a moment and returned with a phone. He said to the actor 'Here's my expert' and passed him the phone."[40] Ellroy chewed the actor out over the phone, who then sheepishly agreed to play the scene the way Hanson wanted.

Ellroy and Hanson would dine together at the Pacific Dining Car and a friendship developed, although it was a competitive one with Helgeland often acting as mediator, "They were both about the same age and knew a lot about the LA of the sixties and seventies."[41] They even had a similar family history. Hanson's uncle Jack Hanson had been a minor Hollywood player and insider, not dissimilar to Armand Ellroy. Jack Hanson owned the magazine *Cinema* and the Beverly Hills clothing store *Jax*. Ellroy had seen Hanson's films *The Bedroom Window* and *Bad Influence* and regarded him as a competent, journeyman director, but in his view Hanson had yet to make a great film. Ellroy was very critical of most modern films. The B-movies and film noirs Ellroy had seen as a child he had enthusiastically absorbed, but as an adult he was caustic about cinema, and that included films that were critically acclaimed. Ellroy was skeptical about any glowing critical consensus that developed around a film.

Prior to the film's release Ellroy and Helen were invited to a test screening in Tacoma in early 1997. They were picked up in a limousine and were driven to the screening with Hanson and Helgeland. Of the two men, Helgeland was the bigger Ellroy fan and felt much more emotionally connected to the original novel than Hanson. Helgeland explained how they had taken the White/ Exley/Vincennes characters and shaped events around them so that the three cops are central throughout, which meant excising many of the subplots and supporting characters in the novel. The screening was from a working print, not yet color-timed and using a temporary soundtrack.

Ellroy's initial reaction to the screening was somewhere between dislike and indifference, but in his heart, he knew this was how he was always going to feel. The filmmakers had free rein to change his novel and having accepted the money he wasn't going to complain about what they had done. Helen sensed how the film was going to be perceived. "I think the critics are going to love this," she told Hanson and Helgeland. However, as Warner Bros were planning a modest September release, critical plaudits were unlikely to be enough to give the film commercial success.

Hanson lobbied hard for *LA Confidential* to be submitted to the Cannes film festival, surmising that it would help gather critical momentum. In May 1997, Ellroy and Helen travelled to Cannes to support the film with Hanson, Helgeland, and the main cast. Ellroy wore his ceremonial Cameron kilt on the red carpet, a brave sartorial choice considering the rest of the men were decked out in Armani, but Helgeland opined that Ellroy wore it so "he'd be easy to pick out."[42] Back in the US, Ellroy and Hanson attended a screening of the film in San Francisco, which was covered by Ed Beitiks, one of the journalists Ellroy most admired, for the *Examiner*. At the screening, an audience member described *LA Confidential* as the greatest crime film since *Chinatown*. Hanson was flattered but tried to play down the comparison, insisting that it was not a homage to film noir. Ellroy was blunter, "This movie is much better than *Chinatown*, which was slipshod, full of anachronisms." Ellroy was happy to criticize Roman Polanski's critically-lauded film, "Just about everything you're looking at there is wrong."[43]

The biggest publicity coup for the film came when Annie Leibowitz photographed Ellroy, Hanson, and Helgeland for *Vanity Fair*. The shoot took place at the Pacific Dining Car. The three men arrived to find the dining tables had been arranged to look as though they had just enjoyed a large meal. Hungry and bored, they spent several miserable hours being photographed. "When we walked into the parking lot," Helgeland recalls, "we exchanged looks as if to say, 'Well that was lame.'"[44] Leibowitz walked out of the restaurant and must have sensed their displeasure. She asked them repeatedly what was wrong, but the three men were too polite, or too intimidated by Leibowitz's lofty reputation, to admit what they were thinking until Leibowitz snapped.

"You didn't like the shoot, did you?"

Leibowitz had intuited their feelings and, not one to be disheartened, instructed an assistant to fetch a polaroid camera. She spent a couple of minutes taking snaps of Ellroy, Helgeland, and Hanson, now visibly more relaxed, in the parking lot. The polaroid shots were reprinted in *Vanity Fair*.

Within a year of its release, *LA Confidential* was already considered a classic of American cinema. At the 70th Academy Awards it lost out to James Cameron's critically panned *Titanic* for Best Picture, which was considered by many critics to be Hollywood hypocrisy at its worst. It won Best Supporting Actress for Kim Basinger and Best Adapted Screenplay for Hanson and Helgeland. Both awards rankled Ellroy. He disliked Basinger's performance and felt that Hanson should not have won the Oscar when his contribution to the screenplay was minimal, "If that had gone to Writers Guild of America arbitration, he wouldn't have got the credit."[45]

The following year another film adaptation of an Ellroy novel was released, although it would not be remotely as successful as *LA Confidential*. Jason Freeland had first come across Ellroy at film school when the author was a guest on a student radio show. Impressed with the Demon Dog, Freeland set about turning Ellroy's debut novel *Brown's Requiem* into his first film as a director. While the film was in development, James Gandolfini was interested in playing the lead role, but he had just accepted the role of Tony Soprano and requested that Freeland wait until he was free of the commitment. Freeland, to his regret, ploughed on with production and cast Michael Rooker in the title role. Despite an impressive cast including Selma Blair, Brion James, and Brad Dourif the completed film was an incoherent mess. Although it was a positive experience for Freeland on a personal level, "So much of the book is about Brown's alcoholism, and halfway through shooting I realized that I was an alcoholic."[46] Freeland embraced sobriety. The film had a brief theatrical release before going straight to video. Freeland had hoped Ellroy would help with the publicity but, after attending a private screening, Ellroy claimed that he had to escape to the bathroom afterwards to contain his laughter and try to think of something nice to say about the film.

Whether the adaptations of his work were good or bad, Ellroy's celebrity status was on the rise. Beginning in 1995, Ellroy appeared as a semi-regular guest on *Late Night with Conan O'Brien*. It was the first of five appearances on the show. O'Brien was an admirer of Ellroy's but found it difficult keeping a lid on Ellroy's outrageous brand of "Dog" humor. The highpoint of which came in 1999 when, seated next to the comedian Dave Chappelle, Ellroy suggested they should start their own "Equal Opportunity Ku Klux Klan Klavern" and they would "let in Jews, Catholics, Irish, Gays—Everybody!" Chappelle and the audience were in hysterics at Ellroy's suggestion. O'Brien was less impressed and Ellroy did not appear on the show for another five years, and when he did O'Brien continually interrupted him, denying Ellroy the latitude to let his schtick work. It was the last time the author would appear on the show.

It was not just showbiz people who were trying to get Ellroy's attention, the publication of *My Dark Places* led to Ellroy being contacted by many people from his past who he had not seen in years. Steve Horvitz, a former classmate of Ellroy's at John Burroughs Junior High School, reached out to the author after reading the memoir.

At first Ellroy didn't remember Horvitz, but when they began talking on the phone it brought back a flood of memories. Ellroy and Horvitz discussed the different turns their lives had taken in the intervening years, but it was Horvitz's memories of attending JB school which really interested Ellroy. They talked about the good and bad teachers, the schoolgirls they had a crush on and the inspiring, funny, or sometimes tragic fates which befell their classmates. Ellroy's conversations with Horvitz began to change his perception of his formal education. After being expelled from Fairfax High, Ellroy had blanked much of his schooling from his mind. He had spent his early years being shuffled from school to school and underperforming at most of them. But now he began to look back on JB with great affection, realizing how many of his experiences there had been formative to his character and regarding it as the only school he really enjoyed attending.

Horvitz had kept in touch with many of the JB alumni and began discussing with Ellroy the possibility of a school reunion. Both men were enthusiastic about the idea, but the planning turned out to be much more complex than expected. Horvitz joined a committee of JB alumni tasked with handling the logistics of the hotel and restaurant bookings. Another committee member,

Donna Lam, had to fight hard for Ellroy to be allowed to attend the reunion. Not all JB alumni remembered Ellroy fondly or were impressed by his reputation as a polemicist, but Donna argued successfully that Ellroy's schtick was just "performance art."[47] Ellroy was not on the committee and restricted himself to the elements of planning which were the most interesting to him— finding people. Ellroy hired LAPD detective Rick Jackson to find JB alumni.

The John Burroughs Junior High School reunion dinner took place at the Pacific Dining Car in November 1998. One large dinner party soon extended to three increasingly large dinner parties on separate evenings when word got around, and more people wanted to attend.

Ellroy was thrilled by the reunion and wrote about it in the *GQ* article "Let's Twist Again." The article angered many of the attendees. What they had not anticipated was that at a reunion where wine and conversation flowed freely, the teetotal Ellroy was absorbing people's memories and experiences as compulsively as the JB alumni were downing the Sauvignon Blanc. Several attendees were surprised and displeased to find their lives laid out in *GQ*. Ellroy, though, was always sympathetic to other people's life experiences. He had made his share of mistakes and endured enough traumas to not judge other people's life choices. Ellroy even took a liking to Howard Swancy, a black evangelical pastor who seemed out of place at a predominantly Jewish reunion. Swancy's strident disapproval of the heavy drinking and choice language which characterized much of the reunion angered some of the attendees. But Ellroy, who always had a degree of religiosity about him, agreed to visit Swancy's Peace Apostolic Church in Carson the following Sunday.

Swancy's fire and brimstone sermon advocated that only those who had accepted Christ as their savior would be accepted into Heaven. This didn't chime with Ellroy's idiosyncratic religious views, as it would exclude "pork dodgers or skeptics or that Moslem guy at my favorite falafel stand."[48] At one point Ellroy describes catching the eye of a "tall black kid" who is clearly bored and attending at the behest of his parents.[49] The boy reminded Ellroy of his younger self when he was dragged to First Dutch Lutheran Church by his mother. He smiled and winked at the lad and made a silent prayer wishing him "imagination and a stern will and lots of raucous laughs. I wished him a wild mix of people to breeze through and linger with over time."[50]

Ellroy was largely unaware of any negative feedback to his *GQ* article. He regarded the JB reunion as a resounding success. Ellroy, Horvitz, and Stoner visited Las Vegas as research for his forthcoming novel. Ellroy was deep into the writing of *The Cold Six Thousand*, the second novel in his Underworld USA trilogy. One of his leading characters, Wayne Tedrow Jr, is a Las Vegas police officer from a wealthy Mormon family. Ellroy visited the Las Vegas Metropolitan Police Museum as research. He stayed at the five-star Bellagio Hotel and Casino, but he wanted to see the more lower-class areas of the city so that his writing would capture Vegas's unique topography. Ellroy drove through North Cheyenne and Rancho Charleston and witnessed scenes of poverty as harsh as could be found in any large American city. It gave him a sense of Las Vegas far removed from the glamor of the Strip. In February 2000, Ellroy and Horvitz visited Las Vegas again as Ellroy was covering the Barrera vs Morales prize fight for *GQ*.

Although he did some research on the novel in Vegas himself, Ellroy was increasingly inclined to hire researchers. Laura Nolan, a junior agent at Sobel/Weber Associates, did much of the research on the key historical figures Ellroy used as characters. It helped Ellroy to make sure, for instance, that a real-life mobster like Johnny Rosselli was not serving a prison sentence at a time when Ellroy wanted him on the street scheming. Ellroy was interested in the most technical of details regarding police work, right down to the regalia on LVPD uniforms.

The writing of *The Cold Six Thousand* was an intense and "tremendously stressful" experience, but Ellroy still found time to enjoy the fruits of his success.[51] On March 4, 1998, Ellroy celebrated his fiftieth birthday. Nat Sobel organized a party for Ellroy held at Gramercy Tavern in New York. Ellroy and Helen flew in from Kansas City to attend. There were around twenty guests, friends of Ellroy who were among the biggest names in publishing at the time—Sonny Mehta, Otto Penzler, Larry Kirshbaum, François Guérif, Chip Kidd and his partner Sandy McClatchy. Later that year, *GQ* bestowed upon Ellroy its Writer of the Year award. The *GQ* Men of the Year awards ceremony took place at Radio City Music Hall on October 21. Ellroy, wearing a tuxedo with a tartan bowtie, gave a raucous speech which was well received by the celebrity audience. At the after-show party, Ellroy found himself flirting with

Jennifer Lopez and, so he claimed, had Salma Hayek bouncing up and down on his lap. He was self-aware enough to acknowledge that "they [Lopez and Hayek] had both been drinking."[52] Ellroy was at the peak of his success but, as was so often the case with Ellroy, hubris would be followed by nemesis.

And Ellroy's nemesis would come in the form of an aging furrier named Albert Teitelbaum.

Ellroy's first anthology of *GQ* articles were released in 1999, titled *Crime Wave: Reportage and Fiction from the Underside of LA*. Aside from the articles, the book also contained short stories featuring a new fictional character named Danny Getchell. Getchell is a quick-thinking and fast-talking *Hush-Hush* reporter in 1950s LA. Ellroy uses Getchell's first-person spiel to indulge in some excessively alliterative, overtly comic experiments. He may have written the Getchell stories to unwind from the pressures of drafting epic novels of historical fiction, but the publication of the short story, "Tijuana, Mon Amour," was the beginning of a myriad of legal problems, expenses, and ongoing stress for Ellroy.

In the story as it was originally published in *GQ*, Ellroy used the real-life character of Albert Teitelbaum. Teitelbaum was known as the "Furrier to the Stars" as he supplied furs to actresses such as Elizabeth Taylor, and briefly served as Mario Lanza's business manager. Teitelbaum was convicted in 1956 of insurance fraud after staging a fur heist at his Beverly Hills clothing store as part of an elaborate insurance scam. Ellroy fictionalized the "robbery" and felt safe in doing so, as Teitelbaum's conviction was a matter of historical record. But Ellroy also adds comic touches with Teitelbaum sleeping with Barbara Graham, the convicted murderer who was executed at San Quentin. Ellroy wouldn't have felt confident writing these scenes unless he was sure that Teitelbaum was dead. Ellroy worked on the principle that it is legally impossible to libel the dead. Unfortunately for Ellroy, the name was more common than he had thought, an obituary check had flagged up a different Albert Teitelbaum.

Teitelbaum was alive and well, an octogenarian with a litigious streak. Teitelbaum sued Ellroy and *GQ* for libel. He was represented by Charles Morgan, a Pitbull attorney who had hounded *The New Yorker* and reporter

Janet Malcolm in a similar case which had dragged on for more than a decade. Morgan eventually lost that case, but the time and resources the lawsuit had drained from *The New Yorker* had been considerable. With Teitelbaum, Morgan knew he had a stronger case as Ellroy had certainly exhibited the recklessness required for a libel suit. Teitelbaum was asking for the inflated sum of $20,000,000. There was little possibility of him being awarded such a figure, but that did not stop the anxiety eating away at Ellroy as he began to contemplate nightmare scenarios such as bankruptcy, and publishers walking away from him.

Ellroy first learned about the lawsuit on February 17, 1999, the same day that Morgan telephoned Condé Nast publications informing them of his client's intention to sue. As it happened, *GQ* were hosting a party in Ellroy's honor at Joe's Pub, Lafayette Street in New York the same evening. It was reported from the event that "Mr Ellroy did not look to be in much of a partying mood. In fact, guests noted that he did not work the room much, and they spotted him talking solemnly with Mr Cooper by the stairway at the end of the bar."[53] Ellroy's legal team was robust in their response. Their research unearthed that over a twenty-year period, from the 1930s onwards, Teitelbaum had been the victim of several suspicious robberies, all of them possible insurance scams. It may have helped them negotiate a more reasonable figure with Morgan, but there was little doubt that Ellroy would have to pay-up eventually. The fact that he had committed libel was indisputable. Ellroy paid Teitelbaum around $180,000. The figure was much lower than he had feared, but the resulting stress had been overwhelming.

Ellroy had written scathing portrayals of members of the Kennedy clan and knew that America's most famed dynasty couldn't touch him as when writing about a person who was deceased there was no legal recourse available to their surviving kin. He had finally been caught out by an elderly ex-con furrier who had retired to Oregon. Teitelbaum always maintained his innocence in the insurance fraud, he even lobbied Governor of California Pat Brown for a pardon. He died in 2010, more than decade after Ellroy had used him in fiction.

Despite these setbacks, Ellroy was still a prized columnist for *GQ*. This was never more evident than when Doug Stumpf, a senior editor at *Vanity Fair*, telephoned Ellroy with the hope of luring him over to the magazine. On his next visit to New York, Ellroy told Art Cooper about the offer from Stumpf. Cooper immediately got Stumpf on the phone and started yelling obscenities at him, warning him against trying to poach his columnists. Cooper and Graydon Carter, editor of *Vanity Fair*, had a clear-the-air lunch at Da Silvano restaurant in Greenwich Village, a few days after the series of phone calls had caused gossip at Condé Nast.[54]

The ruthless nature of magazine publishing entailed editors rarely stayed in post for long at *GQ*. Ellroy's editors included Paul Scanlon who left the magazine in 1996, and Ilena Silverman, who later joined the *New York Times*. He spent many hours on the phone with the magazine's fact checkers. Silverman requested Ellroy write a piece about the death penalty. Ellroy and Jackson flew to Houston to research a death penalty case in November 1999. They visited the convicted murderer Shaka Sankofa at the Terrell Unit in Rosharon where he was being held prior to his scheduled execution. Born Gary Graham, Sankofa was convicted of the murder Bobby Lambert, a drug dealer who was shot dead in the parking lot of a Safeway supermarket. As there was only one eyewitness, and Sankofa's attorney Ron Mock was allegedly drunk for much of his trial, the case had become a cause célèbre among anti-death penalty activists. Ellroy instinctively supported the death penalty, and while he was personally repulsed by Sankofa he reluctantly argued that he should not be executed on the grounds of insufficient evidence in his article "Grave Doubt." Sankofa was executed in Huntsville on June 22, 2000, by lethal injection. Helen hoped that by softening his stance on the death penalty, Ellroy might start to revise more of his conservative beliefs. In the event, the opposite happened. Ellroy viewed the article as an "apostasy."[55] He reverted to full-hearted support of the death penalty and his public conservatism grew more combative than ever, although he seldom, if ever, referred to himself as a Republican. He knew the label would anger most of his readership. Ellroy described his views as being that of a "Tory Mystic."[56]

Ellroy broke new ground when Sobel Weber Associates held "the first auction for an e-book written by a well-known author." The book was titled *Breakneck Pace*, an anthology containing previously unpublished short stories.

The e-book auction was billed as a major step forward in the publishing industry's embrace of digital technology, and who better than an author as popular and innovative as Ellroy to pioneer this transformation. But Ellroy was dismissive, even irritable, about the subject in later interviews, "I don't give a shit about ePublishing. Somebody gave me five thousand bucks to compile these things for that, but that will not prevent me from collecting [the stories] into a regular book. ePublishing will go bust. People want to go into a bookstore and pick up a book."[57] As it happens, the stories were recycled for a later anthology and Ellroy's statement on the durability of the printed book would be vindicated. E-books did not eclipse printed books as many industry analysts predicted. However, as readers increasingly ordered books on the internet bookstores began to disappear from the high street and this meant that authors had to become web savvy to generate publicity and maintain contact with their readership. For Ellroy, still writing all his novels by hand, it would take all his energy and determination to stay in the game, and that meant increasingly resorting to his recognizable and marketable Demon Dog persona.

When "Tijuana, Mon Amour" was reprinted in *Crime Wave*, the Teitelbaum character was renamed Louie Sobel, a sly nod to Ellroy's literary agent. Ellroy and Nat Sobel were still very close, with Sobel sending him correspondence addressed to "Dog" and from "The Money." *Crime Wave* was dedicated to Curtis Hanson. Ellroy and Hanson were still friends, and Ellroy accepted a cameo in Hanson's film *Wonder Boys*. Ellroy flew out to Pittsburgh to film the scene. It was an all-day shoot that stretched into the early morning. The scene takes place at a large house where a literary party is taking place. Several prominent Hollywood actors: Michael Douglas, Robert Downey Jr, Frances McDormand, Katie Holmes, Tobey Maguire, and Rip Torn, appear in the scene. Ellroy was filmed talking to a young woman, but only his back is visible and from their conversation the audience can infer that this is the author of *LA Confidential*. Perhaps Hanson thought the scene was too self-reverential as it ended up on the cutting room floor.

Ellroy's only other acting credit came a year later. Mitch Brian was a Kansas City based screenwriter and director who became friends with Ellroy once he moved to Mission Hills. They would go for coffee and to see movies regularly. Ellroy suggested to Brian that he could direct a film adaptation of *Killer on the Road*, but "I couldn't really see it as a feature that I could get going or that I would want to see, but I loved that interrogation (scene) in it. And I said, can I just make a short film of this section."[58] *Stay Clean*, an 11-minute adaptation of chapter 14 of *Killer on the Road*, was filmed at a rented house in Kansas City in February 2001. In the film, serial killer Martin Plunkett is visited and interrogated at his home by three detectives about his suspected involvement in a double homicide. Ellroy plays one of the detectives, and his lanky frame towers over the three other cast members. His only dialogue is the final line of the film, when he tells Plunkett to "Stay Clean." Ellroy enjoyed joking around with the cast and crew, although he was taken aback by Race Owen who played Plunkett, "He thought the kid was crazy. He was actually a little unnerved by the actor who was playing the killer."[59]

At the same time *Stay Clean* was in production, Ellroy was contributing to another documentary based on his life and work. *James Ellroy's Feast of Death* was directed by Vikram Jayanti. Prior to the production, Ellroy had befriended the *LA Times* journalist Larry Harnisch. Harnisch had done extensive research on the Black Dahlia case and had identified a suspect in the murder—Dr Walter Bayley. Ellroy was fascinated with Harnisch's findings and offered to loan him money to fund his investigation and introduce him to Nat Sobel, as Harnisch was planning a book on the case. Ellroy invited Harnisch to take part in the filming of *Feast of Death*. Two nights of filming took place at the Pacific Dining Car in January 2001. The first night was a dinner with Ellroy and LAPD detectives. The second night features Ellroy and Harnisch dining with LASD detectives. Ellroy invites Harnisch to lay out his Dahlia theory. The response from the detectives present is overwhelmingly hostile. They barely let Harnisch speak, interrupting him constantly with often puerile gags. Ellroy was visibly frustrated and tried to stick up for his friend. A surreal interruption breaks the tension of the scene. Nick Nolte walked into the restaurant wearing a black bathrobe covered in dog hair and hobbling from a leg injury. Nolte's disheveled appearance was completely unexpected and Ellroy was unnerved when he sat next to him at the dinner table. As Harnisch is speaking, Ellroy leans over to Nolte and says, "This guy's getting an awful grilling. What he's found is pretty watertight."[60]

In 1999, Ellroy donated his archive to the University of South Carolina. Acquiring Ellroy's archive had been the brainchild of Matthew J. Bruccoli. Bruccoli was the biographer and leading authority on F. Scott Fitzgerald. With his flat-top haircut, gruff Bronx accent, Brooks Brothers suits covering his considerable girth, and cigar often clasped in his teeth, Bruccoli cut a memorable figure. According to his colleague Richard Layman, Bruccoli was also "brusque, some might say high-handed."[61] Ellroy's assessment was harsher, "the most misogynistic man I ever met."[62] During tense negotiations with Ellroy, Bruccoli telephoned Knopf one day and reduced a female publicist to tears. Ellroy was on friendly terms with the lady in question, and when he heard about the incident, he angrily telephoned Bruccoli and demanded that he apologize to her or "I'll never talk to you again."

"Nobody talks to me that way," Bruccoli snapped back.

The conversation soon descended into a shouting match. Layman, an old friend of Ellroy's, took over the negotiations from that point on. Ellroy told Layman he wanted a South Carolina Gamecocks football jacket. Lou Holtz was the Gamecocks coach at the time and had successfully brought the team back to national prominence. Holtz was adamantly opposed to Ellroy receiving a jacket as he had never played for the team. It took all of Layman's powers of diplomacy to persuade Holtz to let Ellroy have the jacket, and when he finally relented "it didn't even fit."[63]

Ellroy flew from Kansas City to Los Angeles to attend a party at the Pacific Dining Car to celebrate the University of South Carolina acquiring his papers. The choice of setting struck some of the attendees, including Layman as "bizarre."[64] It may have been a calculated snub to the University of Southern California, who had not received Ellroy's papers as "the cocksuckers never asked."[65] The USC campus was only a few miles from the Pacific Dining Car although, as several film producers were at the party, it is more likely Ellroy took the opportunity to show Hollywood his rising critical status. Ellroy would visit the University of South Carolina periodically giving lectures and interviews and updating the archive whenever possible.

A key contact Ellroy made while living in Mission Hills was with the filmmaker Benjamin Meade. Ellroy first met Meade as he was working as an insurance agent at the time and Ellroy was one of his clients. Ellroy and Meade became friendly and when Meade told him that he also directed documentaries, Ellroy was happy to use his celebrity status to help him. The films that Ellroy appeared in for Meade ranged from the banal to the bizarre. In *Vakvagany*, Meade presents home movie footage, supposedly shot from 1948 to 1964, of a Hungarian family consisting of a young boy and girl and their parents. Ellroy is one of three "experts" who provides commentary on the footage, much of which is odd and disturbing. In one scene, the mother appears to be holding the boy's penis while he urinates and Ellroy says, "You can't even really tell if she's messing about with his wang. Looked like she might be fixing his fly or something."[66] Some parts of the film are completely unhinged. Meade travels to Hungary to track down the now aging siblings and breaks into the sister's house to examine her possessions. Ellroy looks like he is not taking the documentary remotely seriously, and his presence does not lend the film the gravitas that Meade was probably hoping for.

Ellroy's next documentary with Meade, *Das Bus*, was a more benign affair concerning the Kansas City public transport system. Meade filmed Ellroy on a bus travelling round the city giving anecdotes about his experiences with public transport.

Ellroy's last, and certainly worst, full-length documentary for Benjamin Meade was released in 2004. *Bazaar Bizarre* tells the story of Kansas City serial killer Bob Berdella who raped, tortured, and murdered six men. The subject matter is promising but the directorial approach is woefully misjudged. The film, which takes its title from the shop Berdella ran in the Westport neighborhood of Kansas City, is a Troma Entertainment production, a company notorious for churning out cheaply made, gore-splattered horror movies. In keeping with Troma's low reputation the film features various reenactment scenes of the hideous torture Berdella inflicted on his victims, as well as a rock band (the Demon Dogs) who perform several distasteful songs about the killer. One of the better moments is an interview with Christopher Bryson, who managed to escape from Berdella after enduring three days of torture and alerted the police. Ellroy gives a semi-humorous narration to the film. Ellroy was deeply unwell at the time and is noticeably bloated. Despite being credited as an executive producer, Ellroy was disgusted with the finished film, calling it "a bad, vile movie."[67]

Ellroy and Meade did have plans to do a documentary adaptation of his anthology *Destination Morgue!* Meade shot some footage of Ellroy on tour to support the book, but a full-length film was never made. As Ellroy detested *Bazaar Bizarre* and was embarrassed by his appearance, he may have felt it would be safer not to make another documentary with Meade.

Ellroy had enjoyed a long run of celebrity with all the perks and stresses that such status entails. But writing was what he was born to do, and it was time he returned to his novels. He could not know that the long-awaited publication of *The Cold Six Thousand* would spark a chain of events that would lead to a nervous breakdown, drug addiction, and the unravelling of his marriage to Helen.

10

The Crack-Up
(2000–2006)

When Ellroy submitted his final draft of *The Cold Six Thousand* the reaction in Knopf was enthusiastic and the author was bullish about its potential. He saw it as his breakthrough into literary fiction. Ellroy, it seems, was right to be optimistic about the novel. It had been six years since the publication of *American Tabloid* and anticipation for its sequel was high. *The Cold Six Thousand* became the first of Ellroy's novels to crack the hardcover bestseller list. Critical reaction was also positive, but from the reviewers who did express dissent, Ellroy received some of the harshest reviews of his career. Tom Cox, who was usually admiring of Ellroy's writing, complained "There's barely a paragraph longer than two lines here, the endless repetition of names quickly becomes irritating, and it seems unrealistic that everyone connected with the American political underworld in the mid-sixties would do their thinking in jive."[1] The Australian writer Peter Temple was blunter, "The book is just a catalogue of psychopathic behavior—graceless, charmless, witless. There is no moment in all of it when time sticks and the mind considers a sentence, sentences, a paragraph. Nothing induces reflection. The only constant reflex is a vague feeling about the pointlessness of it all."[2]

Ellroy's immediate response to the bad reviews was typical of how most people initially react to criticism, he assumed it was wrong and ignored it. He was about to embark on a European and North American book tour in which he would meet thousands of fans who loved his writing. Such an environment may have seemed appealing to shield himself from outside criticism. However, the book tour would become a never-ending nightmare for Ellroy. It would be the culmination of multiple issues which were dogging Ellroy's mental health. Ellroy had more than one traumatic event from his past that was haunting him. He was overworked. The Teitelbaum lawsuit had given him financial worries. His marriage to Helen was under strain. His intense workload, often keeping him away from home for months at a time, was a source of grievance to her.

The first physical manifestations of Ellroy's breakdown began to show on the plane trip to Paris for his book tour. Rather than feeling excitement at the tour ahead, Ellroy was in a very low mood. He became convinced that something was physically wrong with him. He locked himself in the bathroom and "spent 20 minutes looking for rips and tears in my eyes."[3] He was convinced he had skin cancer, or some other serious disease that was affecting his physical condition. It was the start of a series of hypochondriacal and delusional episodes.

After press events in Paris, Ellroy moved onto Rome. He was agitated and had been attacking his own skin like a little boy picking away at a scab. A rash had developed. Ellroy walked around with huge wads of money which he used to pay hotel staff to do tasks for him outside of their job description. It made him feel important and covered for his worrying lack of practical skills. While suffering a panic attack, Ellroy paid a bellman a "C-note" and was huddled into a taxi and taken at speed to a local dermatologist.[4] The doctor told him his cancer fears were unfounded. Ellroy was suffering from "a minor rash exacerbated by scratching."[5] It did nothing to allay his fears.

Ellroy prided himself on always being able to perform for journalists and readers no matter how he was feeling. Certainly, he was functioning well in public given all he was going through, but his paranoid state was beginning to show. After public appearances in Amsterdam, Ellroy travelled to Spain. M.G. Smout interviewed Ellroy at a restaurant in Barcelona. He found the author's behavior to be worrying. Ellroy had "a frightening array of vitamin pills and supplements lined up on the table."[6] He was drinking "copious amounts of green tea" and working out in hotel gyms whenever he could.[7] It helped to ward off his fears that he was physically ill. Smout recognized in Ellroy a developing paranoia, "every blemish, mark on his skin, wheeze, or whatever urges him to seek transatlantic phone help from his wife."[8]

Figure 12 *Ellroy at the Théâtre de l'Odéon in Paris during his 2001 book tour for* The Cold Six Thousand *(French title:* American Death Trip*). The smiles hide the fact that Ellroy was in the midst of a nervous breakdown during the tour. Credit: Jeanne Guyon.*

An error of judgment on Ellroy's part led him to botching what could have been a pleasant reunion. Cindy DePoy, Ellroy's ex-girlfriend from his days in Venice Beach, had been living in Valencia for years and, upon hearing that Ellroy was coming to Spain, had reached out suggesting they meet up. Ellroy had nominally agreed but then made a crass statement in the press that she probably wanted money from him. Cindy was offended and called the meeting off. She was also bemused by Ellroy's handlers' instructions that she must not, under any circumstances, call him Lee. To her, Ellroy was always Lee.

After finishing his European tour with engagements in the UK, Ellroy flew to New York. He met with Helen who was in the city for meetings about her debut novel, *The Ticket Out*. Helen was concerned about her husband's appearance. While Ellroy was usually inclined to shrug off concerns about his workload, he admitted to her that he was exhausted and desperate to go home. But he still had thirty-two US cities to tour.

Ellroy met the journalist Craig McDonald in Ann Arbor. McDonald had been a fan of Ellroy's work for years and was looking forward to interviewing him. However, he had become concerned about Ellroy's wellbeing after monitoring comments the author had been making to the press throughout the tour. They met in the lobby of a busy hotel. The interview was conducted with the bustle of hotel guests and staff coming and going all around them. As soon as Ellroy started speaking, McDonald's worst fears were confirmed, "He was very fidgety. He made intense eye contact, but he was definitely restless."[9] Ellroy talked of how he couldn't sleep and that he was "tired of myself." McDonald presented Ellroy with clippings from interviews which highlighted his most worrying comments, "I posed a question about his health, and I held up my printouts and he took them from me, and he started leafing through them. He became visibly rattled as he was scanning all of these."[10]

After the interview was finished, McDonald sent a message to Mitch Brian who he had been corresponding with in Kansas City, recommending that Knopf release a statement saying Ellroy was cancelling the remainder of the tour. "I don't know if it was due to me, but Ellroy did issue a statement" two days later:

> It is with great regret that I have had to cancel appearances on my US book tour. I have been on the road since March 12 and the effect of this global tour finally caught up with me in Chicago[11]

Back at home in Mission Hills, Ellroy's paranoia began to worsen. He had done the right thing in ending the tour early, but his health struggles were just beginning. Ellroy began compulsively shutting the windows, shutters, and curtains and sitting in the dark, convinced that he had skin cancer.

Helen practiced Iyengar yoga and persuaded James to try it:

> They have all sorts of postures and stuff for anxiety, for what he was going through at that time. I got him mostly restorative stuff, mostly resting the front brain to try to slow it down and stuff, forward bends. It didn't do anything because he was too overwrought to sit still. James was too overwrought to be belted and set up with blankets in these poses which are considered restorative for depression and anxiety.[12]

In the meantime, Ellroy's behavior became increasingly erratic. Helen had to be around him all the time for fear that he would self-harm. On one occasion when she did leave the house to go to her yoga class she returned and found that Ellroy had "tried to saw some kind of freckle on his arm off with a dinner knife."[13] Helen was convinced that her husband needed professional help, but Ellroy refused to see a doctor. Helen sought advice from the University of Kansas Medical Center and was informed that if Ellroy would not seek help then they were not obliged to treat "someone who hadn't threatened violence or suicide and wasn't known to be addicted to a substance."[14]

Ellroy was seeking help, but from dubious sources. Ellroy had met a couple who were followers of Maharishi Mahesh Yogi. According to Helen "somehow James met these two swifties, I can't remember how."[15] They persuaded Ellroy that the teachings of the Maharishi (a tax exile living in the Netherlands) could help with his condition. Ellroy visited the compound Maharishi Vedic City in Jefferson County, Iowa in July 2001. At great expense, Ellroy tried an ayurvedic diet and was "slathered with healing oils and learned transcendental meditation."[16] Helen dubbed Vedic City "Charlatan Central." With mounting bills and no discernible improvement in Ellroy's mental health, Helen decided to "go up there and get him. Get him out of the clutches of these people."[17]

Ellroy finally agreed to see a doctor. He prescribed Ellroy a course of benzodiazepines. Helen described the effect this medication had on Ellroy's mood as miraculous, "Within half an hour of taking these pills, James was on his stairclimber blasting Tchaikovsky."[18] However, it was the beginning of a whole new nightmare for the couple, "He was magically cured and the price for that was addiction."[19] Ellroy was still seeking alternative forms of therapy. In 2002, he visited an astrologer. After reading his meridian lines the astrologer informed Ellroy that the worst place for him to live in the North American continent was the West Coast. It was a sage assessment. LA was the scene of too many traumas for Ellroy, and the City of Angels could beckon him wherever he was on the West Coast.

As it happens, Ellroy and Helen were planning to move and the West Coast seemed like a good alternative to Kansas City. "That was my fault," Helen rued. Ellroy had once viewed his Tudor home in Mission Hills as a monument to his success as a writer. But his recent spate of health problems, the sweltering

Midwest heat, and the ultra-conservative outlook of the community had soured his view of the place. Despite his authoritarian views, Ellroy never fit in with the upper middle-class Republican set at Mission Hills. As Helen recalls:

> Johnson County was a White Flight County and Kansas is still extremely Republican to the point where I wanted out. I couldn't stand it and James never got along with those people. He always upset them because he's not a programmatic Republican and he's not a programmatic conservative. He's just in this category by himself.[20]

They settled on Carmel-by-the-Sea in Monterey County. It seemed to be a good choice, with a temperate Pacific climate and only a five-hour drive from Los Angeles, which was convenient as Ellroy needed screenwriting assignments now that his health problems had put his next novel on hiatus. However, Helen was about to discover that whenever Ellroy was in the orbit of LA, it's gravitational pull would suck him into an orgy of self-destruction.

Ellroy and Helen purchased the former summer home of Clark Gable and his wife Kay Williams in Carmel. They moved to Carmel in July 2002 but stayed in an apartment at first as the house required extensive renovations. Ellroy left Helen to handle all the details of the sale, the logistics of moving from Kansas, and hiring the workmen for the house. His inability to make even the smallest contribution to the move, outside of financing, infuriated Helen.

Ellroy's drug addiction and mental health problems were worsening. He made more and more trips to LA, booking himself a six-week stay at the Beverly Wilshire on the pretense of attending a neurofeedback course for his insomnia. In reality, Ellroy had discovered a pharmacist in Little Tokyo who would sell him prescription drugs under the table and staying in hotel suites was the one place he still felt safe. After overdosing twice, one time at a party he and Helen had thrown at their new home, Ellroy had gone into two separate 72-hour lockdowns at Monterey Hospital. The medical staff informed Helen that Ellroy was bi-polar, a diagnosis that made sense to her at the time but that she would later begin to question.

Helen begged Ellroy to seek help for his addiction at the Betty Ford Center in Rancho Mirage. Ellroy chose a different form of therapy. His addiction to pills had caused his weight to balloon. He decided to seek help in losing weight at the Canyon Ranch Resort in Tucson, a fat farm beloved by Hollywood stars. It would prove a disastrous decision. Ellroy had only been there a short while before Helen received a phone call from the Canyon Ranch staff. Ellroy had been hospitalized after overdosing and hallucinating that he was doing a ride-along in a police car with Rick Jackson. As he was too sick to travel by plane, Helen was now faced with a 1,600-mile round trip to Tucson to retrieve her sick husband. She telephoned Ellroy's friend in LA, the novelist Bruce Wagner, hoping that he might offer to help with the driving. His response surprised her. He told her to ask Carrie Fisher, who had written at-length about her struggles with addiction, for advice.

> It turned out it was a life-changing conversation. There I am talking to Princess Leia for forty-five minutes. I'd never read *Postcards from the Edge*. I never knew about all her lockdowns, drinking and all this kind of stuff. She knew more about the medical psychiatric landscape than anybody I'd talk to during this whole breakdown period with James, starting in 2000. Carrie explained to me how American medicine has evolved so you can't just take an overwrought star, stick a needle in them like in *Valley of the Dolls* and let them rest for twenty-four, forty-eight hours or a week to stop the engines.[21]

Fisher told Helen that the bi-polar diagnosis was premature, "You cannot diagnose somebody as bipolar when they are addicted. The addictions are a screen which you have to stop and remove before you can actually see what's going on mentally with people."[22]

Once he was back in Carmel, Ellroy finally agreed to go into rehab. At Monterey hospital Ellroy discovered that rehab was very different from how he remembered it in the mid-1970s. Now in his early fifties, Ellroy was by far the oldest person there. He became close to Dr. Oscar Reyes, one of the physicians involved in the program. As Reyes was somewhat closer to his age, Ellroy was appreciative of the long conversations he had with someone he could relate to. His attitude towards some of the other patients could be uncharitable. In his addiction worksheets, Ellroy lists "occasional resentment towards perceived stiffs in AA meetings" as a factor which leads him to lose control.[23] He was finally acknowledging the toll his addiction had placed on his marriage. On the same worksheet, Ellroy notes his "frequent frustration on marriage front" and "anger at wife."[24]

The strain of coping with Ellroy's breakdown had almost been too much for Helen, "I nearly went right down with him."[25] However, after attending several rehab sessions with Ellroy she heard horrific stories from the other patients which helped to put her husband's suffering in perspective. On the day Ellroy completed the program, Helen met him outside the hospital with a new Bull Terrier. A gift she hoped would help bring them together. Ellroy named her Margaret, in honor of his idol—Margaret Thatcher.

Helen's hopes for the renewal of their marriage were premature. Ellroy may have beaten his addictions but, as Carrie Fisher had advised, addiction is often a screen of the mental health problems that cause it. Now that he was sober, Ellroy was about to embark on a journey Helen described as an "unchecked descent into madness."[26]

In February 2003, Art Cooper announced his retirement from *GQ*. Cooper had been ousted so that the magazine could be refashioned to appeal to a younger male readership. He blamed this on the popularity of the new lad mags, *Maxim* and *FHM*, which he was loath to try and imitate. "Clearly what everyone wants is babes and boobs and bad jokes. I'm sorry, I don't agree with that at all," Cooper lamented.[27] At his retirement party, Cooper and his wife Amy Levin were presented with around-the-world airline tickets as a belated apology for being forced out of the editor's chair. Sadly, Cooper died of a heart attack in June of that year, while lunching at the Four Seasons. Only weeks earlier he had finished working on his final issue of *GQ*. It was still on the newsstands at the time of his death.

Corpulent, bombastic, and generous to a fault, Art Cooper had played a major role in launching Ellroy's journalistic career, which in turn had led to him writing *My Dark Places*. Cooper was replaced as *GQ* editor by Jim Nelson. Ellroy and a host of other longstanding contributors were fired shortly thereafter. Ellroy interpreted *GQ*'s sudden change of direction differently than Cooper. In his view, he was too macho for the magazine which had embraced the new buzzword—Metrosexual. "I'm a man in my fifties. They fired all the mature guys,"[28] Ellroy complained. He was also a man wrestling with a host of health problems and undergoing emotional turmoil.

Helen found Ellroy increasingly detached when he returned from rehab. He would daydream about women and pay her little attention. He was so aloof in the house that Margaret regarded him as a threat to Helen and would growl at him whenever he was in sight. On the surface, everything was supposed to be fine and Ellroy could still be supportive. He attended, with Helen, the book launch for her debut novel, *The Ticket Out*, which took place at the Pacific Dining Car on January 30, 2003. Although Ellroy was unwell, bloated and so red-faced it looked like his bowtie was strangling him, his standing in Hollywood was never higher. In attendance were Fairuza Balk, David Duchovny (nominally slated to play Ellroy in an adaptation of *My Dark Places*), and Bruce Willis. Willis and Ellroy discussed a mini-series adaptation of *American Tabloid* that Willis was hoping to make through his production company Cheyenne Enterprises. Willis later sent Ellroy a script for a pilot episode and a note in which he added, "please view this as a first draft and not a shooting script."[29] Willis's option on the novel expired before he could produce the series and a later encounter with Ellroy was comically telling. Ellroy and Joel Gotler were dining at the Pacific Dining Car when they noticed Willis was sitting at the next table. Ellroy and Willis chatted amicably for a while before Willis left, and then Ellroy noticed that the movie star had slipped his bill onto Ellroy's table.

With their relationship crumbling, Ellroy and Helen agreed to try an open marriage. Helen's agreement may have only been tacit, and it is not clear how seriously she took it. Ellroy, however, was determined to exploit it to the full. An opportunity would soon present itself.

Ellroy gave a talk at UC Davis on May 28, 2004. During the Q and A afterwards, Ellroy struck up a conversation with a woman named Laura. They agreed to go for a drink afterwards. Intelligent and left-wing, Laura was certainly Ellroy's type, and he may have overstated his marriage problems to draw her into a relationship. He told Laura that a divorce was only a matter of time, whereas at home he was still nominally committed to working on his issues with Helen.[30] Ellroy would see Laura whenever he could, telling Helen that he was visiting a film director friend to discuss work. This ruse continued sporadically until it became untenable in the Winter of 2005. Ellroy confessed to Helen that he had been having an affair. They agreed to divorce.

Laura took a new job in the Bay Area. Ellroy would visit her and even though his divorce to Helen was not yet complete, he proposed, and Laura accepted. Ellroy's divorce was due to be finalized on April 20, 2006. His wedding to Laura was set for less than a month later, on May 13. Friends of the couple confirm they received the Save the Date cards, and some were already booking flights to attend. The people around Ellroy thought he was rushing things. Certainly, he was spending money at an uncontrollable rate. He was generous to Helen in the divorce agreement. Against legal advice, he did not contest her terms, although Helen still had to chase him up to get documents signed. Ellroy had briefly moved into an apartment in Carmel, then he moved to an apartment in San Francisco to be near Laura and plan their wedding.

Prior to their engagement, Ellroy and Laura travelled to Japan together for her fortieth birthday. They stayed in Tokyo and visited Jigokudani Snow Monkey Park. Traveling brought out the irritable and controlling side of Ellroy's personality. The trip "bored and angered" Ellroy and he was "immune to the beauty around us."[31] They started seeing a therapist every Wednesday afternoon to work through their problems. A weekend trip to Seattle was disastrous for the couple. Ellroy and Laura visited a mystic, again with the intention of dealing with their issues. It did not bode well, "the woman had our number."[32] They had a huge row upon returning to San Francisco. Three days later, Laura informed Ellroy that the relationship was over. It would take Ellroy years to get over Laura. However, in the short term he was happy to return to his womanizing ways even as the specter of Laura continued to haunt him.

With no other place to go, Ellroy returned to live in LA for the first time in twenty-five years.

11

Chasing It: Ellroy's Return to LA (2005–2009)

Status was very important to Ellroy now that he was back in his hometown. He rented an apartment in The Ravenswood on North Rossmore Avenue. Built by Paramount Pictures in 1930 to house studio contract players, The Ravenswood, which boasted Mae West and Ava Gardner as some of its former tenants, was a stunning Art Deco monument to LA's movie heritage. Ellroy wasted no time in having his apartment decorated. He requested deep red walls and black leather furniture. The only books on the shelves were his own and black and white photographs of historic LA lined the walls. It was a brood den with a hefty price tag.

Ellroy was making good money as a screenwriter to fund his lavish lifestyle, although his spending was so profligate that he was often one deal behind his expenses. Ellroy's screenplay "The Night Watchman" was generating a lot of interest in Hollywood circles. Spike Lee was attached to direct at one point. Oliver Stone expressed an interest in the project and Joel Gotler arranged for him to meet Ellroy at a Beverly Hills restaurant. Ellroy and Gotler arrived on time, but Stone was forty minutes late. "The one thing you don't want to do is to make Ellroy wait," Gotler recalls.[1] He noticed Ellroy was fidgeting and agitated while they waited for Stone. When Stone finally arrived, he did not apologize for his tardiness but instead "starts to talk about the art of screenwriting." Ellroy noticed Stone had been drinking and finally his patience snapped when Stone told Ellroy that the dialogue of his black characters was weak, and he was going to take him to South-Central LA to pick up the dialect. Ellroy sharply put Stone in his place.

"Mr Stone, you're drunk. I'm not working with you," he told him bluntly.

Stone was shocked that a writer would talk to him that way. They had not yet been served their appetizers and bizarrely, even though the tension at the table was unbearable, the meal still went ahead. "We made it through," Gotler recalls.[2]

"The Night Watchman" was eventually filmed as *Street Kings*, directed by David Ayer, and starring Keanu Reeves. It was a critical and commercial flop.

Coming out of a divorce can be a lonely, depressing period. Ellroy did not lack company, although the nature by which he acquired it often underscored his fundamental emotional problems. He gave a reading at Skylight Books on North Vermont Avenue in which Ellroy admitted "I was at my best and worst."[3] By this time his bookstore performances were fine-tuned to an effective formula. He would begin in outrageous fashion, welcoming the audience:

> Good evening, peepers, prowlers, pederasts, panty sniffers, punks, and pimps. I'm James Ellroy, demon dog of American literature, the foul owl with the death growl, the white knight of the far right, and the slick trick with the donkey dick. My books are written in blood, seminal fluid, and napalm. They will leave you reamed, steamed, and dry cleaned, tied, dyed, swept to the side, blued, screwed, tattooed, and bah-fongooed.[4]

Much of Ellroy's act he had adapted from culture he had been exposed to over the years. The phrase "reamed, steamed, and dry cleaned" was coined by the sportscaster John Rubenstein. Ellroy's love of jive talk was taken partly from 50s tabloid magazines, but also his viewing of *High School Confidential*, a classic beatnik film which was the first picture Ellroy saw in the theaters after his mother's death. Ellroy had experimented with a variety of performance techniques. In London in 1994, Ellroy had given the entire reading in the "voice" of Sniffer, a Staffordshire Bull Terrier which was sat next to him on the podium.

By the mid-noughties Ellroy was less experimental as he had devised a formula he was comfortable with. In his readings Ellroy would avoid reciting long excerpts. His prose was so action-packed he could convey a lot through just a few pages. When it came to questions some members of the audience would be too intimidated to take him on. Women invariably elicited a more charming response from Ellroy, albeit with a lot of showing off. The Q&A would end with a plant question, "Why do you write?" Ellroy would respond with a word-perfect rendition of Dylan Thomas' "In My Craft or Sullen Art." At the Skylight reading seven women in the audience slipped him their number at the signing afterwards. He called three of them and they had dinner dates over consecutive nights. It was not just his public performances that Ellroy had honed to a fine art, he had decided that once he completed the Underworld USA trilogy, he would narrow down both the setting and the subject matter of his writing, "It will be my last non-LA novel. From that point on, I'm a hometown writer exclusively."[5] Ellroy loved reading political biographies and had toyed with the idea of writing historical novels set around the Warren Harding presidency and the governorship of Huey Long, but after the mental exhaustion he suffered after writing *The Cold Six Thousand*, Ellroy decided it would be safer and more beneficial to stick to the LA history and setting he knew so well.

Now that his social life was busier than ever, Ellroy was always eating out with friends at the Pacific Dining Car, going to business lunches and he almost never said no to a benefit gig when asked. Ellroy hired a full-time assistant and continued to spend money recklessly. He purchased dozens of designer suits and indulged in his love of sports cars. Ellroy was frequently seen in the company of the novelist Bruce Wagner. Full of swagger and strikingly bald, Wagner looked like a mirror-image of Ellroy, except that he was usually decked out in black and Ellroy still favored garish Hawaiian shirts. Ellroy acknowledged the similarities between them, "I am the WASP Bruce, and Bruce is the Jewish me."[6] Although Wagner was not responsible for some of the excesses in Ellroy's behavior during this period, he did nothing to discourage him, and may have egged him on at times. Wagner enjoyed hanging out with celebrities and it was through him that Ellroy was introduced, over dinner, to the actress Ali MacGraw and talent agent Sue Mengers.

Wagner introduced Ellroy to Dana Delany. Ellroy had been a fan of Delany's for over a decade, after first seeing her in the film *Masquerade*. Ellroy had watched the film in a cinema in Paris and while it had featured Kim Cattrall and Meg Tilly as the female leads, he had been captivated by the young and beautiful Delany in a supporting role. Now that he was friends with her it felt like a dream come true. Ellroy gave Delany a photo of his mother and told her she was his first choice to play Jean Ellroy if *My Dark Places* was adapted into a film.

"I would have loved to have played his mother," Delany recalls.[7] "I had read *My Dark Places*. I love that book. I think many women do because James is at his most vulnerable, when of course he's also at his most attractive."[8] They also discussed remaking the film noir classic *In a Lonely Place* with Delany in the Gloria Grahame role, "We said, wouldn't it be good to make the story of Dorothy Hughes' novel, rather than Nick Ray's story."[9]

Wagner, Ellroy, and Delany would dine together frequently, and the latter two's perceived closeness drew the attention of some journalists. It was speculation that Ellroy did nothing to quell and played a role in initiating by declaring in a *GQ* article that he loved her "past all reason."[10]

Some of Ellroy's women chasing could certainly be buffoonish. At a reception at the Ravenswood attended by many senior LAPD officers, Ellroy spent much of the evening chatting to Beatrice Girmala, then a Police Captain who later became an Assistant Chief. Ellroy "sensed a vibe" with Girmala, and the next day he sent her flowers.[11] To his astonishment, two uniformed police officers visited Ellroy at his apartment shortly thereafter. The cops politely but firmly told Ellroy that Girmala was "involved with someone, back off."[12]

He didn't need to be told twice.

Ellroy had more success with the woman who had first drawn him back to LA. When he was still seeing Laura, Ellroy had given a talk at the Hammer Museum in LA. It was there that he met Teresa. Teresa was married but in their brief conversation, Ellroy sensed she was attracted to him.

Ellroy contacted the museum offering to speak at another event. Teresa was in attendance. She was by this time expecting a child with her husband. She began spending a lot of time with Ellroy. Teresa told Ellroy she was constantly frazzled and was not finding comfort in her marriage. Ellroy was happy to step into the void, but Teresa had an important condition. An affair between them must not lead to the break-up of her marriage and family, which she described as "inviolate."[13]

Ellroy agreed, enjoying the arrangement for the casual sex it entailed. It wasn't long before Ellroy's feelings for Teresa and his overwhelming instinct to control began to interfere: "It was adulterous, and it was wrong. But we had fun and I loved her."[14] He started pestering Teresa to leave her husband and grew increasingly frustrated when she continually rebuffed his efforts. Ellroy became more desperate. When dining with friends he would try and persuade them to call Teresa and leave messages telling her "to leave her dipshit hubby and marry James Ellroy!"[15] Baffled, several of his friends refused. On one occasion, Ellroy persuaded Rodney Taveira, a young academic who was conducting research on Ellroy to call Teresa, reassuring him that she wouldn't pick up and the call would go through to her answering machine. To Taveira's horror, Teresa did answer the phone.

"Hello, you don't know me," Taveira began nervously, "But I'm calling on behalf of James Ellroy and he wants you …"

"To leave my dipshit husband," Teresa replied, now fully aware of Ellroy's tactics.

Ellroy's campaign soon reached its nadir. He would drive by her house at night and howl outside her window.

Teresa was growing tired of Ellroy's behavior and decided to visit family on the East Coast to take a break from him. By the time she returned, the affair had fizzled out. They parted amicably and agreed to stay friends, although the latter point was more of a platitude as they did not stay in touch. In any event, Ellroy soon became obsessed with other women.

The relationship with Teresa had brought him back to another true love. Ellroy had missed the thrill of writing novels and while he was good at screenwriting and increasingly reliant on the lucrative salary it gave him, he never considered it an art form. He had much of the milieu and plotting in his head for *Blood's a Rover*, the final novel in his Underworld USA trilogy. It would feature the robbery of precious emeralds, an ailing J. Edgar Hoover trying to hold on as FBI Director and the Mob trying to reestablish their casinos in the Caribbean. For the latter point Ellroy employed the journalist Kateri Butler to visit the Dominican Republic and bring him back slides which he studied to accurately portray the setting in the novel. Butler had previously travelled to Vietnam and Ellroy had studied her photography when writing *The Cold Six Thousand*. Ellroy had assumed the Dominican Republic was in Central America. It was only when he was flipping through an atlas that he realized the DR was on the island of Hispaniola. Although he was momentarily embarrassed, Ellroy quickly deduced he could work this to his advantage. The DR bordered Haiti which, with its Voodoo religion and the dictatorship of François "Papa Doc" Duvalier, would make an equally strong setting.

The narrative was developing strongly, but Ellroy felt the story was missing an emotional focus. The novel became clearer to him when he decided to integrate his relationships with Laura and Teresa into the narrative:

> I studied Teresa. I created a Teresa-meets-the-Red-Goddess-narrative in my mind. I pre-aged Teresa to the age of the fictive Joan Rosen Klein. I retained her adultery and two daughters.[16]

Another breakthrough came in the form of the real-life private investigator Don Crutchfield. If the novel was to feature Laura and Teresa, Ellroy knew that he had to somehow be a character in the narrative interacting with them. Crutchfield would provide the means. Ellroy had met Crutchfield at the Skylight Bookstore several years earlier. The loquacious PI told him about his work as a "Wheelman," which required surveilling cheating spouses until he could present irrefutable proof of adultery in divorce cases. Wheelmen had steady work until California law recognized no-fault divorce in 1968.

Ellroy began to realize he could use "Crutch" as the ubiquitous character that most closely resembled him, but instead of spying on women for professional reasons the fictional Crutch would become sexually obsessed with the two leading female characters, "Comrade" Joan Rosen Klein and Karen Sifakis, and be voyeuristically drawn into a violent maelstrom of the Underworld. "I window-peeped four years of History," the fictional Crutch explains in the novel's prologue.[17]

Although he was deep into the drafting of *Blood's a Rover*, Ellroy still needed to make deals in Hollywood to maintain his expensive lifestyle. Ellroy met with Sanford Panitch, executive vice president at 20th Century Fox, in the Fall of 2007. Over dinner the two men discussed ideas. Panitch had a question for Ellroy.

"What's the one dream project you'd like to work on?"

"LA Confidential, Part Two," Ellroy responded without hesitation.

Ellroy dined with Brian Helgeland and Curtis Hanson at the Campanile to discuss the project. They pitched story ideas. One idea they were taken with was that the death of Marilyn Monroe could be used as a narrative starting point. Ellroy was keen to do the movie. Helgeland wanted to do it. They were confident that both Russell Crowe and Guy Pearce could be persuaded to reprise their roles. Only Hanson was apprehensive. While Ellroy and Helgeland would volley ideas back and forth, Hanson kept interjecting with doubts and reservations. The tensest moment came when Hanson flatly rejected Ellroy's idea for a love-triangle subplot. Helgeland recalls, "Ellroy looked at him as if to say 'Who are you to tell me what goes in *LA Confidential*. I AM *LA Confidential*'"[18] The project soon began to fall apart as the funding on offer wouldn't have been enough to cover the production of the original film, and all the principal players were now commanding huge salaries. Ellroy was disappointed but he was experienced enough in Hollywood to know that this had always been the most likely outcome. However, he did not forget Hanson's lukewarm attitude towards making the film.

It was the beginning of the end of Hanson and Ellroy's friendship.

Throughout his life, Ellroy had proved adept at making friends. He craved friendship as much as he was deeply attracted to women. Indeed, the parallels go further as Ellroy tended to become acquainted with people through a form of seduction, showering them with compliments, gifts and being generous and supportive with his time. Just as many of his romances had inevitably ended with a parting, so too had many of his friendships ended suddenly, often with lingering feelings of bitterness. Ellroy's relationship with Duane Tucker soured over an unpaid loan. Ellroy and Alan Marks also fell out over money. Ellroy gave Randy Rice an original manuscript of *Brown's Requiem* and was furious when he later found the same manuscript in a catalogue for a rare books auction. They argued about it and then never spoke again. Ellroy and Jonathan Kellerman lost touch and Kellerman later heard "through third parties that he was badmouthing me."[19] Ellroy's friendship with Steve

Erickson ended abruptly when Erickson wrote an article implying that Ellroy and Helen had ducked out of attending a wedding in LA due to the 1992 riots, "Our relationship was one thing before it suddenly became another thing that I didn't understand for literally years," Erickson said.[20] In fact, Ellroy's flight to LA for the wedding had been cancelled and rumors that snipers were firing at planes that landed in LAX dissuaded him from waiting for another one. Also, the groom was the critic John Powers and he and Ellroy barely liked each other. Ironically, eight years later, Ellroy and Helen did attend Powers' wedding to Sandi Tam.

Larry Harnisch, who felt angry when Ellroy abruptly cut-off contact, complained bitterly:

[Ellroy] eventually tires of all his friends and silently moves on without an explanation. And to anyone who currently considers themselves one of James' friends I can only say 'prepare yourself for him to vanish someday without a word. That's how he is with everybody.'[21]

A pattern could be detected in that Ellroy's books were usually dedicated to women he had broken up with or divorced or friends that he had fallen out with. But in Ellroy's defense there were also many people—Otto Penzler, Chip Kidd, Sonny Mehta, Joel Gotler, Tony Denison, and others—with whom he had maintained a friendship for decades. Ellroy was much more protective of and patient with his friends in Hollywood and publishing. From his early thirties onwards Ellroy had been frequently changing locations, moving from the West Coast to the East Coast to New England to the Midwest and then finally back to the West Coast. It was only natural that he would lose touch with some people.

Now that he was working increasingly in Hollywood, a location not known for being particularly warm or inviting, Ellroy could still be incredibly generous, sympathetic, and kind. But there was an ever-raging conflict in him. Ellroy enjoyed people's company, but at times he was too egotistical and competitive to connect with them emotionally. Indications of this attitude can be found in his writing. Ellroy had made many friends when he first attended AA, but he moved to New York as "I wanted to ditch all the people hooked on therapy and 12-step religion."[22] The attitude seems harsh, that of the artist discarding emotional ties in an endless pursuit of his dream. Part of Ellroy saw himself that way, but for many years he had been drawn back to LA and visited his AA friends often. Indeed, he stuck by them even when they began to see him as an easy mark. Helen despaired at how often Ellroy instructed her to hand money over to his old friends: "I wrote the checks," she lamented.[23]

One day Ellroy bumped into Sybil Blazej, his former neighbor at Ocean Front Walk in Venice Beach. He asked her about Randy and was pleased to hear that his old friend had married and was now living in Arizona. Ellroy promised to visit Sybil at the Library where she worked. As it happened, it took him more than a year to visit and when he did, he was quite taken by one of Sybil's attractive colleagues. "The fact that she was married meant nothing to him," Sybil recalled. "He sent her this huge bouquet of flowers."[24] The gift triggered Sybil's colleague into explaining firmly to Ellroy that she was not interested. Ellroy backed off. If he was disappointed, he didn't show it. He had a non-stop work schedule to occupy his time.

A full-length documentary on Ellroy was commissioned by the European television network Arte. *James Ellroy: American Dog* was directed by the French father and daughter filmmakers Robert and Clara Kuperberg. The Kuperbergs first met Ellroy in the Sofitel hotel in Beverly Hills. Clara recalls, "I said to him, 'Hi Mr Ellroy,' he kindly answered to me 'You can call me Dog!'"[25] They wasted no time in getting to work. From the hotel, "We took his car and went to El Monte directly, to the alley, the place near the Mexican restaurant, where his mother was found dead. It was the beginning of an intense and amazing week with him."[26] The Kuperbergs were working from a script which "was to focus on James Ellroy's life and interests, influences (Film Noir of course, the LAPD, the corruption in Tinseltown, all the themes he wrote about, but also—and especially about his relation to his mother and her death."[27] There was still room for improvisation as they filmed. Ellroy invited several of his friends—Wagner, Delany, Jackson, and Joe and Matthew Carnahan (then working on an adaptation of *White Jazz*) to appear in the documentary. They were filmed over two nights, and two separate dinners, at the Pacific Dining Car bantering back and forth about LA, crime, and Hollywood.

Ellroy also wanted a scene where he is in conversation with a talking dog. A Staffordshire Bull Terrier named Nikki was acquired by the production team and the scene was shot in the parking lot of the Pacific Dining Car. "It was a very long shoot," Clara recalls "because the animal trainer technique was to give peanut butter to the trained dog to look like he was talking. But the dog knew the trick and ate the full jar of peanut butter before we got a good shot."[28] Although that was a difficult scene to film to their mutual satisfaction, Clara declared that "Ellroy was great. He totally improvised the voice of the dog."[29] The Kuperbergs did a good job of capturing Ellroy's life in LA at the time and they found him to be "so generous, so available. He was very honest and patient." Given that he had a rather intimidating reputation, "Frankly we were astonished by his kindness."[30]

Figure 13 *Ellroy with the iconic Parker Center in the background during filming of the documentary* James Ellroy: American Dog. *Credit: Astrid Chevalier. Photo: Courtesy of Clara Kuperberg.*

In contrast to the smooth, fast-paced experience of working with the Kuperbergs, Ellroy found that the production of the TV pilot *LA Sheriff's Homicide* had become a slow, unyielding nightmare. Bill Stoner served as a technical consultant on the show:

[Paramount Studios] ended up filming the show twice with different actors. Miguel Ferrer was the lead character each time. I did the technical advising and James wrote the story. They did a pilot and they filmed it first and they filmed it a second time with new actors and actresses and spent a lot of money on it. The president, at the time, of the station was a Japanese gentleman and there were a lot of Asians involved in the story and James used terminology that street cops would use describing Asian people and the guy told James 'You can't do that on television.' James said, 'I'm not gonna change the way the police talk as that's the way they talk.' The guy said, 'No you can't have them doing that.' They got into a disagreement and the guy cancelled the whole contract and it never got to be shown on television until later when they used it as a cable TV movie (retitled *LA County 187*).[31]

One upside of the experience was that Ellroy became good friends with Miguel Ferrer. Ellroy was thrilled when Ferrer introduced him to his mother Rosemary Clooney. Ellroy had a crush on Clooney as a child and tracking down the stars of a bygone age whom Ellroy had lusted over in his youth became something of an obsession for him. With the help of Rick Jackson, Ellroy set out to find the now aging actresses Lois Nettleton, Shirley Knight, and Suzanne Pleshette. His subsequent contact with them was minimal. He would send flowers and notes of admiration. Ellroy was disappointed when Jackson was unable to locate Kaya Christian, his favorite pinup from the November 1967 issue of *Playboy*.

Miguel Ferrer would join Ellroy, Rick Jackson, and Dana Delany at the Pacific Dining Car for what Ellroy dubbed "dogpad meetings." Their constant lunches were so enjoyable to Ellroy that he came up with the idea of using his friends as characters in three novellas in his forthcoming anthology *Destination Morgue!* After securing permission to use their names, Ellroy set about writing the stories. The first half of *Destination Morgue!* consists of

Ellroy's final articles for *GQ*. Part Two is titled "Rick Loves Donna." Jackson may have expected a serious tone as he had spent many hours talking to Ellroy about his work in Hollywood Homicide with Detective Russ Kuster, who was killed in the line of duty in 1990. Although Ellroy did use Kuster as a character, the tone is not serious. Instead, Ellroy concocted a series of outrageous tales, brimming with his "Dog humor," which culminates in the foiling of a terrorist plot to blow up the Academy Awards ceremony.

When Ellroy showed the work to his friends they were aghast at what he had written about them. As Jackson recalls:

> We read what he wrote, and I said, 'Ahh, James I can't.' I mean I was doing crazy stuff, totally fictional stuff that I wouldn't even contemplate doing. So, I said, 'You can't use my real name.' So, then he came up with 'Rhino' Rick Jenson, and then Dana read it and said, 'Yeah, you can't use my real name.' So, she came up with Donna Donohue, and then Miguel came up with Miguel Figeuroa because he said 'I can't have my name (associated) with some of the stuff you write about.' Even though it was fiction, still you didn't really want your name attached, especially me in my position.[32]

"At the time I had a stalker," Delany explains, "and Rick was helping me with that."[33] Delany and Jackson agreed that having their names published in the novella would needlessly complicate the situation. Even with the name changes Ellroy was rather clumsily hiding his feelings. As by writing a comical love story between Jenson and Donohue (Jackson and Delany), he was trying to offset his own attraction for Delany.

In March 2006, Delany celebrated her fiftieth birthday. At her birthday party, Ellroy was consumed with his feelings for her, which were becoming as painful as a teenage crush. At the NBC All Star party in September, Delany made comments about wanting to get married which were reported in the press, "I would say that for the first time in my life I'm ready to get married. I turned 50 and I'm ready to get married. I'm a slow learner. I don't know who he is yet but I'm ready. He has to be smart, funny and kind." Ellroy may have noticed these comments and intuited the same feelings from his conversations with her. He told one of his friends that he was going to marry Dana.

"When?" the friend asked.

"I don't know. I haven't asked her out yet," Ellroy replied.

He was working up the courage to take an almighty leap of faith.

"We went out to dinner in the Fall of 2008 in NYC," Delany recalls.[34] The venue was the Four Seasons in Manhattan. Ellroy reserved a corner table. He was typically well-groomed, but somewhat less typically he wasn't joking around or showing off. His behavior was that of the perfect gentleman. During the meal, he asked Delany to marry him. Flattered and surprised, Delany told him she would think about it. She told him the answer was no by telephone. She was as delicate as possible in her refusal as Ellroy was a friend she cared for. She needn't have worried about hurting his feelings. Ellroy sent her flowers and a note to state that all was well between them. They did not see much of each other from that point on, "I think life then took over and we all had other work to do. Our triumvirate (Wagner, Ellroy, Delany) had run its course," Delany recalls.[35]

There had been several books written by authors who claimed to have solved the Black Dahlia murder. Most of them lacked credibility, but in April 2003, a book was published on the Dahlia murder which received more critical attention than any of its predecessors. *Black Dahlia Avenger: A Genius for Murder* was written by the retired LAPD detective Steve Hodel. Hodel argued that his father, the physician Dr. George Hodel, murdered Elizabeth Short. Hodel claimed his father was inspired by the Surrealist artwork of Man Ray in how he tortured Miss Short and posed the corpse. After Dr. Hodel died in 1999, Steve Hodel found two photographs of women he believed were of Elizabeth Short in his father's belongings. He began to explore connections between his father and the murder. Hodel had a complex relationship with his father and much of the book reads as a gripping family melodrama. Dr. Hodel was charged with sexually abusing his daughter Tamar but was acquitted at trial in 1949. Steve Hodel also wrote of how, unbeknownst to him, his first wife had been an ex-lover of George Hodel and she had married him partly to reestablish contact with his father. Dr. Hodel moved to the Philippines in 1953, possibly to escape police detection. He returned to the US in 1997, two years before his death at the age of 91.

Ellroy first met Steve Hodel at an LAPD author's night function. Hodel had retired from the LAPD in 1986, so he was not in the circle of friends Ellroy had made in the department from the 90s onwards. Ellroy expressed an interest in *Black Dahlia Avenger* and the two men subsequently met for dinner at the Pacific Dining Car. Ellroy had not been won over by Hodel's argument when he had read the book in hardback, "I was impressed by the scholarship but not entirely convinced."[36] However, Hodel was working on a new "Aftermath" chapter to be published in the paperback edition. Ellroy asked for an advance copy of this chapter and was struck by Hodel's new findings. As Hodel recalls:

> He read it and expressed to me how impressed he was with the new information and that the DA Files independently naming George Hodel as the Black Dahlia suspect, along with the tape-recorded transcripts, clearly were enough to convince him that the 'case was solved.'[37]

Ellroy asked Hodel if he could "help in any way." Hodel asked for a blurb and was surprised with Ellroy's counteroffer to write the foreword.[38] Perhaps sensing that a novelist's endorsement could undermine the book's claim to be factual, Hodel stalled but "after discussing it with and receiving some strong urging from Richard Seaver, my publisher and Editor-in-Chief at Arcade," he accepted the offer.[39] Ellroy's foreword to the hardback edition was measured and well-judged. He lays out objectively why he agrees with Hodel's findings, "There's the multi-point indictment. It's a purposeful accretion of fact, circumstance, and speculation."[40]

Ellroy tries to put his own stamp on the theory by alluding to the Oedipal connections between his novel and Hodel's theory, "This book costs Steve Hodel a father. This book gains him a daughter a generation his senior."[41] Hodel was aware of these links and other more surprising connections such as the Man Ray/Surrealist angle he had unearthed, oddly mirroring Ellroy's fictional explanation in *The Black Dahlia*, a novel he described as "profane and prophetic." Hodel later elaborated that "the 'prophetic' refers to his allusions to the cutting of Elizabeth Short's face in imitation of the painting (of Gwynplaine in *The Man Who Laughs*) which paralleled my real-life belief that George Hodel was creating his own surreal masterpiece as a homage to and imitation of Man Ray's *Les Amoureux*."[42]

Ellroy and Hodel had their last direct contact in 2005 when they dined together at Musso & Frank in Hollywood. At some point thereafter Ellroy began to deeply regret endorsing Hodel's theory. His change of heart was a long process which stemmed from his initial skepticism of the hardback edition combined with Hodel's speculation about the murder of Jean Ellroy. Hodel named George Hodel's associate Fred Sexton as a plausible suspect in the murder of Ellroy's mother. He broached the idea to Ellroy before putting it in print and while Ellroy did not react negatively, other than to tell Hodel it wasn't plausible, he later became angry at the suggestion, describing it as "Just bullshit, and I told Steve that."[43] Also, Hodel's theory that his father had never been charged because he could have exposed widespread corruption in the LAPD angered many of Ellroy's long-standing friends in the department.

Hodel linked his father and Fred Sexton to a number of other murders, many of which Ellroy claimed "were actually solved."[44] Hodel denies they were solved but he remained sanguine about Ellroy's change in attitude, "I know for a fact that James truly regrets writing the Foreword to my book. However, I suspect that his real regret is coming not so much *from the heart,* but rather from Ellroy, the businessman. And believe me James is first and foremost – a businessman."[45] Larry Harnisch took a similar attitude stating that the "various endorsements have more to do with Ellroy's well-established hunger for publicity rather than genuine support of any particular theory."[46] However, Ellroy the businessman felt that he had made a mistake. In January 2010 he told the French journalist Stephane Boulan that he no longer believed George Hodel murdered Elizabeth Short, "I made a mistake. Even God makes mistakes."[47]

The film adaptation of *The Black Dahlia* began shooting in April 2005. Jimmy Harris had first optioned the novel shortly after its release but had left the project when it became clear that he would not have creative control. David Fincher had been attached to direct but his plans for a black and white "five-hour, $80-million miniseries with movie stars" fell through and he moved on to direct *Zodiac,* an epic film about the police investigation into the Zodiac killings.[48] Fincher and Ellroy first met when he was attached to direct *The Black Dahlia.* They became friendly, and when *Zodiac* was released Ellroy was so impressed that he described it as "one of the greatest American crime films."[49] Ellroy and Fincher did a joint interview for the *LA Times* as publicity for the film, and Fincher invited Ellroy to contribute to the DVD commentary. Ellroy couldn't help himself get competitive with the screenwriter James Vanderbilt on the commentary track, criticizing one scene as being "out of a horror movie."

Ellroy had been enthusiastic about Fincher directing *The Black Dahlia*. He had no rapport with the man who was eventually hired—Brian DePalma. Ellroy described DePalma as having "the biggest hips I've ever seen on a man, and he won't look you in the eye."[50] Josh Hartnett was cast as Bucky Bleichert and Scarlett Johansson played Kay Lake, both of whom Ellroy dismissed as "fatuously good-looking."[51] Ellroy saw potential in the film as a book-selling device and tried to not publicly display his skepticism to journalists. To his readers he was indiscreet. "I predict an intriguing flop," he told the audience at one bookstore.[52] The finished film lived down to his expectations. DePalma could not resist falling back into his horror genre roots and there are several sick visuals, including a flashback sequence of Elizabeth Short being tortured.

"Ellroy and I both attended a special screening at the big Samuel Goldwyn Theater in Beverly Hills," recalls Jimmy Harris. "They sent a limousine for us to come because I eventually made a deal to be the executive producer when I bowed out as I realized the picture was not going to be what I intended it to be. Ellroy and I were both disappointed."[53] According to Eddie Muller

> he [Ellroy] kindly invited me to the premiere of the film in Hollywood and that film is a disaster. I remember afterwards we went out and we had dinner with some of his cop buddies and he stood up at the end of the table and said 'Well, the book is now No. 4 on the *New York Times* bestseller list and I wrote it twenty-something years ago, so I got that going for me!'[54]

Despite the film being a critical disappointment and a commercial disaster, failing to recoup its $50 million budget, it led to a bigger surge in sales of Ellroy's books than even the film adaptation of *LA Confidential* had initiated, "It sold fifteen times more books for me in seven weeks than *LA Confidential* did in nineteen years."[55]

Ellroy did some press events for the film and attended a screening at the Venice film festival, standing out from everyone else as always, this time in a white tuxedo. He kept his opinion about *The Black Dahlia* to himself for the duration of the film's run in theaters. He did not hold back on his hatred for it afterwards, "It doesn't even make narrative sense. It's miscast. It's ugly. It's cheap. It's misogynistic. It's no good."[56]

In 2008, Ellroy visited New York to discuss the serialization of his new memoir in *Playboy* with the magazine's literary editor Amy Loyd. Ellroy considered Loyd a fine editor, and when she moved to the eBook publisher Byliner he agreed to write the Fred Otash novella *Shakedown* for them as he felt he "owed her."[57] It was this sort of moonlighting that caused disquiet at Knopf where Edward Kastenmeier had wanted Ellroy for a similar eBook project.

In New York, Ellroy asked Loyd, "Do you know any tall rangy women I could have dinner with?"

"As a matter of fact, I do," she responded.

Loyd arranged a blind date for Ellroy with her friend Nelle Gretzinger. Ellroy and Nelle spoke once on the phone and then met in a restaurant. Matchmaking can be a fraught business, but Loyd appeared to have judged wisely, as Ellroy and Nelle had an instant chemistry. As Nelle put it, "It was a white-hot love affair that burned bright and fast."[58] But even Nelle was surprised when, six weeks into their relationship, Ellroy suddenly announced that he was moving to Brooklyn.

Nelle found Ellroy a house close to where she lived in Brooklyn. She would spend time with him when her kids were visiting their father. They visited Nelle's parents in Cold Spring for Thanksgiving and Ellroy fell in love with the town, later naming it as his favorite town in the US. He was less enamored with "noisy and overcrowded" Brooklyn.[59] Ellroy and Nelle's relationship was happening around the same time as the 2008 economic crash. For Nelle, who ran a family business in the garment district, the economic downturn was devastating, "One day we had a million dollars' worth of sales booked, and we came in the next day and that was just all gone because people were cancelling orders."[60]

Nelle was juggling closing the business with launching a new career. She had accepted the Geoffrey Roberts award for championing new world or emerging wine regions. It required her to spend a month in Belize. Ellroy stayed in Brooklyn, where he quickly became lonely, miserable, and increasingly triggered by the loud, densely populated environment, which was completely at odds with the quiet, contained atmosphere that he needed to both function as a writer and relax.

Nelle was busy in Belize and had very little contact with the outside world, "I was close enough to the Guatemalan border that I was buying Guatemalan phone cards for the phone that I had."[61] She managed to get Ellroy on the phone and was shocked to discover that he had moved back to LA. Being alone in Brooklyn, it seems, was just too much for him. "I remember thinking, wow isn't this bizarre, here I am sitting in this shack on the Caribbean Sea with my Guatemalan cell phone. It all seemed very ephemeral and strange."[62] Ellroy and Nelle's relationship had been so promising that she was left wondering whether things could have worked out in different circumstances, "Our politics were certainly at odds but that never really came up. Interestingly enough, we just avoided the subject of politics."[63] They remained friends and he contacted her when he was in New York. She met him at his hotel only to find him flustered after setting off the fire alarm in his room. Ellroy had placed a plastic-bottomed kettle on the induction burner, and it melted.

Ellroy had provided funding for the restoration of the film noir *The Prowler* (1951). Eddie Muller, who had led the project to restore the film, had been friends with Ellroy for some time. When Muller was co-writing Tab Hunter's autobiography, Ellroy had provided him with a copy of "Portrait of a Murderer," a *Playhouse 90* drama in which Hunter played the killer Donald Bashor. Neither Hunter nor Muller possessed a copy of the film, and it was feared lost, but Ellroy donated a copy from his personal collection, describing it as "one of his favorites."[64] Contrary to reports, Ellroy did not give Muller his sobriquet "the Czar of Noir," but he encouraged him to use it. Muller said, "He knows the power of a good nickname."[65]

Ellroy introduced *The Prowler* at the Billy Wilder Theater on March 20, 2009. He enthusiastically described the film as "Perv Noir." In attendance that night was a young freelance script analyst named Megan Close. Megan was a huge fan of Ellroy's and had seen him at book readings before. She had witnessed the attraction women had towards him as, at one event, her friend brought along a pair of silk panties and asked Ellroy to sign them. Megan's date was late that night and she and a friend ended up sitting in seats that had been reserved for Ellroy and his producer friend Clark Peterson. Ellroy was disarming about the mix-up. He chatted away with Megan. Ellroy had recently celebrated his sixty-first birthday and Megan was only in her mid-twenties, but the attraction was mutual.

It was a double bill showing. By the interval, Megan's date had finally appeared, and she described his behavior as "obnoxious."[66] He was clearly annoyed that Megan was spending so much time talking to Ellroy. Ellroy was amused by his jealousy and at one point grabbed the man's jacket, scrunched it into a ball and launched it into the auditorium. While the date sullenly retrieved his jacket, Ellroy continued to talk with Megan.

Before she left for the evening, Ellroy had not managed to obtain Megan's phone number. Ellroy turned to an entertainment executive who was in attendance and blurted out to him "I'll pay you a thousand dollars if you can find that woman." The executive found Megan within a day and reached out to her, on Ellroy's behalf, on FaceBook. Ellroy and Megan began talking on the phone and subsequently began dating. They liked each other, but Megan admitted the age difference was an issue, "He would ask me 'Dark Questions.'"[67] Ellroy loved to dissect and diagnose women's issues, but Megan was not forthcoming. "I don't think I was haunted enough for him," she recalls.[68]

Their relationship lasted several months and Ellroy was not being monogamous. Things started to fizzle out between them when Ellroy began seeing Erika Schickel and would be drawn into a relationship that would take Erika and him to the brink of self-destruction.

12

The Big Hurt (2009–2015)

In April 2007, at the LA Times Festival of Books, Ellroy met a woman who was going to dominate both his personal and professional life over the next few years. The journalist Erika Schickel was at the festival promoting her "momoir" *You're Not the Boss of Me: Adventures of a Modern Mom*. She was in attendance with her father, the film critic Richard Schickel. Some friends of the Schickels introduced them to Ellroy, who at the time was dating a novelist and screenwriter.

Erika recalls Ellroy was friendly, but the introduction was brief, "He knew who my dad was, but he was looking for (his girlfriend). He was very distracted."[1] It was only when Erika was walking away from the meeting that she had an epiphany about the author, "I thought, Oh My God, if that man knew what was in my heart he would come and get me. He's looking for me and I'm standing right here, but he doesn't know what he's looking for."[2] Erika was married at the time, with teenage daughters, so she assumed her brief meeting with Ellroy would not amount to anything. In fact, she did not see him again until the following year at the same festival.

Erika did not think Ellroy would remember her, but when she approached him, he was both receptive and charming. He talked a little about his writing plans. He was writing a memoir, provisionally titled "The Big Hurt" after the Toni Fisher song, that was being serialized by *Playboy* and would later be published in book form, retitled *The Hilliker Curse: My Pursuit of Women*. Ellroy explained how the book was about his lifelong obsession with pursuing women. Erika tried to hide her response, but its vibrant power surprised her, "I thought holy shit, I am going to be in that book. I didn't know why I thought that. It didn't mean I had any kind of conscious plan. I was still in a great tissue of lies which was my marriage."[3]

Erika began to think about Ellroy constantly, but she made no effort to contact him, nor did she have any plan to, "I had an erotic fixation on him. He was like something I could go to in my mind."[4] She did not see him again until the 2009 Festival of Books, "I was freaked out. I had been so fixated on him. I clammed up and ran away."[5] But she soon saw him again at a birthday party thrown for her at Lou's Wine Shop on Hillhurst Avenue. Erika was enjoying the evening with friends when she spotted Ellroy drinking espresso at another part of the bar, "I walked past him on the way to the Ladies Room to try and catch his eye and he never saw me."[6]

Another chance encounter would bring Erika more success. Ellroy had bowed to pressure from Knopf to create a social media account to drum up publicity for his books. Ellroy, who had still not learned to type, found computers tedious, "I performed this boring duty for three weeks. It was deadening shit work."[7] However, as an author who was obsessed with sex and relationships, Ellroy was about to discover the potential of the internet. Erika noticed Ellroy's new Facebook account and sent him a friendship request, "Hours later this huge, crazy poem comes back to me in my inbox 'my brave bride, I brace at thy breasts.' It was something to behold and I'd never seen anything like it. I was horrified and amused by it."[8]

Ellroy and Erika continued this internet correspondence for several weeks. Then they began talking on the phone regularly. They finally met in person again in July 2009. They had a nominally legitimate reason for meeting up. Erika was planning to write another memoir about her complex relationship with her parents and her time at Buxton College, and an affair with a teacher which led to her expulsion, "The artifice was that we would have this task that he would help me how to do this. I did not know how to write long-form. He is, of course, the master of the big book and of complex plotting."[9] Ellroy soon lost interest in the book, but he was very interested in Erika. Ellroy molded Erika into "HER," the redhead who concludes his pursuit of women in the memoir he was writing.

The relationship meant the inevitable end of her marriage. Erika informed her husband she was separating from him at a Rally's Drive-In in Fresno.

Figure 14 *Ellroy and Erika Schickel. Their fraught relationship would push them both to the brink of self-destruction. Photo: Courtesy of Erika Schickel.*

Whether it was intentional or not, Ellroy had achieved what he couldn't do with Teresa, persuading his lover to leave her husband for him.

The publication of *Blood's a Rover* in September of 2009 marked the end of an eight-year hiatus since Ellroy's last novel was published. The nearly decade-long gestation of *Blood's a Rover*, the longest gap between novels in Ellroy's career, can partly be attributed to the epic, complex narrative Ellroy had constructed, although the breakdown of his marriage, addiction, and mental health problems, womanizing and new focus of working in Hollywood were the more dominant reasons. Nevertheless, for Ellroy's readers the long wait for the conclusion of the Underworld USA trilogy was worth it. *Blood's a Rover* received some of the strongest reviews of Ellroy's career. Preston Jones wrote, "Ellroy's latest is American fiction at its finest, a dexterous, astounding achievement."[10] Ellroy's risky decision to make himself a character in the text, by using Don Crutchfield, and to fictionalize his relationships with Laura and Teresa had, it seemed, paid off. One person who was less than impressed was Crutchfield himself, who privately objected to Ellroy about the way he had been portrayed. Ellroy tried to assure him "he would be the dipshit voyeur kid who ultimately ascends to be the voice of American history" but found that this "was beyond him."[11]

Blood's a Rover

The title *Blood's a Rover* is taken from the A.E. Houseman poem "Reveille" a quotation of which forms the epigraph of the novel:

> Clay lies still, but blood's a rover;
> Breath's a ware that will not keep
> Up, lad: when the journey's over
> There'll be time enough to sleep[12]

Houseman's verse encapsulates Ellroy's portrait of the Underworld. The blood which courses through the veins of a human body also serves as a metaphor for the body politic, which characters such as Ward Littell and Wayne Tedrow have dedicated much of their lives to sustaining. Yet in *Blood's a Rover* many of these same characters are reborn politically as radicals, belonging as it were to a different Underworld, and yearn not for more power and possession through destruction but for the restoration of order on a personal level through fatherhood with the women they love.

Changes in Ellroy's personal life are reflected in the more openly emotional tone of the novel. The novel is dedicated to his ex-fiancée Laura, "*Comrade: For Everything You Gave Me.*"[13] The fictional Comrade Joan politically radicalizes the characters in *Blood's a Rover*. Through their love for strong women, three leading men—Wayne Tedrow, Dwight Holly and Don Crutchfield—become sickened by their longstanding political roles and right-wing allegiances and yearn for legitimacy by moving to the radical left. Aside from Comrade Joan, the other leading female character Karen Sifakis is based on his relationship with Teresa. The issue of illegitimate parentage occurs in the novel, with Dwight Holly convinced he is the father of the married Karen Sifakis' child.

Given this focus on intimacy and fatherhood, Ellroy felt obligated to repudiate the impersonal narrative of *The Cold Six Thousand* which he had come to regard as a career nadir, even though *Blood's a Rover* would be a continuation of many narrative strands and feature some of the same characters from *Cold Six*. Contrary to his earlier defense of the novel, Ellroy embraced the negative reviews: "I think that the book is too complex and somewhat too long and that the style is too rigorous and too challenging in its presentation of a very complex text."[14] Ellroy's constant dismissal of the novel's literary value led Stuart Evers to write an article the *Guardian* titled, "Is James Ellroy the best judge of his own novels?" which cast doubt on the sincerity of Ellroy's volte-face on its literary merit. By switching from an abrasively defensive tone to a relentlessly negative public dismissal of *The Cold Six Thousand*, Ellroy was performing a narrative external to the novels which structured the transition between the two works, preparing the reader for the new style he had embraced. It was a strategy fraught with risk, as readers and critics started to wonder if the author does not hold his past work in high regard, why should they regard his future work seriously? However, it was entirely in keeping with Ellroy's character that he would refuse to let anyone define him, even by his own success. For Ellroy, literary reinvention was revolutionary, throwing off the critical consensus of the past and embracing radical experimentation.

In *Blood's a Rover* the sexual relationships intertwine with the political machinations and conspiracies as Joan and Karen act as a radicalizing influence on the men who fall for them. On this point, however, Ellroy, the self-styled "Tory," has been specific in differentiating fiction from reality: "I wanted to honor in this book the lessons learnt from a woman (Laura) whose beliefs were inimical to mine and to talk in the abstract about the necessity of conversion and of revolution. But I have not moved left. I have just described the journeys of people who have done so."[15] Wayne Tedrow and Dwight Holly had previously been portrayed as violent racists, even if the reader could find some sympathy for them as Ellroy laid bare their demons there was little doubt as to what they remained at heart. When they find in themselves the capacity to love strong women, it triggers a wider moral rebirth as they push America out of the grip of the Underworld. On closer examination, Ellroy is retreading old ground here. He described the main theme of the LA Quartet as "bad men in love with strong women."[16] It is unusual that Ellroy regards women on the political left as "strong," whereas he avoids female characters who share his own Toryism. But then virtually all the women Ellroy has been in relationships with, such as Laura, were left-wing. He used his life as inspiration for his writing, as he did with the history of LA. The more friction and unresolvable conflict that existed in his personal life, the more visceral his art became.

Blood's a Rover begins with an italicized prologue of an unidentified first-person voice, later revealed to be Don Crutchfield's, looking back after many years on the events he witnessed from 1968 to 1972. Crutchfield is referred to in casual conversation by his nickname "Crutch," a name that evokes a mobility or emotional aid. Crutch does not hold the same stature in the Underworld/Intelligence community as Tedrow or Holly. He is an outwardly flawed and pathetic character, yet he is a crutch for others, providing stability through his pure, childlike love of the ideologue Comrade Joan. Crutch is also similar phonetically to crux, which is appropriate as the character who ties the narrative to Ellroy's own life through the voyeurism and love affair with Laura. Crutch also symbolizes the resolution of the historical mystery of the Underworld USA series, as his fate as a voyeur becomes inextricably linked to Hoover's archive of secret files which appear sporadically throughout the three novels:

AMERICA:

I window-peeped four years of our History. It was one long mobile stakeout and kick the door-in shakedown. I had a license to steal and a ticket to ride.

I followed people. I bugged and tapped and caught big events in ellipses. I remained unknown. My surveillance links the Then to the Now in a never before revealed manner. I was there. My reportage is buttressed by credible hearsay and insider tattle. Massive paper trails provide verification. This book derives from stolen public files and usurped private journals. It is the sum of personal adventure and forty years of scholarship. I am a literary executor and an agent provocateur. I did what I did and saw what I saw and learned my way through the rest of the story.

Scripture-pure veracity and scandal-rag content. That conjunction gives it its sizzle. You carry the seed of belief within you already. You

*recall the time this narrative captures and senses conspiracy. I am here to
tell you that it is all true and not at all what you think.*

*You will read with some reluctance and capitulate in the end. The
following pages will force you to succumb.*

I am going to tell you everything.[17]

The role of historian, private eye and sexual voyeur are combined into the
unlikely individual of Crutch: "*I window-peeped four years of our History.*" In
its form, this prologue deliberately echoes Ellroy's direct address to the reader
in *American Tabloid* through its italicized text, its theme of verisimilitude
and its demythologizing of the past so that one historical narrative eventually
triumphs over the other. Although as the timeframe has moved from the era of
Camelot to the sour Nixon years, Ellroy is less concerned with stripping away
idealism than rebuilding it through a positive portrayal of political conversion,
as the hidden conspiracies of the Underworld are gradually exposed to an
angry nation. Ellroy merges historical and literary sources with a tabloid
sensibility. It is the work of both "*literary executor*" and "*agent provocateur.*" It
is both "*Scripture*" and "*scandal-rag*" in its content, thus the salacious becomes
authoritative. Crutch regards this secret history as a form of seduction:
he promises the reader that their skepticism will melt away to the need to
"*succumb.*" It is a bold statement from Ellroy, warning the reader that in its
focus on conspiracies in the shadows of history, the story might seem highly
improbable, but by the end of the novel he will have won them over, making
them "*window-peepers*" as well. The window is the screen through which the
secret history will be revealed.

This first-person narration is only temporary. But although Ellroy quickly
switches the perspective to third-person, Crutch's control over the narrative
remains considerable as the documents the reader will view and the events
described are, to an indeterminate extent, arranged by him. The recorded
transcripts, which appear sporadically throughout the previous two novels,
were compiled and catalogued on Hoover's orders and he was, in a malevolent
and voyeuristic fashion, their author. Crutchfield cannot create documents,
instead they "[*derive*] *from stolen public files and usurped private journals,*" and
he verifies "*credible hearsay*" if it tallies with his own experiential viewpoint.

Ellroy follows Crutch's pensive monologue with a hyper-violent armored car heist which takes place in Los Angeles on February 24, 1964:

SUDDENLY:
The milk truck cut a sharp right turn and grazed the curb. The driver lost the wheel. He panic-popped the brakes. He induced a rear-end skid. A Wells Fargo armored car clipped the milk truck side/head-on.

Mark it now:
7:16 a.m. South L.A., 84th and Budlong. Residential darktown. Shit stacks with dirt front yards.[18]

The opening scene breaks with the established timeframe of the trilogy and jumps back four years, depicting an event which is independent of the events in *The Cold Six Thousand* but runs parallel to them as a series narrative. This is indicated in the very first word in the text: "*SUDDENLY:*" Not only is it italicized, whereas the bulk of the text is not, it is also the only word to appear on the first line, indicating a sharp, unexpected break in the narrative which has detoured from the established chronology of the trilogy by going back in time. Ellroy had already covered 1964 in *The Cold Six Thousand*. This abrupt break followed by a colon leads into the violent events which unfold in the next paragraph. Ellroy forces the reader to consider the effects of the past on the present, as the complex structure of *Blood's a Rover* goes beyond its 1972 cut-off date in the epilogue to, presumably, the present day with Crutch's direct address to the reader. There are essentially three time periods of the novel. Ellroy is restructuring the historical narrative from within, creating new connections and associations between present and past. One of these connections is a specific day, February 24, 1964, and the violent events of this day reverberate throughout the narrative. Consequently, there is a very different tone between the settings of the novel. The heist sequence is described in less than four pages. Four guards and three robbers are killed, and only one man survives. The pace is fast, and the confluence of violence is crammed into a small space and a narrow timeframe: 7:16 to 7:27 a.m. on 84th and Budlong. When the narrative transitions into the novel's main 1968–72 setting, the pace slows and the violent scenes are dispersed.

The opening heist scene is firmly rooted in the crime genre, but as the narrative progresses, Ellroy reveals how this violent robbery is tied to the overarching politics of the era. The direct political aspect of the historical narrative is focused on Hoover's COINTELPRO campaign to discredit the Black Panther movement, which is paralleled by the Mafia's attempts to re-establish casinos in the Caribbean through its courting of the right-wing dictatorships of the Dominican Republic and Haiti. The irrational hatred, and increasing senility, which fuels Hoover's campaign against the Civil Rights movement is mirrored by the religious paranoia which props up Francois "Papa Doc" Duvalier's voodoo personality cult regime in Haiti.

In the grisly demise of Wayne Tedrow in Haiti, Voodoo is a disturbing presence but also oddly indicative of Christian redemption:

> He entered a tavern and ordered a potion. Six *bokurs* watched him drink it. Two men offered blessings. Four men waved amulets and hexed him. He left too much money on the bar.
>
> He walked outside. The sky breathed. He felt the moon's texture. Craters became emerald mines.
>
> An alleyway appeared. A breeze carried him down it. Leaves stirred and sent rainbows twirling. Three men stepped out of a moonbeam. They wore cross-draw scabbards. They had bird wings where their right arms used to be.
>
> Wayne said, 'Peace.'
>
> They pulled their machetes and cut him dead right there.[19]

Tedrow is being watched by six bokurs—black magicians and Voodoo priests. He has already betrayed his Underworld employers and the Balaguer regime which is his host, as he helped to free dozens of heavily doped-up slaves who had been coerced into working on construction sites to build the Mob's casinos. The exact motive of his murder is somewhat ambiguous: he may just be the victim of a violent mugging as "He left too much money on the bar." A "mistake" he repeats as he wanders from bar to bar in a deliberately suicidal, and, thus, redemptive act: Tedrow's sins have become so great he feels the only option left is self-sacrifice. There is a sense of paranoia and cynicism regarding the religion of the bokurs: he is blessed by two and hexed by four others. The potion has a spiritual influence on Tedrow's consciousness of his surroundings. At first this is an uplifting and redemptive experience: "The sky breathed. He felt the moon's texture." But then, as his death draws nearer, it becomes portentous and threatening, yet still a guiding influence: "An alleyway appeared. A breeze carried him down it. Leaves stirred and sent rainbows twirling." The religious overtones to this ritualistic murder reflect how Tedrow has reached this bizarre fate. Tedrow was complicit in the death of an African American preacher. He begins an affair with the preacher's widow, Mary Beth Hazzard. Hazzard is a symbolic name as she ultimately inspires Tedrow to turn on his employers which puts his life in danger.

Tedrow's relationship with Mary links to the armed heist of the prologue. Mary's young son has been missing for years, and Tedrow becomes convinced he is the sole surviving armed robber, who has been periodically sending emeralds from the heist to members of the African American community in LA. For Tedrow, his desire to find and save a young black man atones for his long search and eventual revenge murder of Wendell Durfee, the man who raped and murdered his wife. But Durfee deserved to die, and during the search Tedrow was more conflicted in his inability to find Durfee and exact the vigilante justice which was overdue. Tedrow has a lifetime of extreme Mormonism and Underworld activity to repent for. Tedrow's atonement leads to transcendent feeling in his last moments: "Craters became emerald mines." The beauty and immense value of the emeralds is offset by their capacity for destruction. Whenever the emeralds are the focus of the scene death follows in their wake. This begins with the dizzying, hyper-kinetic violence of the armed robbery and follows through with the dream-like death of Wayne Tedrow right up to the denouement with the death of J. Edgar Hoover.

Upon breaking into Hoover's home, Crutch destroys many of the FBI's director's blackmail files. Crutch's closing monologue alludes to the disbursement of other secret files, and strengthens his position as the character that most strongly links Ellroy to the novel:

> *Documents have arrived at irregular intervals. They are always anonymously sent. I have compiled diary excerpts, oral-history transcripts and police-file overflow. Elderly leftists and black militants have told me their stories and*

provided verification. Freedom of Information Act subpoenas have served me
well. [...] "Your options are do everything or do nothing." Joan told me that.
I have paid a dear and savage price to live History. I will never stop looking.
I pray that these pages find her and that she does not misread my devotion.[20]

As Hoover's grip on power, and life, slowly slips away, the fate of his secret
files becomes the most important consequence of his impending death.
Hoover's identity has always hinged on the power he wields through his
massive archive which he can use for purposes of blackmail. Holly, Tedrow, and
Crutch all find their redemption through women and by extension fatherhood,
even if it is by proxy. Obsessional love leads to extreme and illegal acts being
committed for a political vision. The theft of classified files from the FBI office
in Media, Pennsylvania, on March 8, 1971, and their distribution throughout
the country, confirms the FBI's anti-dissident COINTELPRO program and the
gradual unraveling of the uneasy truce between organized crime and the FBI.

Crutch is sent files anonymously giving him a unique insight into American
history. But the burden of history has been compounded by the tragedy of
lost love. Crutch's search for Joan has radicalized him almost to the extent
of madness, touring warzones hoping to find the revolutionary: "*I have been
to Nicaragua, Grenada, Bosnia, Rwanda, Russia, Iran and Iraq.*"[21] Perhaps
Ellroy goes too far in giving Crutch this claim, imbuing the character with
an impressionistic, even fantastical tendency towards reminiscence which
potentially undermines his entire reliability as a narrator. But in the closing
monologue Crutch reveals details about the real Don Crutchfield which re-
establish his plausibility in typically Ellrovian showbiz terms "*I run a successful
detective agency in Los Angeles. My firm bodyguards celebrities and verifies
stories for tell-all rags.*" Ultimately, Crutch is unable to fulfill the promise of
the opening monologue: "*I am going to tell you everything,*" as history is, by
its nature, always incomplete.[22] The more files he receives, and the greater his
knowledge grows, the bigger the sense of emotional loss and dwindling hope
he will see Joan and their child: "*She's eighty-three now. Our child is thirty-six.
Instinct tells me it's a girl.*"[23] Ellroy ends the Underworld trilogy by merging the
remnants of countless secret files with the novel narrative: "*I pray that these
pages find her and that she does not misread my devotion.*"[24] His reference to

"*these pages*" suggests the history he has conveyed is an authored document or rather a collection of documents and narratives, and that the Underworld novels are a huge fictional archive anchored on an obsession with women.

For the UK tour to promote the *Blood's a Rover*, Ellroy recorded an episode of *Desert Island Discs* for BBC Radio 4. Ellroy had never heard of the show and was unaware that to be invited on as a guest was considered an honor in the UK, previous guests had included royalty and prime ministers. Ellroy found the recording and preparation to be intense. He was given a list of available tracks to play. He picked five by Beethoven, two by Anton Bruckner and one by Jean Sibelius. Then Ellroy and the host Kirsty Young had to decide how they would work them into the show based on the questions she would ask. Ellroy picked *Libra* as his favorite book, fulfilling his vow to Don DeLillo that he would credit him as often as possible. As the recording progressed, the disarming efforts of Young helped Ellroy to relax and take a less self-aggrandizing tone. When she thanked him for his appearance he smiled and said it was "a great pleasure."[25]

After the recording an exhausted Ellroy was interviewed by Miranda Sawyer for BBC 2's *The Culture Show*. Sawyer was such a fan of Ellroy's that after the publication of *My Dark Places*, she went on a pilgrimage to LA visiting the houses where he had lived and the crime scenes he described. Sawyer and Ellroy briefly discussed the nervous breakdown he had suffered on his previous tour, and then a sanguine Ellroy hinted that his issues were behind him, "the book is so hopeful compared to the books that preceded it."[26]

Kirsty Young and Miranda Sawyer were the types of journalists that Ellroy adored—intelligent, beautiful, and patient with him and his outrageous persona. He was about to be interviewed by another female journalist who embodied all these qualities, and it would in turn reopen many of the issues that he told Sawyer he had overcome.

A features writer for the *Sunday Times* interviewed Ellroy at the Langham Hilton where he was staying during the London leg of his UK tour. Her pre-meeting research of Ellroy suggested that this was an author she might disapprove of. She had found footage of Ellroy feigning masturbation in a publicity stunt for the Playboy Channel. But in person, she saw the many facets of his character. The boyishness, the charming and playful gentleman, and the tongue-in-cheek Demon Dog persona. Indeed, it is clear through reading the interview that an attraction is developing.

Although he was still with Erika when he met her, as he acknowledges in the interview, Ellroy was taken with the British journalist. He was skilled at sowing the seeds of attraction but not acting on it, until years later, as though he and the journalist had never been apart.

As his tour continued through Europe, Ellroy appeared at the John Adams Institute in Amsterdam on January 24, 2010. It marked the last significant occasion Ellroy professed his belief in the conspiracy theories surrounding the Kennedy assassination. The moderator, Jan Donkers, a fellow conspiracist expressed his dissatisfaction that there had never been a deathbed confession from one of the principal figures in the assassination. Ellroy responded that Mob Boss Carlos Marcello had confessed, and this would be revealed in a forthcoming true-crime book. He then trotted out his usual line of how Kennedy was killed as part of a "free-floating conspiracy" between organized crime, Cuban exile factions, and rogue intelligence agents, but the tone of his voice suggested that he was struggling to keep the faith. The book Ellroy was referring to was *Carlos Marcello: The Man Behind the JFK Assassination* by Stefano Vaccara. It was published in 2014 and despite the promise of new revelations, it merely rehashed old arguments. A different book would radically alter Ellroy's view of the assassination, and it was written by one of his former colleagues at *GQ*.

Thomas Mallon first met Ellroy when he was working as a literary editor and columnist at *GQ*. According to Mallon, "I would say that our friendship didn't really take off until much later—around, say, 2011. Sonny Mehta or Dan Frank (my editor at Pantheon) gave James a copy of my forthcoming novel, *Watergate*, about which he turned out to be extremely generous and enthusiastic."[27] Shortly thereafter, Ellroy read Mallon's non-fiction work *Mrs Paine's Garage and the Murder of John F. Kennedy*. Ellroy was impressed. Mallon seamlessly navigates between the banality of Lee Harvey Oswald's domestic life and that of his landlady Ruth Paine, with the shattering national consequences of the events on November 22, 1963. More importantly for Ellroy though, Mallon's merciless skewering of the ever-shifting conspiracy theories seemed to be just the argument he was looking for. From now on Ellroy would publicly espouse the "lone gunman theory" and, to the disappointment of some of his readers, expressed his view with the zeal of the convert. He was generous in crediting Mallon with his conversion and appeared with the author at The Paley Center for Media in New York on November 14, 2013, to mark the impending fiftieth anniversary of the assassination and promote Mallon's work. When onstage together, the two authors appeared to have a somewhat unlikely friendship as Mallon concedes, "I'm sort of slight and bespectacled, and my public conversation tends to have a kind of professorial caution to it—whereas James is constantly provocative and entertaining. But there's overlap too: I'm moderately conservative (a rare enough thing in American literary life), and James is—well, way out there."[28]

Once she had split from her husband, Ellroy told Erika that they were now "free and clear."[29] They went public with their relationship at a speaking event at the Hammer Museum on October 19, 2009. It had been planned for Ellroy to be interviewed onstage by Helen Knode, but it was announced shortly beforehand that Helen had taken ill, and Erika stepped into the role. There had been tension between the two women, ex-wife and new lover, from the beginning of Erika's relationship with Ellroy, so there may have been a reason other than illness in Helen's decision to avoid the event.

To gasps from the audience, Erika introduced Ellroy onstage with the words, "maybe many of you came here to see Ellroy in conversation with his ex-wife. You won't have that pleasure tonight, but instead you get his girlfriend."[30] The subsequent discussion was teeming with sexual chemistry between the interviewer and her subject.

Although their relationship was no longer a secret, Ellroy was not prepared to live with Erika. He installed her in an apartment close to the Ravenswood, dubbed it "the fuckpad," and paid her rent. An arrangement which lasted for two years. During their first Christmas together, Ellroy's present to Erika was a gold Rolex. Erika was disappointed because she felt the gift was just Ellroy showing off his wealth, but she accepted it as "it's part of my transformation into HER. I'm gonna be HER so I'll wear the Rolex."[311] However, she had a meeting with her husband to discuss the terms of their divorce and thought it wouldn't be prudent to attend wearing a Rolex. She put her old watch on, and when she returned to her apartment, she forgot to swap it for the Rolex. Ellroy visited that day and was incandescent when he saw she was wearing her old watch, screaming at her for not wearing the Rolex in front of her husband.

Ellroy had a set of rules he expected Erika to follow. Erika was not allowed to smoke pot, she was not allowed to paint her toenails, she could not dance, she could not wear a swimsuit, she could not be naked in a room with another woman, there was to be no contact with ex-partners. She was allowed to contact her ex-husband to make arrangements for their daughters, "no matter what happened he would not come between me and my kids. He was very cool about that."[32] Erika was not sure where these rules came from, but suspected they stemmed from their sex life, "Our relationship, if it was nothing else, it was BIG SEX and that made him too vulnerable. He could not control his fear that any time I went out in the world, any man who saw me would want to fuck me."[33]

Their relationship coincided with an economic downturn in publishing that left Erika out of work. She had freelanced for the *LA CityBeat* which folded, as well as the *LA Times* and *LA Weekly* which were both subjected to deep cuts. In addition, her affair with Ellroy led to many friends abandoning her, "My marriage was over. My kids were in ruins. I lost a lot of friends, and I lost my reputation in the literary community. I was no longer invited to the Festival of Books, the groups, the dinners, anything and Ellroy loved that."[34] To be fair, Ellroy also had friends who disapproved of his relationship with Erika and his casting of her in his new memoir. Sonny Mehta, who considered *Blood's a Rover* to be Ellroy's greatest work, had reservations about publishing *The Hilliker Curse* in book form, and Helen strongly advised him against writing it. "Biography is not fate," she told him, trying to tame his self-destructive pursuit of women.[35]

The Hilliker Curse

A year after *Blood's a Rover* was released, Ellroy's second memoir was published. *The Hilliker Curse: My Pursuit of Women* explores Ellroy's lifelong obsession with sex, and the latter half is focused on his relationships with Laura and

Teresa. Ellroy was repeating a stylistic technique he developed with *My Dark Places*, the memoir which detailed his reinvestigation into his mother's murder and obsession with the Black Dahlia case. Just as his first memoir can be read as a parallel narrative to the novel *The Black Dahlia*, *The Hilliker Curse* is not a linear autobiography, but a narrative closely associated with *Blood's a Rover*, as many of the characters within it appear in both novel and memoir.

The Hilliker Curse was dedicated to Erika Schickel. Although the book ends with the relationship with Erika commencing and indications that Ellroy has moved on from the sexual obsessions and promiscuity that ended his two marriages, things between Erika and Ellroy were always fractious and took a huge toll on them both. *The Hilliker Curse* is Ellroy's most misjudged book and was poorly reviewed. Elaine Showalter aptly summed up why Ellroy could never drop his obsession with women: "When he is secure, contented, domesticated and normal – he risks losing his literary gift."[36] Ellroy's obsession with women had indeed led to some of his strongest work, including *Blood's a Rover*. But in *The Hilliker Curse* the preoccupation with sex is dull and repetitive. The alliterative prose style feels tired, annoying and, most tellingly, disassociated from events in the narrative. As was often the case in Ellroy's later career, the author himself became the book's most severe critic once he had finished publicizing it. Acknowledging that he wrote the memoir solely for money, Ellroy confessed: "I'll be happy to see it go out of print."[37]

Ellroy was increasingly on edge in private and public. Erika loved to dance but she found even if she did a little shimmy, it could induce anger or a panic attack in Ellroy. This became evident when they were both guests at a Hollywood wedding. Clark Peterson and Stacy Rukeyser were married at the Jonathan Club in LA on May 30, 2010. Ellroy was a groomsman and read from 1 Corinthians 13:

> Love is patient, love is kind. It does not envy, it does not boast, it is not proud.
> It is not rude, it is not self-seeking, it is not easily angered, it keeps no record of wrongs.

Figure 15 *Ellroy the Man of God. Reading from 1 Corinthians 13 at the wedding of Clark Peterson and Stacy Rukeyser. Courtesy of Clark Peterson.*

At the dinner afterwards Ellroy and Erika were seated together at a big table, with several other guests. Ellroy was nervous and tetchy. It was not the sort of environment in which he could easily dominate. Guests started dancing the Horah and several people came over to Ellroy's table to bring him and Erika into the dance. This triggered Ellroy, "He yells at the people, drags me out. There's a huge scene. We go home and we're yelling at each other."[38]

Ellroy's mental health was worsening, and it eventually began to affect his public performances. On September 7, 2010, Ellroy appeared at Largo at the Coronet on North La Cienega Boulevard in LA. The warm-up act was the comedienne Laura Kightlinger. Clark Peterson was in the audience and recalls Kightlinger's sexually candid monologue, touching on topics such as oral sex and menstruation, was receiving a mixed reaction. "Suddenly," Peterson recalls "Ellroy appears on the stage and starts yelling 'Get this shit off now.'"[39]

Ellroy continued to verbally harangue Kightlinger until she, doubtlessly humiliated, left the stage. Ellroy had been backstage listening to her monologue and, fragile and easily triggered, had finally snapped as, in his view, it was completely obscene. After he read from *The Hilliker Curse*, Ellroy received an equally mixed response from the audience. The incident with Kightlinger had proved an extreme example of Ellroy's competitiveness and his numerous psychological triggers.

For Erika, the stress of her relationship with Ellroy began to manifest itself physically, "I started having anxiety attacks. I was grinding my teeth. I had an itch that wandered all over my body and I scratched myself bloody."[40] However, it would be Ellroy's mental health that was Erika's paramount concern. When Ellroy returned from the European tour of *Blood's a Rover*, she noticed he was "inhumanly exhausted."[41] Ellroy was suffering from chronic insomnia for which he was being treated by his psychiatrist Dr. Francis Smith. Ellroy began taking Xanax and a host of other drugs. His behavior became increasingly worrying. He would show up at Erika's apartment wearing two left shoes. He would leave his car in places and forget where it was. He would be thrown out of restaurants for erratic behavior. Erika was convinced that Smith was a quack who Ellroy only saw as he was a "prescribing doctor he kept on speed dial."[42] Ellroy's problem with Smith is that he was too trusting and, as someone who never finished high school, a little bowled-over by Smith's qualifications. Ellroy gave a talk about overcoming addiction at a Malibu-based institution associated with Smith. Ironically, Ellroy was sinking deeper into addiction at the time.

One day Erika visited Ellroy at the Ravenswood and he had a shopping bag full of drugs that he had been prescribed, including a brand of marijuana called "LA Confidential." Although he may have enjoyed smoking dope named after his novel, Ellroy was hiding a more serious drug habit. He was drinking alcohol again and Smith had prescribed him amphetamines. Erika occasionally smoked pot, a habit she was trying to quit to help Ellroy in his addiction struggle. One day she confessed to him that she had smoked a joint at her book club and Ellroy exploded at her. In his view, Erika was an enabler whereas his drug use was justified as it had been prescribed, however dubiously.

Ellroy's drug problems came to a head on June 3, 2011. He had booked a suite at the Beverly Hills hotel so he and Erika could celebrate their second anniversary. "We're lying on the bed, and I kissed him and his mouth tastes weird to me. Something is not right in his mouth. Then he gets up to go to the bathroom and he's walking past the foot of the bed and we're talking and then he suddenly collapsed in three parts."[433] At first Erika thought it was a pratfall. It was odd how Ellroy slowly crumpled to his knees, then all fours, and then suddenly he was flat on the ground. She feigned amusement until she realized he was having a seizure. She called 911, but when the paramedics arrived Ellroy had recovered enough to send them away. They had not been gone long before he had another seizure. Erika called the ambulance again and Ellroy was admitted to Cedars Sinai hospital. Ellroy was exhausted and dehydrated and finally admitted to Erika that he had a problem, "He's on a gurney with his teeth knocked out and he confesses to me that he'd been taking speed the whole time."[44]

Ellroy agreed to seek help. Smith recommended a rehab clinic, the One80 Center in Beverly Hills. But Erika, who had lost all faith in Smith, felt that Ellroy needed to address the trauma of his past to improve his mental health. While agreeing that "sobriety is always good" she wanted Ellroy to attend a center in Arizona which specialized in healing trauma.[45] Her analysis of Ellroy's mental state stemmed from her own experience with trauma "If you don't try to understand your trauma it's just going to steer you through your life."[46] Ellroy chose the One80 Center over Erika's advice. When they arrived the attitude of the staff only served to compound Erika's fears. In her view, the staff seemed uninterested in helping Ellroy address mental health issues and she began arguing with them, "Listen to me. You're fucking this up. This isn't going to help him." She became hysterically upset and one staff member snapped back at her, "Well, maybe you need some help with your addictions Erika." Erika was right to be concerned. The One80 Center, which had only opened the previous April, was notorious for indulging the whims of its wealthier clientele.

It was a notoriety Ellroy took full advantage of.

Ellroy was more concerned with a professional quandary than his health problems. In 2005, Ellroy had won the Jack Webb award for his public support for the LAPD. He had subsequently emceed the awards ceremony several times for the Los Angeles Police Historical Society. He was due to host this year's ceremony, but the One80 Center had strict rules about keeping its patients on site during treatment. Attending an event in which alcohol was likely to be free flowing did not seem wise. However, Ellroy was adamant that he needed to go. A deal was struck in which Ellroy would be furloughed from the clinic for several hours to host the event. That night, an inwardly exhausted Ellroy gave a typically flawless performance in front of a large crowd of LAPD Officers. He chatted, mingled, and socialized with police officers who had no idea that Ellroy was a drug addict essentially on parole from rehab for a few hours.

Erika needed a break to get away from the never-ending stress of the situation. She flew out to Cleveland to spend a few days with her sister. When she returned to LA and visited Ellroy at the One80 Center, she walked into his room and was astonished to find him sat up in a chair, with a briefcase on his lap and outlining, by hand on a writing pad, his next novel, "It hadn't been a week since I had scraped him off the floor of the Beverly Hills Hotel."[47]

Ellroy had signed a six-figure deal to write a second LA Quartet, four huge novels set during World War II which would be prequels to the first Quartet.[48] The inspiration came to him one rainy evening in the winter of 2008. He was looking out of his office window and began to imagine "forlorn-looking Japanese in an army transport bus" being taken away for internment at Manzanar.[49] Ellroy began the painstaking process of rereading the original Quartet and sketching biographies of his characters to make sure he didn't write himself into chronological error.

Ellroy had been pleased with his treatment at the One80 Center. He became close to his therapist Dr. Bernardine Fried and was especially delighted when she brought her pet Husky into the Center to spend time with him and the other patients. When Ellroy was released from Rehab, Erika felt that he began to push her away. He started calling her "red" and "tigress" and being more distant around her. Ellroy, it seemed, had hardened in his attitude that Erika had been an enabler. Their relationship had been so volatile that she estimated they broke up and got back together between thirty or forty times, "We would just lie in each other's arms and cry together and say, 'This is insoluble'. Because I couldn't not be who I was, and he couldn't not be who he was. And who we were together in safety and privacy was the most beautiful, connected profound shit I have ever known in my life."[50] They had a major breakup and did not see each other for several months, but then reconciled at the end of 2011.

By this time, Erika was having money problems. She had not been able to write for the past two years, which she attributed to the emotional overload of their relationship. Her writing career, which had seemed promising after the release of her memoir, had slipped away. In desperate need of income, she accepted the offer of a housesitting job from her stepsister in Pasadena. Her interaction with Ellroy was chilly at the time. He told her he would telephone in a month. Erika remembers that he did call exactly a month later, almost to the hour. He informed her that the relationship was over and that they would never speak again. The emotional rollercoaster of the past two years had left him "ground to dust." Years later, Erika is still grappling with her feelings for Ellroy, "We were really good on many levels. It was red hot between us, and I don't just mean sexually. It was red hot."[51]

In Erika, Ellroy had found the "HER" he needed for the mother/lover figure and provide the "happy" ending to *The Hilliker Curse*. Erika though, had tried to stop him idolizing his mother. According to Erika, Jean Ellroy "abandoned him over and over again, was inappropriately sexual around him and was a terrible drunk."[52]

In April 2011, Ellroy closed his Facebook account and left a typically abrasive farewell message to his followers:

Dear FB Friends,

Fuck Facebook!!!!!—It has proven to be worthless as a book-selling device, and is nothing but a repository for perverts, reparation-seekers, old buddies looking for handouts, syphilitic ex-girlfriends looking for extra-curricular schlong and hack writers begging for blurbs.[53]

The harsh tone may be attributed to how he associated the social networking site with his fraught relationship with Erika, but it also reflected some of his genuine views about publishing. In his view, print and television media sold books. International literary tours, establishing good relations with the major bookstore chains, buttressed those sales. Social media and the internet were not only ineffective in selling books, but they were also actively destroying the publishing industry.

Although his relationship with Erika may have led to a nadir in his behavior, Ellroy could still be kind, generous, and inquisitive about other people. This could be seen in a series of friendships Ellroy made around the same time he was chasing women with abandon. Ellroy made a new friend when he met Andrew Quintero at the home of Clark Peterson. Quintero recalls, "I'd been a fan of his and read many of his books and classical music popped up in *Brown's Requiem*. In the very first pages of it the detective is sitting listening to a Beethoven violin concerto. I grew up in a classical music obsessed family."[54] When Quintero mentioned to Ellroy that he was a classical music devotee Ellroy "almost grabbed me by the lapels" with enthusiasm.[55]

Ellroy's interest in Quintero may have been somewhat paternal, "He looked like he could be my son."[566] They would swap CDs and discuss composers. Quintero found that Ellroy's views were strong and vigorously expressed, "He has got no shame in raining down disdain, whether it's on a composer or a performer. He listened to one recording of Rachmaninoff's third piano concerto, and he said 'Oh that guy's a butcher. He's just a butcher playing it.'"[57] But he could be equally enthusiastic about a strong interpretation. After listening to a Brahms symphony by the Berlin Philharmonic, Ellroy gleefully stated "They played the shit out of it."[58]

Classical music often served to deepen Ellroy's fascination with beautiful women. Quintero recalls, "I gave him an early album of Martha Argerich, the pianist. On the cover there was a very lovely photo of her and he had it framed."[59] Quintero introduced Ellroy to the work of the Russian violinist Viktoria Mullova, "He was fascinated by her and her look. He's fascinated by women and there's a line 'cherchez la femme' he'll sometimes bring out."[60] Ellroy liked to joke about the personalities of his favorite composers, "Poor lonely virginal Anton Bruckner and all of his private sufferings." Ellroy was also obsessed with the reputation, if not the music, of the English composer

Havergal Brian. Perhaps he saw in Brian's ability of writing extremely long, ambitious symphonies well into old age a style that he wished to emulate. Brian's "the Gothic" is one of the longest symphonies ever composed and Ellroy would tease Quintero about playing it, "Someday we'll have a listening party. We'll set aside a day, and we'll listen to that whole thing. It was never performed in his lifetime, but we'll do it."

Ellroy formed another close friendship with the novelist Megan Abbott. Abbott first met Ellroy at the Mystery Bookstore at an event for the LA Times Festival of Books, "The managers knew I was a big Ellroy fan, so they put me in the booth next to him. I had him trapped."[61] They talked for hours about crime fiction and the recently released *Zodiac*, "We were both fixated on it."[62] Ellroy and Abbott began talking on the phone and a friendship blossomed. Ellroy appreciated the articles Abbott had written praising his work, "She was a great champion of mine." Ellroy would visit Abbott when he was in New York on business, although Abbott noted that Ellroy could be triggered by "the noise and chaos" of the city.[63] Ellroy was more relaxed with Abbott in LA, "He took me to the Pacific Dining Car for dinner which is where he takes everybody," Abbott recalls. "It was like literally walking into one of his books, an old LA restaurant." Abbott described the friendship as "a dream come true," but even when Ellroy forms a close bond with someone the Demon Dog reputation can hover over the relationship, "I was so nervous to see him, I must admit, every time. He is so much like his books. His persona. It's very hard to tell where that ends and something else begins."[64]

Despite his fame as an author, Ellroy could still meet and befriend people who had never heard of him. Dr. Steven Mandel was Head of Anesthesiology at Cedars Sinai when he first met Ellroy. They met in an optometry shop in Beverly Hills. Mandel was on a break from work and still wearing his smock. Ellroy was being served ahead of him and Mandel noticed the optometrist was fawning over Ellroy, telling him he was "one of the greatest writers in the English language."[65] A slightly embarrassed Ellroy politely informed the optometrist that the man in line behind him was waiting to be served. When Mandel and Ellroy started chatting they soon hit it off. The next day a large box was delivered to Mandel's home, containing all the books Ellroy had authored. Ellroy and Mandel began a movie night tradition which lasted for around eight years. Ellroy would visit the Mandel home every Friday evening and they would watch a classic film noir or popular TV crime drama. He bought Mandel a multi-region DVD player so that they could watch the original Danish version of *The Killing*.

Ellroy met the criminologist Anne Redding at an exhibit on Elizabeth Short held at the Los Angeles Police Museum in March 2012, "I gave him my business card and he called a day or so after that, and we started a correspondence and a friendship."[66] Ellroy appreciated Anne's academic background and her "understanding of some of the hyper-social challenges of juveniles who have challenging upbringings."[67] He agreed to give a lecture, arranged by Anne, at Santa Barbara City College on the Black Dahlia case. In front of an audience Anne noticed how Ellroy could convert to his Demon Dog identity,

> I appreciate that he has a persona that has served him well. I felt that one-on-one, when he and I spent time together, he sheds that and seems much quieter, both in demeanor but also in his soul he seems quieter. I never had a problem with his persona, but I generally preferred the one-on-one James who seemed more relaxed and not feeling the need to display.[68]

In addition to feeling less need to show-off in public, Ellroy had also become a much more regular churchgoer. For several years he attended First Christian Church of North Hollywood, before switching to the First Presbyterian Church of Hollywood.

At AA, recovering from the tailspin of his relationship with Erika, Ellroy was keen on making new friends. Several AA members Ellroy had first met in Venice Beach decades ago, such as Alex Nicol and Richard Katz, reconnected with Ellroy and were struck by how gentle and kind he had become, in stark contrast to the swaggering Ellroy they remembered. Ellroy became close to the musician Richard Duguay. Duguay recalls one occasion when he was driving Ellroy to a friend's five-year sobriety anniversary party on Wilshire Boulevard, "We were listening to some Golden Oldies station and 'Love Train' comes on by The O'Jays. Ellroy turned up the volume full blast and began singing along, bouncing up and down in his seat. 'Here's Mr I Hate-Rock n' Roll and he's singing 'Love Train', not very well, and clearly knows every word."[69]

There had been several ideas mooted for Ellroy to front his own television series over the years. Ellroy finally got the opportunity when Investigation Discovery commissioned *James Ellroy's LA: City of Demons*. Ellroy takes the viewer on a guided tour of LA's criminal history using cases which, as he candidly admitted in the show's preview, have all been covered in his various novels, short stories, and journalism. The show could be viewed as a long advertisement for his backlist. The first episode covers the unsolved murders of Jean Hilliker and Stephanie Gorman. The second episode examines LA's history of organized crime, particularly the rivalry between Mickey Cohen's mob and the Italian crime family run by Jack Dragna. While he was grateful that everyone involved in the production was extremely professional, Ellroy quickly realized that pre-recorded TV was not his forum. He could electrify a live audience at a bookstore, theater, or college venue but when Ellroy was speaking directly into a camera his Demon Dog schtick fell flat. A nervous Ellroy tended to shout his lines at the camera in increasingly desperate attempts to make an impact. Brian Lowry in *Variety* bluntly described Ellroy's performance as "off-putting."[700] The first episode had covered the murder of the teenage girl Lily Burk. Ellroy had been friendly with Burk's parents and had a vague recollection of Lily once waving to him at a family party. Lily's mother, the attorney Deborah Drooz, telephoned Ellroy on the day the first episode was due to air and begged him to pull the segment on her daughter's murder. Ellroy informed her that it was not possible.

There were lighter moments that worked well. Ellroy wrote all his own dialogue and once again requested scenes where he is talking to a dog. This came in the form of Barko, an animated dog voiced by the actor Phil LaMarr. Ellroy was more at ease in the show interviewing Cheryl Crane (about the death of Johnny Stompanato) and Marcia Clark, the prosecutor in the OJ Simpson trial. Nevertheless, the show was cancelled after three episodes due to low ratings and the remaining episodes were not aired.

Ellroy used these well-paid assignments to fund big expenses. In 2012, Ellroy moved out of the Ravenswood and into a Spanish-style bungalow in Bronson Canyon he purchased for just under $1.2 million. Built in the 1920s, Ellroy's new home was straight out of film noir, with hardwood floors and arched windows and doorways. Although he was exceptionally pleased with the house, and in time it would prove a sound investment, there was a part of Ellroy that knew his spending was out of control and his behavior needed to change. But there would be several more affairs before he would begin on this new path. For the moment, Ellroy was too preoccupied telephoning old flames and talking up his expensive new house. Ellroy flew to London to visit the British journalist he had met during the *Blood's a Rover* tour. He enjoyed spending time with her and talking to her pet Staffordshire Bull Terrier, Rupert. Ellroy had a romantic fascination with British moorland and wanted to include it as part of Dudley Smith's backstory in the novel he was currently writing. He and the journalist visited Exmoor together, but Ellroy found it to be "too beautiful" as he had envisaged the harsh, desolate landscape of the North York Moors.[71]

On January 8, 2013, Ellroy met a screenwriter named Vicky at the Smoke House restaurant in Burbank. Ellroy was enjoying a meal with Glynn Martin, a former LAPD officer who he was collaborating with on the archival book *LAPD '53*. They had attended the premiere of *Gangster Squad*, a *LA Confidential* pastiche Ellroy described as "execrable."[72] The Smoke House was a Hollywood hangout and had been used as a filming location in several movies. Vicky was having dinner with a friend. According to her, "by the end of the night we were the only two tables in the place, and we'd all seen the movie and ended up chatting. He was more subdued, definitely more relaxed, not as performative, very polite."[73]

The evening had been pleasant, but Vicky thought nothing of it until she was emailed by an Executive Assistant of IPG, asking her if she would meet up with Ellroy. Intrigued, she agreed, and Ellroy was candid with her that "he essentially tracked me down" and "it was not the first time he had done this."[74] Ellroy and Vicky began a relationship which initially showed a lot of promise:

> It was very strange, sort of a whirlwind. He pursued me I guess is the simplest way to put it, and it was really fun at the beginning and really intense. We were together every day or if we weren't together, it was a three-hour phone call in the evening. At the time it seemed all magical and ultimately the wheels started coming off and it became clear to me that that was just his MO and really none of it had anything to do with me.[75]

Vicky began to worry about Ellroy's "erratic" behavior. One Friday evening, she and Ellroy visited the Mandel home to watch a film noir. Vicky enjoyed the evening, admired Dr. Mandel and his wife, and doted on their dogs. But something she must have done upset Ellroy as on the car journey home he was yelling at her. Ellroy began to disengage from Vicky, but she was not ready to give him up. After a period in which she had been trying and failing to get in touch with him, Vicky began to worry about Ellroy's mental health and feared that he had "gone missing." She drove by his home one Friday evening. Ellroy was returning from Dr. Mandel's house and was shocked to see Vicky's car as he pulled into his drive. A huge row erupted between the estranged couple. It was an unedifying spectacle which permanently ended their once promising relationship.

Ellroy was shaken by the scene and felt a degree of guilt at how his womanizing had brought it on. He later telephoned Vicky to apologize for the way he had treated her. Ellroy knew he had to break his pattern of behavior of seduction and abandonment. A personal intervention from Helen would bring about that change in him and fulfill Ellroy's periodic need for salvation and reinvention.

13

Sanctuary

(Denver 2016–2020)

On the eve of Ellroy's book tour to promote *Perfidia*, the first book of his new LA Quartet, Helen visited him in LA. She was concerned by his appearance. Ellroy had been physically ill with kidney disease and was emotionally exhausted. She spent some time looking after him. Over dinner together, Helen announced she would shortly be returning to her home in Denver. Ellroy started weeping. Years of chasing women had cost him his marriage, burned through his finances, and ravaged his mental health. The woman he truly wanted to be with was sitting right in front of him. Several of Ellroy's friends regarded a reconciliation with Helen as inevitable. His girlfriends had suspected as much. Erika Schickel complained that Helen was feeding Ellroy poison about her on the phone every night, and when a British girlfriend visited Ellroy in LA she grew increasingly frustrated with how much time Ellroy would spend with Helen or even just talking about her.

Helen had several conditions before they reunited. Naturally, there was to be no further womanizing or reckless spending. Also, as she had spent much of their marriage moving around the country at his behest, this time he would move to Denver to live with her. Their living arrangements would be different. Helen lived in an apartment in Denver's LoDo district. She felt that living together had always been one of the hurdles of their relationship, so it was decided that Ellroy would move into an apartment down the hall from her. It became his live-in office, like his old brood-den in Eastchester, while he spent most of his evenings with Helen.

Ellroy was excited about the move. He had visited Helen in Denver and liked the city. It had all the amenities of a big city and none of the traumatic personal history and fame-obsessed, hyper-stressed culture that he associated with LA. He resolved to start planning for the move when he was back from his book tour. Ellroy had high hopes for *Perfidia*. At the Book Expo America in May 2014, Ellroy described the wartime LA setting of *Perfidia* as a "time of fabulous fistfights, brief and passionate love affairs populated by great real-life characters interacting with great fictional characters. It is the secret human infrastructure of enormous public events. It's Ellroy's *Ragtime*."[1]

Perfidia

As a career choice, *Perfidia* could be read as a major gamble by Ellroy. At the same time, it was something of a shrewd and conservative risk. Now in his sixties, and with the gap between the publication of each novel getting longer and longer due to their epic scope, the second Quartet was clearly intended as the last major project of his writing career. If the first novel, *Perfidia*, was not a success, then Ellroy had tied himself to writing three more books in the same series: a commitment he could not back out without considerable embarrassment. Ellroy was betting everything on the belief that readers and critics would want to return to the fictional universe of the LA Quartet and Underworld USA trilogy so that eventually the "three series span thirty-one years and will stand as one novelistic history."[2] As a stylist, he risked looking conventional. The publishing industry, like Hollywood, was contracting and about to enter the age of the endless franchise. Therefore, a re-examination of his past successes may have swayed Ellroy to embark on the project.

By writing a prequel to the original Quartet, Ellroy was more than just reexamining his canon, he was coming at it with a broad revisionism. In *Perfidia*, links with *The Black Dahlia* can be found early in the text through the diary entries of Kay Lake. *The Black Dahlia* is structured entirely as the first-person narration of Bleichert. As a consequence, the reader is not drawn into the thought processes of Kay, but shares Bleichert's external viewpoint of a woman who is both sexy and vivacious, but equally pensive about the demons that haunt her. Ellroy cooled on first-person narration after *The Black Dahlia* as his increasingly complicated plotting and epic narratives required multiple viewpoints. *Perfidia* marks a partial return to this style as instead of a subjective third-person style, as with the other leading characters, Kay's perspective is committed to paper through her own words. Her first diary entry is preceded by the line, "**COMPILED AND CHRONOLOGICALLY INSERTED BY THE LOS ANGELES POLICE MUSEUM.**"[3] The detail is intriguing as the novel was billed as "real-time narration," with the action taking place over three weeks from December 6 to 29, 1941.[4] Kay's diary and the bureaucratic minutiae which precedes the first entry skewers the linear timeframe and sense of real-time as it is Kay looking back through the written word, and it brings the narrative to a point thirty years later in Ellroy's secret history with the death of J. Edgar Hoover and the fate of his archive of files which forms the climax of *Blood's a Rover*.

Kay writes that she began her diary on impulse after seeing from her bedroom terrace "A line of armored vehicles chugged west on Sunset, to fevered scrutiny and applause."[5] This is a similar image to what Ellroy had envisaged looking from his window in the Ravenswood. Just as that served as his impetus for writing the novel, Kay's vision of an impending war has driven her to start writing. As a historical novelist Ellroy was witnessing a flashback to the event whereas Kay lives the war in real-time. The image evokes a series of memories in Kay: her upbringing in Sioux Falls, the brutal murder of a black man by the Ku Klux Klan, her ill-fated involvement with jazz drummer and dope peddler Bobby DeWitt and how this led her to Lee Blanchard and the heart of the LAPD. The memories stop as the convoy passes out of her view, and the diary entry ends: "Nothing before this moment exists. The war is coming. I'm going to enlist."[6] Suddenly the past is of little consequence to Kay, the war will enhance the immediacy of experience in a multitude of ways. Her past demons lose their grip on her as she rushes to embrace new ones. Kay's words are prophetic; the following day the Japanese attack Pearl Harbor, dragging the US into the war and the characters of *Perfidia* into the maelstrom. The switching of timeframes is complicated and fluid. Action unfolds in both real time and reflection, and an entire life is relived in the passing of a convoy. Kay's sudden decision to stop the reminiscence indicates the changed reality; every character's life will be different now the US is at war. But it also shows how Ellroy has completely reinvented the Quartet narrative: "Nothing before this moment exists."

Kay reveals she had feelings for Bleichert long before they are formally introduced. She follows his boxing career and reports on his victories and defeats with some out of character purple prose: "His circumspection in the ring delights me. I have never spoken to Bucky Bleichert, but I am certain that I understand him."[7] Kay telephones his house only to hang up when he replies. Ellroy defers their moment of first contact to the story line in *The Black Dahlia*, which although protected from a complete revision, can never be read in the same way again. Through writing a second Quartet, Ellroy has invited his readers to revisit the first, but some details such as Kay's self-proclaimed love for Bleichert are jarring. Does she really love a man she has never met, or is it merely a powerful crush which, as the circumstances slowly allow over the intervening years, matures into a romantic love?

Another strong link with the narrative of *The Black Dahlia* can be found in the appearance of Elizabeth Short as a living character. In *The Black Dahlia* she haunts the characters and Ellroy himself. In *Perfidia*, she appears in the flesh, and she is revealed to be the illegitimate daughter of Dudley Smith. Having made this significant, and potentially problematic, revelation in *Perfidia*, Ellroy does not ingrain it deeply into the plotting. There are many possibilities about Short's parentage that Ellroy leaves open. The most striking scene between Smith and Elizabeth Short comes when he takes her with his lover, film star Bette Davis, to the theater to see Orson Welles' *Citizen Kane*. Also in attendance is Short's friend from her hometown, the blind Tommy Gilfoyle. There are multiple viewings within the scene. Short narrates the film for Gilfoyle, who, ironically, as Jim Mancall notes, can see a kindness in her the other characters do not: "Short's storytelling allows her, momentarily, to mediate the Hollywood spectacle that will ultimately consume her, and in turn, Gilfoyle sees Short's kindness and talent."[8] Here we have a parallel with Bleichert in *The Black Dahlia*, who also saw virtues in Betty when others, such as the tabloid press, were trying to write her off as a loose woman who invited her fate.

Bette Davis observes Short as she narrates the film, noting the similarities she has with her father Dudley and absorbing her mannerisms for use in future performance: "She would know Beth's every tic by suppertime. She would deftly mimic Beth by dessert."[9] Smith watches the film in a state of agitation. He is the only one not taken in by the "idiot muckraking and invasive technique," and knows details about Welles' lurid personal life that, Beth and Gilfoyle at least, are oblivious to: "Young Welles scrounged coon maids off Beverly Hills bus stops. He bamboozled them with maryjane and magic tricks. He plied them with his cricket dick and drove them home to coontown."[10] Triggered by the film, Smith needs to dehumanize Welles by noting that the genius auteur is as perverted as everyone else in Hollywood. Ironically, the process is not dissimilar to Welles's allusive portrayal of William Randolph Hearst in *Citizen Kane*, particularly in the sexual secret lying behind the mystery of the sled "Rosebud," as Ellroy uses Welles's sleazy reputation to demythologize him. Welles/Smith and Kane/Hurst deconstructions stand in contrast to Kay's love of Bucky, who she has molded into a fantasy figure, in many ways similar to how people fall in love with movie stars. Elizabeth Short has never met Welles but understands his work: "Beth caught the style and conveyed it frame for frame."[11] Fame will allude Short but she comes across as insightful about art she views externally.

Ellroy's work on *Perfidia* had been meticulous. He wanted to portray wartime LA as an around-the-clock city by employing a novelistic version of real-time. Ellroy had to time all the events in the narrative perfectly, "The most difficult part was syncing the air raids accurately to the blackouts and running it around the clock, so if you hand off at 2:59 a.m., and Kay Lake and Hideo Ashida are about to leave the delicatessen in Beverly Hills, Ashida's gotta take-off at 3:01 to drive up the coast and witness the submarine attack."[12]

Many of the positive reviews validated Ellroy's scrupulous attention to detail. However, the novel was by no means universally praised. Dennis Lehane complained that "the ceaseless 'outing' of rumored homosexuals grows monotonous and, worse, predictable [...] The effect isn't revelatory; it's puerile."[13] Ellroy could still count on many strong reviews and a loyal following, but while his writing was as accomplished as ever, his novels were beginning to lose a sense of emotional power, and with it the level of engagement began to seep away.

In June 2015, Variety reported that Ellroy's Bronson Canyon home had been put on the market for $1.395 million. Ellroy moved to Denver in August 2015. When friends visited, they were struck by how rigidly Ellroy and Helen kept to their separate living spaces arrangement, "I saw them separately and then I saw them together,"[14] Eddie Muller remarked. Resuming their relationship nearly a decade after divorcing was never going to be entirely painless. Helen found Ellroy's behavior could still be manic even when he was far away from his old vices in LA, particularly in his need to always be shocking and provocative which he often did when he was slipping into fight-or-flight response, "He continued to talk shit I didn't recognize when we got back together in 2015. The shit would escalate and escalate if I fought him."[15] By patiently working on these issues Helen was satisfied that Ellroy's "fits have diminished significantly."[16]

In LA, Ellroy had found it impossible to say no to an invitation to speak or appear at a public event. He was determined to have a less exhausting schedule, and only make public appearances to promote his own books. However, he made an exception when he befriended Walter Chaw. Chaw was a longstanding fan of Ellroy's work and when he met the author through a mutual acquaintance, they immediately hit it off. Ellroy and Chaw decided to collaborate on hosting a film series at the Alamo Drafthouse in Littleton where Chaw worked as general manager. They called the series "In a Lonely Place with James Ellroy." "He's a savant in regard to film noir," recalls Chaw. "He has an incredible recall of the genre. Films I'd never seen or heard of, based on one viewing, he could place it in the context of its release."[17]

Chaw recommended that a screening of *LA Confidential* would be a good way to begin the series, which began in September 2015. Ellroy's introduction was critical of the film and particularly scathing of Kevin Spacey's performance. A woman on the front row, who Chaw recalls had been drinking, tried to interrupt, "No. He's a brilliant actor."

"You don't know him how I know him," Ellroy snapped back.

Ellroy's views on the film adaptation of *LA Confidential* were increasingly negative and driven by far more than his personal dislike of Kevin Spacey.

Figure 16 *Ellroy introducing a film at the Alamo Drafthouse. Ellroy abruptly cancelled the film series after being angered at how the Alamo had treated his friend Walter Chaw. Credit: Jason Carter.*

On September 20, 2016, Curtis Hanson died at his home in the Hollywood Hills. He had been in declining health for some time after wandering off the set of his last film, *Chasing Mavericks*, and being found confused and disorientated. He was diagnosed with early-onset Alzheimer's disease and spent his remaining years mostly confined to his home. Ellroy had not been in contact with Hanson for years. The last time he saw him was while dining with Clark Peterson in an LA restaurant. Hanson came over to say hello and they could tell from his garbled conversation that he was unwell. He struggled to remember Ellroy's name. When the name finally came to him, Ellroy responded gently "Yes Curtis, it's Ellroy."

Ellroy wrote a tribute in *Variety* to the director who had made a film which was "a signature moment in my life."[18] However, Ellroy spent much of the article damning Hanson with faint praise. Ellroy wrote that "You don't *feel*

Curtis Hanson's films. You admire their allegiance to craft."[19] As for Hanson's adaptation of his novel Ellroy opined, "What I failed to feel, I admired. What I lost in emotional pop, I regained in a rush of breathtaking craftsmanship."[20] Despite ending the article with a vow to "introduce the film to a hundred more audiences before I go myself," Ellroy made a promise to himself.[21] His lingering affection for Curtis Hanson had stopped him from doing this before, but now that Hanson was dead, Ellroy decided that whenever someone asked him about *LA Confidential*, he would not hold back on his negative opinion of the film.

When people drift apart it's often difficult to identify a single reason or juncture in time. For Ellroy and Hanson it was the culmination of many things. Ellroy's perception that Hanson had treated Brian Helgeland shabbily. Hanson's reluctance to make a sequel. Ellroy's decisiveness contrasted sharply with Hanson who he described as "the most circumspect man I've ever met."[22] The nature of Hollywood does not lend itself well to enduring friendships. People often work together intensely on a project, form a close bond and then they don't see each other for years afterwards unless it is connected to work. But what most bothered Ellroy about Hanson was that, because of him, his legacy as an author was now inextricably tied to a film that he never really cared for.

Despite his feelings for the film, Ellroy had continued to work on the idea of sequels and spinoffs. Ellroy was not involved in a 2003 TV pilot episode of *LA Confidential* which starred Kiefer Sutherland as Jack Vincennes. Ellroy did write a new TV pilot in 2013 which was never produced. Ellroy envisioned the pilot opening with scenes from the film, followed by voiceover by the character of Sid Hudgens Jr. In a riposte to fans of the film Hudgens Jr says, "You thought the story ended *then*. Fools, you were wrong. It's just kicking into high gear *now*."[23]

In 2018, Ellroy was in New York on business when he received a call from Brian Helgeland. Helgeland told him there was renewed interest in Hollywood for "LA Confidential 2." Ellroy offered to meet with Helgeland in LA, but Helgeland said he would fly out and meet him at his home in Denver, displaying the sort of decisiveness Ellroy admired. In Denver, the two writers discussed the nature of the project. It had been more than twenty years since the original film. To acknowledge the passing of time Helgeland felt the sequel should be set in the mid-1970s, with a plot that involved the kidnapping of Patty Hearst by the Symbionese Liberation Army. Russell Crowe and Guy Pearce were likely to resume their roles, and Helgeland wanted to throw in a Black cop to make up a trio of leading characters. He had Chadwick Boseman in mind for the role. Helgeland was now one of Hollywood's hottest screenwriters and directors, commanding multi-million-dollar fees per film, but he was going to lay down a condition to the studios. Helgeland would only make "LA Confidential 2" if Ellroy was attached to the project. Ellroy was deeply moved by the gesture.

Ellroy and Helgeland flew out to LA to pitch the project. Everything appeared to be moving positively, and actors were getting attached to the production. They spent several days trying to sell it to Hulu, Netflix, Amazon. Helgeland let Ellroy do most of the pitching as he was a commanding speaker, and no one knew these characters better than the author himself. But everywhere they went the studios said no. "We came to realize that whatever filmmaking was in 2018 it was not going to make 'LA Confidential 2'," Helgeland recalled.[24] Ellroy was by now exhausted with Hollywood. For years he had taken lucrative screenwriting assignments on the happy assumption that the films were unlikely to be made. Every so often a dream project such as 'LA Confidential 2' would come along and reignite his interest in the craft, but then with seeming inevitability the project would fall apart. It was a soul-sapping process that took his time and energy away from writing novels. Given his age and the epic scope of the Quartet novels he knew he needed to refocus on his first writing passion. He called up Helen in Denver and said, "It's over."

Ellroy was through with Hollywood.

Ellroy maintained his campaign against the reputation of the original film. He introduced a twentieth anniversary screening of the film at the Alamo Drafthouse in December 2017. Although his opening comments were positive, describing the adaptation as "extraordinarily witty and lively" he soon reverted to what he disliked about the film, including how it is "markedly overpraised" and "you feel nothing for Kevin Spacey, and you feel less than nothing for Kim Basinger and Russell Crowe."[25] Ellroy's public attempts to discredit the film reached their peak in LA the following April. Ellroy was invited to the Egyptian Theater for a pre-screening discussion of the film with Eddie Muller. At the time the novelist and screenwriter Jordan Harper had been working on a new TV pilot adaptation of *LA Confidential* for CBS.

Ellroy and Harper met at the Egyptian Theater. Harper told Ellroy that the pilot and the planned series, which hopefully would follow, was not going to be entirely faithful to the novel, "I told Ellroy that he would not like the pilot, and I stand by that. Adaptation requires changing. The goal of adaptation should not be just to place a faithful replica of the book onto the screen, because in that case people should just read the book."[26] Harper found Ellroy to be very supportive of his plans and he left immediately after their talk. If Harper had stuck around to witness Ellroy's onstage discussion of the film, he may have been surprised by the author's sudden change in attitude. Ellroy's take on the film was vitriolic. According to Eddie Muller:

> I was very taken aback and surprised when James made public comments disparaging of Curtis Hanson, and seemingly not aware that the auditorium was filled with people who were personal friends of Curtis, and that they were still hurting because of Curtis's recent death. A lot of people felt—wow, we don't understand why James is saying these negative things, especially in light of Curtis's very untimely death.[27]

Figure 17 *Ellroy and Eddie Muller introducing a screening of* LA Confidential *at the Egyptian Theater on April 14, 2018. Ellroy's campaign against the film would reach its peak at this event, shocking many of the people who were in attendance. Credit: Film Noir Foundation.*

After the talk Ellroy flew back to Denver leaving Muller to handle the backlash, "That was the opening night of a ten-day film festival and I had ten more days of people coming up to me saying 'What the hell was wrong with Ellroy? Why would he say those things?' and I got a little exasperated as I was getting the flak, not James."[28] Muller telephoned Ellroy and explained the amount of negative feedback his talk had created. Ellroy apologized. He considered Muller a good friend and regretted causing him any embarrassment. It began to change his attitude. To answer questions honestly when journalists and readers asked him about the film was one thing, but the scene he had created at the Egyptian Theater had been unedifying. Ellroy promised himself that he would no longer introduce screenings of the film.

Jordan Harper's TV pilot of *LA Confidential* was a multi-million-dollar production. Despite a positive reaction from the few industry insiders who saw it, CBS decided not to air the pilot and Harper's plans to tell the story of the novel over five seasons fell through. "When you talk to people who don't work in Hollywood, it's very difficult to explain and I don't know how to explain it other than to say it's just what they do," Harper said.[29] When it was first published in 1990, *LA Confidential* had brutally skewered the perception that LA was the city where people came for their dreams to come true. The characters who bought into that dream were left jaded, disappointed, and ultimately broken on the Wheel of Fortune. Thirty years after the book was published, the novel seemed to be having the same effect on the people who were still trying to adapt its story to the small and silver screen.

Ellroy severed many ties when he moved to Denver. He found this to be a necessity as LA had so many negative memories for him. Many of his friends in the LAPD had retired. In June 2018, Michael Moore was appointed Chief of Police. Ellroy received word that Moore was not a fan of his. In the age of Black Lives Matter, having Ellroy, the self-styled "Tory Mystic" who speaks in jive as an unofficial LAPD spokesman did not seem wise. The era of the apologist was over. Organizations like the LAPD began to reposition themselves. If anything, they tried to emulate their social activist critics.

Ellroy's most acrimonious split did not occur in LA. Nat Sobel had been Ellroy's literary agent for more than three decades. In the book industry,

Sobel's reputation was legendary. At the 2015 Edgar Awards, when Ellroy was appointed Grand Master, Otto Penzler presented him with the award and paid tribute to Sobel's contribution to Ellroy's success, describing him as "the greatest agent alive." In his acceptance speech, Ellroy exclaimed "I am devoutly religious. I see God's hand in every moment of every day, and God's intercession in all events large and small." Afterwards, Sobel admonished Ellroy for these lines. He felt that religious declarations could do nothing but damage to his writing career. Ellroy ignored him. He had become increasingly religious with age and was regularly attending an Episcopal Church in Denver. If anything, he found the Episcopalians were too liberal for his tastes. Ellroy enjoyed reading the work of the Calvinist theologian Timothy Keller.

Ellroy was nearing seventy and Sobel was an octogenarian. Ellroy thought that Sobel's skills as an agent were beginning to slip. Sobel Weber Associates had represented Helen Knode in the sale of her first two novels, and while she claimed to have left the company on good terms, Ellroy was not satisfied with the way she had been represented. Over the years, Ellroy had become increasingly tetchy around Sobel. When Sobel wrote to Ellroy asking him to contribute to a collection edited by Michael Chabon, Sobel mentioned in passing that Chabon was a Pulitzer Prize winner. Ellroy defaced the letter with the words "So What?"[30]

Ultimately, Ellroy and Sobel's friendship and professional collaboration ended abruptly over a relatively minor incident. The titles of several Ellroy's novels had been released online via the Sobel Weber website, before Ellroy wanted them to be known to the public. This led to reports that the third Underworld USA novel would be titled "Police Gazette," when Ellroy never considered it to be anything other than a working title. Ellroy stated to Sobel that he did not want this to happen again. Sobel assured him that it would not, although at his advanced age he may have been as computer illiterate as Ellroy. All the forthcoming titles by Sobel Weber authors were listed on the agency website, including Ellroy's latest novel *This Storm*. Sure enough, an online article appeared on a crime fiction website revealing the new title.

One Sunday evening Ellroy had introduced a film at the Alamo Drafthouse. In the bar of the theater afterwards, Jason Carter, a regular attendee of the film series, approached Ellroy "I had the phrase 'This Storm' written on a scrap of paper. When I first saw Ellroy, I said, 'I saw something on Nat Sobel's website ...' and handed him the paper. He looked shocked and hurt and tore the paper in half."[31]

"This is clearly not the title you intended for volume two," Carter said.

"Not at all," Ellroy replied. "Jason, I'm not upset with you, but this pisses me the fuck off."

Ellroy fired Nat Sobel the next day over a curt two-minute phone call. Later that day Sobel telephoned Otto Penzler and said, "I've had the best news and the worst news."[32]

The best news was that one of Nat Sobel's discoveries, Viet Thanh Nguyen, had won the Pulitzer Prize for his debut novel *The Sympathizer*. The worst news was that Sobel had lost James Ellroy as a client, a man he considered a true friend.

Ellroy had long suspected, due to their completely different backgrounds, that Sobel had always looked down on him. But perhaps he was wrong in this assessment. According to one mutual friend, "I know for a fact that there was no other author who Nat felt so close to."

Ellroy took Jason Carter out to dinner at his favorite Denver haunt, Elway's Steakhouse in Cherry Creek, as a thank you for bringing the matter to his attention.

Ellroy felt that his split from Nat Sobel was long overdue, and that he had only stayed with him for so many years out of a sense of loyalty. Here was the fracture in Ellroy's personality in full play, the sentimental loyalist prone to sudden outbursts of ruthlessness. It did leave him with the question as to who was going to represent him from now on. He discussed the matter with Thomas Mallon. Mallon was in no doubt as to who should represent Ellroy. He recommended his own agent, Andrew Wylie.

Wylie had gained the nickname "the Jackal" from his reputation for swooping down and stealing other agents' clients. But he didn't need to steal Ellroy from anyone. Mallon recommended Ellroy to Wylie by email, "I do believe that James is touched with genius and that he has great things in front of him as he heads into his fourth quarter."[33] By this time Ellroy and Wylie were already in touch. Ellroy had managed to get Wylie on the phone when the agent was in London on business. He asked Wylie to represent him and received an unequivocal response, "I'd love to be your agent, James."[34]

The two men lunched together in New York. Wylie's sharp business mind was a good fit for Ellroy who was ambitious as ever. Ellroy was proud to be with the Wylie Agency which he described as "the greatest literary agency in the world." The move appeared to pay-off. In 2019, Everyman's Library republished the entire LA Quartet and Underworld USA trilogy in three new volumes as part of its Everyman's Classics series. It was an honor Ellroy felt was overdue, but Sobel had been reluctant to lobby for it. Wylie had played a key role in making it happen.

One of the melancholiest aspects of aging is to witness friends pass away one by one. Don Crutchfield died in 2016. His passing did not receive any press coverage and Ellroy did not find out about it until sometime later, when he telephoned the Crutchfield home to discuss royalties, only to be told by a relative that he had died. Crutchfield had been the friend to Ellroy that Fred Otash never was. Ellroy had genuine affection for him and trusted him enough to make him a leading character in a novel, knowing that he would never break their agreement.

Dick Contino, the accordionist whose career Ellroy had helped to revive, died in April 2017. Ellroy was giving a post-film discussion on *Rififi* at the Alamo Drafthouse when he heard the news. Merri O'Neal Contino wrote on Facebook, "It's been many years, but thank you (Ellroy) for the friendship you shared with my father. You were a bright spot in his life, professionally and personally."[35] Randy Rice died in April 2018. He spent his final years with his wife Rae Jones in Bisbee, Arizona, which coincidentally is the small town the character of Lynn Bracken is from in *LA Confidential*. Ellroy did not find out about Randy's passing until two years later. He was deeply affected by the news. Ellroy and Randy had not seen each other in years and had a difficult parting, but there are some friendships, especially those forged in childhood, that exist on a different plane.

One friend Ellroy had stayed in close contact with from the moment they met until his final days was Sonny Mehta. Mehta had encouraged Ellroy to be the type of writer he wanted to be. There were crime writers whose sales had proved more robust than Ellroy's, but Mehta never urged his friend to be more commercial if it compromised his vision. "He was always too circumspect to ask me—why hadn't I written a novel that sold as well as *The Black Dahlia*," Ellroy recalled.[36] Mehta died of pneumonia in December 2019, after being admitted to New York Presbyterian Hospital.

In January, the following year, Ellroy attended a memorial event to Mehta at New York Public Library. Around five hundred people were estimated to be in attendance, including many authors and luminaries in the publishing industry. Ellroy paid tribute to the man who had made his dream come true by inviting him to Knopf. He described Mehta as "the greatest publisher in the world of English-language books" and read from A.E. Houseman and the Book of Revelation.[37]

The passing of so many old friends could be enough to induce a depression in any author, but Ellroy took it as a sign to accelerate his working schedule and use whatever time he had left to fulfill his still grand ambitions. Ellroy was still fanatically loyal to his younger friends. In July 2018, *Westword* reported Walter Chaw had left his position at the Alamo Drafthouse on "mutual terms."[38] Ellroy was disgusted by the Alamo's treatment of Chaw. The last film Ellroy introduced at the Alamo was the heist-flick *Charley Varrick* in June 2018. He then abruptly ended the film series. Ellroy issued a statement on his website:

> I have severed my connection with the Alamo Drafthouse in Littleton, where for two years I was pleased to present monthly screenings of (mostly noir) films from my personal canon. Thanks to all who attended the screenings and the Q&As at the pub. I hope you enjoyed them as much as I did.[39]

This Storm was published in May 2019. Ellroy seamlessly interweaves the internment of Japanese Americans in the wake of the Pearl Harbor attacks, the grisly discovery of a corpse in Griffith Park, a gold heist, fifth-columnist agitators, attempts by the Japanese to establish a political and military foothold in Mexico. To convey the theme of anti-war, pro-fascist propaganda, a large swastika dominated the front cover of the novel. This came about through a farcical communication error. Ellroy had requested to Chip Kidd that he design a symbol which merged the Swastika with the Nazi Eagle and Soviet Hammer & Sickle. In the novel, Hideo Ashida is working on such an image while interned at Manzanar. Perhaps Ellroy wasn't clear enough or his instructions became garbled as they were passed along by third parties, as Kidd opted for a single swastika formed out of the merging of directional arrows. It was a potentially controversial image that could have been easily avoided. "Nothing ever came back to me," Kidd recalls, "but when the book was published in paperback the swastika was gone."[40]

Many of the reviews of *This Storm* were positive, but even among Ellroy's admirers a certain weariness was creeping in. Anthony Cummins wrote "Relentless and disorienting it may be, but Ellroy has never been a five-pages-before-bed kind of writer; his vision is more the fever dream after lights out."[41] For all its technical brilliance, *This Storm* was more a text to be admired rather than one that engaged the readers emotionally.

Ellroy toured the UK and Ireland in promotion of the book in May and June of 2019. Kate McQuaid was his publicist for the tour. From the first moment they met, a friendship developed. Kate was amazed by Ellroy's energy. He wouldn't flinch at six hours of press interviews. The tour began with an appearance at the Southbank Centre, and moved on to Manchester, Glasgow, Dublin, and ended with Ellroy being interviewed onstage by Mark Lawson at the Hay Festival. Kate witnessed Ellroy's spiritual side. During one restaurant meal with publishing colleagues, Ellroy said grace and used the memorable phrase, "Thank you for the professional regard at this table."[42]

For his bookstore appearances audiences were directed not to ask questions about Donald Trump. The chaotic Trump presidency was viewed with a mixture of fascination and horror in Britain. Always a conservative, Ellroy had most likely voted for Trump or abstained in 2016, if only to halt the creation of a Clinton dynasty. Ellroy's hatred of the Clinton family knew no bounds. In private though, he held a very low opinion of Trump and his few public utterances confirmed this. He told the journalist Edward Luce that "I have never seen more volcanic, pathetic self-pity in a man. Trump revels in his own grotesque. I know something about men. Real men do not wallow in self-pity."[43]

In September 2019, Ellroy travelled back to London to accept the *GQ* Writer of the Year Award. Ellroy was shocked at what had become of the magazine that had once employed him. In his view, *GQ* had become a "politically-correct rag" and the awards ceremony held at the Tate Modern was "just another hot overcrowded room."[44] Kate McQuaid was present at the ceremony. She and

Figure 18 *Ellroy, the artist Ray Richardson, and Ray's dog outside the Southbank Centre in London, May 27, 2019, taken while Ellroy was on a book tour for* This Storm. *This would be one of Ellroy's last trips abroad before the Covid-19 pandemic brought international travel to a standstill. Credit: Kate McQuaid.*

Ellroy were seated at a table with the Chinese artist Ai Weiwei. She sensed Ellroy's displeasure with the event, "It's not the Man Booker Prize. It's a corporate event to promote *GQ*."[45]

Ellroy improvised a brilliant speech, declaring himself an anglophile and praising many of his colleagues in publishing. Now a septuagenarian, Ellroy had amassed a huge number of literary awards, including the coveted Order of Arts and Letters in France where he was still a superstar. He was always grateful, but nothing beat the thrill of the work itself, and there was already another project that he was preoccupied with.

In a *New York Times* interview Ellroy was asked who he would like to write his life story, "Either the estimable Tom Nolan, biographer of Ross Macdonald, or Adam Sissman, biographer of John le Carré. These guys know their subject and craft."[46] In October 2019 Ellroy visited the University of South Carolina for a week-long series of events related to his archive. He had dinner with Richard Layman and showed him a list of potential biographers. Layman was unimpressed with his selection.

"Pick someone who has written on you," he advised.

In February 2020, Ellroy had recently returned to his Denver apartment after speaking at a tribute to Sonny Mehta in New York. The previous month, the first US citizen had been diagnosed with COVID-19 in Washington State after returning from a trip to Wuhan, but the virus was still not causing a major alarm with the US media or the public, and Ellroy thought little of it. He checked his answering machine and received a message he was not expecting:

Hello James. This is Steve Powell. We last met in Manchester during the UK tour of *This Storm*. I've written three books on you to date. I have some news. I'm writing your biography for Bloomsbury. It's a scholarly biography. It's gonna be a great book. By the way, I've discovered the identity of your mother's first husband. His name was Easton Ewing Spaulding ...

"I always get what I want," Ellroy wrote in *The Hilliker Curse*. "It comes slow or fast and always costs a great deal."[47]

Figure 19 *Lord of all he surveys: Ellroy in Denver, 2021, recording his "Hollywood Death Trip" podcast for AudioUp. Credit: Jimmy Jellinek.*

Notes

Chapter 1

1   *LA Times* 1958a.

2   *KCET* 2018.

3   *Los Angeles Times*, 1958c.

4   Ibid.

5   Ellroy 1996: 83.

6   Ibid., 344.

7   Ibid., 345.

8   Ibid., 346.

9   Ibid., 346.

10   Ibid., 346.

11   Ibid., 346.

12   Terr 1994: 188.

13   Ibid., 188.

14   Ellroy 1996: 346.

15   Ibid., 347.

16   Ibid., 347.

17   Ibid., 347.

18   Ibid., 347.

19   Ibid., 347.

20   Ibid., 347.

21 Ellroy 2010: 13.

22 Ellroy 2006: 362; Ellroy 2010: 13.

23 Ellroy 1996: 348.

24 Ibid., 348.

25 Wedner 2008.

26 Ellroy 2010: 13.

27 Ellroy 1996: 348.

28 Wolfe 2006: 29.

29 McKinty 2019.

30 Ibid.

31 Ellroy 1996: 85.

32 Ibid., 109.

33 McDonald 2001: 123.

34 Ellroy 1996: 348–9.

35 Epstein and Morella 1983: 20.

36 Leaming 1989: 17–24.

37 Slater 1965: 139.

38 Leaming 1989: 21–2.

39 Ibid., 22.

40 Ellroy 2010: 13.

41 Ellroy 1996: 84.

42 Akel 2017.

43 Ellroy 1996: 349.

44 Terr 1994: 187.

45 Ellroy 1996: 84.

46 Ibid., 349–50.

47 Ibid., 349.

48 Ibid., 340.

49 Ibid., 350.

50 Hodel 2004: 226–7.

51   Ellroy 1996: 363.

52   Ibid., 107.

53   Slater 1965: 137.

54   Ibid., 137.

55   Ibid., 143.

56   Ibid., 144.

57   Rich 2008: 177.

58   Epstein & Morella 1983: 153.

59   Slater 1965: 153.

60   Ibid., 156.

61   Terr 1994: 188.

62   Ellroy 2004a: 31.

63   Epstein & Morella 1983: 183.

64   Ellroy 2010: 13.

65   Ibid., 13.

66   Ibid., 12.

67   Ellroy 1996: 106.

68   Rich 2008: 177.

69   Rooney 1991: 235.

70   Stiefel 2019.

71   Ibid.

72   Rich 2008: 178.

73   Haffner 2011: 324–6.

74   Ellroy 1996: 85.

75   Ibid., 85.

76   Ibid., 86.

77   Ellroy 2010: 4.

78   Ibid., 14.

79   Ellroy 1996: 351.

80   Ibid., 352.

81 Ibid., 320.

82 Ibid., 87.

83 Ellroy 1997: xvii.

84 Ellroy 1996: 85.

85 Ibid., 83.

86 Ibid., 83.

87 Ibid., 83.

88 Ibid., 87.

89 Ibid., 85.

90 Ellroy 2010: 10.

91 Ibid., 10.

92 Ellroy 2020.

93 Ellroy 2010: 11.

94 Ellroy 1996: 89.

Chapter 2

1 Ellroy 1996: 89.

2 Ibid., 89.

3 Ibid., 89.

4 Ibid., 89.

5 Ibid., 272.

6 Ibid., 90.

7 Ibid., 90.

8 Ibid., 90.

9 Ibid., 90.

10 Ibid., 91.

11 Ibid., 269.

12 Johnson 2010.

13 Ellroy 1996: 335.

14 Swaim 1987: 14.

15 Ellroy 1996: 94.

16 Ibid., 49.

17 Ibid., 14.

18 Ibid., 16.

19 *LA Times* 1958b.

20 Ellroy 1996: 82.

21 Ibid., 81.

22 Ibid., 81.

23 Ibid., 82.

24 Ibid., 13.

25 Ibid., 13.

26 Ibid., 93.

27 Ibid., 83.

28 Ibid., 94.

29 Ellroy 2021.

30 Ellroy 1996: 77.

31 Ibid., 77.

32 Ibid., 95.

33 Ibid., 105.

34 Ibid., 108.

35 Horvitz 2020.

36 Ellroy 1996: 107.

37 Jacobson 2021.

38 Ibid.

39 Ibid.

40 Ellroy 1996: 107.

41 Ibid., 109.

42 Ibid., 96.

43 Ibid., 108.

44 Powell 2014.

45 Akel 2017.

46 Ibid.

47 Rich 2008: 177.

48 Ellroy 2004a: 33.

49 Silet 1995: 46.

50 Ellroy 2005: viii.

51 Ibid., viii.

52 Webb 1958: 35.

53 Ellroy 1996: 103.

54 Ellroy 2006: 367.

55 Ibid., 363.

56 Ellroy 1998—correspondence.

57 Ellroy 2020.

58 Ellroy 1996: 114.

59 Ibid., 107.

60 Ibid., 116.

61 Swaim 1987: 14.

62 Ellroy 2020.

63 Ellroy 1996: 111–12.

64 Ibid., 116.

65 Ibid., 118.

66 Robson 2019.

67 Heaney 2014.

68 Ellroy 1996: 126.

69 Kihn 1992: 29.

70 Ellroy 1996: 115.

71 Ibid., 113.

72 Ibid., 91.

73 Ibid., 91.

74 Kinsey 1948: 167.

75 Ellroy 1996: 114.

76 Ibid., 114.

77 Kihn 1992: 20.

78 Ellroy 1996: 117.

79 Ibid., 119.

80 Ibid., 111.

81 Ibid., 120.

82 Ibid., 105.

83 Ibid., 115.

84 Ibid., 120.

85 Ibid., 120.

86 Ibid., 121.

87 Ibid., 121.

88 Ibid., 121.

89 Tucker 1984: 7.

90 Ellroy 1996: 122.

91 Ibid., 122.

92 Ibid., 122.

93 Ibid., 123.

94 Ibid., 123.

Chapter 3

1 Ellroy 1996: 125.

2 Ibid., 124.

3 Cao 2017.

4 Ellroy 1996: 125.

5 Ibid., 124.

6 Ibid., 124.

7 Ibid., 124.

8   Ibid., 124.

9   Ellroy 2020.

10   Ellroy 1996: 125.

11   Ibid., 125.

12   Ibid., 124.

13   Ibid., 125.

14   Williams 1991: 88.

15   Swaim 1987: 15.

16   Ellroy 1996: 126.

17   Ibid., 126.

18   Ibid., 126.

19   Ibid., 129.

20   Ibid., 129.

21   Ibid., 130.

22   Ibid., 130.

23   Ibid., 131.

24   Ibid., 131.

25   Ibid., 132.

26   Ibid., 132.

27   Ibid., 132.

28   Didion 1979: 42.

29   Silet 1995: 41–2.

30   Powell 2009: 196-7.

31   Ellroy 1996: 128.

32   Ibid., 128.

33   Ibid., 130.

34   Ellroy 2010: 31.

35   Ellroy 1996: 129.

36   Erickson 1989: 18.

37   Ellroy 1996: 134.

38   Ibid., 134.

39   Ellroy 2010: 30.

40   Ellroy 2021.

41   Ibid.

42   Ibid.

43   Helenius 1971.

44   Ellroy 1996: 136.

45   Ibid., 136.

46   Ibid., 136.

47   Police records for James Ellroy, 1968–1975.

48   Ellroy 1996: 137.

49   Ibid., 137.

50   Ibid., 137.

51   Meade 2003.

52   Powell 2009: 189.

53   Ibid., 189.

54   Ellroy 2020.

55   Ellroy 2010: 28.

56   Ellroy 2021.

57   Ellroy 2010: 29.

58   Mollett 2021.

59   Ibid.

60   Ellroy 2020.

61   Mollett 2021.

62   Ibid.

63   Ellroy 2020.

64   Ellroy 2010: 27.

65   Ellroy 2020.

66   Ellroy 2010: 27.

67   Ellroy 1996: 140.

68   Ibid., 140.

69 Ibid., 133.

70 Ibid., 133.

71 Jayanti 2001.

72 Ellroy 1996: 140.

73 Ibid., 135.

74 Ellroy 2004a: 131.

75 Ibid., 131.

76 Swaim 1987: 14.

77 Ibid., 18.

78 Police records for James Ellroy, 1968–1975.

79 Ibid.

80 Ibid.

81 Ellroy 2021.

82 Ellroy 1996: 142.

83 Ellroy 2010: 203.

84 Ibid., 203.

85 Ellroy 1996: 144.

86 Ibid., 145.

87 Kihn 1992: 26.

88 Ibid., 25.

89 Ellroy 1996: 147.

90 Kihn 1992: 25.

91 Ellroy 1996: 150.

Chapter 4

1 Ellroy 1996: 149.

2 Ibid., 150.

3 Kafesjian 2021.

4 Ellroy 2020.

5   Ellroy 1996: 151.

6   Morneau 2020.

7   Ibid.

8   Rich 2008: 181.

9   Powell 2008a: 163.

10 Ellroy 2021.

11 Ibid.

12 Morneau 2020.

13 Ibid.

14 Ellroy 1996: 151.

15 Duncan 1996: 64.

16 Ellroy 2020.

17 Ibid.

18 Meeks 1990: 22.

19 Ellroy 2021.

20 Ibid.

21 Swaim 1987: 15.

22 Ellroy 2020.

23 Ellroy 1996: 153.

24 Chamales 2021.

25 Marchetti 1999.

26 Chamales 2021.

27 Ellroy 2021.

28 Swirkal 2021.

29 Swaim 1987: 16.

30 Duncan 1996: 64.

31 Kennedy 2020.

32 Ellroy 2020.

33 Ibid.

34 Blazej 2020.

35 Ibid.

36 Ibid.

37 Ibid.

38 Miller 1996.

39 Huttner 2020.

40 Smout 2001: 109.

41 Huttner 2020.

42 Ellroy 1981: 97.

43 Huttner 1980.

44 Ibid.

45 Ibid.

46 Ellroy 2010: 57.

47 Terr 1994: 209.

48 Huttner 2020.

49 Kihn 1992: 31.

50 Sabin 2020.

51 Kennedy 2020.

52 Ellroy 1980 Correspondence.

53 Sabin 1980 Correspondence.

54 Ellroy 1980 Correspondence.

55 Ibid.

56 Ibid.

57 Ibid.

58 Ibid.

59 Ellroy 1981 Correspondence.

60 Ibid.

61 Ibid.

62 Ibid.

63 Ibid.

64 Sabin 1981 Correspondence.

65 Ursin 2021.

66 Sabin 1981 Correspondence.

67 Blazej 2020.

68 DePoy 2020.

69 Ibid.

70 Ibid.

71 Ibid.

72 Ellroy 2020.

73 DePoy 2020.

74 Van der Vort 2021.

75 Ibid.

Chapter 5

1 Phipps 2004: 126.

2 Ellroy 1981 Correspondence.

3 Ellroy 2010: 67.

4 Ellroy 2021.

5 Ellroy 2010: 67.

6 Huttner 2020.

7 Sabin 2020.

8 Ibid.

9 Ibid.

10 Ellroy 1981 Correspondence.

11 Huttner 2020.

12 Ibid.

13 Ellroy 2010: 66.

14 Sabin 2020.

15 Ellroy 1996: 207.

16 Sabin 2020.

17   Ellroy 1981 Correspondence.

18   Millard 2020.

19   Ibid.

20   Ellroy 2010: 66.

21   Millard 2020.

22   Ibid.

23   Ellroy 2020.

24   Ferrari-Adler 2008.

25   Kihn 1992: 31.

26   Penzler 2020.

27   Kihn 1992: 32.

28   Tucker 1984: 9.

29   Rich 2008: 185.

30   Kihn 1992: 31.

31   Ferrari-Adler 2008.

32   Ibid.

33   Douglas 2020.

34   Ibid.

35   Ibid.

36   Ibid.

37   McDowell 1983.

38   Ellroy 2021.

39   Tucker 1984: 9.

40   Ibid.

41   Ibid., 7.

42   Ibid., 10.

43   Sabin 2020.

44   Ellroy 2010: 67.

45   Lerner 2020.

46   Ibid.

47   Ibid.

48   Ellroy 1998: i.

49   Ibid.

50   Meade 2003.

51   Ellroy 2021.

52   Pyne 2014.

53   Ellroy 1984: 436.

54   Ellroy 1998: i.

55   Douglas 2020.

56   Silet 1995: 44.

57   Rich 2009.

58   Penzler 2020.

Chapter 6

1   Powell 2008a: 164.

2   Milward 1997.

3   Stinson 2021.

4   Ellroy 2021.

5   Delany 2020.

6   Ellroy 2020.

7   Palwick 2020.

8   Ibid.

9   Ibid.

10   Ellroy 1990: 278.

11   Palwick 2020.

12   Revelle 2020.

13   Ibid.

14   Ibid.

15   Ibid.

16 Ibid.

17 Ibid.

18 Ibid.

19 Ellroy 2021.

20 Erickson 2020.

21 Ibid.

22 Ellroy 1990: i.

23 Kellerman 2020.

24 Ibid.

25 Ibid.

26 Ibid.

27 Grady 2020.

28 Ellroy 1996: 209.

29 Penzler 2020.

30 Ellroy 1987: 3.

31 Ibid., 3.

32 Ibid., 3.

33 Ibid., 3.

34 Ibid., 1.

35 Ibid., 3.

36 Ibid., 11.

37 Ibid., 63.

38 Mancall 2014: 88.

39 Ellroy 1987: 71.

40 Ibid., 31.

41 Ibid., 71.

42 Ibid., 77.

43 Ibid., 135.

44 Ibid., 141.

45 Ibid., 169.

46 Ibid., 170.

47 Ibid., 170.

48 Ibid., 192.

49 Swaim 1987: 13.

50 Ellroy 1987: 358.

51 Ibid., 358.

52 Ferrari-Adler 2008.

53 Kirshbaum 2020.

54 Ibid.

55 Revelle 2020.

56 Ellroy 2020.

57 Taveira 2012: 367.

58 *Publishers Weekly* 1988.

59 Gross 1988.

60 Schulman 1988.

61 Ibid.

62 Penzler 2020.

63 Helgeland 2021.

64 Harris 2020.

65 Ibid.

66 Ibid.

67 Ibid.

68 Ibid.

69 Mary Ellroy 2020.

70 Ibid.

71 Ellroy 2010: 74.

72 Mary Ellroy 2020.

73 Ibid.

74 Ibid.

75 Ibid.

76 Ellroy 2020.

77 Penzler 2020.

78 Ibid.

79 Mary Ellroy 2020.

80 Ellroy 2010: 75.

81 Ibid, 75.

82 Ellroy 2021.

83 Ellroy 2020.

84 McDonald 2009: 79.

85 Ellroy 2021.

86 Ibid.

87 McDonald 2009: 79.

88 Mary Ellroy 2020.

89 Guérif 2020.

90 Ibid.

91 Champenois 2020.

92 Guérif 2020.

93 Manchette 1987.

94 Guérif 2020.

95 Mottier 1989.

96 Powell 2009, 172.

97 Ferrari-Adler 2008.

98 Ibid.

99 Davis 1990: 45.

100 Ibid., 92.

101 Frommer 1993: 39.

102 Powell 2013.

103 Ibid.

104 Duncan 1996: 78.

105 Powell 2008b: 171.

106 Ellroy 2021.

107 Ellroy 2010: 73.

108 Mary Ellroy 2020.

109 Ellroy 2010: 73.

Chapter 7

1 Ellroy 2010: 80.

2 Knode 2020.

3 Gilmore 1992: 164–71.

4 Knode 2020.

5 Ibid.

6 Ellroy 2010: 85.

7 Ellroy 2010: 88; Ellroy 1987: 279.

8 Ellroy 2010: 92.

9 Mary Ellroy 2020.

10 Douglas 2020.

11 Ibid.

12 Kirshbaum 2020.

13 Vachss 2021.

14 Abrams 1992.

15 Grimson 1992.

16 Johnston 1994: 16.

17 Knode 2021.

18 Kidd 2020.

19 Ibid.

20 Ellis 1992.

21 Ibid.

22 Ibid.

23 Ellroy 2021.

24 Ibid.

25 Tartt correspondence.

26 Ibid.

27 Larson 2021.

28 Ellroy 2021.

29 Ibid.

30 Duncan 1996: 79.

31 Powell 2009, 191.

32 Ellroy 2020.

33 Ellroy 2021.

34 Lehner 2020.

35 Ibid.

36 Jud 2020.

37 Grady 2020.

38 Ibid.

39 Cooper 1999: xi.

40 Duncan 1996: 76.

41 Ellroy 2020.

42 Stein 2021.

Chapter 8

1 Ellroy 2010: 96.

2 Ellroy 1992: 1.

3 Girardot 2021.

4 Stoner 2020.

5 Ellroy 1996: 206.

6 Stoner 2020.

7 Ellroy 1996: 212.

8 Ibid., 213.

9 Ibid., 213.

10 Stoner 2020.

11 Silet 1995: 51.

12 Jayanti 2001.

13 Ibid.

14 Ellroy 1996: 215.

15 Ibid., 218.

16 Ibid., 218.

17 Ibid., 221.

18 Stoner 2020.

19 Canavese 2006: 156.

20 Stoner 2020.

21 Silet 1995: 51.

22 Ellroy 1996: 225.

23 Ibid., 253.

24 Ibid., 254.

25 Ibid., 180.

26 Ibid., 256.

27 Ibid., 242.

28 Ibid., 263.

29 Stoner 2020.

30 Ellroy 1996: 265.

31 Hogan 1995: 55.

32 Ellroy 1996: 266.

33 Ibid., 267.

34 Ibid., 267.

35 Black 2020.

36 Ibid.

37 Ellroy 1996: 269.

38 Ibid., 272.

39 Ibid., 273.

40 Ibid., 274.

41 Ibid., 277.

42 Ibid., 248.

43 Ibid., 290.

44 Ibid., 326.

45 Ellroy 1999: 244.

46 Ellroy 1996: 307.

47 Ibid., 292.

48 Ibid., 292.

49 Powell 2008a: 167.

50 Ellroy 1999: 247.

Chapter 9

1 Patterson 1996.

2 Ellroy 1996: 338.

3 Beck 2020: Klock 2020.

4 Birnbaum 2001.

5 Ellroy 1995: letter to Mehta.

6 Ibid.

7 Ibid.

8 Ellroy 1995: 4.

9 Ibid., 4.

10 Ibid., 4.

11 Ibid., 4.

12 Ibid., 4.

13 Ibid., 4.

14 Silet 1995: 50.

15 Rich 2008: 186.

16 DeLillo 1995.

17 Ibid.

18 Hogan 1995: 59.

19 Duncan 1996: 81.

20 Ellroy 1997a.

21 Kidd 2020.

22 Ibid.

23 Ibid.

24 Lilja 2008.

25 Ripley 2021.

26 Rankin 2021.

27 Ibid.

28 Ibid.

29 Ibid.

30 Johnston 1995: 283.

31 Cave 1995.

32 Olson 1997.

33 Gotler 2020.

34 Powell 2008a: 166.

35 Jayanti 2001.

36 Ellroy 1997b: xvi.

37 Ellroy 2021.

38 Moors 2021.

39 Ellroy 2020.

40 Helgeland 2021.

41 Ibid.

42 Milward 1997.

43 Beitiks 1997.

44 Helgeland 2021.

45 Ellroy 2020.

46 Freeland 2020.

47 Lam 2021.

48 Ellroy 1999: 287.

49 Ibid., 288.

50 Ibid., 288.

51 Ellroy 2021.

52 Ellroy 2020.

53 Swanson 1999.

54 Kelly 2000.

55 Ellroy 2021.

56 Ellroy 2006.

57 White 2013.

58 Brian 2020.

59 Ibid.

60 Jayanti 2001.

61 Layman 2020.

62 Ellroy 2020.

63 Layman 2020.

64 Cogan 1999.

65 Ibid.

66 Meade 2002.

67 Powell 2013.

Chapter 10

1 Cox 2001.

2 Temple 2019: 165–6.

3 Ellroy 2010: 106.

4   Ibid., 109.

5   Ibid., 109.

6   Smout 2001: 105.

7   Ibid., 105.

8   Ibid.

9   McDonald 2020.

10 Ibid.

11 McDonald 2001: 115.

12 Knode 2020.

13 Ibid.

14 Ibid.

15 Ibid.

16 Ellroy 2010: 114.

17 Knode 2020.

18 Ibid.

19 Ibid.

20 Ibid.

21 Ibid.

22 Ibid.

23 Ellroy Worksheets.

24 Ibid.

25 Knode 2020.

26 Ibid.

27 Carter 2003.

28 McDonald 2006: 134.

29 Willis 2003 correspondence.

30 Laura declined to be interviewed for this biography, but she did confirm that "I had an on-again/off-again (really, mostly off-again) relationship with Ellroy."

31 Ellroy 2010: 156.

32 Ibid., 158.

Chapter 11

1   Gotler 2020.

2   Ibid.

3   Ellroy 2020.

4   Ibid.

5   Ellroy 2006.

6   Ellenson 2006.

7   Delany 2020.

8   Ibid.

9   Ibid.

10   Ellroy 2003.

11   Ellroy 2021.

12   Ibid.

13   Ellroy 2010: 167.

14   Ellroy 2020.

15   Taveira 2021.

16   Ellroy 2010: 169.

17   Ellroy 2009: 1.

18   Helgeland 2021.

19   Kellerman 2020.

20   Erickson 2020.

21   Harnisch 2014.

22   Ellroy 1996: 207.

23   Knode 2020.

24   Blazej 2020.

25   Kuperberg 2020.

26   Ibid.

27   Ibid.

28   Ibid.

29 Ibid.

30 Ibid.

31 Stoner 2020.

32 Jackson 2020.

33 Delany 2020.

34 Ibid.

35 Ibid.

36 Lopez 2004.

37 Hodel 2011.

38 Ibid.

39 Ibid.

40 Ellroy 2004b: xxi.

41 Ibid, xxi.

42 Hodel 2011.

43 Powell 2008a: 165.

44 Ibid, 165.

45 Hodel 2010.

46 Harnisch 2010.

47 Hodel 2010.

48 Davis 2014.

49 Powell 2013.

50 Meade & Pryor 2005.

51 Ibid.

52 Ibid.

53 Harris 2020.

54 Talking Books – Eddie Muller.

55 Guérif & Rauger 2016.

56 Ibid.

57 Ellroy 2021.

58 Gretzinger 2020.

59 Ibid.

60 Ibid.

61 Ibid.

62 Ibid.

63 Ibid.

64 Muller 2020.

65 Ibid.

66 Close Zavala 2020.

67 Ibid.

68 Ibid.

Chapter 12

1 Schickel 2020.

2 Ibid.

3 Ibid.

4 Ibid.

5 Ibid.

6 Ibid.

7 Ellroy 2010: 189.

8 Schickel 2020.

9 Ibid.

10 Jones 2009.

11 Ellroy 2021.

12 Ellroy 2009: ii.

13 Ibid, i.

14 Powell 2008a: 158.

15 Peace 2010: 216.

16 Rich 2008: 185.

17 Ellroy 2009: 9.

18 Ibid, 3.

19   Ibid, 421.

20   Ibid, 639–40.

21   Ibid, 640.

22   Ibid, 9.

23   Ibid, 640.

24   Ibid, 640.

25   Ibid.

26   Pick 2009.

27   Mallon 2020.

28   Ibid.

29   Schickel 2020.

30   Schickel—Hammer Museum.

31   Schickel 2020.

32   Ibid.

33   Ibid.

34   Ibid.

35   Knode 2020.

36   Showalter 2010.

37   Ellroy 2020.

38   Schickel 2020.

39   Peterson 2021.

40   Schickel 2020.

41   Ibid.

42   Ibid.

43   Ibid.

44   Ibid.

45   Ibid.

46   Ibid.

47   Ibid.

48   Page 2009.

49   Collis 2019.

50 Schickel 2020.

51 Ibid.

52 Ibid.

53 Powell 2011.

54 Quintero 2020.

55 Ibid.

56 Ellroy 2020.

57 Quintero 2020.

58 Ibid.

59 Ibid.

60 Ibid.

61 Abbott 2020.

62 Ibid.

63 Ibid.

64 Ibid.

65 Mandel 2021.

66 Redding 2021.

67 Ibid.

68 Ibid.

69 Duguay 2020.

70 Lowry 2011.

71 Ellroy 2020.

72 Ibid.

73 Vicky 2020.

74 Ibid.

75 Ibid.

Chapter 13

1 Amazon Books 2014.

2 Ellroy 2014.

3 Ibid., 24.

4 Lindquist 2014.

5 Ellroy 2014: 24.

6 Ibid., 30.

7 Ibid., 25.

8 Mancall 2014: 88.

9 Ellroy 2014: 588.

10 Ibid., 582.

11 Ibid., 582.

12 Ellroy 2021.

13 Lehane 2014.

14 Muller 2020.

15 Knode 2020.

16 Ibid.

17 Chaw 2020.

18 Ellroy 2016.

19 Ibid.

20 Ibid.

21 Ibid.

22 Ibid.

23 Ellroy LAC Pilot script.

24 Helgeland 2021.

25 Carter 2017.

26 Harper 2020.

27 Muller 2020.

28 Ibid.

29 Harper 2020.

30 Sobel letter to Ellroy – on Chabon.

31 Carter 2021.

32 Penzler 2020.

33 Mallon 2016.

34 Wylie 2020.

35 O'Neal Contino 2017.

36 Ellroy 2020.

37 Milliot 2020.

38 Harris 2018.

39 Carter 2018 website.

40 Kidd 2020.

41 Cummins 2019.

42 McQuaid 2021.

43 Luce 2019.

44 Ellroy 2020.

45 McQuaid 2021.

46 NYT 2019.

47 Ellroy 2010: 74.

Works Cited

Abrams, G. (1992) "How "Bout Some More Words" *LA Times* (Aug 30) <https://www. latimes.com/archives/la-xpm-1992-08-30-bk-8612-story.html> [Accessed May 27, 2018]

Akel, J. (2017) "Scene of the Crime" in *At Large Magazine* <https://atlargemagazine.com/features/scene-of-the-crime/> [Accessed May 17, 2018]

Amazon Books (2014). "James Ellroy on WWII, Perfidia and his Second LA Quartet" (Sep 9) https://www.youtube.com/watch?v=YN33NkbD7Xo&list=LL&index=148 [Accessed Nov 28, 2018]

Beitiks, E. (1997) "To Live and Die for LA Confidential" *SFGate* (Sep 14) <https://www.sfgate.com/style/article/To-live-and-die-for-L-A-Confidential-3101105.php> [Accessed Jan 5, 2019]

Birnbaum, R. (2001) "James Ellroy" *Identity Theory*, http://www.identitytheory.com/james-ellroy/, [Accessed 8 Oct 2010]

Canavese, P. (2006) "James Ellroy: The Black Dahlia, LA Confidential" in S. Powell (ed.) (2012) *Conversations with James Ellroy* (Jackson: University Press of Mississippi), pp. 149–57

Cao, L. (2017) "Five Myths About the Vietnam War" *Washington Post* (Sept 27) https://www.washingtonpost.com/outlook/five-myths/five-myths-about-the-vietnam-war/2017/09/29/467ef3e0-a474-11e7-ade1-76d061d56efa_story.html [Accessed Aug 22, 2019]

Carter, B. (2003) "Art Cooper" *Guardian* (Jun 11) https://www.theguardian.com/media/2003/jun/11/pressandpublishing.guardianobituaries> [Accessed Aug 3, 2019]

Carter, J. (2017) "L.A. Confidential the Movie – Twenty Years Later" *Venetian Vase* (Dec 20) https://venetianvase.co.uk/2017/12/20/l-a-confidential-the-movie-20-years-later/ [Accessed Aug 19, 2019]

Carter, J. (2018) "James Ellroy's Lonely Places: A Retrospective" *Venetian Vase* (Dec 5) https://venetianvase.co.uk/2018/12/05/james-ellroys-lonely-places-a-retrospective/ [Accessed Jan 7, 2019]

Cave, N. (1995) "A Letter from Nick" *Bad Seeds Newsletter* (Mar).

Champenois, S. (2020) "Death of Freddy Michalski, great translator of the Anglo-Saxon black novel" ArchHyde (May 24), https://www.archyde.com/death-of-freddy-michalski-great-translator-of-the-anglo-saxon-black-novel/ [Accessed July 16, 2019]

Cinematheque (2016) "Dialogue Avec James Ellroy" (Sep 14) https://www.cinematheque.fr/video/983.html [Accessed Apr 5, 2019]

Cogan, D. (1999) "Gamecock Confidential" *LA Weekly* (Dec 9) https://www.laweekly.com/gamecock-confidential/ [Accessed Aug 5 2018]

Collis, C. (2019) "James Ellroy on his new novel This Storm and why Citizen Kane is a 's—ty film'" *Entertainment Weekly* (Jun 2) <https://ew.com/books/2019/06/02/james-ellroy-this-storm/> (Accessed Jun 4 2019)

Cooper, A. (1999) "Introduction" in *Crime Wave: Reportage and Fiction from the Underside of L.A.* by James Ellroy (New York: Vintage Books) pp.xi–xiv

Cox, T. (2001) "Powders, Treason and Plots", *Observer*, (22 April), http://www.guardian.co.uk/books/2001/apr/22/crime.jamesellroy, [Accessed 22 Sept 2011]

Cummins, A (2019) "This Storm by James Ellroy review – Nazis, orgies and Orson Welles" *Observer* (June 16) https://www.theguardian.com/books/2019/jun/16/this-storm-james-ellroy-review [Accessed July 1 2019]

Davis, E. (2014) "David Fincher & James Ellroy Plotting 1950s Noir Series for HBO" *IndieWire* (Sep 8) https://www.indiewire.com/2014/09/david-fincher-james-ellroy-plotting-1950s-noir-series-for-hbo-272728/ [Accessed June 5, 2019]

Davis, M. (1990) *City of Quartz: Excavating the Future in Los Angeles* (New York: Verso).

DeLillo, D. (1995) Colombia, University of South Carolina, Correspondence, (Mar 4)

Didion, J. (1979) *The White Album* (London: Weidenfeld and Nicolson)

Duncan, P. (1996) "James Ellroy: Barking", in S. Powell (ed.) (2012) *Conversations with James Ellroy* (Jackson: University Press of Mississippi), pp. 61–91.

Ellenson, R. (2006) "The Mean Dahlia: A Night out with James Ellroy" *New York Times* (Sep 10) <https://www.nytimes.com/2006/09/10/fashion/10nite.html> [Accessed May 13, 2016]

Ellis, B. [1992] Colombia, University of South Carolina, Correspondence (October)

Ellroy, J. Colombia, University of South Carolina, Correspondence, Business, October 16, 1980 – October 1, 1981

Ellroy, J. (1981) *Brown's Requiem* (New York: Avon).

Ellroy, J. (1984) "Because the Night" in *L.A. Noir* (London: Arrow, 1998) 227–561.

Ellroy, J. (1984c) Colombia, University of South Carolina, MS Correspondence, Business (18 Nov 1984) 4, 1–4.

Ellroy, J (1987) *The Black Dahlia* (New York: Warner Books)

Ellroy, J (1990) *LA Confidential* (New York: Warner Books)

Ellroy, J. (1992) *White Jazz* (New York: Knopf).

Ellroy, J. (1995) *American Tabloid* (New York: Knopf).

Ellroy, J. (1996) *My Dark Places* (New York: Knopf).

Ellroy, J. (1997a) "Sam Fuller Tribute" Non-Fiction Journalism, Colombia, University of South Carolina.

Ellroy, J. (1997b) "Introduction" in C. Hanson and B. Helgeland, *L.A. Confidential: The Screenplay* (New York: Warner Books) pp. xv–xx.

Ellroy, J. (1998) Colombia, University of South Carolina, Correspondence, Personal, Walter McIntosh.

Ellroy, J. (1999) in *Crime Wave: Reportage and Fiction from the Underside of L.A.* (New York: Vintage Books)

Ellroy, J. (2003) "Dana, Anne and Jean: Three Women, One Man" *GQ*, June, 226–7

Ellroy, J. (2004a) *Destination: Morgue!* (New York: Vintage)

Ellroy, J. (2004b) "Foreword" in S. Hodel, *Black Dahlia Avenger: A Genius for Murder* (New York: Perennial) pp.xix–xxi.

Ellroy, J. (2005). "Introduction" in J. Webb (1958) *The Badge*. (New York: Thunder's Mouth Press) pp. vii–ix.

Ellroy, J. (2006) "Hillikers: an Afterword to The Black Dahlia" in *The Black Dahlia* (New York: Warner Books) pp. 361–71.

Ellroy, J. (2009) *Blood's a Rover* (New York: Knopf).

Ellroy, J. (2010) *The Hilliker Curse: My Pursuit of Women* (London: Heinemann).

Ellroy, J. (2014) *Perfidia* (New York: Knopf).

Ellroy, J. (2016) "L.A. Confidential Author James Ellroy on Curtis Hanson: 'He Was a Voyeur, He Was a Camera' *Variety* (27 Sept) https://variety.com/2016/voices/opinion/la-confidential-james-ellroy-curtis-hanson-1201870744/ [Accessed 9 Oct 2018]

Epstein, E. & Morella, J. (1983) *Rita: The Life of Rita Hayworth* (London: Allen & Co).

Erickson, S. (1989) "James Ellroy: Crime Fiction Beyond Noir" *LA Weekly*, Jul. 21–27 pp.18–26.

Ferrari-Adler, J. (2008) "Agents & Editors: A Q&A with Agent Nat Sobel", *Poets & Writers* vol. 40, http://www.pw.org/content/agent_amp.editors_qampa_agent_nat_sobel, [Accessed 8 Mar 2011]

Frommer, M. (1993) "An Interview With Mike Davis" *Chicago Review* Vol. 38, No. 4, pp. 21–43

Gilmore, M (1992) "A Life in Crime" *Men's Journal*, Nov.–Dec: pp.164–71

Grimson, T. (1992) "The White-Hot Extreme: White Jazz by James Ellroy" *LA Times* (Aug 30) https://www.latimes.com/archives/la-xpm-1992-08-30-bk-8598-story.html [Accessed 7 May 2019]

Gross, J. (1988) "Books of the Times: A Nondescript Victim and Los Angeles Shames" *NY Times* (Sept 9), https://www.nytimes.com/1988/09/09/books/books-of-the-times-a-nondescript-victim-and-los-angeles-shames.html?auth=login-google&pagewanted=all&src=pm [Accessed 22 May 2019]

Guérif, F. and J. Rauger (2016) "Dialogue avec James Ellroy" *The French Cinémathèque* (Sept 14), https://vimeo.com/200653511 [Accessed 14 August 2020]

Haffner, G. (2011) *Hands With a Heart: The Personal Biography of Actress ZaSu Pitts* (Denver: Outskirts Press)

Harnisch, L. (2010) "The Pitfalls of the True Crime Genre" *Venetian Vase* (22 Mar), http://venetianvase.co.uk/2010/03/22/the-pitfalls-of-the-true-crime-genre, date accessed 10 Nov 2011.

Harnisch, L. (2014) "James Ellroy and the Remake of 'Laura': Doomed from the Start" *The Daily Mirror* (Aug 27) https://ladailymirror.com/2014/08/27/james-ellroy-and-the-remake-of-laura-doomed-from-the-start/ [Accessed May 17, 2019]

Harris, K. (2018) "Walter Chaw Leaves Alamo Drafthouse During Expansion to Westminster" (July 11) <https://www.westword.com/arts/walter-chaw-leaves-alamo-drafthouse-during-expansion-to-westminster-10527336> [Accessed July 13, 2019]

Heaney, M. (2014). "James Ellroy: "Whatever I Conceive, I Can Execute" *Irish Times* (Nov 23) https://www.irishtimes.com/culture/books/james-ellroy-whatever-i-can-conceive-i-can-execute-1.2008762 [Accessed July 22 2019]

Helenius, S (1971) "Returning the Dykes to the Dutch" in *Everywoman* (Jul 9) page unnumbered

Hodel, S. (2004) *Black Dahlia Avenger: A Genius for Murder* (New York: Perennial)

Hodel, S. (2010) "An Open Letter to French Journalist Stephane Boulan re. James Ellroy and Black Dahlia Avenger", *Steve Hodel's Squad Room Blog* [blog] (25 January), http://207.56.179.67/steve_hodel/2010/01/cut-author-james-ellroy-some-s.html, [Accessed 1 Feb 2010]

Hogan, R. (1995) "The Beatrice Interview: 1995", in S. Powell (ed.) (2012) *Conversations with James Ellroy* (Jackson: University Press of Mississippi), pp.53–60.

Huttner, R (1980) University of South Carolina, Correspondence, Business, (Dec 15)

"Inventing LA: The Chandlers and Their Times" 2018, *KCET* <https://www.kcet.org/shows/inventing-la-the-chandlers-and-their-times/timeline-history-of-the-los-angeles-times> [Accessed May 21, 2019]

Jayanti, V. (dir.) (2001) *Feast of Death* [film].

Johnson, R. (2010) "Writers Salvador Plascencia and Michael Jaime-Beccera share a city and a common inspiration: El Monte" *Los Angeles Times*, April 25, 2010. Avaialble at <https://www.latimes.com/entertainment/la-ca-el-monte-20100425-story.html> [Accessed August 12, 2019]

Johnston, I. (1994) "King Noir" *Purr Quarterly* pp.12–17.

Johnston, I (1995) *Bad Seed: The Biography of Nick Cave* (London: Abacus)

Jones, P. (2009) "Book Review *Blood's a Rover* by James Ellroy" *Dallas Morning News* dallasnews.com [Accessed August 1, 2009]

Kelly, K. (2000) "Authors Feud with 60 Minutes" *New York Post* (Oct 11) <https://nypost.com/2000/10/11/authors-feud-with-60-minutes/> [Accessed Jan 6, 2015]

Kihn, M. (1992) "Doctor Noir" in S. Powell (ed.) (2012) *Conversations with James Ellroy* (Jackson: University Press of Mississippi), pp.25–35.

Kinsey, A. (1948) *Sexual Behavior in the Human Male* (Philadelphia: Saunders)

LA Times (1958a) "40 Dead in Runaway Mountain Train Dive," June 23, p.1

LA Times 1958b "Blond Woman Sought in Nurse Killing," June 23, p.1.

LA Times 1958c "Nurse Found Strangled, Body Left in El Monte Lane," June 23, p.2.

Leaming, B. (1989) *If This Was Happiness: A Biography of Rita Hayworth* (New York: Viking).

Lehane, D. (2014) "The Big Sweep" *New York Times* (Sept 4) https://www.nytimes.com/2014/09/07/books/review/james-ellroys-perfidia.html [Accessed Dec 5, 2015]

Lilja, T. (2008) "An Evening with James Ellroy" *Blackbird's Nest* <https://www.blackbirdsnest.net/ellroy.html> [Accessed May 5, 2019]

Lindquist, M. (2014) "James Ellroy's 'Perfidia': dark doings on the eve of WWII" *Seattle Times* <http://seattletimes.com/html/books/2024460599_perfidiajamesellroyxml.html> [Accessed Sept 6, 2014]

Lopez, S. (2004) "Writing the Last Word on a Mystery?" *LA Times* (May 23) < =https://www.latimes.com/archives/la-xpm-2004-may-23-me-lopez23-story.html> [Accessed May 28, 2018]

Lowry, B. (2011) "James Ellroy's LA: City of Demons" *Variety* (Jan 18) <https://variety.com/2011/tv/reviews/james-ellroy-s-la-city-of-demons-1117944317/> [Accessed Nov 18, 2018]

Luce, E. (2019) "James Ellroy on his Dark Places" *Financial Times* (May 31) https://www. ft.com/content/8849ea5a-8136-11e9-b592-5fe435b57a3b [Accessed October 2, 2019]

McDonald, C. (2001) "James Ellroy: The Tremor of Intent" in S. Powell (ed.) (2012) *Conversations with James Ellroy* (Jackson: University Press of Mississippi), pp.114–24.

McDonald, C. (2006) "James Ellroy: To Live and Die in LA" in S. Powell (ed.) (2012) *Conversations with James Ellroy* (Jackson: University Press of Mississippi), pp. 132–48.

McDonald, C. (2009) *Rogue Males: Conversations & Confrontations about the Writing Life* (Madison: Bleak House Books)

McDowell, E. (1983) "Suspense: A Theme of Library Talks" *New York Times* https://www. nytimes.com/1983/12/04/books/suspense-a-theme-of-library-talks.html [Accessed June 1, 2020]

McKinty, A. (2019) "James Ellroy Walks Into a Streakhouse and Orders Clams" in *Crime Reads* <https://crimereads.com/james-ellroy-walks-into-a-steakhouse-and-orders-clams/> [Accessed June 13, 2019]

Mallon, T. (2016) Email to Andrew Wylie, April 19

Mancall, J. (2014) *James Ellroy: A Companion to the Mystery Fiction* (Jefferson: McFarland & Company)

Manchette, J. (1987), "James Ellroy Du Crime" *Libération* (April 3) https://www.liberation. fr/livres/2014/04/03/james-ellroy-du-crime_992977/ [Accessed May 16, 2019]

Marchetti, M. (1999) "Selling Saved Their Lives" *Fortune* Vol. 151, 2 http://www. equityvaluegroup.com/Fortune.html [Accessed July 1, 2019] p. 36–44

Meade, B. (Dir.) (2002) *Vakvagany* (FILM)

Meade, B. (Dir.) (2003) *Das Bus* (FILM)

Meade, B. and B. Pryor (Dir.) (2005) *Destination Morgue* (FILM) Unreleased

Meeks, F. (1990) "James Ellroy" in S. Powell (ed.) (2012) *Conversations with James Ellroy* (Jackson: University Press of Mississippi), pp. 20–4.

Miller, L. (1996) "Oedipus Wreck" *Salon* (9 Dec), http://www.salon.com/1996/12/09/ interview961209/ [Accessed 19 Nov 2010]

Milliot, J (2020) "Hundreds Turn Out to Remember Sonny Mehta" *Publishers Weekly* (Feb 20) <https://www.publishersweekly.com/pw/by-topic/industry-news/Obituary/ article/82466-hundreds-turn-out-to-remember-sonny-mehta.html> (Accessed March 1, 2020)

Milward, J. (1997) "L.A. Beyond Your Wildest Nightmare" *Los Angeles Times* (Sept 7, 1997), http://articles.latimes.com/1997/sep/07/entertainment/ca-29564/3, [Accessed 3 Aug 2010]

Mottier, C. (Dir.) (1989) *Cinéma Cinémas* [Film]

New York Times (2019) "By the Book: James Ellroy" (June 8) https://www.nytimes. com/2019/06/06/books/review/by-the-book-james-ellroy.html [Accessed July 16, 2019]

O'Neal Contino, M. (2017) https://www.facebook.com/JamesEllroy

Olson, R. (1997) "James Ellroy on Nick Cave" *Bad-Seed.org.*

Page, B. (2009) "Second LA Quartet to William Heinemann" *The Bookseller*, http://www. thebookseller.com/news/second-la-quartet-william-heinemann.html, [Accessed 10 Nov 2011]

Patterson, L. (Dir.) (1996) *Unsolved Mysteries* [Film]

Peace, D. (2010) "James Ellroy and David Peace in Conversation" in S. Powell (ed.) (2012) *Conversations with James Ellroy* (Jackson: University Press of Mississippi), pp. 212–19.

Phipps, K. (2004) "Interview: James Ellroy" in S. Powell (ed.) (2012) *Conversations with James Ellroy* (Jackson: University Press of Mississippi), pp. 125–31

Pick, K. (2009) *The Culture Show* [Film]

Police records for James Ellroy, 1968–1975, Colombia, University of South Carolina,

Powell, S. (2008a) "Engaging the Horror" in S. Powell (ed.) (2012) *Conversations with James Ellroy* (Jackson: University Press of Mississippi), pp.158–68.

Powell, S. (2008b) "Coda for Crime Fiction" in S. Powell (ed.) (2012) *Conversations with James Ellroy* (Jackson: University Press of Mississippi) pp.169–75.

Powell, S. (2009) "The Romantic's Code" in S. Powell (ed.) (2012) *Conversations with James Ellroy* (Jackson: University Press of Mississippi), pp. 189–200.

Powell, S. (2011) "Ellroy Opts Out, Goodbye to Facebook and Other Stories" *Venetian Vase* https://venetianvase.co.uk/2011/06/26/ellroy-opts-out-goodbye-to-facebook-and-other-stories/ [Accessed 23 June 2018]

Powell, S. (2013) "Unpublished James Ellroy Interview" *Venetian Vase* (9 Feb), http://venetianvase.co.uk/2013/02/09/unpublished-james-ellroy-interview/, [Accessed 9 February 2013.

Powell, S. (2014) "James Ellroy: In My Craft or Sullen Art" in *Venetian Vase* <https://venetianvase.co.uk/2014/11/06/james-ellroy-in-manchester-in-my-craft-or-sullen-art/> [Accessed August 2, 2019]

Pyne, H. (2014) "James Ellroy" in *Shortlist* (Feb 19) https://www.shortlist.com/news/james-ellroy [Accessed August 10, 2019]

Publisher's Weekly (1988) "The Big Nowhere" https://www.publishersweekly.com/978-0-89296-283-9 [Accessed June 6, 2019]

Rich, N. (2009) "James Ellroy: The Art of Fiction" in S. Powell (ed.) (2012) *Conversations with James Ellroy* (Jackson: University Press of Mississippi), pp. 176–88.

Robson, L (2019) "James Ellroy Finally Has Happiness in His Sights" *The Economist* <https://www.1843magazine.com/features/james-ellroy-finally-has-happiness-in-his-sights> [Accessed August 1, 2019]

Rooney, M. (1991) *Life is Too Short* (New York: Villard)

Sabin, N. Colombia, University of South Carolina, Correspondence, Business, 1980–1

Schulman, S (1988) "Crime/Mystery: Bigots & Bashers" *New York Times* (Oct 9) <https://www.nytimes.com/1988/10/09/books/crime-mystery-bigots-and-bashers.html> [Accessed August 2, 2019]

Showalter, E (2010) "James Ellroy, the Ancient Mariner of LA Noir" *Times Literary Supplement* (Nov 3)

Silet, C. (1995) "Mad Dog and Glory: A Conversation with James Ellroy" in S. Powell (ed.) (2012) *Conversations with James Ellroy* (Jackson: University Press of Mississippi), pp.40–52.

Slater, L. (1965) *Aly: A Biography* (New York: Random House)

Smout, M. (2001) "Lunch and Tea with James Ellroy" in S. Powell (ed.) (2012) *Conversations with James Ellroy* (Jackson: University Press of Mississippi), pp.104–13.

Swaim, D. (1987) "Don Swaim's Interview of James Ellroy" in S. Powell (ed.) (2012) *Conversations with James Ellroy* (Jackson: University Press of Mississippi), pp.11–19.

Swanson, C. (1999) "A Furrier with a Shady Past Sues James Ellroy for Libel" *Observer* (Jun 7) <https://observer.com/1999/06/a-furrier-with-a-shady-past-sues-james-ellroy-for-libel/> [Accessed Sep 13 2018]

Talking Books (2016) "Chapter 114: the demon dog of crime fiction" https://www.newstalk.com/podcasts/talking-books/page/24 [Accessed 27 Dec 2017]

Tartt, D. Colombia, University of South Carolina, Correspondence, [Undated]

Taveira, R. (2012) "Interview with James Ellroy" in *Comparative American Studies* Vol.10 No.4 pp.362–75

Temple, P. (2019) *The Red Hand: Stories, Reflections and the Last Appearance of Jack Irish* (London: River Run)

Terr, L. (1994) *Unchained Memories: True Stories of Traumatic Memories, Lost and Found* (New York: Harper Collins)

Tucker, D. (1984) "An Interview with James Ellroy" in S. Powell (ed.) (2012) *Conversations with James Ellroy* (Jackson: University Press of Mississippi), pp. 3–10.

Webb, J. (1958) *The Badge* (New York: Thunder's Mouth Press)

Wedner, D. (2008) "It's urban life plus suburban life, squared" *Los Angeles Times*, Feb 3, 2008. Available at <https://www.latimes.com/archives/la-xpm-2008-feb-03-re-guide3-story.html> [Accessed August 4, 2019]

White, M. (2013) "Off the Record with James Ellroy" Cahiers du Cinemas (Jan 14).

Williams, J. (1991) *Into the Badlands: A Journey Through the American Dream* (London: Paladin)

Willis, B. (2003) Colombia, University of South Carolina, [Feb].

Wolfe, P. (2006) *Like Hot Knives to the Brain: James Ellroy's Search for Himself* (Lanham: Lexington Books)

I had hundreds of hours of conversations with James Ellroy from January 2020 onwards for this book, and many hours of conversation with Helen Knode. It would be redundant to date them all. Therefore, I have cited them simply as Ellroy 2020/21 or Knode 2020/21 in the endnotes depending on the year they were conducted.

Below is a list of other interviews I conducted. The list is not comprehensive and only covers interviews cited in the text:

Megan Abbott, interview by author, July 7, 2020
Jean Beck, email conversation with author, December 2, 2020
Nicola Black, interview by author, June 3, 2020
Sybil Blazej, interview by author, January 8, 2020
Paul Bogaards, interview by author, October 8, 2020
Mitch Brian, interview by author, July 27, 2020
Jason Carter, interview by author, January 2, 2021
Gerald Chamales, interview by author, May 5, 2021
Walter Chaw, interview by author, October 13, 2020
Megan Close Zavala, interview by author, November 18, 2020
Benoit Cohen, interview by author, June 8, 2021
Dana Delany, interview by author, September 3, 2020

Samuel R. Delany, email conversation with author, January 28, 2021

Cindy DePoy, interview by author, 20 April, 2020

John Douglas, email conversation with author, December 15, 2020

Richard Duguay, interview by author, 27 February, 2021

Mary Ellroy, email conversation with author, May 6, 2020

Steve Erickson, email conversation with author, August 10, 2020

Jason Freeland, interview by author, August 28, 2020

Frank Girardot, interview by author, January 23, 2021

Joel Gotler, interview by author, August 20, 2020

James Grady, interview by author, February 26, 2020

Nelle Gretzinger, interview by author, June 23, 2020

François Guérif, interview by author, April 5, 2020

Larry Harnisch, interview by author, November 5, 2020

Jordan Harper, interview by author, July 10, 2020

James B. Harris, interview by author, April 19, 2020

Brian Helgeland, interview by author, April 29, 2021

Steve Hodel, email conversation with author, May 5, 2011

Steve Horvitz, interview by author, June 2012, 2020

Richard Huttner, interview by author, March 9, 2020

Rick Jackson, interview by author, March 28, 2020

Leslie Jacobson, interview by author, May 16, 2021

Ian Johnston, interview by author, April 29, 2021

Rae Jones, interview by author, March 27, 2021

Reinhard Jud, interview by author, September 29, 2020

Anthony Kafesjian, interview by author, March 20, 2021

Edward Kastenmeier, interview by author, October 30, 2020

Richard Katz, interview by author, May 11, 2021

Jonathan Kellerman, interview by author, November 29, 2020

Deirdre Kennedy, interview by author, April 1, 2020

Chip Kidd, interview by author, July 1, 2020

Larry Kirshbaum, email conversation with author, December 30, 2020

Janet Klock, email conversation with author, December 12, 2020

Clara Kuperberg, email conversation with author, August 15, 2020

Donna Lam, interview by author, August 11, 2021

Darrell Larson, interview by author, June 14, 2021

Richard Layman, interview by author, July 17, 2020

Wolfgang Lehner, interview by author, September 27, 2020

Betsy Lerner, email conversation with author, August 22, 2020

Craig McDonald, interview by author, July 25, 2020

Kate McQuaid, interview by author, May 29, 2021

Thomas Mallon, email conversation with author, June 25, 2020

Steven Mandel, interview by author, February 7, 2021

Michael Gregg Michaud, email conversation with author, August 15, 2019

Martha Millard, email conversation with author, June 11, 2020

Chrystine Mollett, interview by author, May 29, 2021

Rick Moors, interview by author, June 9, 2021
Tim Morneau, email conversation with author, May 8, 2020
Eddie Muller, interview by author, May 20, 2020
Alex Nicol, interview by author, June 28, 2021
Laura Nolan, interview by author, February 8, 2021
Susan Palwick, interview by author, November 21, 2020
David Peace, interview by author, April 7, 2021
Otto Penzler, interview by author, March 21, 2020
Clark Peterson, interview by author, February 18, 2021
Andrew Quintero, interview by author, September 29, 2020
Ian Rankin, interview by author, March 9, 2021
Anne Redding, interview by author, January 31, 2021
Glenda Revelle, email conversation with author, August 19, 2020
Mike Ripley, email conversation with author, March 13, 2021
Nellie Sabin, email conversation with author, May 16, 2020
Erika Schickel, interview by author, July 15, 2020
Jeff Stein, interview by author, September 8, 2021
Jay Stiefel, email to author, July 6, 2019
Joseph C. Stinson, interview by author, January 21, 2021
Bill Stoner, interview by author, March 29, 2020
Rick Swirkal, interview by author, May 1, 2021
Rodney Taveira, interview by author, August 4, 2021
Marya Ursin, email conversation with author, March 26, 2021
Andrew Vachss, interview by author, May 16, 2021
Anne Van der Vort Purky, interview by author, May 19, 2021
Vicky, interview by author, December 20. 2020
John Williams, interview by author, April 15, 2021
Andrew Wylie, email conversation with author, November 10, 2020

Index